PERSONA NON GRATA

PERSONA NON GRATA

A Memoir of Disenchantment with the Cuban Revolution

Jorge Edwards

Translated by
Andrew Hurley

PARAGON HOUSE
New York

First American edition, 1993

Published in the United States by

Paragon House
90 Fifth Avenue
New York, New York 10011

Originally published in Spanish under the title *Persona non grata*.
Copyright © 1973, 1985, and 1991 by Jorge Edwards
Introduction copyright © 1993 by Jorge Edwards
Translation copyright © 1993 by Andrew Hurley
Preface copyright © 1993 by Octavio Paz

Manufactured in the United States of America

Library of Congress Cataloging-in-Publication Data

Edwards, Jorge.
[Persona non grata. English]
Persona non grata / Jorge Edwards ; translated by Andrew Hurley.—
1st American ed.
p.   cm.
A memoir of disenchantment with the Cuban Revolution.
Includes index.
ISBN 1-55778-576-7
1. Edwards, Jorge.   2. Diplomats—Chile—Biography.   3. Cuba—
Politics and government—1959–   4. Chile—Politics and
government—1970–1973.   I. Title.
F3101.E33A3413   1993
327.2′092—dc20

[B]   92-44638
                                                        CIP

Je ne connais que deux partis,
celui des bons et celui des
mauvais citoyens.

ROBESPIERRE

Contents

Preface

This book by Jorge Edwards is one of the truly vibrant classics of modern Latin American literature. Its strengths are threefold: historical, psychological, and literary. As a historical document it is a chronicle, at once absorbing and terrifying, of the upper reaches of the political and literary hierarchy of Havana during the years in which the Castro regime began to show its teeth. In this sense, *Persona Non Grata* is the history of the disenchantment of a generation of intellectuals; thanks to this book, many men and women were able to see the true nature of the Cuban regime, which combines the tyrannical elements of supposedly bygone Latin American dictatorships with the gray impersonality of every totalitarian bureaucracy of the twentieth century. This book, however, is not simply a chronicle: It is simultaneously a psychological, social, and moral study of the internal workings of a dictatorship and that government's relations with intellectuals. It is a book that Balzac, had he known it, might well have included among the series of novels that compose his "Scenes of Political Life." What is remarkable about Edwards' story is that it can be read as *testimonio* (that hybrid Latin American genre which combines a counterofficial version of historical events with the psychological immediacy of first-person narration) and also as a work of fiction. And so the third of the book's recommendations: its clear, terse, rapid, and ironic style. Its language fuses those most difficult of qualities—transparency with intelligence, incisiveness with a smile. This is a civilized book, which attempts not so much to condemn and denounce as to illuminate and understand.

—Octavio Paz

Author's Introduction to the American Edition

Persona Non Grata was the first book written by a left-wing Latin American intellectual—as I might be defined in those distant days—that was openly critical of the Cuban regime. Anthony Burgess, whom I met in Barcelona and who read the book in its first English translation, wrote that it was a "devastating critique of Castro's Cuba," and he was probably right. My purpose, however, has never been to write a devastating book, but instead to tell the story as it really happened. I wrote *Persona Non Grata* as both a personal memoir and a historical chronicle of one of the most critical moments in Latin American history.

In 1964, as a result of a resolution adopted in Montevideo, Uruguay, by the Organization of American States, every country in Latin America, with the sole exception of Mexico, broke off relations with Fidel Castro's regime. This was a decision made under strong pressure from Washington, of course, and it was never popular in my country or anywhere in the region. In 1970, when Salvador Allende won the democratic Chilean elections on a left-wing Marxist ticket, one of his first measures upon taking office as president was to reopen diplomatic relations with Cuba.

At that time I was known in Chile and in Spain as a writer—I had written one novel and four books of short stories—but since 1957 I had also been a member of the Chilean foreign service. I belonged, then, to a long tradition of diplomat/writers in Latin America, a tradition that was broken by the military coup of September 1973 and has not been renewed in our current transition to democracy. Like most Latin American writers of the early sixties who were left-wing intellectuals, I had declared my sympathy for the Cuban Revolution from its very beginnings, and I had visited Havana in January 1968 as a guest of the Island's official cultural authorities. During that first visit I had established important contacts with the writers and general literary world of Cuba. Before that, in 1964, during the presidential elections in Chile, I had openly supported the candidacy of Salvador Allende. My background might have led one to see me, at least at first glance, as the one diplomat of my generation most suited to open the Chilean Embassy in Havana and to prepare for the arrival of the fully invested ambassador.

In every sense, Cuba was very far from Chile in those days, and this distance helped us maintain a dangerously naïve approach to Cuban matters. After my first twenty-four hours on the Island, I knew that I was precisely the *least* appropriate person for the job. I had talked and drunk Chilean wine with Fidel Castro himself till very late the first night of my arrival. The next morning, in the huge lobby of the Habana Riviera Hotel, I received some of his better informed, more able and implacable critics, including the poet Heberto Padilla. Many of the Cuban writers I had known before my arrival had turned in the meantime into fierce dissidents, and they certainly didn't mince any words after the first round of frozen daiquiris. Even as early as 1970, it was their view that the economy was destroyed, that the political situation was disastrous, that Fidel was utterly mad. The secret police, always concealed but omnipresent in the spacious hotel lobbies of Havana, took note of my company and our conversations. What kind of revolutionary had the Chilean socialist government sent as its first diplomatic envoy to Cuba? From that very moment, every step of mine was carefully watched, and my final conflict with the authorities was inevitable. Four months later, in late March 1971, Padilla was imprisoned—one hour after he and an Italian Communist correspondent had come to see me in the Habana Riviera. He was accused of having given me, the diplomatic representative of Chile—the only friendly country that Cuba had at the moment in all of Latin America—"a negative image" of the Cuban Revolution. In other words, Heberto Padilla was accused of high treason.

Castro managed the case, the Island's first imprisonment of a well-known writer, with great skill. Padilla, pressured and mistreated (to say the least) in prison, soon came around: He produced and starred in an act of public self-criticism, following to the letter the script prepared for him by State Security, and accused his best friends, both Cuban and foreign, of being counterrevolutionaries. I was omitted from the list of the accused for obvious reasons: I was still an official Chilean diplomat, and in consequence a representative of the Allende government, however much that might irritate the officials of the Castro regime.

Fidel managed within a short time, one or two months, to get some of the important Latin American and European intellectuals who had been protesting

Padilla's treatment to withdraw their protests, or at least to continue to be friendly to the regime, and this achievement created the first sharp and almost unbridgeable division, lasting even until today, between the writers of Latin America. From that time forward, Julio Cortázar and Gabriel García Márquez would head the ranks of those unconditionally committed to Castroism, while the dissident ranks, openly critical of the regime, would be captained by Octavio Paz, Mario Vargas Llosa, and Juan Goytisolo. Years later I learned that Cortázar, who was one of the finest short story writers of the Spanish language and who died in Paris in the eighties, was irritated in his last days because Cuban officials put pressure on him to try to take him from France to a Cuban hospital. Having a first-hand knowledge of his love for the city of Paris, I can imagine very well his reaction. And Gabriel García Márquez, too, who once traveled frequently to the Island and stayed in the luxurious mansion that the government kept always open for him in Havana, now appears to be rethinking his alliance, discreetly distancing himself from his old friend Fidel Castro.

As for me, Fidel asked his friend Salvador Allende to throw me out of the diplomatic service as soon as possible, or at least to punish me for what Castro himself defined on my last night in Havana as "conduct hostile to the Revolution." I, being a writer, that most suspect of characters for any strong State, had the wretched idea of writing a narrative of the whole case—and worse, of putting it in nonfictional form.

I began writing it in Paris, where I had been posted as counselor to the poet/ambassador and Nobel Prize-winner Pablo Neruda. I later took a leave of absence and finished the book. I drew upon my post-Havana experience as a diplomat, and upon the dark and disturbing news that was coming out of Chile after Pinochet's takeover in September 1973, to draft an epilogue to my Havana story.

When the book was published, it provoked a scandal on the Left and was received with mixed feelings, with a sort of uncomfortable satisfaction, by the Right. In an extraordinary instance of dictatorial symmetry, the main body of the book brought down upon itself the censorship of Fidel Castro, while its epilogue brought the book the censorship of Pinochet. The worst, however, came about as a result of the notorious discomfort caused by the book in certain supposedly progressive Western literary and publishing circles: There was a conspiracy of silence. In Spain and other Spanish-speaking countries, the book (published in Barcelona by another left-wing intellectual, Carlos Barral) was read with irritation or with enthusiasm, but always intensely. It even turned up on the best-seller lists, with no advertising or promotion of any kind, leading Carlos Barral to exclaim, "The books I publish *never* make those lists!" In England and France it was praised by liberal intellectuals or intellectuals of the "critical Left." The person in charge of the Italian edition, however, Enrico Filipini, told me he lost his job at Bompiani, a prestigious Milan publishing house, for having published *Persona Non Grata*. With the recent death of Oliveira Salazar, the Portuguese had just been freed from a long dictatorship, and the Left believed they could at last take power. In the spring of 1974, coinciding with the blooming of the flowers throughout the land, the so-called Carnation Revolution took place; rights to the book were bought, and plans were made for its publication. But then the revolution entered a temporary Stalinist phase, and the Portuguese prudently refrained from publishing it. An important German publisher went further: They sent a telex to my agent in Barcelona to inform us that they did not even want to be sent a copy of the book to read; they already knew what it was about. On the other side of the Atlantic, some American publishers optioned the book, but they ended up "opting out." The only person who dared try to bring out the book in the United States was José Manuel Vergara, a Chilean publisher who operated out of Barcelona (Editorial Pomaire) and had dreams of setting up shop in New York under the imprint of Pomerica Press. Vergara was a generous, enthusiastic, and somewhat deluded publisher. The copies of the book printed by Pomerica Press, an enterprise founded on the hopes and desires of my friend and on little else, never even reached the bookstores.

In spite of all these setbacks—all the censorship—the book has had an extraordinary life from the very first. It has been defended by people such as Octavio Paz, Mario Vargas Llosa, Hugh Thomas, Graham Greene, Pierre Daix, Max Gallo, and Emir Rodríguez Monegal. Some intellectuals of the Left, of course, accused me in writing of being an agent of the CIA. These implacable accusers would later set themselves up in American universities where they enjoyed the best fellowships, honors, and invitations offered by the capitalist world.

Felipe González, the prime minister of the Spanish government, told me at a reception in the Moncloa Palace in Madrid that the book had been widely discussed by him and his friends inside his party (the Workers Spanish Socialist Party) in the days before Franco's death and that he had mentioned it to Fidel Castro.

"And what did Fidel Castro say?"

"He took it very well, very calmly," González replied, and I suspected that Fidel, probably surprised by the readings of his distinguished host, had no other way of taking it.

The book entered military-controlled Chile surreptitiously, smuggled in by people arriving from Argentina or Spain; it was even "imported" in small quantities by some booksellers. The official censorship was lifted in 1978, but afterwards, by one of those unexplained whims of dictatorial regimes, it was censored for a second time when the 1981, complete, edition reached customs in Santiago. With the aid of lawyer friends of mine I took the matter to court. At last we reached the Supreme Court of Chile, and although the decision, like so many decisions in those days, was worthy of a Pontius Pilate, it served at least to call attention to the subject, and eventually it led to the elimination of prior censorship of books by the military regime. General Pinochet in person, in a speech delivered in the plaza of a small town in the provinces, announced that it would no longer be necessary to request government permission before books would be allowed to circulate and be read. This turn-around, which came in 1983, opened the gates, and from that point on, many other books critical of the regime—"controversial" books, as they were called; in Spanish, *conflictivos,* which simply means "conflicting with the official view of things"—found their way into the hands of Chilean readers.

Things in Cuba have been much more difficult, but I know that the book, in spite of all, has enjoyed quite an underground following. I was very happy to learn, for example, that José Lezama Lima, a great poet and novelist who remained till the end in Havana, had managed to read it before his death. Fidel Castro told a Chilean politician visiting Cuba that he, Fidel, "didn't read things like that," but he later indicated his fierce displeasure at some of my descriptions of his physical deterioration, his apparent weariness, his lined, tired face when he announced the failure of the ten-million-ton sugarcane harvest in December 1970. But the most gratifying story out of Cuba reached me in this way: In the mid-eighties, after a lecture I had given at Tulane University in New Orleans, an older gentleman came forward from the rear of the auditorium. He spoke with an unmistakable Cuban accent, and he told me that he had been a political prisoner in Cuba for many years. During that time in prison, he said, he had once paid ten Cuban pesos to rent the book for a night's reading. I felt I had made it as an author: The censorship, the intrigues, the accusations (in some cases vile and willfully mean) all just came with the territory. I reached the conclusion that all censorship was imposed with the complicity of the mediocre intellectuals of the world.

At one point in his life, Franz Kafka was a member of a committee to help the psychological victims of World War I. Today it would have to be a committee to aid the psychological victims of contemporary dictatorships. In this book, of course, there is much talk of psychology, and even of paranoia. I was often accused by Castroites of having written this book out of some sort of persecution complex. Guillermo Cabrera Infante, who knew about such things, once wrote me a letter containing this memorable phrase: "There is no such thing as a persecution complex where persecution is so complex." I am often consoled by that phrase; I feel like a person who has also passed his *saison en enfer* and who has managed to get out with some of his hair a little singed, but otherwise safe and sound.

Through all these long years, and in spite of its powerful censors, the book has always found its way. It has opened the eyes of many to the inner workings of a dictatorship. For me, and later for others, it began a process that allowed us to escape from the mental prisons that were typical of the intellectual life of the sixties and seventies.

A Polish leader who in time became an open dissident and one of the heads of Solidarity quietly said to me in a bar on the Ramblas in Barcelona, years before the fall of the Communist regime in his country: "The only thing you've done is report that the emperor was walking around without any clothes on."

Today, twenty years later, the emperor continues to go around naked, and we foresee no short-term ending of the Cuban tragedy. The division in the Cuban world is insurmountable. Castro stubbornly refuses to begin any kind of negotiations, but worst of all is that he has nobody with whom to negotiate, no valid interlocutor. The Cuban opposition in Miami seems willing to accept nothing but unconditional surrender, and is just sitting back waiting for the spoils of the Island. It seems we are headed toward an apocalyptic ending of the story, and nobody seems to be aware of or concerned about the problem. There is a germ of democratic opposition on the Island as well as in exile, but in my view it is still a minority and has no real support from the United States or anywhere else in the Western world. Maybe Castro has come to believe that he is eternal, but are we also forced to believe it? And ought we not, just in case Castro is not eternal, to begin to work out a peaceful, reasonable, democratic outcome for Cuba?

Persona Non Grata, however, is not only about Castro and the Cuban dictatorship, but also about the dictatorship that devastated Chile in those days—and in fact, about the madness of all dictatorships. When the book first appeared, people constantly approached me and whispered in my ear: "I know that everything you say is true, but this is not at all the right time to say it. Don't you see what General Pinochet is doing at this very minute in your country?" The answer to this question didn't seem easy in those days, but I had not the least doubt about it. If we didn't look at the deviations and monstrosities of real socialism in the face—and the socialism of Cuba was the closest thing to real socialism available to us—we would never be able to get rid of the Chilean dictatorship through a peaceful and mature process. The discourse of the military junta always manipulated two things that we badly needed if we were to recover the health of our society: language and historical memory. That is why the writing of memoirs of the very recent past was a therapy then, and the reading of them today a necessity.

Georgetown, 1993

PERSONA NON GRATA

1

Someone had already hinted to me in Santiago that I might be getting a new posting, so the telephone call I received in Lima did not take me entirely by surprise. The caller asked me, at the request of the president of Chile,[1] to be in Havana within ten days; I was to open Chile's first embassy there since relations between the two countries had been broken off six years earlier. I was to go first to Santiago for a couple of days to receive instructions, and then to fly at once to Havana, via Mexico.

Since leaving Cuba, I have spent weeks, off and on, trying to make it all add up. Much of what seemed accidental or coincidental at the time has taken on new, and often sinister, meaning; the pieces of the puzzle, in which I have begun to make out a more somber picture of reality than I once saw, have silently and precisely begun to fall into place as obsessive recollection has done its work. I now hear the siren song of that telephone conversation, full of insinuating hypocrisy, and I see, too late, what was behind it. The caller had to make that call; he had a dangerous vacancy that had to be filled as soon as possible. "A very brief mission, just till the ambassador arrives, and you'll be off for Paris." And besides—how was one to refuse a presidential request?

---

[1] Since January 1970 I had been the Chilean Embassy counselor in Lima, Peru. When this story begins, in November of that year, Salvador Allende had just assumed the presidency of the Republic of Chile a few days before.

1

When I had met with him in Santiago, the president had admitted that he had opposed my appointment. The "people from the ministry" had insisted, however, that I was the only person suitable for the job. My own view was that Cuba's friendship with Chile, after the reestablishment of diplomatic relations, depended not in the slightest on my performance, while my work in Peru, at least during the period when the Chilean ambassador from the Unidad Popular government[2] was being installed and getting his bearings, was useful.[3]

It occurred to me even then that the eternal bureaucrats of the ministry had tricked me, using that "request" of the president's without warrant, but I told myself that the experience would be worth it. The experience, as it turned out, was rougher than I, or even they (*"possibly* they," I should say), expected. Because maybe they did expect it. That siren call across the telephone wires, luring me into the edges of the spider web, definitely meant something. But it also may be that the experience actually was worth it after all. Unless my slow fall into the center of the web, into the devouring jaws, is not over yet, in which case there will be no way back from the experience—and that is a possibility that cannot be discarded either. One would have to admit, if this latter scenario were true, that those who prefer not to have the experience, those who choose simply to "opt out" and turn their backs on the experience, are right. But I am not one of those who fear to tread, which makes me a candidate for destruction, or for suicide. Of course, I may not yet have returned to a normal way of seeing things. It may be that in spite of my illusory sense that I have indeed returned to a normal way of seeing things, I am still suffering from that paranoia that made me, upon my return to "the world," imagine that the Barcelona apartment of a friend of mine was bugged. The truth is, I could speculate *ad infinitum*. This book could turn into a labyrinth of imaginings, uncertainties, ambiguities. And so the best thing to do must be to set forth the unembroidered succession of events, even when knowing "what it was all about" leads one to doubt its very plausibility. It is sometimes easier to see

---

[2] The Unidad Popular government was a coalition of leftist and progressive liberal parties headed by Salvador Allende. It took power in October 1970.

[3] All through 1970 there was a great deal of talk in Peru of war with Chile. It was election year in Chile, and many people thought that the CIA was behind the anti-Chile propaganda in Peru, since its purpose would have been to prevent Peru's leftist military-revolutionary government under General Velasco Alvarado and Chile's Unidad Popular government (assuming, that is, that Allende won the Chilean elections) from forming a solid socialist block in South America.

"what it was all about" in the course of the telling, as the verbal gears turn and as the rhythm of the words falls, perhaps, into a bottomless well that swallows all.

"I've been had," I told myself, "because what we're now learning about the Cuban situation gives no one much cause for celebration—but I'm going anyway, willingly, even conscious of being the victim of a trick."

By the time I took the plane for Mexico City, I was truly looking forward to being in Havana again, after my visit of January–February 1968.[4] I was both curious and excited. Images of that previous trip crowded my memory, the newspaper publicity that accompanied this second trip, the sensation of local renown, the special attention from the airline employees, who treated me "ambassadorially," all lent me (with some help from personal vanity) a sense of optimism, as though I had been suddenly plucked up out of the limitations of everyday life. My impressions were no doubt similar to those of the nine-to-five Joe who's just won the lottery—I traveled in a state of drowsy, blessed unconsciousness. The contradictions between the siren song of the telephone and the doubt in the presidential voice should have been more than sufficient cause for reflection. One or another warning, the mocking insinuations that my stay in Havana couldn't possibly be as brief as I had been told, were dismissed as the kind of comment that one might expect from those poor souls that always spoke more out of envy than of clairvoyance in situations such as these. Incurable optimism, as it has a way of doing, seized upon what suited it, and brushed aside the rest.

Seen from the air, the multitudinous reddish lights of Mexico City added fuel to that enthusiasm and kept it alive. It was six o'clock of a cold morning at

---

[4] At that time, while on unpaid leave from the Chilean Ministry of Foreign Relations, I had gone to Cuba as a writer. I had been invited to attend the Havana Cultural Congress but also to be a member of the jury for the annual literary prizes given by the Casa de las Américas. These literary prizes were important, the Cuban (or Caribbean, or even Latin-American) equivalent of the Booker or Pulitzer prizes. The Casa de las Américas is itself a fascinating subject for a book: Especially during the first ten or so years of the Revolution, through the sixties, it was a sponsor of many kinds of cultural events as well as literary prizes, and in many ways acted as a kind of Ministry of Culture. Through it, Cuba's national and international cultural policies were channeled (and in a government whose policies were as centralized as Cuba's, that meant its ties to Castro himself were very close); its director had virtual cabinet rank within the government. The importance of the Casa de las Américas as a patron of literature and the arts, especially early on, at a time when virtually all liberals (and therefore, almost by definition, virtually all poets, playwrights, writers, and other artists) were eager supporters of the Cuban experiment, can hardly be overestimated.

the airport, and the reception line of the Cuban embassy awaited me. With them stood, in an act of diplomatic solidarity, the Chilean cultural attaché, who had not gone home to bed at the end of a late party.

The Cuban ambassador to Mexico, a tall, reserved man with an intelligent look about him, has invited Burchard[5] and me to have a cup of coffee and a glass of rum with him at his residence, before my departure for Havana. Near the barred gate of his residence stand a group of those young athletic types with short hair and hard stares that I will discover everywhere I turn in Havana. My eye is not yet practiced, so I pay them no mind.

Nor do I see any symbolic meaning in the blinds drawn closed during the day, the cold and darkness of the room, an atmosphere that well befits the frigidity of the relations between Cuba and Mexico.[6] The flavor of the thick coffee and the rum are like a rich foretaste of tropical Cuba. I speak to the ambassador about my first trip to his country, early in 1968, at the invitation of the Casa de las Américas, and he smiles with enigmatic courtesy. Today I think back about what that smile masked: my invitation as a *writer,* that is, as a bourgeois intellectual; my defense of José Norberto Fuentes' submission, a book of short stories, which after its publication was attacked by *Verde Olivo,* the official Army magazine; my friendship with certain dissident writers . . .

Conditions could not have been less auspicious for me, but who in Chile knew that the crisis had gone so far? Everyone was predicting that a stunning reception awaited me, that all my difficulties would be smoothed away immediately, that we would be installed in a magnificent house (one no doubt already selected for me). Afterward, Mario Monteforte Toledo[7] told me: "When I learned of your appointment, I was struck by how terribly inopportune it was. Writers, as a class, tend to be critics of the regime nowadays. There's nobody less appropriate to be Chile's first diplomatic representative in Havana than a writer." They knew more about Cuba in Mexico than we did in Santiago. But it may be that President Allende did know, or at least had some intuition about,

---

[5] The painter Pablo Burchard, cultural attaché to the Chilean Embassy in Mexico City.

[6] This at the moment when the regime of Gustavo Díaz Ordaz had just ended and Luis Echeverría was assuming the presidency.

[7] A well-known Guatemalan writer and politician who had been living in Mexico since the military takeover and ouster of Jacobo Arbenz's reform regime in Guatemala in 1954.

the situation, and that his coolness to the idea of my appointment derived from that knowledge.

The ambassador stood, all amiable stiffness, and walked with us to the door. I was told that shortly after that meeting he commented that "the Edwards family is immortal: The last ambassador of the reactionaries, before relations were severed, was an Edwards. The first diplomat from the Popular regime, after relations are reestablished, is named Edwards. An immortal family, indeed."

From my first day in Havana, I would find myself every morning in the pages of *Granma,* and every afternoon in the pages of *Juventud Rebelde,* with allusions to the "Edwards clan," the "Edwards empire," the "center of reactionary conspiracy," et cetera. This publicity inspired countless questions from Cuban citizens, scattered jokes from Western diplomats, and an impeccable silence from the representatives of socialist countries, who could only trust in the envoy from "our comrade President Allende," and who, especially in the case of the Orientals, would address to me, through the offices of their interpreters, speeches burning with enthusiasm and revolutionary solidarity.

As I entered the departure area at the airport in Mexico City, I believe I caught the flash of a flashbulb out of the corner of my eye. If someone were intent on keeping tabs on me, all they would have to do would be use the newspapers of Chile and Cuba judiciously. But the police are more efficient— and at the same time more stupid, with that imperturbable mechanical stupidity of theirs—than I thought at the time. My passport was submitted, like all the other passengers', to a prolonged scrutiny. In consideration of my diplomatic investiture, my passport was spared the indignity of the accusatory stamp, in inch-high letters, that read *TRAVEL TO CUBA,* and I myself was spared the useless, though humiliating, ceremony of a mugshot (useful, perhaps, on second thought, for its power to humiliate one).

As I reached the end of a long passageway under repair, my fingers sliced by the cord tied around a box containing twelve bottles of the best Chilean wines, I could see the Soviet-made Ilushin turbojet painted with the colors of the Cuban flag on its tail. It was Enrique Bello and Rebeca Yáñez, whom I ran into at the market at Providencia a short while before I left for the Pudahuel airport in Chile, who had urged me, with almost frenzied enthusiasm, to buy this wine. They had also not let me leave the market without a few bunches of *cochayuyo,* a dark brown seaweed used in the preparation of certain dishes which (according to Enrique) Fidel Castro and Nicolás Guillén loved. In one of his typical fits of generosity, this one aggravated by his passion for gastronomy, Enrique scribbled a recipe on a piece of paper, arguing heatedly over the details of it with Rebeca, while the cashier, looking on skeptically, told us the market was closing. Enrique's mouth had watered at the very thought of that plate of *cochayuyo,* but the crackling bunches of the marine delicacy were finally too much of a burden to bear, and they were left behind, under the care of Margarita, my Lima cook.

The stewardesses' distinctive accents, the dry rum on the rocks, that morning's edition of *Granma,*[8] the latest edition of *Bohemia* (on one of whose pages I discovered myself, leaning on the railing of a balcony of the Hotel Habana Libre three years earlier, during my previous life as a mere writer, making a statement for the official Cuban press agency Prensa Latina)—it all brought back to me, almost with a shock, the hours spent by this chargé d'affaires before he had been one, on that same balcony looking out over that same city. It had been three long years, as all these years were. But to take my seat on the Ilushin was to erase with one stroke the time elapsed and to be transported to the soil of Cuba—that "first free territory of the Americas," as so many voices, in such diverse circumstances, would repeat untiringly for the three and a half months to come.

After flying for several hours over the Caribbean, I suddenly recognized, not without emotion, the palms and the reddish soil of the Island. The plane came to a stop near several other Ilushins and an old Bristol Britannia (a plane on which I had crossed the Atlantic twice in 1968). I felt a bit nervous, as the plane halted, at the thought of having to step outside the plane and walk down the steps as a public personage, besieged by reporters and subjected to the rounds of handshakes prescribed by protocol. I thought I might find one or another of my old friends there; their pleasure at the opportunity to greet me as the first of Chile's new envoys had been reported in Lima in the cable dispatches of Prensa Latina.

When I saw no one at the foot of the steps, I experienced a confused sensation, a mixture of relief and disappointment. Walking ahead of me, a small group of people was now nearing the airport building. It was the reception party for two Scandinavian ambassadors who were stationed in Mexico City but who were also accredited in Cuba, and who had come on a fifteen-day visit in order to make a token appearance there and to perform some of the rites of the profession. The group entered a large room, apparently

---

[8] December 7, 1970.

the area reserved for Protocol. I started to follow them, but at the gates stood a Gabriel whose finger pointed out the alternate route that I, as a mere mortal, was to take.

"This is not the Protocol area?"

"That way!" my Gabriel intoned imperiously, not deigning to give me a direct answer but pointing a long finger instead in the direction of the common areas.

"I am the Chilean chargé d'affaires," I said.

The guard wavered a second, as though he could not quite believe what he had heard, and then, when he saw that I was starting to pull out the black passport with gold letters that my country's diplomats carried, he lurched into sudden and intense activity. Within seconds I was ushered into the Protocol area, into the presence of an assistant secretary of Protocol who began, with the suave manners possessed by functionaries of that ministry all over the world, to offer me a long and most sincere apology—the error had been altogether theirs, how could this have happened, no one had told them! And what a pity, compañero![9]—they had so much wanted to have a magnificent welcome in my honor, the reception merited by the representative of the Unidad Popular government of Cuba's brother country Chile!

My arrival had been communicated by the Chilean Ministry of Foreign Relations to the Chilean Embassy in Mexico City, which in turn had notified the Cuban Embassy there. Had the Cuban Embassy forgotten to forward the information to its government? For his part, the Prensa Latina agent in Lima had promised to report the news. Had he also been negligent? While I listened to the courteous apologies of the Protocol officer, who was playing his role to perfection, I was struck by the thought that my error had lain in not requesting the Chilean Foreign Ministry to communicate the time of my arrival directly, by cable, to their Cuban counterparts. I even offered this argument in his favor to the Protocol officer, since he insisted upon taking all the blame upon himself. From the other side of the large room, the Scandinavian ambassadors,

---

[9] *Compañero/-a* is the Latin American equivalent of the Russian "comrade" in some ways, though it is used in many more contexts. A man can talk about his "*compañera*," for example, meaning perhaps wife, perhaps girlfriend; a "compañero de trabajo" is quite literally and unpolitically an office mate or fellow office worker. The word signifies social and political solidarity, and is used throughout Latin America (and not only in Communist or socialist regimes) for many purposes. Here and throughout this book, of course, it indicates a "true believer" in the Cuban experiment—like "brother" or "sister" might be used by a church group.

who had the red cheeks of heavy drinkers and with whom I had not exchanged introductions, were looking over at me out of the corners of their eyes, with the slight skepticism of old European diplomats.

Soon there appeared beside the assistant secretary of Protocol a tray loaded with large frothy daiquiris. The man's apologies never stopped. The head of Protocol, who had tarried a few minutes with the Scandinavians, at last came up and began to repeat the explanations and apologies, but his style was more concise and direct, and he did not so slavishly follow the rhetoric of the traditional diplomatic formulas. He seemed to trust immediately in the lack of offense I took at the incident. He said they would put me up in a hotel and that my situation would be seen to at once, and he himself led me to a small private automobile, a chocolate-colored Volkswagen.

For reasons which it would be premature to set forth in the first pages of this story, I do not now believe that this ignorance of my arrival was real and fortuitous. But let us not get ahead of ourselves . . .

Meléndez, the head of Protocol, set me up in a suite on the eighteenth floor of the Hotel Habana Riviera. The Habana Riviera was one of the American-style luxury hotels built in the El Vedado section of Havana during the tourist boom years that preceded the fall of Batista. It was built to face the ocean; one steps outside the lobby onto Havana's famed Malecón, the seawall-road that runs for a long stretch along the ocean front. The Malecón has wide sidewalks, those on the ocean side punctuated at intervals by ventilation holes so there is some escape valve for the waves as they break along the rocks below. In the old days the Malecón was the axis of the tourist area of Havana, a place for strolling, chatting, seeing and being seen. The Hotel Habana Riviera sat in lordly splendor on its privileged site. It had a large, and rather grand, cabaret, which was frequented by the likes of George Raft, Frank Sinatra, and Ernest Hemingway—and where in the early years of the Revolution, some of the Revolution's leaders might be seen as well. Now it was closed on weekdays, while on weekends it opened to a motley crowd of more common folk, dressed in their party best. In another room, a casino before the Revolution, there was dancing to the music of Cuban standards. There was something a little old-fashioned about it all, something in those Pérez Prado songs, and the odd absence of rock and pop, that for me evoked the atmosphere of adolescence.

The bar attracted foreign journalists, experts, businessmen, writers, politicians who were the guests of the country, short-term diplomats such as myself, with no official residence yet, and also gave harbor to the occasional inmate of the hotel who had dropped anchor there after the Cultural Congress of 1968, carrying out none-too-well-defined activities. There was a table of young Czechs who drank heavily every Saturday night and who kept strictly to themselves; I never saw them socialize with anyone. At another table one could often see Pierre Gollendorf, a photographer I had met in Paris sometime around 1964, and who had been under the wing of Violeta Parra there.[10]

I discovered that the top three floors of the hotel—floors 18, 19, and 20—were reserved for the use of the Prime Minister. Meléndez informed me that Castro would be speaking to the nation that night, on the occasion of the close of the Plenary Assembly of Basic Industry, and he said he would have a television set sent up to my suite so I could watch.

Meléndez gave the appearance of a happy-go-lucky sort of fellow; he was athletic, with small eyes, a low and somewhat beetling forehead, and short hair. I do not know whether he took part in the struggle against Batista. More than one person thought it necessary to tell me that before the Revolution he had sold ties in one of the big El Encanto department stores, which had later been burned down in an act of counterrevolutionary sabotage. Meléndez walked bowlegged, hitting his fist against his palm like a boxer. I cannot recall ever seeing him wear a long-sleeved shirt; when the sleeves of his jacket rode up, they revealed thick, muscular forearms.

No more than fifteen minutes had gone by when two workers brought a huge cardboard packing case up to my room, with a Bulgarian or Soviet television inside. Its imitation of Western TV sets was a little crude, with a few touches of outright bad taste, but the set worked well, in spite of its looks, and in spite of the hesitancies of the workers who installed it and who seemed to be seeing this model for the first time in their lives.

I took off my suitcoat, poured myself a whisky from the bottle I had brought in my bag, and sat down in shirtsleeves to watch Fidel's speech. A light breeze, heralding the Cuban winter, helped dissipate the humid heat. The breeze was more effective, in any case, than the air conditioner that the bellboy had turned on with a certain ostentation, reminiscent of times gone by, as he left, and which only weakly emitted a stream of coolish air. I afterward learned that Fidel had used similar rooms as his residence and general headquarters in the days just after his triumphant entry into Havana in early 1959. At about eight-thirty, his face, a bit aged in comparison with the face I was accustomed to seeing in photographs, came on the screen.

*   *   *

---

[10] Violeta Parra was a very well known Chilean singer and songwriter, the sister of the distinguished poet Nicanor Parra.

It had been years since I saw Fidel close up for the first time, in a hall at Princeton University in April 1959. Eleven and a half years, in fact, the precise age of the Revolution. That once-youthful Revolution was beginning to age, to lose the freshness and fury of its beginnings, to mature—and with it, its leaders. Part of the legacy of maturity, of course, is the deterioration that inevitably accompanies it. Just since my trip to Havana in January 1968, little less than three years ago, the changes had been enormous; the faces of the city and of Fidel had suffered parallel and implacable erosion. The walls of Havana were peeling; strips of masking tape held together the broken panes of glass in the windows of many buildings; there were houses abandoned; rubble sometimes covered the sidewalks right up to the foundations of the buildings and blocked the way to pedestrians; skeletons of rusted automobiles lay about the streets. And the same erosion could be seen in Fidel; it had left his eyes sunken and had brought out the bones in the hand that he used, with a certain tenseness, a trace of nervous hesitancy not seen in him before, to smooth his beard or make his characteristic gesture (that now seemed to stop halfway sometimes) of pushing aside an invisible piece of paper or holding it up for the spectator to contemplate.

Reality had taken fierce vengeance on the dreams that accompanied the beginnings of the Revolution, that stage of it that might be called its spontaneous, romantic period, when it had not only stirred the hopes of the Latin American masses but also awakened the enthusiasm of the young people and the intellectuals of aging Europe. For its enemies, arguments against the Revolution were easy to come by—so much so that I allowed myself, weeks later, a bad (counterrevolutionary) joke: The campaign managers for Alessandri[11] should have organized tourist excursions to Cuba . . . A bad (counterrevolutionary) joke that held its pinch of truth. And yet, alongside the serenity and stable sadness that come with maturity, that come when one descends from the heights of juvenile euphoria, there was a pathetic veracity that one had almost to admire, a quixotic pride in the act of showing those cracked and peeling walls, the dusty rubble that blocked the sidewalks, the rusted hulk of the 1950 Chevrolet that one day, in the middle of the street, with the bang of an exploding tire or the shiver of a gasping engine, had simply and forever died. Havana, the world-famous whore of the Caribbean in the fifties, now showed herself without makeup, regenerated, defiant in her poverty. And Fidel himself, sitting

---

[11] The candidate of the right defeated by Salvador Allende in the September 1970 elections in Chile, the last popular elections for president held in accord with the old Chilean constitution.

before the TV cameras, showed a face likewise without makeup, pathetic in its weariness, in the intense worry that he neither could nor cared to hide.

I recalled the scene that had been described to me not long ago by one of our diplomats in Washington. Richard Nixon was giving a dinner at a grand hotel in California in celebration of the first landing of man on the moon. Diplomats had to take a plane, put on their tuxedos, and find their places in an enormous dining room of gleaming and garish bad taste. When everyone, according to instructions from the Protocol section, was seated, the host and the guests of honor yet to appear, there was a movement behind some curtains near the table of honor. Hundreds of spotlights were turned on the spot; the television cameras began to film in unison. Nixon then made his appearance, in full makeup and a false smile. From his place he made gestures of greeting, or rose to shake hands with some public figure nearby—the Soviet ambassador, for example, or the chief justice of the Supreme Court. When the astronauts' turn came, they stood and said a few innocuous words, listened to by millions of American viewers as they chewed the insipid food they had served up to themselves on TV tables in their living rooms.

One of the basic ways of understanding the Cuban Revolution is as a reaction to the "American way of life," and as an opposition to it. Given the golden calf, given the noisy, mendacious vulgarity of *el Norte,* the Hispano-Afro-American world was offering its bearded face lined with weariness and care, its honest visage with no makeup to mask the hard, stubborn reality that it reflected. It repeated, in new terms, the confrontation described by Rubén Darío in his ode to Teddy Roosevelt. The poem is simply called "To Roosevelt," and here are its first lines:

> It would be with the voice of the Bible, or
>   some verse from Walt Whitman,
> That one could reach thee, Hunter!
> Primitive and modern, simple and complex,
> with one part Washington and four parts Nim-
>   rod.
> Thou art the United States,
> thou art the future invader
> of those innocent Americas that still have
>   native blood,
> that still pray to Jesus Christ, and still
>   speak Spanish.

I had first seen Fidel, as I said, during his famous trip to the United States in early 1959. I was studying public and international affairs at Princeton. A

wealthy American interested in Latin America had made it possible to invite
Fidel to speak at the university. At that time there was a degree of sympathy for
Fidel in the United States, but I could see, especially after his visit to Princeton,
that distrust and even open hostility were the predominant attitudes toward him.
President Eisenhower went off to play golf so that he would not have to meet
him, so Richard Nixon, then vice president, saw to the job of speaking with him
and of writing up a report which, as we later discovered, directly opposed
collaboration of any kind with the new regime in Havana.

In Princeton, the university, and in fact the entire city, was in an uproar
over the visit. With the most refined hypocrisy, the university authorities
made sure that Fidel's speech would give rise to no student demonstrations in
support of revolutionary Cuba. Instead of holding the activity in a large
auditorium, they scheduled it for one of the classes given by a Professor
Palmer, whose course principally dealt with the American Revolution. Fidel's
talk, then, would be held in the building housing the Woodrow Wilson
School of Public and International Affairs, in a hall meant for about fifty
people, with invitations strictly controlled. In that way the speech would be
invested with a suitably intellectual cast and a sort of antiseptic cordon would
be placed around it (foreshadowing the cordon that would later be set up
around the entire Island). At the same time, the Princeton authorities could
give proof of their liberalism, the inheritance of that other revolution that
constituted the academic specialty of Professor Palmer.

In my role as "Latin American" and as a student of the School, and thanks
to the good offices of Fidel's host (who was later sanctioned, in the little world
of Princeton, for his incipient Castroism), I obtained two tickets to Fidel's
speech. In spite of the fact that my wife and I arrived quite early, we found that
the main doors to the Woodrow Wilson School were heavily guarded. Behind
the police lines a compact mass of students had gathered, among whom were
some Cubans who had come in from New York. There was a festive sort of
atmosphere generally, an effervescence, which from the standpoint of today
might be seen as a foreshadowing of student demonstrations of somewhat later
years—the Vietnam years—although there was not the charged atmosphere in
this demonstration that would be seen in so many subsequent ones. At this time
the conscience of the American dissident movement had begun to mobilize
against the hydrogen bomb, against war preparations, against the oppressive
forms that capitalism so often took, and the presence of those young people
shouting, laughing, waving, as though they were waiting for some sports idol
or rock star to appear, was an unequivocal sign—precisely for *not* being
inspired by that baseball champ or Hollywood star, but rather by a revolution-

ary hero from the unknown subworld of the Latin South—of the disquiet, the crisis of conscience that was so deeply to affect the United States in the following years.

At about this same time a handful of shabby, bearded poets had passed through Princeton, leaving few echoes among those walls that had eavesdropped on the classical words of Thomas Mann and the difficult teachings of William Faulkner. They had come on foot, or hitchhiked, or ridden the Greyhounds from faraway San Francisco, and their names were Allen Ginsberg, Gregory Corso, and Lawrence Ferlinghetti (and others even less well known in those times). But even stranger and more unsettling than the beatniks' appearance against the peaceable Princeton backdrop was that of the guerrillas from the Sierra Maestra. Students of economics, political science, and history were not accustomed to studying leaders like those that strode into the hall in the Woodrow Wilson School through a back door, surrounded by a guard of police: bearded men in olive-green fatigue uniforms, their long hair tied up in braids or a ponytail, marching into the hall with an ironic smile, their youthful bodies springing at every step. There were girls in uniform and beret as well, and much like the men in the distrustful or overly cocky expressions their faces wore—expressions reasonable in view of the waiting crowd, whose attitude seemed to swing between hostility and the curiosity of the audience at a circus or a bullfight.

The room stood and applauded, the crowd's excitement mixed with curiosity, when Fidel strode through the door at the rear of the hall, returning greetings left and right as he walked down the center aisle to the dais at the front of the room. His entrance through the rear obeyed security considerations, and a few agents came in with Fidel, along with still more Cubans in their olive-green fatigues.

Speaking to his Princeton auditors, Fidel used a hesitating, rudimentary English, which he employed, nonetheless, with his customary oratorical skill, that pleasure in the management of words and that ear for the rhythm of the phrase—reiterative, repetitive—that he never abandons, or that if he ever abandoned it was precisely in those long stretches of the speech that I would hear on the day of my arrival as chargé d'affaires in Havana. Some people have told me that the speech I heard that night in Havana was the worst speech of Fidel's life, that it pained them to hear him, for they had seen in the Commander-in-Chief's unaccustomed lapse of rhetorical control a sign that the Revolution was passing through one of its most serious crises. Someone likewise observed that a comment like that was one way of smuggling in criticism. Still, the crisis that followed the disastrous "ten-million-ton harvest"[12] was one of the circumstances that was to determine the nature of my fate in Cuba.

In Princeton, though, it was the beginning, the stage of mad hopes and of dreams. The youthfulness of Fidel and his compañeros symbolized the youth of the Revolution, and was one key to the novelty of the phenomenon in the world's eyes. Fidel revealed in his speech that a Hollywood producer had offered him a million dollars to film the odyssey of the ship *Granma* as it crossed the Caribbean from Mexico to Cuba, and of the long struggle waged from the Sierra Maestra. But the producer was mistaken; Fidel and his followers were not interested in money. Fidel did not need to say it at that moment, but the producer's error was revelatory of the whole American attitude toward the Cuban Revolution—revelatory and premonitory.

The speech at Princeton was a long plea for collaboration between the United States and the new government in Cuba. It was, perhaps, the most eloquent and convincing plea that could be made in its favor, and the very fact that it was made in a halting and rudimentary English, to a group dedicated to the study of the American Revolution, made it all the more meaningful. Meanwhile, Eisenhower was playing golf and his advisers had taken refuge behind that impenetrable wall thrown up by deaf men who have no desire to hear. Unless I am mistaken, mine (that of the only Latin American present in the hall) is the only memory that remains of that speech.[13] I will now try to summarize it, even if my doing so embarrasses the American authorities (and perhaps Fidel himself somewhat).

Fidel, who tried to stay within the bounds of Professor Palmer's seminar, said that the Cuban Revolution was a new, original stage in the history of revolutions. Unlike the Soviet revolution, unlike the Marxist model of Revolution with the capital *R* of some grand abstraction, Cuba's was not based on the principle of the class struggle. Exactly the opposite had occurred in the Cuban Revolution, said Fidel: Members of all classes had taken part in the fight against tyranny. The explanation for this phenomenon lay in the fact that the Batista dictatorship had become unbearable at every level, the sole exception being those directly profiting from its excesses. Nor, said Fidel, did the

---

[12] See p. 184 for a fuller description of this failure and the crisis it brought on.

[13] Colin Harding, translator of this book for the Bodley Head edition in England, reminded me that I had gone with Pilar, my wife, and asked me whether she weren't Latin American as well. Good question! Criticism from feminists here will be entirely justified. I modified the phrase in the British edition, but here, in order to be faithful to the original, I leave it, with my sincere apologies to female opinion.

Revolution intend to do away with private property. In a country in which land was in the hands of a very few, agrarian reform would create new owners; these would constitute an important consumer base for the industrial development of the Island.

Fidel's words, in those first months of the Revolution, were not far from those that President Kennedy, inspired by the Keynesian experiments of Franklin Roosevelt, would later employ to explain his plans for the Alliance for Progress. One must not forget that Fidel was speaking in Princeton, one of the most influential academic centers in America, during a tour whose admitted purpose was to win over the good will of the people of the United States for the Cuban experiment. By the time Kennedy became president, Fidel had already allied himself with the Soviet block. In response to a series of countercoup attempts, the Revolution had radicalized, and the Bay of Pigs invasion at the beginning of the Kennedy administration marked the point of no return. Besides, as everyone knows, Kennedy did not launch his Alliance for Progress as a means of building bridges with Cuba; he did it to pacify and neutralize the rest of Latin America—that is, precisely so that the Cuban example would not be followed throughout South America.

In spite of everything, one can always speculate about the fate of the Cuban Revolution if it had been Kennedy in the White House instead of Eisenhower in the spring of 1959. One must not forget that a short while before Kennedy's assassination, there was a rumor that he would attempt to bring the United States closer to the Castro regime.

As I recall in detail the scenes of that visit to Princeton, it occurs to me that there was nothing the Republican administration could do but slam the door in Fidel's face, as Eisenhower the golfer and Nixon the boxer effectively did. The explosive influence of the Cuban Revolution in Latin America would have been felt even within the borders of the United States. The Princeton authorities' idea to confine Fidel to a small hall, and to an audience of specialists, was a reflection of the same political mentality that moved the White House to place Cuba under quarantine. During Fidel's speech at Princeton, it seemed to me irritating and stupid that Washington should not show a more understanding attitude; now I see that Washington's reaction followed the logic of the system perfectly: however irritating the reaction may have been, it was the inevitable outgrowth of that logic.

Washington could not look kindly on the fact that the young men and women of Princeton, after waiting three hours behind the police lines, had cheered the revolutionary *caudillo* and lifted him over their heads in spite of all the shoving and pushing the security agents could do—it took those agents several minutes to "free" him from the student mob and shove him into a car. In the midst of the hullabaloo, one could hear Cuban voices and see chubby, olive-skinned men jumping up and waving their arms to get Fidel's attention, frantically calling out, driven to a frenzy by the presence of their famous compatriot.

At the end of his talk, Fidel Castro had brusquely shaken off the squad of American bodyguards that were assigned to the rear door of the auditorium and he had left the hall alone, through the smiles and applause of those who had heard his speech, and walked into the arms of the young crowd outside. There was a good dollop of hypocrisy in the applause inside. As the official cars pulled away and the tumult in the street began to die down, one of the most outstanding students, handpicked to attend the speech, remarked to me, "He is going to destroy the economy." The absolute certainty behind that prediction deeply angered me. I told him that there was nothing *left* of the Cuban economy to destroy, that everything was yet to be done.[14] I could have used the terms that Jules Michelet used when he stated, in his *Histoire de la Révolution Française,* that we should not be talking about "revolution," but rather about "founding." But I was without Michelet's support, and the student, whose intellectual arrogance would have been argument-proof anyway, shot me an ironic look and shrugged his shoulders.

I remembered this and other things—my trip to Cuba by invitation of the Casa de las Américas in January 1968, Fidel's speech in the Chaplin Theater to the participants at the Cultural Congress in Havana, the return trip, via Prague, at the peak of liberalization and the ascent of Dubček—as on the TV screen in my hotel room I saw a more thoughtful, less euphoric Fidel, no longer young, who as he spoke seemed to search for words. And though he raised his voice from time to time, it was not with that furious conviction of other times, for he was not attacking a foreign enemy now, but rather going through an examination of Cuba's internal problems—absenteeism, disorganization in production—with the members of the Plenary Assembly of Basic Industry. This was one of the public examinations, true collective self-criticisms, that

---

[14] Now I see that the economists of the Unidad Popular in Chile acted out of much the same convictions that I held in my twenties when they maintained, in all innocence, that "inflation would destroy the power of the bourgeoisie." "Inflation is going to destroy us *all*," the taciturn Pablo Neruda, a sixty-year-old man who had never studied economics anywhere, said to me, and the results were not long in being seen.

became relatively common after his famous speech of July 26, 1970, in which he had recognized the failure of the "ten-million-ton harvest." This sort of discussion of issues at a basic level was part of the process of democratization laid out by Fidel, and its intention was to avoid future errors in guiding the economy.

If certain criticisms had been listened to early on, there would have been no need to make such a mistake about that harvest. The Cuban Revolution, which always advances somewhat gropingly, and in reaction to events rather than by initiation of action *per se,* was now urging a vast movement of reflection and debate in labor centers. Some people thought this process would turn out to be dangerous, that it would let out too many tensions, too much of the pent-up discontent which up until this moment there had been no opportunity to express. Others believed that Fidel, after indignantly rejecting René Dumont's thesis (Dumont himself now beginning to be accused of being a CIA infiltrator), was attempting to correct one of the main faults that the French economist had pointed out: the arbitrariness of decisions and the lack of democratic control of decision-making.

To all of this, the Commander-in-Chief, or *Comandante,* as he was universally known, pronounced the Cuban equivalent of the proverbial saying "Slowly but surely wins the race." He seemed to be meditating on the full implications of this concept, and the meditation involved a long self-criticism, then a repetition of the concept in other words. Sugarcane, he explained, is a difficult, implacable crop, but the only way to reap sugar is by harvesting sugarcane. When the Revolution came to power, there were four hundred thousand professional sugarcane cutters, *macheteros,* on the Island; now there were only sixty thousand. Because nobody, in this new society, aspired to be a *machetero.* And yet if you wanted to reap sugar, you had to cut sugarcane. Suddenly, the Comandante was talking about Chile, whose reopened relations with Cuba had been announced two or three weeks earlier. Chile, Fidel was saying, was in a very advantageous situation: Copper production requires relatively little manpower. A sugarcane harvest, on the other hand, needs five hundred thousand men.

In the middle of the speech, which the Bulgarian TV set was bringing to me quite well, the telephone in my room rang. The director of Protocol announced that he was coming by to pick me up. He was going to take me "somewhere." Ingeniously applying the experience of other diplomatic missions, I thought for a moment that Meléndez must be trying to make up for the cool reception at the airport with an excess of amiability. After several days of taking planes, opening and closing suitcases, seeing too many people, going from Lima to Santiago, back to Lima, then to Mexico City, and then from Mexico City to

Havana, the only gesture I would have appreciated, at least that night, would have been being left in peace to sip a glass of whisky and watch Fidel's speech on television. But there was no excuse, no way under those circumstances that I could reject the attentions of the head of Protocol, who I figured intended to take me to a restaurant or something of the sort. So I stood up and put on my jacket again, once more cursing the gilded shackles of diplomacy that do not allow one the simple right to say no, the right to reply "Perhaps another day, thank you" once in a while, yet which are so envied by the foolish men and women of my country, and in fact of the entire continent, that we seem to have inherited the French taste for the pomp of "the career."

Tieless, the director of the Office of Protocol was waiting for me downstairs at the door of the hotel in a little Volkswagen, his own car. We had hardly gotten in when he speeded off toward the old part of the city, colonial Havana. I was never afterward able to recognize the streets we drove down that night. They were narrow, dirty, smelly streets, paved with potholes. The houses looked gloomy and rundown. A soldier stopped us at one corner, but after two words from Meléndez he let us continue on.

The Volkswagen stopped beside a high, blank wall. There were militiamen armed with machine guns posted along the sidewalks. Emaciated black and mulatto faces, their expressions closed and somewhat self-absorbed, could be seen at the black holes of windows, peeking out through the clothes hung out to dry and the broken windowpanes. We went through a steel door, and suddenly I was greeted by the voice on the television, its words, amplified by loud-speakers, now echoing in the theater that lay just on the other side of those curtains. The silence, the audience's attention, was almost palpable; from time to time they would shout, answer a question from the speaker, break into laughter or applause.

Backstage, there were a number of militiamen seated or standing about, looking bored. They would exchange a few words from time to time in a low voice. The head of Protocol introduced me to a relatively young-looking "comandante" (I had not yet figured out the exact meaning of the name and rank of "comandante") with a red beard; his name was Manuel Piñeiro (nor was I aware of the significance of that name), and he began to converse with me in the most natural manner, asking me questions about Chile and various people in the government. The head of Protocol left us chatting alone for a while, but then suddenly Comandante Piñeiro brusquely excused himself. I'm sure he was insulted by my relative indifference, since I thought I was talking with some simple squad leader, perhaps of these very soldiers. But when Meléndez came over to sit down with me again, he asked me where Piñeiro had gone, and something about the tone of Meléndez's question suddenly made me think—maybe this red-bearded comandante, in spite of his simplicity and naturalness, his total lack of stiffness and formality, was really a person of importance. The European custom of introducing people with all their titles and degrees, a custom which we in Latin America have such scorn and disdain for, had its obvious advantages!

A short while later, Comandante Piñeiro returned to his seat and picked up the conversation we had left off. The voice in the background, meanwhile, was announcing to the assembly that Christmas celebrations would not be held that year—they were a foreign tradition imported from old Europe by colonized Cubans, and totally alien to the climate and working conditions in Cuba. At the end of December the harvest would be at its peak, its most crucial moment; interruption of the cane-cutting by celebrations, with the aggravating factor of the absenteeism that inevitably preceded and followed the fiestas, would create a delay whose impact on the economy would be intolerable. Christmas and New Year's celebrations, seen from a revolutionary perspective, were a typical case of cultural dependency; the time had come to free ourselves from *that* sort of dependency as well, by holding celebrations that corresponded to the climate and production cycles of Cuba. Were not European festivals linked to the seasons, the rhythms of agricultural production, the end of planting, the grape and cereal harvests? This year, Cuban end-of-year celebrations would be postponed until after the sugarcane harvest. Did the assembly agree to that? The assembly unanimously cheered and applauded enthusiastically. Among that applause there was quite possibly, Piñeiro whispered in my ear, the sound of Chilean hands clapping: Delegations from the National Society of Agriculture and the National Airlines were present in the hall, as were former senator Baltazar Castro and his family.[15]

As the final applause was slowly dying down, some of the Chileans began to appear backstage. Soon there was a compact little Chileo-Cuban assembly standing in the wings, and it was joined almost immediately by the imposing presence and physical stature of Fidel. Someone (I can't recall whether it was Piñeiro or Meléndez) told Fidel that Chile's first diplomatic envoy was present. Fidel, surprised, turned to me and shook my hand warmly.

---

[15] Senator Castro was at this time viewed by the Cuban government, with some justification, as one of the main proponents of Chile's breaking the blockade against Cuba. Senator Castro also exported wine to Cuba.

"If I had known that you had arrived, sir," he said, "I would have announced it in my speech," and then he added, smiling and emphasizing each word, as though it were a little piece of mischief he could allow himself now and then, "I'd have broken with protocol!"

I thought nothing of it at the time, but today I wonder: Could he not have known? And if he really didn't, who was it that kept the news from him, and for what reasons? Cuba's embassy in Mexico City knew perfectly well, and I had arrived at José Martí Airport three hours before the Prime Minister began his speech. It was hard to believe that no one in his retinue knew of my arrival, and if one considers the importance given in Cuba to the arrival of the first South American diplomat, the representative of the Unidad Popular government of Chile, after more than six years of severed relations, how is one to believe that the failure to communicate the news to Fidel was not deliberate? This is another of the mysteries of my stay on the Island. Besides being a memoir and a story, this book is a retrospective investigation into those months, an effort of memory not greatly different from the methods of psychoanalysis, and in which the very writing of the text brings not a few revelations to its own author.

Raúl Roa, the Cuban minister of foreign relations, was backstage, too, wearing an old navy-blue sport shirt. He offered to take me back to my hotel, and I signaled to Meléndez, in the midst of the hullabaloo of the mass departure, that I was going with Roa.

"Wait for me in the hotel, then," Meléndez said. "I'll come by to pick you up and take you to *Granma*—they want to interview you."

In the midst of the confusion caused by Fidel and the other leaders and the militiamen, all of whom wanted to get out the narrow steel door at the same time, there was no way to beg off this new invitation of Meléndez'. This was no hour to be interviewed. But, I figured, there would be time to sleep later.

Roa sat in front, beside the driver. As he spoke he opened his bony hands and gesticulated vigorously, with ungainly movements that made me think of a pelican. He immediately established a cordial, simple relationship between us, symbolized perhaps by that old shirt, and certainly helped by his conversation. It was the total opposite of the sort of conversation that one might have held with a minister of foreign relations anywhere else in Latin America—or the world, for that matter. In those first moments, Roa's attitude seemed to show me the human face of the Revolution.

Our conversation continued for some twenty minutes on the sidewalk in front of the Habana Riviera. We stood beside the seawall, where one could see, in the darkness below, the white spray of the breaking waves, and we talked about one thing and another—the Peruvian military leaders and the international policies of the Christian Democrat government; former Chilean foreign minister Gabriel Valdés and Christian Democrat Tomic; Socialist party leader Carlos Altamirano and Salvador Allende. In Raúl Roa's opinion, Allende was the most experienced politician of the Chilean Left, the man with the deepest understanding of the country. Nor did Roa try to hide his sympathies for the government of Peru: he revealed to me that he had suggested to General Velasco Alvarado that he should not rush to reestablish relations with Cuba, but rather wait for a moment when that action would cause fewer repercussions that might endanger the stability of his administration.

I later heard it said that Roa was the foremost intellectual figure of Cuba. (This judgment, which came from officials of cultural institutions, was probably in part a way of downgrading such creative figures as Alejo Carpentier, José Lezama Lima, Nicolás Guillén, and the younger writers.) But I also heard young Party militants criticize the grandiloquence and ornamentation of Roa's prose and his speeches. Those young people, in whose intransigence could already be seen a certain ambitious desire for power, considered Roa a benign survivor of the age of politician-orators out of which Latin America had only barely emerged. Roa had published a book about the deeds of a grandfather or great-grandfather of his, a prominent figure in the wars of independence, and the truth is that the style was a bit overcharged, and slightly anachronistic. At the same time, Roa's passion for the history and politics of Latin America was refreshing. We had conversations more than once afterward; once or twice he offered me invitations to his house that never quite materialized, and looking back, that doesn't surprise me. Throughout these conversations he talked to me about all sorts of things, but now that I reflect back, I believe that he tellingly avoided many others.

I said good-night to Roa, and at once Meléndez's Volkswagen, whose presence I had not noticed, slid up out of the darkness. Meléndez was unwilling to release his prey, although the prey could hardly keep his eyes open. Besides, Havana was not the best place one could have chosen for a rest cure.

It took me a couple of months to recognize the place where the *Granma* building was located, near the Plaza de la Revolución, in spite of the fact that I passed nearby almost every day. That night we walked through a lobby under repair and took the elevator to a high floor in the building. There was great activity in the offices, as though it were the middle of the day. I was shown into a meeting room with wood-paneled walls and the ubiquitous posters of the heroes of the Revolution. Capitán Mendoza, the editor of *Granma,* was there, along with the assistant editor Ramón Perdomo, and there were also Comandante

Piñeiro, the journalist Marta Rojas (known for her reports on Vietnam), and some others, I don't recall exactly who else. I sat down and waited for the interview to begin, but my interlocutors, sitting around the circular table, smiled at me, asked me occasional questions about my trip, made small talk, and generally leaned on their elbows. I was beginning to think that Meléndez had dragged me up there at two o'clock in the morning to talk about the weather, when Fidel Castro came into the room. It was only then that I realized that everything had been prepared for this, even the vacant chair beside me, but that Fidel's movements, for security reasons, were never announced ahead of time. Fidel, who had had a long and difficult night, looked as tired as I'm sure I did. His eyes were sunken, and he rubbed them two or three times. Nonetheless, he soon got his second wind. He said he was very happy with the reception his speech had had, in spite of the fact that he had demanded a new round of sacrifices and had announced the suspension of the Christmas and New Year's festivities.

"It was a hard speech," he said, raising his eyebrows, as though he himself were amazed at having passed the test so successfully.

But now there was the arrival of the envoy from Chile to celebrate. How was it possible that there was no Chilean wine on the table? Diligent souls jumped up, as though someone had tripped a switch, and disappeared through a door at the rear to go find wine.

The fact that I had just been working in Lima especially interested Fidel Castro. There was talk of the anti-Chilean feelings that still survived in Peru. Fidel said he had done a great deal to convince the Peruvians that Chile had no aggressive intentions toward them. Speaking of certain members of the military junta, Fidel said he was convinced that General Velasco Alvarado was a leftist. His popular origins, most unusual in a high military commander in Latin America, Fidel felt to be revealing.[16]

---

[16] As is common knowledge, Velasco Alvarado was removed from power a few years later, and soon after died. The military revolution fell into total discredit, and the Peruvian people acted with great political common sense by electing president Fernando Belaúnde, who had been overthrown in 1968 in Velasco's coup. It is interesting to remember now, in the light of Fidel Castro's words above, that in the days following the fall of Allende, Velasco's regime entertained serious thoughts of attacking Chile, in order to recover the provinces lost in the Pacific war during the last century. There is good reason to believe that these guerrilla plans had the sympathy, and the practical support, of Cuba. Soviet armaments bought by the Peruvians would be complemented with Cuban military advisers. This dangerous combination of actors would have brought on the downfall of Velasco, who was, at any rate, gravely ill. The cancellation of these plans influenced Castro's later decision to launch his large-scale military intervention in Angola.

The Commander-in-Chief thought that Chile would sooner or later come under attack by the Yankees. Since a confrontation could not be avoided, the best strategy would be to have such a confrontation on favorable terrain. According to Fidel, the battle ought to be fought over something worth fighting for—copper, for example—and the problem presented to the country in such a way that the people, every Chilean man, woman, and child, would immediately see the necessity of, and the economic advantages to be gained from, nationalization. Suddenly, in one of the outbursts so typical of him, Fidel assured me that we should not hesitate to ask his aid if we had any problem of armed intervention. After all, he said, his aid to the Algerians had been decisive in their war of liberation. He had sent them a ship with guns and soldiers! He added the following phrase, as we clinked our glasses (now filled with the white wine that had at last appeared on the table): "We may not be very good at producing, but we're great at fighting!"

Later I made the connection between this phrase and the nineteenth-century wars between the Spaniards and the Cuban rebels, the *mambises,* fighting for the liberation of the Island, and I realized that the legendary deeds of those times—battles in which machete-wielding *mambises* charged well-armed Spanish troops, in which the rebel generals Gómez and Maceo showed mythic courage and military genius—were the episodes from Cuban history that were most insistently and proudly cited in Revolutionary Cuba, so that an uninterrupted line of continuity was drawn from those struggles to the struggles of the present.

Moving on then to Chile, Fidel maintained that Allende had so far managed things extremely well. He did say that he felt that Allende should go slow, and I recalled the phrase Fidel had used in his speech a couple of hours ago: "Slowly but surely wins the race." Now was the time to nationalize copper, said Fidel, and leave socialism for later. Otherwise, the necessary leadership cadres would not be in place, Allende would have to fight against too many enemies at once, he would face acute production problems, and so on. Speaking from hard Cuban experience, Fidel counseled a prudent advance. I had the impression that if Fidel could have been heard in Chile at that moment, he might have been able to exert a moderating influence on our leftist extremists; those words, and the attitude behind them, explained why certain extremists were choosing to invoke the slogans and exhibit the posters of Ché Guevara rather than those of Fidel. Later I learned that René Dumont, in his last book about Cuba, insistently contrasted the figures of Ché and Fidel, in a critique from the Left that was taken to be very confrontational and that was, in the eyes of many officials, suspect.

That night, drinking Baltazar Castro's white wine, we talked of many things in an atmosphere of great camaraderie and trust. Fidel and his retinue were favorably impressed with Darío Saint-Marie, the owner of the *Clarín*,[17] who had just made a trip to Havana. Obviously well-disposed toward Saint-Marie, the group at the round table began to tell anecdotes about him: In that very room, using such and such arguments, Saint-Marie had praised Cuban journalism very highly. Saint-Marie had said that *Granma* was the best newspaper in Latin America. No praise could have achieved greater effect! I was very careful, of course, to tell them that Saint-Marie had called General Ibáñez, during his second presidency (1952–1958), a Renaissance prince!

When we all stood at last, at the end of the meeting, Fidel, thumping me on the chest in a way that I found to be characteristic of his moments of humor, asked me, "Do you think I ought to buy off Matte?"[18]

"Why not!" I replied. "I think it would be best for everyone."

"Then I'm going to have a talk with him!" Fidel said.

Naturally, that exchange was decided upon in advance, especially since my response was perfectly predictable, but the way Fidel "asked my advice" had a tone of general friendly banter about it. Fidel immediately told Piñeiro to talk to me, since I "must know a lot about Peru." I always found Fidel to be fascinated by Peru, by the paradox that a traditionally reactionary institution such as the army could impose measures which within the historical and social context of Peru turned out to be revolutionary. His enthusiasm reminded me of his speech in January 1968, at the Cultural Congress in Havana, in which he made a clear distinction between the revolutionary force and impetus of a traditional institution such as the Catholic Church, and such supposedly avant-garde institutions as orthodox Communist Parties, for example, which acted, in practice, in reactionary or hyperconservative ways. By December 1970, his position with regard to Communist Parties had changed, but not his Quevedian and Unamunian[19] delight in contradiction and paradox, a delight quite possibly rooted in Fidel's Hispanic ancestry and that of the Island itself.

Later, when it was too late to fit my actions to the discovery, I found out that the luxury of dialectics was reserved for the Commander-in-Chief, and no one else.

---

[17] A large-circulation Chilean newspaper, not overly sober in its reporting, that was published in the days before the 1973 *coup d'etat*. Much later it was learned that a short while before the fall and death of Allende, Saint-Marie had put together a deal by which he sold his newspaper to the Chilean government with credit from the Banco Nacional of Cuba.

[18] Matte was the president of the Chilean National Society of Agriculture, a bastion of landowners and private farmers, and was visiting Cuba at the time.

[19] I am referring to Francisco de Quevedo, the seventeenth-century satirist, poet, and master of Baroque style, and Miguel de Unamuno, a leading Spanish philosopher of the early part of this century.

2

As he left *Granma,* Fidel had told Meléndez to find me the best available house. I can still hear his voice, a little hoarse from the late hour and the long speech, as he called out to Meléndez from the door of the meeting room: "Give 'im the best house!" I took the opportunity to speak to Meléndez as well. I told him about my problems in getting around; I had no car, and I couldn't buy one just for the two or three months I would be in Havana. Meléndez promised to send me one of the Protocol cars right away. But time in Havana seemed to move at a different rhythm than the one I knew. Two weeks passed before I began to be shown office space. And for the first two or three days I remained, with the exception of the brief ceremony of official presentation of my credentials at the Ministry of Foreign Relations, anchored in my hotel, lacking even the transportation that was provided any official guest of the country. As I left messages for Meléndez at his office (all unanswered) or strolled through the streets around the hotel, contemplating the Caribbean, I would recall with wry humor how my friends in Chile had made such rosy predictions of a brilliant posting—*They'll treat you like a king, you'll be given a mansion in Miramar or Guanabacoa, with a swimming pool!*

Later, some of my Cuban friends—Pablo Armando Fernández, Heberto Padilla—were accused of having "surrounded" me from the beginning of my stay, of "monopolizing" me, and for the specific purpose of giving me a negative impression of the Cuban Revolution. Isolated in my two rooms in the Hotel Habana Riviera, I was not hard to surround. Besides, was there anything wrong with my friends from 1968, from years gone by in Europe, or friends of friends, members of a worldwide literary brotherhood, coming to visit me? They didn't even come as fast as I, who threw wide the doors of my suite on the eighteenth floor—my residence and at the same time, for the moment, the Chilean embassy—would have liked. But there is nothing to be gained by defending them, now that they themselves have confessed their various guilt. All that's lacking is the confession of my own guilt—and so I will confess, in words I imagine the State Security apparatus will wholeheartedly accept: Even as I went about my austere duties as diplomat I committed the apparently unpardonable indiscretion of throwing open my doors to those literary friends, and, with them, to the humor of Cuba, its wit, its poetry, even though those qualities of spirit had been rendered suspect by virtue of their association with precisely my friends, and even though, to make matters worse for me, those qualities of wit, humor, and poetry as often as not served as the sauce to venomous criticism, acid intelligence.

But even before the writers, came the journalists. These latter, reading the dispatches from news agencies in Santiago, had made arrangements to be on hand as I got off the plane, but their expectations had not been met. I gave a long interview to Ramón Perdomo, that young assistant editor of *Granma* who had been sitting directly opposite me at the round table during the conversation with Fidel Castro. He began by defining me, into the microphone of his tape recorder, as a "thirty-nine-year-old lawyer." For the young revolutionary journalist, the decrepit profession of the law, the number of whose practitioners has become a virtual scourge in Latin American societies, was still, as it was for my father's generation, a cause for pride. "Not lawyer!" I said. "It's true that I studied law once upon a time, but I never practiced. More than a lawyer or a diplomat, I'm a writer. That is my only real vocation, in the true sense of the word."

My interviewer smiled submissively. The next day, the text of the conversation, occupying two full pages in *Granma,* faithfully reproduced that initial misunderstanding. I gave the fact no importance, nor could I understand the importance my friends gave it, the jokes and sarcastic remarks it provoked. That self-definition of mine had hit a nerve that I didn't know existed—but at least in early December 1970 the situation I unwittingly created for myself could still be talked about frankly and freely, in typical Cuban style, and even be laughed about. The tone of the comments gradually changed, though, and the joke began to take on a more serious cast. When Heberto Padilla read my disclaimer in the interview in *Granma,* he predicted (clamping his cigar between in his teeth and making much, as was his style, of his powers of clairvoyance) that I wouldn't last long in Cuba. But at that point no one dared consider the fuller and more serious consequences this foreboded down the line. While a minimum of analytical rigor would have led us to conclude that our situation was precarious and that what was called for was simple prudence, nothing, it seemed, would alter our cheerful, inconsequential loquacity. It turned out, though, as Padilla had predicted: With the triumph of the Unidad Popular and the installation of Allende as president, Chile had made History (with Padilla's typical capital *H*), and I, the first South American diplomat in Havana after the breaking-off of relations, was a participant, whether I wanted to be or not, in the process of that History. I myself once said, using an expression common in Chile, that without realizing it I had stuck my finger in the fan. I can still hear the laugh that got from Padilla and his friends. You either roared with laughter, or you cried. And that laughter, three months later, did become tears. But today I have received a letter from Havana saying that Heberto has gone off to the beach at Santa María to recover after "his problem"; that the Revolution has been very generous with him; that Belkis, his wife, "is very happy, too, and acts as though nothing had happened." Probably what we are faced with here is the fact that the worn formulas put forth by European intellectuals, those loose cannons of the Left—formulas, too, which are really quite rigid, given their pretended liberty—are useless in dealing with, or explaining, the Cuban situation. Who knows! Because what one sees, with some surprise, is that in spite of the bitterness, the frustrations, the disillusionments and disappointments, the thick heads of the police—in spite of everything—certain sectors of the Revolution also possessed a kind of happiness, a sense of the gratuitousness of things that went beyond formulas and that while not redeeming the entire situation perhaps redeemed the essential things.

I had flown to Cuba with mountains of books and letters sent to various people by friends in Peru and Chile. My indefatigable Peruvian friend Emilio Westphalen, confidential poet, a man of higher culture than his surroundings, and who within his perfect manners was a tiger when it came to *Amaru*, the magazine that the Engineering University of Lima was allowing him to publish at the time, had sent copies of his magazine to everyone he could think of. Mauricio Wacquez, who had returned to Santiago after living for a year in Havana, had sent countless letters and messages with me. Enrique Lihn sent his regards to Heberto, to Pablo Armando, to Pepe Rodríguez Feo, to Roberto Fernández Retamar. Heberto often quoted a phrase written by Enrique shortly after Enrique left Cuba: "The Revolution, seen from a distance, grows . . ."

The third or fourth day after my coming to rest in the Habana Riviera, then, I went to the Casa de las Américas, loaded down with some of the letters, books, and copies of *Amaru* that I had brought with me. Since I have always liked to walk, and since the car promised by Meléndez had never appeared, I made the trek on foot. The tower of the Casa de las Américas building didn't look too far from the hotel.

The problem I had not counted on was the humidity of the tropics, which doubles all distances. Then there was the weight of the books. I began to shift them from hand to hand and to walk faster, thinking I'd get there soon, but the tropics took their implacable revenge. Within a few minutes, my arms had stiffened on me, I was perspiring heavily, and the blue building of the Casa de las Américas, with its thirties architecture, was no closer than before. One could hear, under the regularly spaced black holes drilled into the pavement of the sidewalk of the Malecón, the powerful suction and violent crashing of the waves. The past few days had been cloudy, with fleeting moments of sunshine alternating with long stretches of gray skies; it was the end of an extremely dry fall. Facing the sea, the buildings of Havana, which had once formed an impressive skyline à la New York or Chicago, now stood peeling and in decay, their broken windows patched with cardboard. The walls of some abandoned houses had begun to crumble. From time to time one saw mounds of rubble, hulks of rusted automobiles, as though tongues of fire and salt had passed across the city.

At the Casa de las Américas, they were holding one of the meetings leading up to the 1971 literary prizes. Haydée Santamaría, who was at the time living with her husband Armando Hart in the province of Oriente, though maintaining the chairmanship of the Casa, had come from Santiago de Cuba to attend the meeting. I was greeted by Manuel Galich, Mario Benedetti, Roberto Fernández Retamar, the painter Mariano Rodríguez, a young woman named Chiki Salamendi (a kind of literary groupie *avant la lettre*); there were also other faces I had met during my 1968 trip, although not all the faces of 1968 remained. On the wall, the portrait gallery of "friends of Casa de las Américas" had grown; I recognized more than one face that I had bade my farewells to in Santiago or Lima.

Although I gave my walk no great importance, Haydée was astounded that I had come on foot. The Chilean chargé d'affaires! The first diplomatic envoy from the revolutionary Chilean government, walking all that way! It was not just that the tropical climate discouraged one from walking; certain remainders of the American presence in Cuba made the identification of the automobile with power even stronger than in other countries. My arrival on foot was a gesture of modesty that ran the risk of not being appreciated; it might even be interpreted, in fact, as weakness in confronting Meléndez's machinations— and Meléndez was, to all appearances, a figure that inspired explicit and unanimous antipathy at the Casa de las Américas.

"Have you been shown your house yet?" Haydée went on. "They haven't done that, either!" Well then, Haydée formally authorized me to tell Meléndez that since she now lived in Oriente, she had offered to lend me her house, especially in view of the delay in the actions of the Office of Protocol. I should watch, she said, with a hint of anticipatory pleasure, Meléndez's reaction.

Haydée and her team were very pleased with the statements of support and sympathy for the Casa de las Américas that I had made to the Prensa Latina correspondent in Santiago. The Casa's policies were under fierce attack, and they deluded themselves into thinking that statements of mine might help them. They were overly optimistic—an error that was committed frequently, during the three and a half months of my stay in Cuba, by my friends in the literary and cultural circles of Havana. The frontal assault had already been decided upon by the Commander-in-Chief, who was just waiting for the right moment to attack. "We may not be very good at producing, but when it comes to fighting, we're terrific. . . ." Our incurable optimism, our imprudence, our loquacity were to be toys in the hands of the Maximum Leader. The repeated (and recorded) echo of our conversations would serve to feed his anger, to polish his arguments against the "bourgeois intellectuals," and these arguments he would declaim in the certainty that the young people of Latin America would ever afterward repeat them word for word.

When I said my good-byes at the offices of the Casa de las Américas, I was sent off, again, with armfuls of publications—this time publications from the Casa—and with all sorts of friendly, congratulatory promises, and I was driven back to my hotel in a broken-down American automobile whose driver I had met on my previous trip. My eye was not yet trained to see that the rusty old heap that drove me home, with its rattling of loose bumpers, was the unequivocal sign that the Casa and its chairwoman were in trouble. Otherwise I would have been riding in the silent, well-upholstered comfort of an Alfa Romeo 1750.

At nine o'clock the next morning, I received a call from the front desk. The Casa's automobile, sent over by compañera Haydée Santamaría, was at my disposal for as long as I needed. Four minutes later, the solicitous voice of Meléndez, who had been totally inaccessible for days, came on the line.

"Listen, Edwards," he said, "I'm sending over a car from Protocol."

"I appreciate that, Meléndez," I replied, "but I won't be needing it . . . Haydée Santamaría has just sent one over from the Casa de las Américas."

"Send that car back, man! Send it away! The driver of your car is named Agustín. He's on his way."

Two months later, Aldo Santamaría, Haydée's brother and head of the Cuban Navy, made a vague allusion to the car incident—just one phrase, and a slight smile, but I saw that the detail had been worthy of attention. I told the story to a colleague from a socialist country, and my colleague's comment was: "It's that Meléndez does nothing but that."

"Nothing but what?"

"Listen in on our conversations. He doesn't have a minute to solve your problems of getting set up, but he'd no more than heard that Haydée was sending you a car, and he sent you one. Understand?"

Although I was beginning to understand quite well, the only comment I made was to raise my eyebrows and shrug my shoulders.

One of those first nights, I attended a cocktail party at UNEAC, the Cuban Writers and Artists Union. I found myself among several friends and acquaintances from my previous trip. Juan David and his wife, who had been cultural attachés in Paris back in 1966, were there, as were the painter René Portocarrero, the poet Nicolás Guillén, several young writers, and so on. Suddenly a woman, a Cuban friend for many years, approached me and whispered in my ear (with that intonation and syntax that have always endeared Cubans to me): "I suppose you know that you're no longer a *persona grata* in Casa de las Américas, *chico*?"

The news, coming from a well-informed person, hit me hard. I had had nothing but the friendliest relations with the Casa de las Américas. Yet my friend was in a position to know these things. What brought all this on, then?

"My friendship with Neruda?"

She only smiled. I asked again: "My being on the jury that gave the prize to José Norberto Fuentes?"

"Yes," she said, giving me to understand that the case of Neruda was too thorny for her to venture a comment on. I was nonplussed. All this went so counter to appearances—the attentions of Roberto Fernández Retamar, the plans for my collaboration on an issue of the Casa de las Américas magazine to deal with Chile, the car Haydée had sent me. What contradictory elements had suddenly entered the picture? After Salvador Allende's triumph, Fernández Retamar had written me a pleasant note asking me to send him some unpublished piece of mine for the magazine. During those first days of December 1970, he was given to praising me enthusiastically to anyone who would listen (and who seemed willing to pass his words on to me). And he spoke of Pablo, referring to Neruda by his first name, as though nothing had ever happened.

I had already realized that the literary split was deeper, more irreconcilable, than ever. Padilla did not speak to Lisandro Otero, or Roberto Fernández

Retamar, or the Uruguayan writer Carlos María Gutiérrez, and in fact had no qualms in saying that they were State Security agents. But even though I was Padilla's friend, I was also the official envoy of the government of Chile, and State Security agents supposedly understand that sort of thing very clearly. I could understand that previously, when I had taken part in the decision to give the prize to José Norberto Fuentes (a literary decision which I am still happy with today) and when Fuentes later had had problems with the Army and with State Security, I had no doubt been a *persona* little *grata*. But now the situation had changed, and my personal statements in support of the Casa de las Américas were received as an unexpected pat on the back from the Unidad Popular in Chile. But it is possible that State Security, from that time on or even long before, had decided to invalidate that backing, "neutralize" the writer now wearing the dangerous hat of diplomatic representative of Allende's Chile.

Within a few days of my arrival, Padilla had said to me, "Don't talk about anything. Don't trust anybody. Not even me. They can get information out of me anytime." From what I now see, Padilla understood the situation—and knew himself, as well. He did not stand up very long to the police onslaught. Somewhere—in some file, on some tape—his version of our conversations and of my movements in Havana (a version doubtlessly tailored to the specifications of State Security) must surely exist. The file must be available to Chilean security agencies, as well, in case police-socialism should come to power in my country.[1] That is to say, I should have listened to Padilla: Not trust anybody, not even him—least of all him. As someone observed to me in Paris after Padilla's "self-criticism": Padilla left the people who stood up to defend him in a pretty pickle. In the history of socialism, other people have assumed the ultimate consequences of following a divergent (perhaps erroneous, but always principled) line; it took Padilla almost no time to recant. Why talk so much, then, if he was not capable of standing up under the first little squeeze? Why not do what others did who recognized their own fear—keep his mouth shut?[2]

---

[1] The notebook in which this phrase is written is the second of the manuscript notebooks of *Persona Non Grata,* dated "Paris, June 6, 1971." On that date, Piñeiro had already seen to it that a thick file on my case, padded out no doubt with Padilla's statements while he was in jail, was sent to his trusty friends within the Chilean government. It is entirely probable that the file disappeared after the coup and Allende's death on that fateful September 11, 1973, but surely there is still a copy, for some twenty-first century researcher, in the secret files of Havana.

[2] This observation was made to me by the Cuban-born painter Wilfredo Lam, an important figure in *avant-garde* French painting who organized the journey of the Salon de Mai from

Padilla always thought that international literary opinion would protect him. At the beginning, Fidel had courted that opinion, feeling that it was one of the Cuban Revolution's best lines of defense, an instrument that could be used not only to break the trade embargo but also Cuba's general ostracism from the "family of Western nations." But in the last two years, everything had changed. Independent intellectuals of the Left, who had once been Cuba's strongest defenders, had now begun to make known their reservations about the Revolution. Fidel and the government were extremely sensitive to these attacks, no matter how moderate and limited they were, because they came from those once thought to be Cuba's best friends and therefore they accentuated the dangerous feeling of isolation, of cultural alienation, that Cuba suffered.

The most telling crisis involving the intellectuals of the Left, and especially the Europeans, occurred when Fidel did not denounce, but rather approved, the invasion of Czechoslovakia by the Soviets. For the European Left, Cuba had represented the possibility of a libertarian socialism, with freedom of thought and of artistic creativity. But Cuba was a remote, even exotic, possibility. For many of those intellectuals, right or wrong, the Prague Spring had become the most solid and tangible hope. And that hope had been crushed with tanks, and with Fidel's mind-boggling applause. In some circles Fidel's speech in support of the Soviet tanks was the greatest political scandal of those gloomy days of August and September 1968, and became the most painful of failed illusions. It had been a stab in the back to that particular option for socialism that Fidel, thanks perhaps to an acquiescent ambiguity, had come to represent in the outside world. According to some gossips, Fidel had justified his stand to a Spanish Communist leader with two arguments: (1) the invasion gave him a splendid opportunity to achieve a closer relationship with the USSR; and (2) the Czechs hadn't fought back, while they, the Cubans, had defended themselves to the last man against every real or possible attack. Fidel's supposed reasons were, as is clear, a perfect symbiosis of cynicism and machismo.

The fact is that ever since that speech, European intellectuals had begun to treat Cuba a little differently—the kid gloves were off. And by the time I

Paris to Cuba in 1967. The comment came, as I clearly recall, as we left Bistro 121, on the rue de la Convention—an expensive place frequented by well-known, and knowing, patrons. I now think that judging Padilla's conduct from that point of observation was too easy.

arrived in Havana, Fidel in turn had decided, with the demonic arrogance that characterizes him (and certain, too, that he could count on the sympathies of the USSR), that he could live without the opinion of those intellectuals and that he would violently break with them at the first opportunity that presented itself. This was the circumstance that Padilla didn't, or pretended that he didn't, get quite right. He believed that the solidarity of the non-Communist Left would defend him, when in fact that solidarity with Castro's latest *bête noire* would sink him. There was nothing to do but renege on his European friends, denounce them as hostile, venomous, decadent agents of the Enemy. And the best way for Castro to implicate them all in the accusation of "counterrevolutionaries" was to have Padilla confess that he, their friend and contact in Cuba, had been a counterrevolutionary from the very beginning. That way, the "international Left" would be shown for what it was, and branded for life. And when Fidel broke with those "leftist anticommunist liberals" he gave additional proof of his own alignment with hardline Soviet orthodoxy. It is entirely probable that Fidel saw in the USSR the only serious threat to his internal power, and that he determined to give proof of his loyalty to the "party line." Was it not true that K. S. Karol, René Dumont, even Hans Magnus Enzensberger himself, all showed suspicious tendencies toward Maoism? In his self-criticism, Padilla cited personal contacts or friendships with each of these men. Was it not true that a Chinese diplomat was sitting in the first row at the reading that Padilla had given, in early January 1971, at UNEAC—a reading of a book of unpublished poems whose title was *Provocations*?

In another of his surprising political about-faces, performed with his habitual virtuosity, the Commander-in-Chief had used Padilla as a pawn in his decision to play, or pretend to play, the game of Soviet cultural orthodoxy. The surrealistic babble of the Casa de las Américas and its friends on every continent had ended. As the motto of the time had it: "Inside the Revolution, anything." But that "anything" had been restricted to the tightest boundaries of State Security police sectarianism.[3] Fidel said as much to me, on the eve of my departure, and quoted the examples (the *inevitable* examples, as he saw the situation) of Stalin and of Mao's Cultural Revolution.

---

[3] "Sectarianism" in the sense of anti-pluralism, that is. When, later, a diplomat observes that "President Allende appears not to be sectarian," what that implied was Allende's tolerance for a degree of pluralism. Coalitions, in fact, were the order of the day in constitutional Chile.

"There will be many disappointments yet for you to suffer," he added, and he was right, in spite of the fact that I am beginning to get over my shock at disappointments.

The case of Pablo Neruda in all this process is most revealing. Neruda had gone to Havana at the beginning of the Revolution and had written the first important book in support of Cuba, *Canción de gesta* ("Song of Great Deeds"). But Neruda, who was stepping back from Stalinism, had perceived disturbing signs of a cult of personality. For those who were listening, some lines from one poem, dedicated "to Fidel Castro," said as much, and Neruda felt that Fidel, if no one else, had indeed understood:

> This is the cup. Take it, Fidel.
> It is filled with so many hopes
> that as you drink you will learn that your victory
> is like the old wine of my own country:
> not made by one man but by many men,
> not by one plant but by many plants,
> it is not one drop, but many rivers,
> not one captain, but many battles.

Neruda's view of Stalinism was that it began with the destruction of the Party as the center of any possible discussion or control of power, and that its next step was the formation of a party-instrument that cohered around the figure of the beloved leader, father of the people, and teacher and guide for present and future generations.

Using well-aimed internal coups, Fidel was, at the time of Neruda's visit, working on the destruction of the old Popular Socialist Party, one of the most solid Communist parties in Latin America and one of those with greatest worker support. The hard-line, pro-Moscow orientation of the Cuban PSP was still very much in evidence in the early sixties, and this circumstance was used by Fidel with his customary shrewdness. Leftist intellectuals, meanwhile, applauded. By striking out against the Cuban PSP, Fidel was giving proof of his seeming independence from Moscow, his "revolutionary" rather than "revisionist" line, all of which the Revolution would carry at gun-point into Latin America while at the same time allowing the free flowering of the arts, letters, and thought.

Within this context, the attack on Neruda—an attack aimed by extrapolation at the Communist Party of Chile, which was embarked on the "revisionist" road of labor-union, parliamentary, electoral struggle, and destined by definition to failure—had seemed "opportune."[4]

As I was told the story, things had occurred more or less like this: Following orders from their superiors, four literary sergeants[5] had met to draft the letter: Roberto Fernández Retamar, Edmundo Desnoes, Lisandro Otero, and Ambrosio Fornet. The accusation was based on two "serious" actions his Cuban "compañeros" and "friends" interpreted as double-dealing on Neruda's part: his trip to New York at the invitation of the PEN Club, and his acceptance of a decoration in Lima that was bestowed upon him by President Fernando Belaúnde. It did not count that Neruda had defended the Vietnam cause in New York before a group of wildly enthusiastic young pacifist rebels whose protests would, years later, at last force Richard Nixon to rethink the U.S. role in Vietnam, and that the writers of the Peruvian Left had obtained from Belaúnde a medal for the poet of Machu Picchu. The young Roberto Fernández Retamars and Lisandro Oteros of Cuba, who had come home from their universities in the United States to discover the Revolution when Fidel had already entered Havana,[6] were now attacking the poet of *España en el corazón* ("Spain in the Heart") and the *Canto general* ("Universal Song") with all the ferocity

---

[4] In the late sixties, Communist leaders in Chile were expressing their serious private reservations about the Castro regime. Sometimes these divergences became visible, like the upper slopes of the iceberg. The 1973 *coup d'etat* and the installation of the reactionary military regime paved the way for the reconciliation of the Chilean Communists and the Castro regime. It was a reconciliation carried out under the ægis of the strictest sort of pro-Soviet orthodoxy, only permitted by Fidel's clear and unswerving adhesion to that line, after his more lukewarm "tendencies" of the sixties.

[5] This was an expression used later by Neruda to refer to Roberto Fernández Retamar. When he wrote in a later satiric poem about "Marcos Chamudar" and about "Retamúdez Gordillo," Neruda was comparing Fernández Retamar to Marcos Chamudes, who was a young Communist militant in the forties characterized, according to Neruda, by a remarkably doctrinaire and accusatory zeal, and who afterward, during the years of González Videla and "creole McCarthyism," shifted to the right lock, stock, and barrel.

[6] Guillermo Cabrera Infante, in a letter written after reading *Persona Non Grata,* corrects this information. Roberto Fernández Retamar and Lisandro Otero, he explains, participated with some militancy in the 26th of July Movement *before* the Revolution. Those who were in the United States, but who "saw the Revolutionary Light in time," were Desnoes and Fornet. The accusation against Neruda was owed more than anything, according to Cabrera Infante, to the envy of Nicolás Guillén. Neruda knew of this envy and he praised the other Guillén, Jorge, as "the Spanish one, the good one," but he also saw in the letter, I believe rightly, larger political motivations.

of the Red Guard. The letter soon appeared in public, signed by Alejo Carpentier, a friend of Neruda's for many years, by Nicolás Guillén, by all or almost all the poets, writers, and intellectuals of Cuba.

I was told that some of the signers had discovered their signatures and learned of the text of the letter on the day of its publication. Some people, alarmed because their signature did not appear (a disturbing symptom of the health of their official literary life), had rushed to ask to be included. One of the very few well-known writers, perhaps the only one, who did not appear on the list of signers, and who also did nothing to get on the list, was the old, and very Cuban, Enrique Labrador Ruiz, a friend of Neruda's since the forties in Mexico. Labrador Ruiz chose to shut himself up in his big rundown house high up on Calle Reina, shielded by his acidic humor, his legendary memories, and his crotchetiness, and to wait, like the experienced player he was, for all this to pass. [7]

When we saw or learned of the letter, we Latin American writers felt ourselves divided between our respect and admiration for Neruda and our unconditional support of the Cuban Revolution. A comfortable mental operation softened the conflict: Neruda represented Stalinism and the revisionism of the old CPs; Cuba, on the other hand, was freedom and spontaneous, authentic revolution. We did not realize that in Cuba, under our very noses, there had begun to flourish a sectarianism of another sort, much less bloody than Stalin's[8] but with more than a few similarities in the essential mechanisms. And the first of those similarities was our own gullibility; we accepted everything, wishing at all costs to avoid a break, and the airing of dissension. We had had no great trouble establishing our distance from the Neruda of *Las uvas y el*

---

[7] Labrador Ruiz was able to leave Cuba later, and he wrote me a letter telling me that he had spent a year in Madrid, aided by friends. He was planning to meet members of his family in the United States, but the U.S. authorities would not give him a visa because of his trip to China in the fifties. He told me that the situation in Cuba had gone from bad to worse after I left: "more hunger and more terror." Labrador went from Madrid to Caracas, where he worked as a journalist, at the age of seventy-something, and finally was able to enter the United States, where he died in Miami in late 1991.

[8] This is a Stalinism that brings about the literary and civil death of its opponents in the sphere of culture, rather than their physical death, and which is therefore less bloody—but I am not certain it is any less cruel, to judge by such testimonies as that of Reinaldo Arenas, to cite just one case. The case of Neruda was very visible, but accusations against "foreign sympathizers," for example against Carlos Fuentes, Nicanor Parra, and many others, began to multiply long before the "Padilla affair."

viento ("The Grapes and the Wind"),[9] the Neruda of the frozen Stalinesque moustache. Were we not now revealing, however, an even more serious intellectual submissiveness to the dictates of Havana? Another similarity was the reasons for keeping silent: The fragility of the revolutionary Island and the terrible force of the blockade could be compared to the socialist solidarity of the Stalin years. But history had changed, while we ourselves, dazzled by the arrogance of youth and, in some cases, by rapid success, had not fully learned its lessons.

Agustín, the first driver assigned to me by Protocol, was a young mulatto man who walked with a swagger, glancing to one side and cracking his knuckles a little halfheartedly. He was friendly and polite, but moody. Sometimes he would be in a foul humor, but he wouldn't say why. I had qualms about hiring him for my entire stay—though personally driving the Protocol car would have been indelicate—but he insisted that he was entirely at my service, for as long as I wished. Each time I told him that would be all for the time being, he would announce that he was going to go "catch a few winks" or he would ask if there were time for him to eat. Eating and sleeping were his principal concerns. He often told me, somewhat unctuously, that he liked working for me—perhaps because of my tolerance for his eating and sleeping habits. One Friday or Saturday night he showed up with his wife and sister at one of the hotel ballrooms. He must have been on the lookout for me, because as soon as he saw me out in the lobby he invited me to sit down and have a beer with them. As etiquette required, I invited Agustín's sister to dance. She was a dark-skinned woman whose round face has left not a trace in my memory. I do recall, though, that she told me I danced the Cuban steps "like a dream." I have always been a mediocre dancer, conscious of my own mediocrity. So I smiled, unconvinced by the unconvincing compliment, and soon I went upstairs to sleep.

I now ask myself what Agustín was after in bringing his sister there. It's true that they might have been sitting at the table in the cabaret like any other family group, and that in Cuba it was quite common for young couples to go out with a mother, a sister, or some other relative. But it was also possible that Agustín was wandering around the lobby waiting for me to come in, while the wife and

[9] *Las uvas y el viento* is a good example of the dogmatic Stalinist phase of Neruda's career.

the sister, this latter introduced into the picture by an unseen hand, were waiting patiently in the bar, bait for an off-guard diplomat. The mind behind that unseen hand, informed by Agustín's gossipy tongue, knew that I often stuck my head in the bar when I came in late on weekend nights and music was still playing.

In Cuba I became more suspicious and mistrustful than I had ever been before. That is what people often mean, no doubt, when they say "I learned a lot." Well, I did learn a lot; and I haven't finished learning yet, either, or, as I said at the beginning of this book, putting two and two together, and finding in the sum new causes for perplexity. The idea even occurs to me, as I write these lines, that Agustín's sister was not his sister at all, that the ostensible sister was in fact someone the unseen hand[10] had sent me through Agustín as intermediary. Someone had studied me and determined my real or supposed weaknesses. I suspect that in practice those weaknesses are discovered and analyzed only part way, with a certain clumsiness, since I did say good-night and go up to my room, where I continued reading one of the books by the authors then fashionable in the intellectual underground: Karol or Dumont—no matter, they were both recalcitrant agents of the CIA, as we later learned from Padilla's self-criticism.

But let's not get ahead of ourselves. It is also possible, and perhaps probable, that Agustín was out with his wife and sister that Friday or Saturday night, knowing that I, in keeping with my odd habits, had gone out to visit my long-haired drunken friends, the ones given to versifying and even perhaps, in private, to other even more shameful depravities.

Suddenly I got a call from Meléndez telling me that he was replacing Agustín with a driver named Tomás, who was more serious and responsible, more "militant," as Meléndez put it, a member of the Party. A short while later I saw Agustín, in shirtsleeves, wandering through the lobby of the hotel like a soul in purgatory. Later I learned that he had had some sort of run-in with the son of a Chilean politician who lived in the hotel. The story was that he had pressured the Chilean youngster to get him a bottle of rum from the Diplomarket.[11] The boy had resisted, and the impulsive Agustín had threatened to

---

[10] The unseen hand of Big Brother, I add now, now that I am more experienced in the ways of all those big brothers that protect us, watch over us, and punish us if we stray from the straight and narrow.

[11] In the Havana of shortages and rationing, the Diplomarket served the government, diplomatic, and VIP clientele. One could purchase goods there, for hard currency (usually dollars), that were simply unavailable otherwise on the Island.

hit him, at which the boy, rising to the full dignity of the son of Chilean VIP, had called in the appropriate authorities. As those things usually went, Agusasín was about to wind up a *machetero* on a government sugarcane plantation. But in spite of Agustín's pleas, my defense of him was somewhat grudging. Not long before, he had forgotten that I asked him to wake me to go to the airport to see off Mario García Incháustegui, Cuba's ambassador in Santiago. I awoke half an hour late, dressed on the run, and rushed downstairs. There I had to wait for Agustín, who was, incredibly, still fast asleep. Unless the unseen hand had suggested that he oversleep. I later learned that Manuel Piñeiro, the red-bearded young *comandante,* was also to go to the airport to see off García Incháustegui, and it could be that he preferred not to see me there. I had earlier refused an invitation from him to dinner because of a previous engagement with Lezama Lima, Pablo Armando Fernández, and Heberto Padilla. Naturally, a dyed-in-the-wool revolutionary like Piñeiro could not bear that rejection. Unless he invited me to dinner knowing that I had prior engagement, with the clear intention of testing me.

I saw Piñeiro two months later on the deck of the Chilean training ship *Esmeralda,* cracking jokes and laughing with the young cadets, trying to make them like him, and I associated his work of pulling in young men and women with that same work of some of my old Jesuit preceptors. Had he wanted to invite me to dinner on the same day I had an engagement with my friends—a birthday celebration, if I recall correctly, for Lezama Lima—so as to test me, so that after I had failed the test, as it was perfectly predictable that I would do, he could put me on his black list, his Inquisitorial Index?

"Stay here for a year, and you'll turn into a classic of socialism, my boy," Padilla would say, laughing and looking at me wickedly through his round, alert eyes.

With Agustín and my brand-new Alfa Romeo (whose color, either dark red or blue, I can't recall, was that generally given to the most important of the Very Important People, or so I was told), I began to make my rounds of visits to the Cuban authorities and to the heads of diplomatic missions. I would make three or four visits a day, sometimes more, racing in my Alfa through Miramar, Cubanacán, El Vedado, along the Malecón toward Old Havana. This was my first experience as head of an embassy, and a rather peculiar experience it was. During the first few days I had had to take on the roles of ambassador, typist, telephone operator, and doorman. Chile's new embassy in Cuba was an establishment composed of myself, my long-suffering portable typewriter, and a few files on the possibility of trade between Chile and Cuba; its headquarters was a two-room suite in the Habana Riviera. The first person to join my team was Agustín, with the Alfa. It would have been strange for us not to arrive at a certain solidarity with each other, for Agustín not to have come to feel a certain loyalty toward me, even when the unseen hand immediately ordered him to betray me. I often think that that was the only reason for replacing Agustín with Tomás: in my three and a half months in Havana, I was assigned three drivers. I recognize, however, that my suspiciousness, sharpened by subsequent events, may have become a bit exaggerated.

We drove, at any rate, through the almost deserted streets from one embassy to another, from one ministry to another, trying to keep up with my very full schedule. That activity, in the brilliant light of the tropical winter sun, speeding along the Malecón where one often had to swerve to avoid the sudden surge of the waves, produced in me, I can now confess, a great exhilaration. It made me feel, as I neared forty, that I was young, full of energy, interested in—even impassioned by—my work.

Every visit enriched my stock of knowledge. Monsignor Zacchi, the papal nuncio, who had been in Havana since 1960, talked to me about his attempts to achieve a *modus vivendi* bridging the government and the Catholic church. It was his view that since in Cuba the war of independence from Spain had come at the end of the nineteenth century, very late in comparison to the other colonies of Latin America, anticlericalism was still very much alive and well in Cuba in the last half of the twentieth. Zacchi pointed out to me that there was Protestant influence in the emancipation of slaves, owed in part to the intervention of the United States, and of course there was liberal or Masonic influence from the lay community. I confirmed the monsignor's insight for myself later in the port city of Matanzas, which I passed through several times: The Masonic lodges occupied one-story houses with prominent façades that faced the street; they were very neat, painted in various colors, and their names were written above their doors.

During the years of the Republic, after independence had been gained from Spain, religious education had been confined to the parish level, and this situation had continued after the Revolution. What was important, then, was the presence and training of priests. It was not hard for Zacchi, in his defense of the cause, to find parallels between Christian doctrine and the objectives of the Revolution: the austerity, the attention to the humblest and the weakest members of society. He preferred the role of bridge between government and church to that of ecclesiastical negotiator. To his religious colleagues he was the Revolution's advocate, or devil's advocate, if you will, with a fervor that could well have been disturbing for orthodox mentalities. He once told me that he hoped that within the near future a Catholic could be a militant in the Communist Party. And he would look out at one with eyes half innocent, half calculating as he held a cigarette between the fingers of his upheld right hand: "Why not?" My years in school, now somewhat distant, had taught me that atheism was an essential element of Marxism, and because of my religious indifference I had not reflected much on the matter. It may be that Monsignor Zacchi, swept up in the dialectics of the Cuban situation, got a little carried away. By now he had cut sugarcane (with the corresponding publicity) and had taken the sixty or seventy seminarians of Havana off to work at the harvest, performing an experiment that in his opinion had yielded excellent results. The church, according to Zacchi, was far from serene in its view of all this: It expected the Revolution to yield in all things, though it would not, in turn, make concessions of any kind.

Zacchi was a curious mixture of young priest of the church, bordering dangerously close on heterodoxy if not stepping over the line altogether, and Florentine diplomat and artificer—smiling, courteous (courtly), and shrewd. He was capable of falling into a certain affectation. I believe, however, that he was well-intentioned, that he handled a difficult situation with intelligence and good will.

Every embassy was a separate world, with its own special atmosphere accentuated by the particular political situation of the country it represented. Spain, whose empire after centuries of failing health had breathed its last (in fact, with the loss of Cuba in 1898), occupied a manorial building, with a certain *fin de siècle* baroque excess about it, that faced the old harbor. The antechambers and halls were filled with a gloomy, silent crowd of people who seemed to have issued from Pérez Galdós' late nineteenth-century novels of Madrid: shopkeepers, innkeepers, greengrocers, butchers, hairdressers, lawyers' clerks, solicitors. The hurricane of the Revolution had left them stunned, slumped on their benches, seized with repressed anxiety or bilious hesitancy, and looking up with supplicating eyes. After having cut fabric out here in the New World for years, or selling groceries, passing the purchases of flour or beans over the counter with the coins of the customer's change, they now found they had to go back to Spain again, to Galicia or Extremadura, with empty hands. They were familiar with the realities of power from historical tradition, so they knew it was futile to complain about their lot. Fidel Castro might as well have been a *caudillo* out of the Carlist wars, but they were not ones to rely on any *caudillo* who did not guarantee them, above all else, their bag of flour, their few coins, their scales. I remember the words of one Franquist clerk: "With Franco, there's a chicken in every pot in Spain." These were the eternal Sancho Panzas, swept overboard in the unlikeliest place in the world, in that last of the colonies, in the tropics, by a sudden squall, a squall ironically unleashed by Fidel, the quixotic son of a Spaniard like themselves. The Basque writer Miguel de Unamuno, whose philosophy was linked to the Spanish defeat in Cuba in 1898 and who wrote one of the best modern interpretations of Miguel de Cervantes' novel, might have been intrigued, in spite of his fierce anti-socialism, by the paradoxes of the case. Because Castro, that tropical Quixote, had something of Sancho Panza about him as well; he had learned, through the years, quite a lot about the wisdom of Sancho Panzaism, while some of his compañeros, those who had not got down off Rocinante's saddle (a metaphor used by Ché Guevara himself a short time before being killed in the Bolivian jungle), were still on the road—as enemies or as heroes, but at any rate outside the daily activity of governing the Island.

While the Spanish Embassy had done its work in that rundown building, the American Embassy had raised a fortress of concrete and glass in the aseptic architectural style of the fifties. There, the most important of the embassies, it had once held sway over the Malecón, along which passed a thick, noisy parade of Cadillacs, Oldsmobiles, and sports cars every after-noon, making their way past the crowds on the sidewalks. From its windows, the American Embassy looked out upon a scene which showed in microcosm the social disparities that led within a few years to revolution: Black kids would jump into the paths of pedestrians to beg for nickels, while the young people from the university, in shirtsleeves, their teeth decayed, looked with scorn on the spectacle of yachts cleaving the blue waves of the Caribbean. At the gaming tables in the hotels nearby, the sound of the chips grew louder and louder, at the La Torre bar enormous daiquiris flowed like water, and in a sordid apartment with dirty walls, thugs shot a man in the back of the head and blew his brains out.

The Swiss were in that old American Embassy building now, but in the same office where the Swiss chargé d'affaires delivered the business of representing Chile into my care, the United States ambassador must have rubbed his hands together, puffed at a Havana cigar, and looked out on his city, his ocean, the skyline whose many-colored lights were beginning to wink on—the symbol of progress, of the boom in business—and where his unconditional, uncountable followers contributed to keeping the structure, the apparently impregnable system of control, solid and solidly in place.

In the room from which it was still hard to realize that the United States ambassador had disappeared, the Swiss diplomat smiled as he handed over to me receipts of all kinds. Then suddenly I found myself holding the inventory of the library and other personal effects of Emilio Edwards Bello, "don

Emilio," as many Havaneros still remembered him. I realized the Swiss gentleman, a subtle man with a good sense of humor, must have found it strange and somewhat amusing that a relative of don Emilio's had been named—and by the Unidad Popular government of all people!—to reopen diplomatic relations with Cuba. Although Chile had not intended it, nor had anyone paid the coincidence the slightest attention, the detail, seen from the Swiss perspective, must have shown how pluralistic, how antidogmatic the Chilean Revolution was. But perhaps for the very reason that the detail was the product of the simplest sort of lack of attention on the part of the Foreign Ministry in Chile, it was not quite so amusing to official circles inside Cuba.

The phrase spoken by the Cuban ambassador to Mexico was revelatory enough, and *Granma* dedicated at least one line per day to the Edwards family, the symbol and nucleus of the reactionary right; in these lines, no exception was made for the new Chilean chargé d'affaires.

Western ambassadors would make courteous small talk with me, more than once recalling pleasant times in Chile or giving me practical tips for living in Havana. They lived, or pretended to live, very well. Since their governments, or the press in their countries, were often violently anti-Cuban, they themselves didn't have to attack Cuba—in fact they could sit back and enjoy Havana, within limits. Why complicate one's life by taking security precautions? The safest thing of all was not to have secrets: Look for the sunny side of things, "accentuate the positive," make apologies for the failures, and dedicate the rest of one's time to bridge, golf, and anodyne conversations—never refusing to take part, when the occasion demanded, in the symbolic sessions of cane-cutting organized by the office of the Director of Protocol.

I was always struck by the heaviness and bad taste of the socialist embassies. There must have been a huge factory somewhere turning out statues of Lenin. In fact, since the cult of personality of the head of state had supposedly been suppressed,[12] Lenin's omnipresence no doubt constituted progress.

In all, or almost all, of the socialist embassies, there would be a toast, accompanied by a little speech—a mixture of politics (with wishes for the success of the people of Chile, its government, and Compañero President Allende) and personal greeting. The North Korean ambassador's tone turned angry when he began speaking, in his syncopated and explosive language,

---

[12] Or so it appeared to me in mid-1971.

about Yankee imperialism. The North Vietnamese ambassador, on the other hand, was a suave, serene, smiling man, who briefed me on the war situation with absolute confidence in the victory of his nation.

I can still see the Chinese ambassador's living room: high ceilings with quotations from Mao Zedong on the walls, written in large red letters on white canvas. The ambassador, a round-faced, smiling man, looked to be some sixty years old. He was always accompanied by a young interpreter wearing eyeglasses; the interpreter was as cheerful, and even more jovial, than his boss. We drank a toast of some clear liquor to the friendship of Chile and China, and to the prompt establishment of diplomatic relations between the two countries.

A few days later, the ambassador came to visit me at my hotel; he informed me of the official establishment of relations. We exchanged the ritual phrases of courtesy and the little speeches required by the occasion. I left the ambassador at the door of the hotel, where he entered the shadowy depths of a huge black automobile bearing a red flag. He waved good-bye, smiling in a way that reminded me of undersea divers seen through the portholes of submarines.

Every time I ran into the Chinese ambassador at a cocktail party, he would grasp my hands and greet me with great affection, his words translated, and apparently enthusiastically seconded, by the young interpreter. I was once at a reception at his house. He suddenly called me over, his interpreter repeating his emphatic gestures; he handed me a cordial glass, picked up another, and ordered them filled. Then he launched into a long toast of friendship. Someone later told me that these toasts have great meaning for the Chinese, which I do not doubt, judging by the ambassador's attitude, and that of his impeccable interpreter. Both men distinguished themselves at the diplomatic parties with their Mao-blue uniforms, their red Mao button on the lapel, and their eternal smiles, accentuated by sporadic laughter and movements of their head in unison.

One must mention, because the contrast is most telling, that the Soviet Embassy was generally much more temperate and restrained, at least with the Chilean chargé d'affaires. They were extremely amiable, but they took their time in returning my initial visit, and they did not, as the saying goes, shower me with attentions. They appeared to want me to understand that they were not ones to believe in love at first sight—they had too much experience in the matter for that—and that the part played by the Communist Party in the government structure in Chile was more interesting to Chileans than to anyone else.

Exactly two weeks have passed since my arrival. Today I finally saw a house suitable for the official home of the Chilean Embassy. I now have a person to help me during the morning, a young Chilean who has worked in the INRA (the National Institute of Agricultural Reform) and who is about to return to Chile, after nine or ten years, with his Cuban wife and their children. His wife's exit visa is long in coming, and he has begun to get nervous, but his work in the office is very efficient and useful.

Pilar arrives in Mexico City early on the morning of the twenty-ninth. I'll go meet her there and we'll spend New Year's in Mexico City with some friends: Carlos Fuentes, Fernando and Blanca de Syzslo, who are coming in from Peru, etc.

As one can see, I am beginning, little by little, to get organized, while my ministry remains mute. Being head of mission without a word from headquarters or any support is worse than being an office boy. The arguments against my continuing in the diplomatic service have become unanswerable. As a political ambassador, no matter how briefly, I pass. But that implies dedicating oneself to politics, not to diplomacy, which seems to me more and more everyday a profession for the long-suffering meek of the earth, those who can content themselves with swallowing their pride for a living. (I hope my colleagues will forgive me for this.) Of course twenty years from now, if I survive, I may still be plodding along and still, like the great majority of diplomats, complaining. Never say never. Life can be very perverse, and ironies abound.

As for the condition of the writer, the poet, I can see it clearly in some Cuban cases—Lezama Lima, Pablo Armando, Pepe Rodríguez Feo, Heberto, José Norberto Fuentes (whom I have yet to see, as he's apparently in hiding), Fayad Jamís (a friend from my previous visit who's now making himself scarce too), Miguel Barnet and his impassioned researches into the Afro-Cuban

---

[13] Scattered through the pages that follow are excerpts from the diary I kept in Havana. I include this first one because it has a description of Ché Guevara that I thought would be interesting. These few pages are the only pages of my diary that could be rescued. It was stolen from me at a hotel in Cali, Colombia, in August 1974, during a Writers Congress. Political robbery? Literary? The diary was in a new suitcase crisscrossed with zippers and mined with secret compartments, and it had been a gift from Carmen Balcells before I left Barcelona. There was no doubt that it was an attractive object for common burglars and the like, who must have found in it, in some inside pocket, the useless notebook and thrown it into the murky river that ran in front of the hotel. But there was also a little money on the table, and it wasn't taken. Perhaps it was too little to bother with.

elements of the island. They keep the torch lighted, while suffering difficulties that from almost comic egocentrism they tend to exaggerate, yet at the same time enjoying comforts granted them by the Revolution. By tacit order of certain establishment types, Lezama Lima's *Paradiso* has a circulation that is virtually clandestine, but on the other hand, in the past no one would have dared to publish it. They, the writers, are critical, caustic, biting, but within the Revolution. Because the truth is that in this part of the Americas people perceive only two alternatives: be a branch-office of the USA (*viz.,* Guatemala, Puerto Rico), condemned to lose your identity in a flood of ugly opulence while still struggling to free yourself of the bonds of poverty, or else take the path of the battered island of Cuba, with its whopping errors and its grave ideological deviations (since, as René Dumont points out, the idea of socialism has suddenly become confused with a military dictatorship of socializing tendencies, a political phenomenon bordering dangerously on a fascism of the Left). Still, I have no doubt of the outcome of such a choice. The best argument in the Revolution's favor is, for me, the humor, the satire, of the intellectuals, who in spite of all are tolerated.

In Havana one can also understand the phenomenon of Ché Guevara, whose words during dinner at the home of Ramón Huidobro, then Chilean ambassador to the international organizations in Geneva, where I met him, seemed to me at the time quite inopportune.

In that room full of experienced diplomats and government officers, Ché Guevara spoke of leaders' need to take part in the popular life of a country, and he cited the concrete case of Ho Chi Minh. In that setting, Ché's words seemed shocking, but it is hard to dispute Ché's argument that the leader should identify with his community, his people, his nation even in the way he lives, and should know, or make himself discover, the opinions of the masses.

The lack of real popular participation in political and economic decision-making in Cuba, at all levels, might explain many errors there. According to a Chilean official who has lived in Cuba, a young agricultural "technician" ordered hundreds of hectares of land plowed up so that a grass called pangola could be planted, when in fact the plant that he saw growing in those fields *was* pangola. But the Cuban peasants, the *guajiros,* not daring to object, followed his instructions. It is also possible that the young ship's captain who sailed out of the bay at Rio de Janeiro without weighing anchor, and thereby ripped up the international cable, also failed to hear the voice of his more experienced crew.

Unless it might be that the glorification, the external trappings of personal power, the huge portraits in the public squares and the small sanctuaries manned by the CDR's (the Committees for the Defense of the Revolution) at the entrance of every building serve not just to produce that reverential fear which prevents the government from sharing its decision-making or consulting the populace in the process, but also to combat the anarchy which is so much a part of Hispanic peoples. There may be a parallel between Ché-Fidel and Carrera-O'Higgins. Ché Guevara and José Miguel Carrera[14] were guerrillas and martyrs. Fidel Castro, like Bernardo O'Higgins, has had to assume the colder role of strategist and builder, the supreme leader (or director) who must keep factional struggles at bay, or use them to his advantage, and who must, at all costs, prevent the boat from taking on water.

That dinner in Geneva that I mentioned in my Havana notebook took place during the first United Nations Trade and Development Conference in March 1964. Ché Guevara, who was still Cuban Minister of Industry, was there as head of the Cuban delegation. In Chile, it was the period of Jorge Alessandri and the moderate Partido Radical before the break with Cuba had occurred. At Huidobro's table there was a group pretty well representative of one strain of Latin American liberalism: two leading theorists of the economics of under-development, Raúl Prebisch and Felipe Herrera; Edgardo Seoane, who was then vice president of Peru, at the beginning (if I remember correctly) of the Belaúnde era; Carlos Lleras Restrepo, who was not yet the president of Colombia; the representative from the leftist Brazilian government of João Goulart, who was to fall within a few days; Carlos Martínez Sotomayor, who had just become ambassador to the United Nations after a term as minister of foreign relations. It was a gathering of liberals and technocrats in dark-blue suits, old acquaintances whose conversation, within the limits of formality, was spiked with jokes, allusions to a mysterious body of common knowledge, witty barbs and ripostes. Ché, who came late, was dressed in olive-drab; there was a tense look about his sallow face (though it would sometimes suddenly change into a smile), and his conversation "curdled the milk," as the Spanish expression goes. For my part, I thought his attitude was unnecessarily aggressive and undiplomatic. It was my view that Cuba needed to break out of its increasing isolation, but Ché, at least at that dinner, seemed determined to take the contrary course. The group of persons he was speaking to could hardly be categorized as the most Neanderthal in all of Latin America; one need not have

---

[14] A hero of Chilean independence shot by a firing squad on the order of the Argentine general José de San Martín in 1820.

discarded any possibility of a dialogue with these gentlemen. Still—how could she take such an attitude at the time without abandoning the revolutionary position? How could one demand such "maturity" from a revolution as young and as isolated as Cuba's was at that moment? Ché no doubt saw no alternative to being the killjoy at Ramón Huidobro's dinner party. Because that *was* Ché's attitude that night—the attitude of the wet blanket—unless my memory of that dinner is playing tricks on me.

He began by saying that he felt absolutely out of place in the international atmosphere of Geneva and that conference, that the entire show was pointless and futile. He belonged to another world, he said. He liked to get up at sunrise on Sunday morning and go off with the *guajiros* to cut sugarcane at 5:00 A.M. When he talked about Vietnam he said he liked the sort of socialism in which the leaders lived in huts like the people around them. He was probably implicitly contrasting that sort of life with what he'd seen on his recent visit to the Soviet Union, which had deeply marked him, left him disappointed and disaffected, and may in fact somehow have been decisive in his final destiny. Ché said he wouldn't stay out the conference, that he would be going back to Havana—the conference struck him as being a total waste of time.

Every word Ché spoke must have been like a pail of cold water thrown in the faces of Raúl Prebisch, who for some time had devoted all his energies to organizing this conference; of Felipe Herrera, unwavering participant and moderator at international forums such as this; and of many others who sat around the table, men who were the lions of international organizations and conferences. I had been invited as the secretary of the Chilean delegation to fill out the table, as in diplomatic circles embassy secretaries were often invited, since one's jobs in that position include legal expert, speechwriter and preparer of erudite reports, translator, cicerone, messenger, gofer (as they say in Holly-wood), sometime procurer, driver, porter, errand boy, and of course, diner number fourteen when the news of an unforeseen and ill-timed absence leaves the host or hostess with thirteen for dinner. I had been invited, then, to fill in for someone who had "fallen ill" a few hours earlier, and so I could observe the spectacle from my relative anonymity, inwardly enjoying it all though a bit shocked at the same time by what appeared to me to be an unnecessary, impolitic, and *a priori* belligerence on Ché's part.

Ché left early, and the comments of those who remained, though hardly friendly, could not be said to go beyond the limits of civility, moderation, and tolerant good humor. The evening ended pleasantly.

Within a few days there was a military coup in Brazil. For one entire afternoon alarming and confused news poured in. The next morning we all filed in to the plenary assembly hall and found that in the seats assigned to

Brazil, and theretofore occupied by one of the largest delegations, there was but one man, a third secretary. The hallways of the Palace of Nations buzzed with unaccustomed activity. Ché was standing over in one corner, surrounded by a small group of people. In answer to a question, he maintained that although the Brazilian coup appeared to be a setback, it would turn out to be good for Latin American revolution in the long run. The truth was that the Goulart government had been little better than a bourgeois democracy gradually stagnating and growing corrupt; the presence of a clearly reactionary and repressive military leadership would provoke a polarization of forces and act as a catalyst for armed struggle in Latin America.

Ché's revolutionary apologetics did not convince me at the time, but until the end of his life his actions were always consistent with his words at Huidobro's and in the hallway of the Palace of Nations. Many nights I would see him in the meeting and conference rooms of the hotel holding conversations until past two in the morning with members of other delegations, mostly from African or Asian countries. During that period we had dinner with him at the home of a Cuban diplomat, and he told me that his mother, whom I met once in Paris as she was in transit from Cuba to Argentina, had been imprisoned when she returned to Buenos Aires and had died a short time after being released from prison. Mario Vargas Llosa, who was married to Julia Urquidi at the time, had put Ché's mother up in his little apartment on the rue de Tournon, in St-Germain-des-Prés, and I recall that he compared her case to that of the mother of any Peruvian minister, who would be staying at the Ritz or the Georges V and have the entire embassy at her beck and call. It now seems strange to me, however, that the Cuban Embassy should take so little notice of the mother of one of the greatest heroes of the Revolution. Was it simple Latin American carelessness or deliberate coolness? Did Ché's mother—her departure from Cuba and her death in Buenos Aires after being released from prison—have some influence on her son's later fate? One is always in danger of being over-subtle in one's analysis of these matters, but the Cubans are more subtle than one sometimes imagines. My three and a half months as a diplomat on the Island made me believe much less in the workings of chance and much more in secret premeditation.

Just as Ché had announced at Huidobro's dinner party, he soon fled the unbreathable air of the Palace of Nations and returned to Cuba. Afterward he also fled his ministerial office and took up weapons, as the Vietnamese leaders he admired had done, and went off to create in Latin America another Vietnam. The indigenous peoples of Bolivia would understand the message he brought, and the polarization of forces in Brazil foretold by him in Geneva would allow him to spread the popular wildfire of revolution throughout the entire central region of the continent. But his calculations, perhaps for being premature, failed him, and he met the bitter and solitary death we all recall. The least that can be said of him is that he was consistent in every act and word, and that this attitude, when stubborn reality refused to adjust to it, cost him his life.

I soon realized that Western diplomats in Cuba, who traveled in long official automobiles back and forth between their residences, the Ministry of Foreign Relations, and the residences of their colleagues, where they invariably found the same *hors d'oeuvres* served by the same waiters to the same guests, had little opportunity to observe the real life of the country. This must have reassured Meléndez and his men, for whom the world was divided into the bad guys from the CIA, whom they had the duty to keep under surveillance, and the good guys (they themselves). These two gangs (or sides, to put it in a more neutral way) carried out their respective missions among a vast, harmless, and manipulable multitude of compliant officials and complacent peddlers of Western goods who could be counted on to keep their rose-colored glasses firmly in place so long as their purchase orders went through without too much trouble.

The Swedish chargé d'affaires, who would take short trips out into the provinces and try to inform himself of the social and agricultural situation by talking with *guajiros,* agricultural experts, and people in the streets of small towns, and who would often pay me a visit to compare notes, would of course (as is the custom in diplomacy) transmit his findings to his government—so he was cast, as I learned later, as an agent of the enemy. Meléndez' bunch preferred diplomats of the old school, the *salon* and cocktail-party diplomats. It had come to that state, well-known in other latitudes, in which a socialist society favors cynicism and mental sloth.

As for my own journeys into the hinterland beyond Havana, they were seen by the authorities as evidence that, if I had not yet joined the CIA, it couldn't be long until I did. It was reported that I couldn't stand the revolutionary process that was transforming Chile, and that sooner or later I would become a *gusano*—a "worm" or "maggot," as counterrevolutionary turncoats were known in Cuba—and an agent of the CIA.

On one of those trips outside Havana, I was witness to a curious spectacle. A foreign journalist had come by my hotel after dinner with two young ladies, friends of his, to pick me up and take me out for a ride. We drove to the beach at

Santa María and went for a walk alongside the moonlit sea. The young woman I was walking with was quite innocent, and she was totally ruled by the taboos of old Spanish Catholicism, in spite of the fact that the Revolution was just a few years younger than she; I, in turn, in spite of what local gossip columns might have been saying, am far from considering myself a Don Juan, that incorrigible rapist portrayed in García Lorca's poem. During our walk, my companions explained to me that not long ago, when there was an imminent threat of invasion, it was forbidden to walk along that beach at night, but that those times were gone.

As we were returning to Havana about one-thirty in the morning, we met a long file of people walking in the direction opposite our own. It was a straggling, irregular column that went on literally for miles. Some people were limping; others carried children in their arms or on their backs. My companions weren't sure what all this was, but they said it looked like some sort of religious procession.

Friends of mine to whom I later told the story explained that I had witnessed the resurrection of the cult of San Lázaro—not the Lazarus of the Christians, but the San Lázaro of the Afro-Cuban cult of *santería*. They could hardly believe that the procession had stretched for miles, though I had seen it with my own eyes.

"There's been no procession of San Lázaro since sixty-one, sixty-two," they said.

But the embers of superstition still lay beneath the ashes, and suddenly, when one would least have expected, the flame had flared again. Everyone agreed that this was most revealing. The failure of the "ten-million-ton harvest" had led to a strange and disquieting climate in the country.[15]

"You can't imagine what it was like. Nobody dreamed of blaming the government. On the contrary! There was a tremendous identification between the people and Fidel during those days. Every Cuban felt the failure of that harvest as his own. You could feel it in the streets. Every Cuban wept when the harvest failed."

But the ten-million-ton harvest had taken on an almost mythic character. With that harvest, it was promised, shortages and self-denials would be ended. When the mirage faded, however, and economic reality brought on even more stringent rationing, a dangerous void was felt. Into that void rushed the creative spirit of myth. The *babalú* cult of San Lázaro (one of the many

---

[15] The reader is referred to p. 184 for a fuller discussion of this devastating blow to the Cuban Revolution's dream of agricultural abundance.

subcults of the *santería* religion), having been for a time muted by the rational-ism of the Revolution, was reborn with sudden, harsh vigor. I later heard stories of other almost incredible events that occurred around this time. Some people were predicting great popular uprisings. In diplomatic circles, there were murmurs that Fidel would remain as party secretary and that Carlos Rafael Rodríguez, a man trusted by the Soviets, would become the new prime minister. (All this was said out of the range of possible bugs, out of earshot of the inquisitorial apparatus of the government.) Another rumor had it that Carlos Rafael would assume the presidency and would have more power than the current president Osvaldo Dorticós; that way Fidel could be gotten out of the way without violence. It was also rumored that Raúl Castro, through his control of the Army and the State Security apparatus, was the real strongman. Did not Raúl give the Soviets some guarantee of orthodoxy? During my stay in Cuba, the rumors grew. The air at times seemed charged with omens. I would go out onto the balcony of my hotel room and lean against the grimy railing and look out over the peeling and flaking city, the half-deserted streets, the Caribbean, where every morning a ship would be riding low in the water from its cargo of sand—the sign that somewhere in the world, far from El Vedado and the old bourgeois and tourist neighborhoods, there was, in spite of all the rumors and predictions, construction going on—I would stand there on the balcony, with the hope of escaping the omnipresent and invisible microphones, and I would relate to the consul the latest speculation that had come to my ears.

Despite Fidel's announcement of the suspension of Christmas and New Year's festivities, a few days before Christmas I received a huge turkey with the compliments of Foreign Minister Raúl Roa. I also found in my room a large basket brimming with fish and other seafood, a gift from the Prime Minister. Lacking a house, what was I to do with these gifts, which in the midst of rationing and the suppression of holiday festivities took on a certain fairy-tale quality? I mentioned the turkey to several friends of mine, whose eyes widened in surprise and covetousness, and at last we decided to cook it in the home of the poet César López. We would have it for lunch on a Sunday before I left early the next day for Mexico City.

I will never forget the euphoria of the preparations for that turkey, its juicy, meaty presence—the way it received the ingredients for the stuffing through the opening behind; the archaic instrument used to introduce the stuffing, as though for some medieval laxative; the way it began to turn golden in the oven. At the Diplomarket I had bought vegetables, condiments, fruit, and Chilean

and Spanish wine. The mere thought of Lezama Lima's inexhaustible gastronomic sensuality, of the pleasure he would experience after years of hard
denial, the salivation that would flood his palate as he stood before the golden
succulency of the bird, made the idea of inviting him more necessary than it
already was. Padilla and Belkis were also invited, as were Maruja and Pablo
Armando, Pepe Rodríguez Feo, and Miguel Barnet. All was carried out within
the strictest bounds of secrecy; if the news of my good fortune spread through
the literary circles of Havana, we would be certain to receive more than one
unforeseen visit; more than one would fall "like a turkey," as we said in Chile,
into our midst—and that meant we would run the risk of having very little
turkey for ourselves. In spite of our precautions, though, there were certain
mysterious telephone calls, voices that inquired what was happening in López'
house. Was this culinary curiosity, or the police? We never found out, but I
have the impression that the turkey was consumed in an atmosphere of some
tension, which my friends tried valiantly to lighten and dissimulate for my
sake.

Lezama and his wife, who was invariably well-mannered and calming, left
early. It must have been Agustín who drove them, in my Alfa, to their home in
Trocadero near the old Paseo del Prado to which so many pages of the *Paradiso*
are dedicated. I can still see Lezama eating that day: He was sitting in an
armchair, his ankles crossed and his head bent slightly over his plate, which he
balanced on his belly and his huge flabby thighs with a plump hand. He ate and
talked without pause, in that monotonous droning (or better yet, ritual) voice
he had, his words hanging in suspense at the end of each phrase as he tried to
overcome his asthma and get his breath again and tie that phrase to the next, in
a process of association of ideas and images that might be prolonged, with
historical allusions and quotations from books, to infinity. Fidel, with his
energetic sports, his distrust of literary speculations, could not bear a man like
Lezama. What need had Cuba for such extemporaneous erudition, such verbal
labyrinths, when the task of forming a new society, under heroic conditions
and starting virtually from scratch, had just begun? Fidel's stern cult of
activity, his near-worship of action (which one presumed he had learned from
his Jesuit preceptors, for whom idleness is the root of all evil) was utterly
irreconcilable with Lezama's extraordinary contemplative sensuality, a character unique in all the culture of the Spanish language. Lezama's intellectual
hunger, almost gluttony, was only matched by his appetite—its beginning and
end, like his appetite, lay in himself, in his own navel. There can be no doubt
that Fidel would have preferred some tireless man of action, like some of those
produced by the Chilean middle class, to that man of gustatory, verbal, and
literary passion that lived on Trocadero Street. Fidel, as I have said, struck me

as some Quixote influenced and to a large degree conquered by the spirit of
Sancho Panza. Lezama, in spite of his Sancho Panza physique, was an intellectual Quixote; his long verbal weavings were as filled with archaisms and
bizarre flights as that other Knight of the Woeful Countenance.

Heberto Padilla looked upon the curious spectacle from a revolutionary
perspective, and he was transported with delight at it—even savoring (sparks
of malign intelligence lighting up his eyes) the anticipation of what might turn
into a dramatic crisis. He talked about History that day, licking his chops and
rubbing his hands together, as though he had discovered some masochistic
pleasure in subjecting himself to its implacable machinery, meanwhile lifting a
glass of Paternina wine aloft or lighting and savoring the Montecristo cigar that
I had bought especially for him at the Diplomarket. Those innocent
pleasures—food, drink, cigars, and the conversation of speculation—had by
this time already begun to take on a sense of the forbidden, the sinful, which of
course made them doubly attractive but which dragged us to the edge of a
precipice, to the verge of a dizzying fall which we had no very lucid awareness
of being so exposed to. For Heberto, the fall ended in prison and the act of
public self-criticism which we all know of. He'd have done better not to play
with fire. I managed to remain in the diplomatic service because in Chile power
is less concentrated and one force tends to counteract another.[16] Thank good-
ness for that. But let's not get ahead of ourselves.

After Lezama left, the rest of us stayed on, in César López' library, drinking
the whisky that I had brought and talking about literature. From time to time
somebody pulled a book off the shelf and read a poem—a sonnet by Quevedo
or a stanza from some classic by Rubén Darío. There was also a sort of contest
to see who could recite poems from memory, and people recalled unforgettable
lines from García Lorca, Neruda, or the French.

The Cuban writers that I knew had large houses (though they were falling
apart), books, and jobs that allowed them lots of time to write. But they were
nervous, excited, filled with angst and anxieties, sometimes rightly so but
more often because of some irrational quirk or vanity,[17] and they all seemed to
have become obsessed with backbiting and gossiping, with criticizing the
regime, though there was no possible way they were going to have any
influence on the course of events. The worst thing, perhaps, was the sense they

---

[16] I remind my most kind and long-suffering reader that these pages were written in
mid-1971.

[17] Even though, in private, I had been critical of certain aspects of Cuban socialism, in early
1971 I was doing some wishful thinking about it as well.

had that they were prisoners in their own land, with no future of any kind: They were not allowed to travel even when they received invitations from abroad, with all expenses paid. It was not a question of monetary exchange, but of political control, and we all knew that the regime would make no concessions.

We Chilean writers, at least in the last few years, had not had houses, or libraries, or time, or sometimes money to pay the grocery store or the doctor for our children's medical bills. Still, most of us managed to survive, and almost all of us had become, under the auspices of leftist organizations, or the diplomatic service, or American or Canadian university fellowships, inveterate travelers. Of course one could count on the fingers of one hand the people in Chile who were writing seriously and constantly, and not simply resting on the laurels of a past book or two. The literary life of the Latin American countries has always seemed to me fictitious—fictitious and imitative. In the diplomatic service, which I entered on the basis of an examination and in which I rose strictly through the ranks, I did not always sleep, contrary to general belief, in a bed of roses. But I did achieve some contact with national and international reality, I did have direct experience of certain basic facts that make the world go 'round and that are not picked up at literary evenings. This is the sort of experience that is inaccessible to those who live on fellowships, and the "fellow" is a well-known figure in writers' circles. Such experience is inaccessible, too, to the eternal idler who is the protegé of some aunt, or the heir to a fortune, or the simple sponger that cuddles up to literary types and their slightly acidic wines. I wasted too much time at those gatherings as a young man, and now I make it a practice to flee them.

The curious thing is that in Cuba, due perhaps to the very fact that it was a country "on the margins of things," and to the fact that in 1968 the writers were my first contact with the Island, I neither could nor wished to flee those gatherings. I think the writers in Cuba were more pleasant, more cultured, more gracious, and less provincial, than the great majority of my Chilean colleagues.

My Cuban friends' exasperation stemmed above all from seeing the meteoric rise of certain opportunistic writers, who always seem to be the most mediocre members of the creative clan. It is my belief that the Cuban Revolution at one stage trusted too much in the prestige of literature as an instrument with which to break through the blockade and gain foreign support. At one period, moreover, literature, culture in general, did serve to show that the Cuban brand of socialism was "different," since unlike other countries Cuba did not curtail intellectual freedoms. But the root of the evil, the basic error, was the idea of "using" literature. When this idea crystallized, there

immediately appeared those "writers-as-tools," those ever-available opportunists, who had never lifted a finger for the Revolution but who were suddenly
heroically determined to make an *a posteriori* show of their revolutionary
merits, hymning the libertine freedom[18] or the rigorous calligraphy of the New
Man, according to the tune played at the top. My friends, meanwhile, rather
than going the route of writing books for the present moment or for the future,
sat in their ramshackle houses among broken lamps and rickety old furnishings
and indulged in obstinate and unrelenting bad-mouthing, bitter and sterile
backbiting. One must admit that it was hard not to fall into that attitude. Two or
three of the younger ones resisted, and they kept themselves, for good reason
as it turned out, at a prudent distance from my rooms in the Habana Riviera.
Of those two or three, one was later summoned, in spite of having kept himself
away from the rest of us, to perform a public act of self-criticism, and with a
gesture unheard-of in those days unexpectedly "spoiled" what everyone present unanimously declared to have been a night to remember.[19]

But back to that Christmas dinner: That Sunday evening before my trip to
Mexico City we were reading poetry and talking about literature in César
López' library, absorbed in the pleasures of the music of words (a pleasure at
the time, as I've said, increasingly politically suspect) in an atmosphere
vaguely alcoholic and hazy with cigar smoke, with the waves beating against
the Malecón across the street, throwing up walls of spray and licking the
houses and other objects of Havana with their tongues of salt, when I caught
sight of a dark-skinned young woman who had come in as silently as a cat and
sat down among us. She was smiling, listening without surprise and as though
she were long accustomed to our cries of admiration for the poems and to this
talk of ours, that often grew heated and confused. The young woman kept
looking at me out of the corner of her eye with an attentiveness that I attributed
to curiosity about the Chilean chargé d'affaires. I use the correct term here,
but most people thought of me as Chile's first ambassador, a misunderstanding
that not only increased people's curiosity but also their surprise when they saw
that I "surrounded myself" with ragged, and out-of-favor, poets and writers.

Drawn by the magnet of that gaze, as my late friend Jorge Sanhueza would
have said in a parody of the Spanish classics, I suddenly found myself sitting
beside the stealthy visitor. I talked with her for a long time, and we decided to

---

[18] The stale surrealism of the early years and the Stalinism, the socialist realism that dares
not speak its name, after the crisis in March 1971.

[19] The person who would not follow the script for the evening was José Norberto Fuentes.

go later that night to the house of a painter who'd invited me over for drinks—
drinks that I myself would supply. She said she had an engagement for dinner,
but that we could meet later. I went out into the hallway to ask one of my
friends who the girl was.

"They sent her to you," my friend guffawed. Then he turned immediately
serious and added: "Be careful! She's very dangerous."

"Then I'd better call our little date off."

"No! Not yet, anyway . . . But don't say a word!"

I recalled a party at the Chilean poet Enrique Lihn's house in 1968, during
the time he was working in Havana at the Casa de las Américas. Somebody
pointed out a certain person to me and told me to be careful.

"Why would you let a policeman in your house?" I asked Enrique Lihn.

Enrique shrugged his shoulders. "They just come," he said. "There's no
way to avoid it."

The exchange shocked me at the time, but in the rush of all the other
experiences I had during that visit to the Island, I had forgotten all about it. Nor
was I, back in 1968, a figure that merited special surveillance. But between
the writer invited for one month in January 1968 and the diplomat representing
the Chile of the Unidad Popular at the end of 1970 there was a difference
that the security services recognized much better than I myself did.

Agustín, my driver, drove me at precisely midnight to the address given me
by the Mysterious Visitor. It was a modern building in the city's best residential area. In a few moments she emerged from the elevator, opened the car door,
and slipped inside, greeting Agustín with the greatest friendliness and as
naturally as one could imagine, as though she already knew him or at least had
met him on other occasions and vaguely remembered his face. At my hotel
they had not, until then, allowed anyone up to my rooms. The insurmountable
obstacle so far had been the elevator operators. I had had to enter into long
negotiations with them once in order to persuade them to let the young Chilean
man who was helping me out as secretary during my first days even step into
the elevator. It was quite a surprise, then, to see that a movement of the
Mysterious Visitor's eyebrow was all it took for the desk clerk to hand me the
keys and for the doors to the elevator to slide wide open.

"How did you do that?" I asked.

"It's my job," she said. "It brings me here all the time, at all sorts of hours."

"What work is that?"

"Public relations."

Following my friend's counsel, I only opened my mouth to utter trivialities.
I thought myself clever, doing that. But she was cleverer than I by far. Every
detail of my room, every word I spoke must have been seized upon for that

public relations job of hers. I gave her, at her request, a bottle of whisky, and to keep her warm at that hour of the night, she took a black sweater I had just bought in Chile—in Havana it represented the height of luxury. She also asked me to bring her cosmetics from Mexico. As one can see, her work in public relations had no ill effects on her femininity. Quite the contrary. She left my room as stealthily as at five o'clock the previous afternoon she had entered the house of César López. She even took the trouble to call me two or three hours after leaving the hotel to be sure I didn't oversleep and miss my plane.

The nights of Havana now were, in the best of circumstances, far less dazzling than they had been in the past. Its lights had dimmed, its once-glittering skyline and neon signs had been blasted and scarred by the revolutionary wind. Now only a few faded letters still sputtered on the sign bearing that brand name (and the brand name itself only remembered by people older than thirty) that harked back to some once-powerful family (now fled to Miami, New York, the Canaries, or some other place far from the risk of revolution) whose banishment had been demanded by stern justice, for the once-powerful family's name would inevitably be linked, on that dramatic Island, to acts of crime, thievery, or corruption. But the salt air would eat away even the little that was left of that name on the cracked and peeling wall, the little that was left in the memory of the young generations, who now marched down the streets singing anthems or crying out revolutionary slogans after studying in classrooms that had once, before being expropriated by the Revolution, served as the grand *boudoir*—1940s Hollywood-style—of the wife of the man who had borne that name and owned the factory that made the product that likewise bore it.

After the dimness and the darkened nights of this new Havana, after the silence and the gloom of those cracked seawalls with the crumbling sidewalks that were for some people (once again, those past thirty) the site of nostalgic reminiscences and thoughts secretly hostile, if not openly opposed, to the Revolution—after all that minor-key experience—the colored lights of Mexico City's Paseo de la Reforma were frankly dizzying, as though without realizing it, and in a very short time, I had become used to Havana and were now acting like some country bumpkin in the big city. I had been picked up at the airport in Mexico City by my friend the Chilean cultural attaché, and now, dazzled and timid, almost fearful, suffering an odd sort of culture shock, I could only blink as I sat in his almost fabulous Chevrolet, the outside covered with chromework and painted psychedelic green or blue, all knobs and dials inside, and listened to it throb as it swam swiftly and silently through the schools of other equally swift and silent machine-creatures, through the noise and the rush, through the beckoning calls of glittering signs and shop-windows, through the smog that burned my eyes and made a mockery of Fuentes's famed region of transparent air, swam past a gigantic monument erected in honor of bad taste, in honor of the rhetorical inflation of our Latin American republics, swam past a park where country women dressed in red, white, or green strolled and, as though in some painting by Diego Rivera, herds of children followed them—a confirmation that nature, in the broadest sense of the word, imitates art.

"The people with money live up in the hills of Chapultepec to get out of the smog, which is as bad as New York's or Tokyo's, maybe worse."

Through the trees, outside the broad clearings in which the monuments of Mexico City stand, the windows of office and apartment buildings sparkled like emeralds.

"Surely the Aztecs had more genius for monumental architecture."

"Look at a building built during the period when Mexico was subject to European culture. The modern building style has not only managed to banish the European *fin de siècle* styles but to reincorporate the indigenous, pre-Columbian style as well. It is going back to the country's deepest traditions. The style, the tradition, began to be used again several years ago, and the country has not the slightest complex about it."

"I know. I know there was a revolution here."

Without taking his eyes off the expressway, which required his full attention as it snaked through a neighborhood filled with baroque cupolas, my friend smiled gently.

Later, on the crowded, noisy patio of a restaurant in the Zona Rosa, with a green *salsa* on the table that made even the bones in your skull burn, I told Carlos Fuentes the story of the Mysterious Visitor whose mere arched eyebrow had made the Cerberus of the elevator sheathe its fangs, whose presence had inspired obliging smiles and gestures of accommodation, and whose dangers I had been warned about in whispers by my friend in the hallway of César López' house. I told Carlos Fuentes how her eyes took in everything and how she feigned interest in the literary, allusion-dotted conversation, and how she had spoken not one word I could remember. "They've sent her to you. Be careful! Don't talk! Remember that that big mouth of yours is your Achilles' heel." A cloud of smoke issued from Carlos' mouth, and his eyes grew as round as saucers—it was hard to tell whether he was mocking me or actually scared. I could carry her to my hotel room, he said, but I had to put an absolute muzzle on that Chilean loquacity of mine, ignorant as I was of the subtle workings of the machinery of History.

"In my time things hadn't come to that yet. What a pity I missed that scene!" Carlos' comic frivolity was perfectly deliberate and yet showed that as an intellectual on the well-upholstered margins of the Latin American subworld, and in spite of his well-known (and well-earned) reputation for critical insight, he really did not know how fearsome those mechanical, implacable gears could be.

His New Year's Eve party also had an air of deliberate frivolity about it— rock music, with blowups of newspaper photographs of Emiliano Zapata, Pancho Villa, Luis Buñuel; long-haired young painters in Cossack boots and thick leather belts; young Englishwomen with pale shoulders and milky-white bosoms, dressed in pre-Raphaelite anachronism; distinguished ladies of the new school with intoxicating voices that held for the Chilean (an eternal islander, however much he might travel) a charm that plucked him up out of this world and left him hypnotized and paralyzed, for these were women whose conversation, though leavened with frivolity, was charged with wit, cunning, and sheer information—though they too were ignorant of the fell workings of those grinding gears. The solid foundations of the Mexican Revolution, the new order which had been established after and on top of all the blood that had been shed in that place which before the coming of industry had indeed been the most transparent region of the air, allowed these still-young men and women, the children (or grandchildren, really) of the revolution, to dance to the rhythm of rock and roll under the larger-than-life eyes, faded with time, of Emiliano Zapata, without any risk or consequence for themselves whatever.

They might write the most ornate and complex poems, paint fierce and angry paintings, and write novels with impunity. The ancient Aztec and Toltec stones, the broad avenues and esplanades between the pyramids, the gold of the baroque altars, the cannon- and rifle-shot still buried in the walls of a provincial town square, the color of the markets and fiestas, the sudden outburst of violence served them as inspiration or as backdrop. Occasional acts of political repression, however bloody they might be, were never more than relatively slight shocks to the life of the country, like the tachycardia that hypochondriacs and those who know little about medicine sometimes confuse with the onset of a myocardial infarction. Faced with the habitual squawking of the protests of intellectuals, the Powers That Be even allowed themselves the luxury of a certain irony.

"You ask me about Mr. Octavio Paz's resignation?" the Mexican president Díaz Ordaz once remarked on television. "Well, according to my information, Mr. Paz did not resign, he requested permission to be allowed to retire. . . . So of course . . ."

"Il était très emmerdé, le pauvre Octavio, avec son travail d'ambassadeur . . . ," said one of the ladies at the New Year's Eve party. "Poor Octavio. He came out covered with shit from that ambassador's job of his."

For the Chilean traveler, for that native of a small country that was just a stone's throw away from the crossroads of History (as Heberto Padilla would say, with a touch of pomposity and provocative malice, as he puffed on his ever-present Havana), the easy and insouciant happiness of the host and his friends was cause for serious meditation, for slightly melancholy reflection, as he sat on a handsome colonial chest and looked at the room where people were dancing and sipped at his whisky.

Fernando de Syzslo, pointing at the host, said, "Look at him! Doesn't he look like some Mexican general?"

With his moustache, his wide smile, his navy blue pinstripe three-piece suit, his spotless white shirt and gleaming tie, our host, circulating, whisky in hand, among his guests, under the grim gaze of the heroes that had been nailed to the walls, displayed the most delighted and expansive side of his personality.

The blockade could be seen at its clearest, for the flagrant and brazen thing it was, in the way I was treated at the airport in Mexico City when I went to catch my return flight to Havana. As on my first trip, less than a month before, I caught the flash, somewhere in the confusion at the entrance to the passenger area, of a flashbulb; I don't know whether it was aimed at me. In those days I had not yet lost my Chilean innocence respecting the existence of secret police. The loss of that innocence came later, so that now, retrospectively, I suspect that I was indeed the target of that flash of light. (The CIA? Mexican authorities? Cuban State Security?) Though my picture had been published in the newspapers (as I told myself in those days in order to rid myself of those suspicions, which I wanted to think of as more a product of egocentrism or paranoia than of cool reason), I now know that security services must maintain up-to-date images: the spare tire, the beginning of a jowl, the bald spot, the expression, even one's favorite suit, and on such a day, at such an hour, and under such and such circumstances. No detail can be irrelevant in the mosaic of information, and since they could hardly photograph me, a diplomat, openly, as I later saw them do, one by one, to the bearers of ordinary passports (after a wait that would make anybody lower his resistance), I now think it was more than likely that that flash of light, which I just caught out of the corner of my eye and whose source was lost in the crowd of people, was aimed at me.

Going through the line to have our passports checked for Havana, I had to wait more than an hour at the airport for my passport to be returned to me, in spite of the fact that it lay on top of the stack, within inches of the unattended photograph machine, and was supposed to be given preferential treatment. It was returned to me at last, without the supposedly denunciatory words *TRAVEL TO CUBA* stamped on it in letters so large that even blind customs and police officers could be sure to read it, and my flight was called. I and the other passengers walked down a long corridor of temporary wallboard and glass, and we came out beside the Ilushin with the colors of Cuba painted on its tail, gleaming in the midday sun. I must confess that the Cuban flag and the modesty of the Ilushin brought a flush of emotion to me. I felt at home suddenly, and I believe that I made a small, self-satisfied demonstration of my familiarity with the language of the crew for the sake of my wife.

In the seat in front of me, a Chilean official of international connections was traveling; he was one of those diplomats whose conversation is inevitably peppered with the names of a long list of influential friends. His list, of course, included the name of Salvador Allende: "We've been friends for more than twenty years." And as he said that, the international official, who had already been at pains to tell me how well he was treated by Chilean embassies around the world, looked at me out of the corner of his eye to see whether I'd sat up at that or not, whether I was the sort of professional who would defer to him and with whom the complicities and tacit understandings of the profession could be established, or whether I was some insubstantial johnny-come-lately to the world of diplomacy, a person whose future in the higher spheres of international dealings was in no way assured.

"I still don't have an embassy," I told him, to prevent the gentleman at the outset from having too many illusions.

"You don't have an embassy! I would have thought you'd be set up royally by now."

I had no residence yet, no embassy building, no offices, I explained. It was not easy to find a good house in Havana that wasn't already occupied. The residences of the old wealth had been taken over for student housing, in accord with the new plans for public instruction.

The international traveler was understanding, though his sidewise, yellowish gaze never left me. He asked what had become of this one and that one, old friends of his, but I wouldn't let myself be dragged into that sort of game: Every reply I made revealed a greater degree of familiarity with the intimacies of our foreign service, but I made them only little by little and almost grudgingly, and I managed to keep the gentleman in some perplexity. I could see that he was making calculations as to who I was, why he didn't know me, why (with this last name of mine that had always stood so perfectly for the forces of the reactionary right in Chile) his "friend of twenty years" Salvador Allende had named me chargé d'affaires in Havana under circumstances in which such a posting, even if only temporary, could not have been done merely administratively, but rather would have had to have secured the acquiescence of the highest spheres of government. His ignorance of my identity caused my companion profound distress, for he feared that he had suddenly been passed over by events, confronted with the necessity to meet new, perhaps impenetrable, faces, people who perhaps even knew things that he, who thought he knew everything and everybody, did not know, and who could return his intense, scrutinizing gaze with a calm, and even perhaps ironic, one.

The international traveler, who had spent half the time he'd been on board the plane turned around in his seat to face me, returned to his normal position, in an apparent decision to adopt a strategy of retreat, which he later would complement with circuitous and probing condescension. The plane, meanwhile, was no longer flying over open sea but rather now descending over stands of palm trees and red-clay roads. One could see, off in the distance, the concrete towers of the city and glinting sunlight on the Caribbean. The Ilushin touched down at last at the airport at Rancho Boyeros; it rolled quickly past a formation of army trucks parked beside the runway and then ever more slowly taxied toward the terminal, past some of the big-bellied old turboprop Bristol Britannias I had seen on my 1968 trip. The Ilushins were the Alfa Romeos of Cuban aviation, while the Bristol Britannias, with their sky-blue interiors flecked with artificial stars out of some old Hollywood movie, were the rickety, chrome-fendered Oldsmobiles that still limped down the Havana streets, gasping and wheezing and leaving a trail of black smoke and oil stains.

My international compatriot was awaited by a little group of functionaries of several nationalities; they had taken the trouble to bring along a photographer to record the historic round of handshakes that ensued. I began to conceive for my traveling companion a secret and almost embarrassing admiration. No detail escaped him; what happened to me on my first arrival in Havana—when the cord tied around the case of wine cut my fingers and I had been within an inch of being expelled from Protocol's receiving area— would never have happened to him. Surely nothing of the sort had ever happened to my traveling companion, nor would it. He was now advancing, smiling, his briefcase borne by another functionary, toward the official arrival area, whose doors were wide open to him; nearby there stood the black official vehicle, whose soft seats had been prepared hours earlier to receive the dignitary's posterior when it arrived.

The head of Protocol, as eager and efficient as always, greeted us most cordially. My Alfa, with Agustín at the wheel, speeded off toward Havana. On the other side of the highway stood the buildings, recreation fields, and baseball diamonds of a model insane asylum. The rows of new red or green tractors still stood neatly in formation on an embankment beside the road.

Some were still in their huge packing crates beside other rows of yellow farm machinery.

"Why don't they use that machinery?" I had asked, the first time I saw this phenomenon.

"Ah!" My interlocutor had raised his hands and answered me in a hushed voice, looking around secretively to see if there were any invisible electronic ears. "If you're here a year, you'll see them rust and slowly fall apart."

"In an underdeveloped capitalist country—in Chile, for instance— agriculture's not very highly mechanized, but if a farmer buys a tractor, since he's either got to invest his own savings in it or get up to his neck in debt with the State Bank for it, he treats it like a baby, and he gets all the use he can out of it."

"You'll see!" my interlocutor had insisted. "The most striking characteristic of a socialist economy is its waste. Workers, clerks, who only have the right to one pair of shoes a year, look at those tractors and they see their shoes sitting there, rotting."

"A certain kind of socialist economy, you mean."

"Of course! True socialism doesn't work that way. But the problem is, we're surrounded with incompetents—idiots! Idiots!"

My interlocutor, red-faced, exasperated, seemed to have forgotten all about the electronic ears—tiny, tiny things, by all reports, that testified to the marvelousness of modern technology. According to well-informed persons one talked to, they were hardly larger than the head of a pin, and they could be aimed at precise locations inside a room, or even on balconies, so that even the subtlest, most surreptitious and muted sound waves could not escape their secret spying.

"Take the Lenin Park," another Cuban interlocutor would say to me, this time in Paris. "Fifteen hundred acres of lush grounds for the recreation of the citizens of Havana, while Havana itself is falling to pieces. It's a little like the Metro in Moscow in the time of Stalin, with its marbles and its crystal chandeliers. Of course the Metro is used by people every day."

Now, in Agustín's presence, I simply pointed out to Pilar the rows of tractors, adding that the Revolution had mechanized agriculture. I would make further comments about this in our room—where the ears buried in the walls, much more reliable than Agustín's, would take careful and meticulous note! But we were now at the Plaza de la Revolución, and I pointed out to Pilar the public buildings, the statue of José Martí, and the huge posters with portraits of Ho Chi Minh and Ché Guevara (who had of course wanted to resemble Uncle Ho in his self-denials and heroic determination). We then drove down streets shaded by huge, kindly *jagüeyes,* wild banyan trees, their roots emerging even from high branches. We circled the monument to the fathers of the republic, and at last we drove to the hotel, always under the gaze of the inexpressive eyes of groups awaiting the unpredictable and long-delayed coming of the next bus.

When I was growing up, I went to the Colegio de San Ignacio, a Jesuit school, and at various times in my years there it was my lot to officiate as first student of the class at certain ceremonies—as leader of the Marian Congregation; as altar boy to Archbishop and then Cardinal José María Caro (passing him the silver censer, whose newly lit incense would give out great intermittent puffs of smoke at the *missa solemnis* on the school's patron-saint day, July 31); and even as precocious Catholic orator standing before the cardinal now far along in years (who'd fallen fast asleep midway through my speech). I participated in the life of the school to a degree I might now call excessive, swept along by a certain spirit of ostentation which my Jesuit mentors, with a probable view to using me as a shining example of their cause, never seemed to see the need to discourage. This excess, I believe, finally left me sated on ceremony, what nowadays might be called burned out on it, and today I feel a sort of anarchic aversion to all that pomp and show. At the time, the result was a withering acid I tended to sprinkle over the flowers of the rhetoric I would use at the altar or later in parliamentary gatherings of one kind or another, and my words began to take on a telegraphic nakedness, close to paralysis, from which I have been decades recovering.

That is why I liked the style of the Cuban Revolution from the beginning. Fidel's oratory, especially what I heard of it at Princeton, in that rudimentary English of his, was literally a pole away from the empty phrase-making by our own Latin American brand of "public figures," whose overused and over-blown images made them the butt of endless jokes and parodies among my friends and me at the university. When one particular statesman spoke, we would wait in barely contained glee for him to pull out his never-failing Pandora's Box. The Ship of State and Sword of Damocles were part of the same arsenal, and several years ago someone had the brilliant idea of putting together a Museum of Rhetorical Objects made up of such legendary items. The Sword of Damocles would be displayed in a showcase on a velvet pillow, and beside it, that other mythic blade, The Two-Edged Sword. (The Trojan Horse, the Horse of a Different Color, and other Rhetorical Animals would be in a separate wing.)

But revolutions, which sweep away the clichés of the past, themselves tend after a while, and perhaps inevitably, to engender their own new rhetoric. It is

in that attitude to language that one can find the root of all political perver-
sions. An old Soviet poet, Semyon Kirsanov, who attended a Communist
demonstration in Chile a few years ago, told Pablo Neruda that the meeting had
reminded him of the beginnings of the October Revolution. Why? asked
Neruda. Because of the homemade signs and posters, Kirsanov replied, and
the amateur lettering, and the drips of paint running off the letters down the
signs. In today's demonstrations, Kirsanov said, looking back nostalgically on
those early years of the Russian Revolution, the posters are made on an
assembly line, by professionals, and the paint on the perfect letters doesn't run.

In Cuba, that same change was already taking place; spontaneity was
inevitably and perhaps necessarily being supplanted by premeditation. Or to
put it another way: The Revolution was beginning to outgrow its spontaneous
stage. I could see this clearly in the inaugural ceremony of the Congress of the
International Organization of Journalists. The heads of the diplomatic missions
of the socialist and "friendly" countries were all invited. We had reserved
seats in the first rows. On the stage, sitting beside the Cuban political leaders
and under the huge revolutionary slogans hung from the rear curtains, I saw a
Chilean journalist I had known during my university days. He winked at me in
recognition and smiled what might have been a false smile. In spite of his
current leftist radicalism, he had the ashen, melancholy face of the perfect
bureaucrat. A platoon of militant children came on stage and recited something
and then they began to tie the kerchiefs that symbolized their brigade around
all our necks, as the occupants of the stage looked on in approval, crossing
their hands in their laps and smiling beatifically. A Frenchman with a waxed
moustache and the slightly antiquated look of a *bon vivant,* and with that
somewhat incongruous kerchief about his neck, stepped up to the podium and
opened the convention with a resounding and "inspirational" speech. He
delivered it with the calm security, the sensuous delight in the well-turned
phrase that characterizes the French and represents the theatrical side of their
talents. One could see that the French gentleman had been chosen after long
deliberations and compromises as the person most likely to please everyone on
the organization's board. His oratory, his very presence vaguely evoked the
period of Romain Rolland and the Society of Nations, though he must have
been just a youngster in those days.

Immediately afterward, Raúl Roa took the podium, and he spoke as brilliantly and skillfully as always, in spite of the slight verbal excess that had
become a habit of his. The warmth of his words was convincing.

As the session broke up, I spotted the white, well-barbered head of Nicolás
Guillén, who in an impeccable dark suit, and wearing a large medal on his
lapel, was making his way to the front of the auditorium. I made some remark

about the medal, thinking that he would erupt with the laughter that had made him famous at parties and gatherings in Chile, but he remained stonily silent. My error in calculations as to Guillén's reaction was symptomatic of that Chilean openness that Padilla had once remarked on. I found it strange that the person I had known in the Café Bosco in Santiago and the Latin Quarter in Paris would not take a joke about a medal. But we were not in the Café Bosco, and the joke was, as the saying quite aptly has it, "out of place."

Out in the lobby, all the mission chiefs were standing in a tight little group, in obedience to the inveterate inability of all diplomats of all times and places to mix with other mortals. There was an exhibit of photographs, as I recall, that portrayed the Angolan National Liberation Movement. A member of the editorial staff of *Juventud Rebelde* came over to me and asked what I thought of Roa's speech. My first answer did not satisfy him.

"Didn't you find it too wordy, too rhetorical? Don't you think he used a rhetoric out of the past?"

"No, not really. I think his rhetoric was very effective, *is* very effective, even today."

My interrogator, after studying me out of the corner of his eye and seeing I wouldn't be drawn into indiscretions so easily as all that, retreated. The group of mission chiefs began to say their good-byes, with the usual smiles and bows, and to file off to their long black cars. . . .

"And you, my friend the chargé d'affaires from Chile, were you invited to the opening session?"

"Yes, Mr. Ambassador."

"Well, I wasn't," the ambassador from Mexico said.

"The invitation arrived quite late; only a few hours before the ceremony," I said, even while knowing that this detail would not calm my colleague's ruffled feelings. (I now think that the late arrival of my invitation might have been calculated by Meléndez to keep me from going.)

"Mine never arrived," the ambassador said; and then, after a short silence, he added, "It's a pity for them to make distinctions, don't you think?"

I shrugged my shoulders.

"Your position is very delicate," the ambassador said, "and you have acquitted yourself admirably. We've said as much to some of our colleagues."

"Thank you, Mr. Ambassador!"

"You must not take it as a compliment. I would not say so if I did not think so."

The Mexican ambassador's words of praise, which were repeated on several occasions, should have put me on guard, but I went on—and would go on to the end, or near the end—as frankly and openly as before.

"Important journalists are here from Mexico. What will they say when they don't see one among those who were invited? They will think, I imagine, that one is not doing one's job well here, or that one has caused some distress. Do you understand, my friend?"

The ambassador had got a whiff of the poison that might find its way between the journalistic lines when his terrible compatriots returned to Mexico, and the mere idea gave him heartburn. He no doubt hoped that I would present his case to the Cuban Foreign Ministry, since Chile was in its good graces, and since Chile and Mexico were on such good terms, etc. But the line had been drawn with unerring eye: The socialist countries and the "friendly" countries had been invited, and Mexico was not at the moment one of those countries, after the incident of the Mexican diplomat who had been accused by the government of Cuba of being a CIA agent and the announcement of the termination of air agreements between the two countries.

After he had made these complaints, the ambassador came around to his favorite subject: socialism à la Sweden, which in his view had none of the drawbacks of either capitalism or socialism and all of the advantages of both.

"Don't you think so, my friend?"

Another of the subjects that he continually returned to was the issue of people seeking political asylum; he would panic at the mere mention of the problem. He advised me to continue to reside in the hotel, and told me I should not accept a house that did not have high walls and that could not be thoroughly protected. His, a fortress in every sense of the word, was guarded by soldiers with machine guns. And besides the huge front gates with their triple locks, an iron barrier cut off all access at the vehicle entrance.

"Imagine, my friend—a bus once burst through the gate, drove all the way to the rear of the garden, and the driver and all the passengers requested asylum. It was perfectly planned."

Now the barrier was there to prevent another such accident from occurring.

The ambassador sighed. The ambassador would not lose his optimism. He puffed at his Havana, as short and stubby as the ambassador himself, and emitted a cloud of smoke. At the other end of the large living room, young people in bathing suits ran barefooted over the shining tiles of the floor and out the door. Seconds later one heard the splashing as their bodies hit the water in the pool.

"They go to the University of Mexico," the ambassador explained, "but they come here for their vacations."

"That's very convenient for you."

"Indeed."

The ambassador nodded. He had stopped, as he was accompanying me to the door, before the full-length portrait of a young woman.

"She is the daughter of the former owner of this house."

The young woman, halted in that hypothetical time that precedes revolutions and that is seen, after the revolution has triumphed, through a lens of legend—the time of Talleyrand's *douceur de vivre,* of the "happy few" of Stendhal, echoing Talleyrand—that young woman, caught by the hand of the painter as she stood in the idyllic *entr'acte* of a history whose scenes were bloodied with outbursts of violence and struggle, standing now in remoteness from the convulsions of the present as she had stood in remoteness from the convulsions of the past (convulsions that even as she posed for her portrait were about to deliver forth their new progeny, and that delivery to come much sooner than she could ever have imagined), smiled at the two of us out of a setting of roses and white water lilies under a sky of flawless blue. Her shoulders curved gracefully, the skin of her arms looked fresh and cool under the near-transparent tulle of her dress, and her hem brushed the grass, allowing a glimpse of ankle and of delicate shoe. The ambassador looked up at the portrait with evident satisfaction, as though between himself and the girl there lay some sentimental and mysterious bond.

But the times had changed, there was no doubt of that, and the ambassador, eager to keep in step with those times, was an ardent advocate for socialism à la Sweden. He had begun his diplomatic career in Sweden, and of Sweden he had imperishable memories.

"Oh yes, my friend, an admirable country! If you ever have the opportunity to be sent to Stockholm, go without a second thought!"

We stepped out onto the portico, and Agustín (who was sleeping on the hood this time) woke with a jump and ran to start the car. It is possible that in the midst of his nap a pocket tape-recorder (whose uses in today's world I only fully discovered in Europe, months later) was running. If so, the conversation I had with my Mexican colleague, in which I showed myself entirely too tolerant of Swedish-style socialism, and even spoke some incriminating (to use Heberto Padilla's favorite adjective) words, may have added its bit to the file that was growing against me.

Meanwhile, from the entrance of his mansion, the ambassador was making the gestures of farewell that are *de rigueur* in the world of protocol. The gates swung open and the barrier that guarded the sleeping and the waking serenity of the diplomat lifted to allow us to pass. The machine gun-toting soldiers, bored with a posting that had recently lacked all surprise, since no one any longer dared entertain such ideas as hijacking a bus and driving it, via the

Mexican Embassy, to Miami, watched us pull out of the driveway, turn, and speed away, tires squealing, just the way Agustín liked it, especially when there was an audience.

When the Cuban ambassador to Mexico remarked that the last Chilean ambassador, the ambassador from the *ancien régime*, as it were, had been an Edwards, he was referring to Emilio Edwards Bello, brother of Joaquín Edwards Bello[20] and my father's first cousin. Don Emilio, as everyone in Cuba and Chile called him, had been ambassador for many years; he had fallen in love with the country, had married a Cuban woman. He became one of that list of characters that lived in and about Havana in the years before the Revolution. Many members of the revolutionary government had known him, and some still held warm, friendly memories of him.

On those diplomatic visits to other embassies, the memory of don Emilio was always popping up. His ex-secretary, now no longer young, came to me for a job. She knew embassies inside and out, and she spoke to me of her warm personal relations with President Allende, whom she had had the honor of serving when he paid his first visits to Fidel's Havana. I didn't much like the idea of hiring a member of the old mission, even if it were but a question of an administrative secretary, but the idea had to be discarded entirely when Meléndez baldly asserted that the former secretary had ties to the CIA.

"The CIA?" I asked.

"The CIA," Meléndez repeated. "After she stopped working for Chile she went to the Swiss embassy. There she made connections with the CIA. We found out that not long ago she got a new contact. Of course, *chico!*"

Anything was possible, but in any case Meléndez's warning effectively vetoed the nice (or not-so-nice) lady's job. Hiring her would be tantamount to a direct provocation of the director of Protocol.

On another occasion I visited a friend's apartment, and my friend told me that the staff of the building, former employees of don Emilio's, were looking forward with great excitement to meeting me. I went downstairs to say hello to them. They were a man and his wife, very old now, who seemed unable to believe that this meeting with a relative of don Emilio's, in 1971, could be real.

---

[20] Joaquín Edwards Bello was a writer well known not only in Chile but throughout Latin America for his fiction and his chronicles.

The old man, pale and mute with emotion, took my hands. His wife looked at me as though I were a vision from another world, and she asked me about don Emilio's children and grandchildren, of whom I had only the vaguest knowledge. What was curious, and perhaps dangerous to my diplomatic standing, was that they saw a family resemblance, and that this resemblance even further heightened their emotion and disbelief. It was overwhelming proof—I had to have come from that other world, and their trembling hands touched my own otherworldly, and apparently time-traveling, ones.

A similar encounter occurred at a diplomatic gathering, a dinner at the French Embassy. The waiter who had served me was a man some sixty years old, with gray hair and pink skin and obsequious eyes that were at once soft and probing. He retained all the appearances and gestures of the old times, and one knew that in his day he had been a submissive witness (though one perhaps gnawed at times by rebelliousness or quiet indignation) to the life of the *haute bourgeoisie* of Cuba. He accompanied me to the door, and as my car was brought around he asked me if I were not a relative of don Emilio. My affirmative brought on emphatic demonstrations of delight. Afterward, at every cocktail party, the moment the waiter saw me enter he would make his way through the crowd of guests, tray held professionally aloft, and offer me my drink the way I liked it, with lots of ice and just a splash of water, or spin the tray around to set the most toothsome appetizer before me. I later became familiar with—or rather guessed I had fathomed, because familiarity was out of the question—the full subtlety of the Cuban State Security apparatus, and that knowledge (if I may be allowed to claim my experience as knowledge) does not permit me to discard the possibility that the waiter who had served don Emilio was an agent for that apparatus. At the receptions I attended at the French Embassy, his soft keen bright eyes would observe me with an air of protective sympathy. But would he, later, in some mysterious office as he stood before some official with blurry and impersonal features, report on my attitude, or on snippets of my conversation? Did the pocket of his impeccably white jacket contain a tiny tape-recorder, the latest version of the breed, the spawn of some electronic wizard—in keeping, paradoxically, with the taste for such electronic devices that the Cubans had inherited from the USA? The plausibility of the suspicion could not but shock a "bourgeois intellectual," as Fidel, in a conversation with certain Chilean politicians, revolutionaries free of any taint of contamination whom he could entrust with such a confidence, would call me after my departure.

Of course faced with the blockade, the quiet campaign of sabotage, and the attempts on the life of Fidel, the Revolution had seen it necessary to organize its defense. Though don Emilio's waiter may have contributed to that honorable mission as a member of the State Security apparatus, his nostalgic sympathy was no less sincere as he evoked for me the old man-of-the-world who'd been seduced by the charms of Havana. It was that nostalgia which led him to choose for me, don Emilio's nephew—a diplomat, too, though one set down in very different circumstances, slipperier and definitely more dangerous, and who possesses, no doubt, about a tenth the experience of his tight-lipped and resourceful uncle—to choose for me the most appetizing canapé and to bring me the whisky of exactly the color and density he had discovered that I, the nephew, worthy inheritor of the sybaritism of those men in whose service the waiter had learned his trade to the pitch of perfection, liked.

"Don Emilio didn't give a shit about the Revolution, *chico,*" Roa told me one afternoon in his office. "But he couldn't live anywhere else but Cuba. When he came to say good-bye to me, when Chile broke off relations, he was crying, I tell you. He stood right there where you're sitting and he cried!"

Meanwhile, the Edwards name continued to take up a considerable percentage of the space in the columns that *Granma* and *Juventud Rebelde* dedicated to Chilean politics—and to be mentioned in increasingly pejorative and sordid ways. And to top it all off, in a sleazy operation almost surely organized by the CIA and aimed at damaging Chile's export market in copper, the main protagonist was an American citizen whose name was Howard Edwards.

"That name!" Padilla exclaimed, opening his eyes wide in an expression of feigned consternation.

I actually came to suspect that someone, probably from the Santiago office of Prensa Latina and probably, too, in connivance with journalists in Cuba, was using the excuse of my being a distant relation of "the Edwards clan" to put me in a difficult position—and with me, my colleagues and friends. It was altogether possible that some information demon, at some spot along the circuit on which information ran, was with calculated insistence inserting that patronymic that carried so many ominous connotations. Was this a deliberate and concerted provocation? That is another of the questions I will never have an answer to.

During mid-January I wrote some more in my diary. I would later have to break the habit. Along with my patience I began to lose my equanimity. Even on television, moreover, one saw reports, openly broadcast, on the surveillance methods employed by State Security. In consequence, I realized that there was no way I could just hide my little notebook behind an old suitcase in the bottom of the closet.

Havana, January 10, 1971

In *El árbol de la ciencia* (*"The Tree of Science"*), the novel Baroja wrote during his sixth year of medicine, he says, "In Spain, one is not paid for one's work, but for one's submissiveness."

Certain truths apply to Spain and to all of Latin America as well.

Someone observed not long ago that Cuba's problem is that everything has to be decided by Fidel. Nothing works, nothing functions, nothing runs without the Comandante's intervention. He is *l'etat par excellence,* but the Island would be paralyzed by the mediocrity of its middle-level bureaucrats. In my few contacts with young people of university age, I have seen that there are great reserves of energy, self-denial, and talent there. Are those energies, those abilities taken advantage of in the administration, or in the economic sphere? I suspect that in the realm of officialdom, at least while I was a witness to it, the system was much more receptive to bureaucratic conformity—that is, to submissiveness—than to work of quality. It has been rumored that discontent among the students worried the government, and that one outstanding student from the Universidad de Oriente had interrogated Fidel aggressively during one of Fidel's conversations with the students. As one version of the story had it, the student had gone so far as to call Fidel an autocrat, in fact using the very word. This rumor went on to say that his comments had cost the student his university career. It was not possible to determine what part of the story was true and what part tendentious fantasy, nor to say what motives impelled those who spread such "news." Cuban gossip reminded me of the "snowballs," as they were called, of Lima, which grew as they rolled along, and which showed what the true greatness of the old Spanish pastime must have been.

At the end of January or the beginning of February something happened, though, on which all the oral versions could agree. In a café in El Vedado, in the middle of Havana, a group of boys started harassing a girl, making off-color jokes and suggestive remarks about her. She was sitting with a young painter at a table near the boys'. Apparently the painter stood up and very politely and respectfully, and using the socialist-approved word "*compañero,*" asked the jokers at the other table to leave his companion alone. One of the boys stood up, insulted the painter in the most vulgar way, and finally pulled out a pistol and killed him. A soldier who had been passing by managed to catch the murderer as he ran away, and the young man was sent to the nearest police station, where reports had it that he confessed his crime with appalling cynicism.

Several times I heard complaints about how unsafe the streets were. More and more often one heard talk of muggings and robberies. The funeral of the painter, who was beloved by his friends at the university, apparently became a silent demonstration of protest. "Things are very bad," a young woman said to me, almost immediately falling silent and fixing her eyes on some invisible spot in the distance. She appeared to be at the verge of tears, and very moved. I was later informed that the young woman worked for the CIA. What Cuban was not accused of being in the service of one security force or another during those days?

Havana, January 12, 1971

Someone has said that "the intellectuals are too nervous," that they are all suffering from some sort of persecution complex.

The truth is that the situation favors neurosis. I see myself surrounded by allusions to my bourgeois origins, and I think: Isn't a rich businessman who owns thousands of acres of land and who sells his products—sells them, in fact, at prices inflated by the blockade—more of a bourgeois than I am, in spite of the apparently "proletarian" family name that he has? The thick underbrush of symbols—names, slogans, posters, monuments—prevents one from seeing the forest. And weren't there children of bourgeois merchants who helped to form revolutionary thought?

Of course there were. The problem is that cold reality, balanced truth, reason, matter little. On the contrary. Psychological pressure, which favors neurosis, fantasy, paranoia, has a political upshot: All criticism will be invalidated under some pretext or other—bourgeois origins, opportunism, moral debility, et cetera—all solidarity coopted unmercifully, all power nipped. All that will remain, free of its past, free of all original sin, is the Sole Power.

In mid-January, my work began to be more organized, in a rudimentary sort of way. I had something resembling a registry of correspondence, the beginnings of a file, the seals of the old consulate and embassy. I even had paper and envelopes with a letterhead that read "Embassy of Chile in Cuba," a gift from Protocol. Protocol had also lent me an ungainly old safe that sometimes would open with various combinations of the keys, depending on its whim of the moment, and sometimes would remain hermetically sealed, unmoved by any attempt to conjure it open.

I had managed to get living quarters separate from the office. Both quarters were on the eighteenth floor of the Habana Riviera, but my "residence" was at one end, overlooking the Malecón and the sea, while the "chancery" occupied a two-room suite with a balcony that overlooked the streets of El Vedado. The third-secretary and consul (one and the same person) had arrived shortly after New Year's; with him was his young wife, a son three or four years old, and a newborn baby. They were installed across the hall from me, in a three-room suite identical to my own. Since the air conditioners dated from the bygone days of Yankee tourism and only emitted a distant rumble and a current of room-temperature air, on the hottest days we would sometimes open all the doors to get some breeze from the cross-ventilation. Someone, I can't recall whether it was a Chilean or a Cuban, told me that the air-conditioner vents were a favorite place for bugs, a notion that did little, as one can imagine, to cool the rooms.

During this time, the Chilean Senate rejected the first ambassador to Cuba proposed by the government. I was forced, therefore, to contemplate the possibility of a considerably longer stay than I had bargained for. The situation was not pleasant. Some ambassadors had told me that it had taken them a year or more to find a house. It seemed foolish to buy a car only to sell it a few months later: The only people authorized to buy cars were the members of the diplomatic corps. Though I was told that the state also bought cars, no one could give me hard information, let alone assurances. I could not even think, then, about having my own house and my own transportation for several months more.

Given all this, many Western and socialist ambassadors were quite insistent in their assertions that the representative of Chile, given the political situation between the two countries, ought to be able to enjoy the normal facilities of an embassy. To make my own feelings worse, I had been told that my Chilean compatriot Baltazar Castro, a personal friend of Fidel's though no relation, and much appreciated in Cuba for having broken through the trade embargo a good while before Allende's coming to power, had occupied a suite on the twentieth floor of the Habana Riviera during his last visit to Cuba, which had coincided with my own arrival. Apparently the air conditioning worked perfectly on the twentieth floor.

"Don Baltazar may have broken the trade embargo," I told myself, "but I'm the one, when all's said and done, who has broken the diplomatic blockade— even if only symbolically." My lack of experience in countries where central planning is practiced (as the jargon of international organizations will have it) was enormous. I went to Protocol and spoke to them about the suites on the twentieth floor. At first they acted as though they knew vaguely about their existence. Then they promised to find out about them and "get back to me." The conversation took place with lower-level officials, called "attachés," since Meléndez had become more and more difficult to locate, and only appeared when he himself took the initiative.

Two days later, I spoke with one of the attachés, a boyish young man with a frank, open face and a constant smile. It was he who had lent me the famous safe which served to give the appearance of security in my offices.

"Listen, Eguar," he said (using the pronunciation of my name that had become standard among the government employees I was dealing with at the time), "I found out about the twentieth floor. It seems the twentieth floor is under repairs."

"And how long will these repairs take?"

"Oh, I couldn't say."

It was best not to try to corroborate the attaché's information. The elevator operators maintained a strict vigilance over the passengers, a vigilance softened in my case by certain considerations of protocol. The consul and his wife had experienced at first hand the severity of the keepers of the gate; more than once they had been asked for identification before they could be taken to their rooms. The consul was quite young, and somewhat self-conscious of his investiture; after each of these incidents he would come to me flustered and upset, pale, and in a frenzy of ill-contained anger.

One simply could not, then, discover for certain whether those supposed repairs were or were not being done. The elevator operators were on constant guard, the stairways were sealed. But I did have good relations with one of the desk clerks, whom I had found to be more alert and efficient than the others. He had asked me for a job in the Chilean embassy. Had it been his idea, or was he put up to it? There was no way of knowing. At any rate, one afternoon while he was handing out keys and giving messages and mail to arriving guests, he called me to one side.

"Would you like to see the twentieth floor?"

"I've been told it's under repairs."

"Let's go up and have a look around," he said, as though he hadn't heard me.

He went off to get a key, and soon reappeared over by the elevators. We went up in the car reserved for luggage, and so stopped at no intermediate floors.

The doors opened onto a silent, timeless world with gilded moldings on the walls, little statues here and there, and a thick red carpet that had survived intact the Revolution's twelve years of cannibalizing desirable goods. The rooms reminded one of the Hollywood *boudoirs* of the fifties—satin bedspreads, the red of the curtains contrasting with the pastels of the furniture and walls, glass-topped tables, bars with elegant barstools, and a table and four chairs in the corner. The bathrooms and closets were sumptuous. One could imagine Barbara Stanwyck, Linda Darnell, the young Rita Hayworth, or Marilyn Monroe (before she'd truly made the "big time") staying there.

The desk clerk was likely fascinated by all this decoration, and perhaps too by the exclusive, secret nature of the rooms, to which elevators ascended only on exceptional occasions. I, on the other hand, was attracted by the space, the air conditioning, and the idea of living for the next few months in something that resembled a private apartment more than a hotel room.

"You'll just have to persuade them to give it to you," the desk clerk said.

In Protocol they took note that the repairs had been finished, and that the rooms on the twentieth floor were in impeccable condition. I alleged that I was going to have to be in the hotel for several more months, that I had to receive visits from the diplomatic corps and other important visitors. Protocol said they'd see. Protocol would do all they could to satisfy the Chilean chargé d'affaires' request.

The next day Protocol informed me that the Prime Minister had ordered that the rooms on the twentieth floor be reserved for a delegation from Canada that was to arrive within the next few weeks. Well! I supposed that if the order came from the Prime Minister himself, that was that, then.

3

Varadero, January 16, 1971

Joaquin Edwards Bello, the Chilean novelist and essayist, wrote a series of chronicles about many of the "Founding Fathers" of Latin American Republics including Francisco de Miranda, the Venezuelan hero of Independence. The great figures of Latin American history occur during the continent's revolutionary period: Miranda, Bolívar, Bello, Carrera, San Martín, O'Higgins, and so on. And what about now? Edwards Bello was impressed by the shadow of influence that Miranda cast over Europe. And what about Fidel's, or Ché's? Neruda's? J.E.B. writing before '60. Very South American obsession with the triumph in Europe.

Problem of a country like Chile, that it gets used as a tool in the power struggle between the Big Ones (conversation with the ambassador from Yugoslavia). The periphery of Yankee imperialism seriously threatened for the first time. Before, it was Yankee bases surrounding the USSR. The Korean War and today's war in Indochina have put China on the defensive. The situation could well change now. Struggle for hegemony in the Pacific. "Assistance" from other revolutions for Chile's.

Foreseeing the possibility of uninvited reading, I tried to write nothing but what was strictly indispensable in my notes: pills for keeping the memory of things alive. I now believe, however, that I must have either mistrusted memory or been addicted to note-taking, because my notes were pretty explicit. It

78

might also be that as a bourgeois liberal brought up, in spite of the efforts of the Jesuits to the contrary, in the Voltairean tradition of the Republic of Chile, I did not believe in the real existence of the police-as-devil. I came from the least police-ridden country in the world, in spite of the fact that the Frei administration had not been exactly unschooled in State Security tactics, and I had come to a state that had always had a security apparatus, aimed in the past against the forces of progress and now dedicated, after hundreds of aggressions against it, to the necessary, indispensable task of defending the Revolution, even as it sometimes engendered, as is unfortunately inevitable, its own bogeymen. The machine which Chile had the fortune never to have possessed[1] and which is always sinister, even when it works on behalf of the central current of history, often invents the enemies that serve as its fodder.

I had never seen the machine up close; therefore, I did not believe it was real. I hid my notebook on a shelf in the closet, behind an empty suitcase, and when I found it in the same place the next day I was reassured. I knew vaguely of the existence of the machine, but what I did not suspect was its extreme subtlety. How could service everywhere be so inefficient, my breakfast arrive as often as not an hour late, coffee instead of tea, one cup for two people, three cups for one, the cream pitcher without cream (or milk), or no bread to accompany the ice-cold eggs—how could the service be so bad and the functioning of the machine so impeccable, so precise, as though in *its* case the improvisation, absenteeism, and general sluggishness of the tropics simply did not apply?

It was hard to believe, especially for a person from Chile. The Yugoslav ambassador, who came from a part of the world that had its conflicts and had experienced the phenomenon—*he* might believe it. There was one detail that stuck in my mind, but that I did not think prudent to consign to my diary. In the middle of our conversation, the ambassador, moved by a sudden contemplative, poetic impulse, invited me out onto the balcony where we might look out over the ocean. Were we free from bugs out there, standing in the wind off the water and listening to the roar of the waves? I wouldn't say now categorically that we were. What the ambassador had to say to me, in a whisper, was that Chile should turn to its own advantage the rivalry between the two super-

---

[1] Need I remind the reader again that this was written in our pre-history—that is, before September 1973? And if I use, even ironically, the word "pre-history," does this mean that discovering the police aspect of the world, our world at least, is equivalent to entering modern history, that succession of social cataclysms in which the motive power is, as Marx said, the class struggle, but in which the norm, the direction, is determined by reasons of State?

powers rather than taking sides with one of them. We should not even consent
to allow Soviet warships to be painted in Chilean ports. That was exactly the
way Stalin had tried to insinuate himself into Yugoslavia—the ships were in
port, being painted, and the crews would be on shore, but Tito, though on the
friendliest of terms with Moscow, had not authorized the repairs. By the
way—had I noticed all the Cubans who were traveling to Chile?

"You never know who they're working for," the ambassador whispered.

In spite of everything, Cuba's relations with Yugoslavia, which had gone
through a very bad time—because Yugoslavia had sold arms to Batista during
the time Fidel was in the Sierra, and also because the Yugoslav newspapers
had mocked the memory of Ché Guevara—in spite of all, the relations had
improved a bit. The ambassador hoped that we in Chile would not repeat the
errors of other socialist countries, that we would create an attractive, different
sort of socialism, a socialism with space for true freedom, so that the other
countries of Latin America would follow our example.

We returned from the balcony talking about the beauties of the ocean, the
delights of the pool at the Habana Riviera, and other trivialities. The ambassador believed I was not familiar with Yugoslavia? He understood that Chile
was an extraordinarily pleasant country as well as an interesting one, with
great wines, magnificent seafood, and a breathtaking landscape.

"A good description of my country, Mr. Ambassador!"

With one thing and another, then, the interview had lasted for more than an
hour, and the ambassador excused himself.

Varadero, January 17, 1971

At the house once belonging to the American millionaire Irenée Dupont, on a
spit of land to the west of Varadero. There are still several albums of family
photos lying on a table. Many photographs of iguanas, which are apparently
abundant on the grounds. I am shocked by the vulgarity of the captions written
on them by the owner of the estate; they reflect, perhaps not altogether
consciously of course, his Spencerian philosophy, his "struggle for life" social
Darwinism. Outfitted in Bermuda shorts that revealed flabby thighs, Dupont's
wife makes the iguanas jump for their food in one photograph, while the old
man, in another, "fills their bellies." There are other photos in which one sees
the old man goading them to fight; the iguanas, nose to nose, threaten each
other with sinister, prehistoric jaws.

Immense lawns, a private golf course and beach. Art Nouveau house and
furniture. Marble bathrooms. On the top floor, a mirador with black tiles and
columns. A huge telescope, now pitted and weathered with salt air and disuse,

once employed for contemplating the farther limits of the Dupont domain, standing proudly before the vastness of the Caribbean. The enameled tiles of the mansion's roof are green.

In the bookshelves of the salons on the first floor, the collected works of authors such as Kipling, Robert Louis Stevenson, Balzac in English translation. Probably purchased by the yard. Insignificant pocket books, as well, and these have in fact been read. The tables of the restaurant are set with tablecloths and plates which still bear the Dupont monogram. In the central salon, a small orchestra, its musicians mulattos, and a handful of spectators. People whose hand Dupont would never have shaken. Tomás says that he never knew such estates as this gringo's existed. Now Tomás has access to the beaches, which were almost entirely private before, and to many other things, in spite of the fact that this access is limited by the general rationing. But rationing implies investments for the development of the country, and implies moreover a fair and equitable distribution of goods.

In the snapshots of Dupont, the Cubans of the time look fawning and submissive. In one photo, of a party on the terrace, they look euphoric, thrilled at the idea of drinking the Yankee millionaire's whisky and treading his gleaming tile floors. They've been getting ready for this for a week, ironing their seersucker "Palm Beaches" and traveling from the capital. He, in turn, has opened his doors as a sporadic and gracious concession to the native population. It costs him but a small effort once a year to keep them happy. But his equals—his equals are the other gringos he is photographed with, drinking aperitifs, playing golf, sunbathing in special sunglasses to protect themselves from the tropical sun.

Tomás tells me his father was relatively well-to-do. He began with a stall out of which he sold sausages and roast pig served on "trenchers" of fresh bread. A Spaniard, his partner, furnished the beer. Tomás' father wound up a rich man, the owner of slot machines in Havana as well as other businesses. Even so, he refused to recognize Tomás as his son or pay for his schooling.

Meléndez himself told me that Tomás is a faithful member of the party. The difference between Tomás and Agustín, my previous driver, who could think of nothing but eating and "catching a few winks," is like that between night and day. Tomás tells me that you don't see anybody around Camarioca anymore, the Varadero airport from which flights to Miami take off. I don't believe that, and I suspect that he doesn't either.

The Island has lovely scenery, with its hills, palm trees, and the geometrical bright green patches of its sugarcane fields. In some places there are birds like turkey buzzards. The intense red of the evening, above the landscape of palms and hillside, and the emerald blue of the ocean are quintessentially Cuban.

This is what a Cuban artist like Lezama Lima must love; part of what holds him is his land, and it is also what allows him to live and to write. That love should be the sufficient justification of a country's writers. From it everything else derives. The Cuban Revolution, in its origins and in its ultimate meaning, is a *national* revolution. In breaking from a humiliating past of internal arbitrariness and foreign dependency, the Revolution was bound to identify socialism, the modern shape of social organization, with the struggle for the liberation of the country. Thence the special sense of alliance with Vietnam and now with the revolution in Chile. The problem is that sectarianism, insofar as writers are concerned, emerges everywhere, in everything, and under every imaginable disguise, and there is no way to reach a balanced judgment of anything. There is, of course, no lack of petty opportunists, writers both native and foreign who are at the same time agents for the State Security apparatus, and who are more than glad to stir things up a bit. Balance may take a while. The road that's been embarked upon is long.

In one of his chronicles of Miranda, Edwards Bello shows Miranda in England, attempting to use the Anglo-Spanish rivalry for the cause of independence in the New World. The struggle between France, England, and Spain, reflected in the various stages of our own Wars of Independence, is still instructive today. The episode in which the English government, after allying itself with Spain against Napoleon, allows Miranda to fall, is wonderfully narrated.

J.P. meets me in the hotel lobby and we go out for a walk so we can talk. It is a winter afternoon, just at nightfall; the waves crash high against the Malecón and wash across it. A military truck has stalled in the middle of the street; water comes more than halfway up its tires. A rickety old Chevrolet, on the other hand, manages to back up and avoid the flood of seawater.

Although we are walking down the Avenida de los Presidentes (as I recall its name now), some three hundred yards from the ocean, we can feel gusts of spray. This gray, wintry atmosphere makes us feel, perhaps erroneously, that we are being watched, being followed by secret microphones, indiscreet eyes and ears. There are a few lights, people waiting for the bus (the *guagua* as the Cubans call it), on Línea Street (whose name, like that of Avenida de los Presidentes, I may be misremembering). There is a crowd at the exit of a movie theater, farther down the street.

The stalled truck reminds me of a story told me by a Chilean man just before he returned, forever he said, to Chile. I tell J.P. the story—there was an engineer who spent months in his garage at night fitting up his old car so it would float. He treated the underside somehow so it would be waterproof, and made a keel; he soldered and welded and closed up every seam and chink; he installed a rudder and a propeller on the rear and camouflaged them. One afternoon he loaded up his family, drove off like a man going on a little visit— Be right back!—headed for the beach, drove into the ocean, and sailed the eighty miles to Miami. There he was interviewed by every newspaper and radio and TV station in the world, and General Motors, in return for the publicity, gave him a brand new car.

J.P. smiled; he neither accepted nor denied the truth of the anecdote. The life of an exile is sad. No true Cuban ever manages to fully adapt to life outside Cuba. The difficulties within Cuba, however, are terrible.

"The other day I heard a black woman arguing with a CDR[2] member in the street. The devil himself can't quiet those black women, you know how they are. They're not afraid of the CDR or anybody else. 'Before,' this woman was saying, 'when I didn't have any food for my child, there was always at least a little bread and guava paste to give him. Now you can't even find a guava. How can that be, compañera? Before, when my baby needed something, I could go out onto the street, turn a trick, and I could make a few pesos to buy some milk and meat.' "

We talked about the new harvest, which was now in full swing. J.P. said that running a sugar mill is terribly hard, self-sacrificing work. He recalled the old owners of the great sugar mills before the Revolution, who even when they were in Havana never took their minds off the way the wind was blowing, the weather reports; they would constantly be on the telephone to the mill, where they had a hand-picked, very well paid manager, in spite of which they themselves would supervise the harvest when it reached a critical point, working from six o'clock in the morning until late at night.

Now the machinery at the mills is old, finding spare parts is hard, the network of trucks and locomotives, which is the key element in the harvest, is in terrible condition.

"Do you think they'll come close to the seven million tons that Fidel is asking for?"

J.P. purses his lips and moves his right hand in a gesture of doubt. Six at the outside, if that.

---

[2] CDR: *Comité para la Defensa de la Revolución,* or Committee for the Defense of the Revolution. The reputation of the CDRs, while I was in Cuba, turned sinister. For many Cubans, they were synonymous with neighborhood surveillance and "squealing."

"Some people think discontent has reached a level that's actually dangerous; they think there's a possibility of outbreaks of violence like last month in Poland."

My friend's forehead furrows again in scepticism.

"I doubt it," he says. "We'll probably just go on struggling along, more or less the way we're doing now, for a good while yet. We have the ocean, the sun that gives us vitamins, and Cubans are long-suffering. Once we finish paying the Russians for the fishing port, which we are paying off with production, we'll have more fish than we know what to do with."

I recalled the words of the woman, the Mysterious Visitor, I had met at the Christmas celebration at César López' house.

"A hundred thousand people will die here," my Mysterious Visitor had told me, looking at me attentively as she waited for a reply (which never came), while the wind beat with fury against the four sides of her peeling, rundown tower that was being eaten away by the seaspray and the sand from the Caribbean. "We'll probably die ourselves. Because of this Revolution that we've fought, that is a part of our lives. What shit!" She looked at me intensely, her eyes so wide they seemed ready to burst from their sockets. We were talking, calmly, in a corner of her room almost totally occupied by a double bed. The open door revealed another room where there was a mulatto woman and where the voice of a child could be heard. There were posters in the house, but they were peeling away from the walls, and there were three or four pieces of furniture in ruins. There were cats, a lot of them, and a dog howled in the attic, apparently terrified by the howling of the wind. When they saw me come in, the two friends of the Mysterious Visitor had picked their pistols up off the table and left with a vague wave.

When I finally left the tower I felt tremendous relief. My secretary told me that Tomás had been desperately looking for me.

"Pistols!" said Padilla. "That means State Security." And after a moment of reflection, Padilla added that the government was on alert those days. In his view, it was the most critical situation the Cuban Revolution had yet faced. Under the pretense of an interest in sugar, a few weeks later I persuaded the Powers That Be to take me to visit the Camilo Cienfuegos Sugar Mill, one of the largest in the country, if not the largest. The railroad cars loaded with green sugarcane were pulled up to metal tanks sunk into the ground. One side of the car opened up and huge steel pincers on the end of a crane tilted them ninety degrees, so the sugarcane rolled into the tanks by gravity. The cars were then righted and pulled away, while the cane was transported upward on conveyor belts and spilled into a system of knives that started the milling process. I was led along steel catwalks as we followed the cane into the mill. One way flowed the sugary liquid; another way went the dry, squeezed-out stalks. The machine floor was enormous; to one side was a huge complex of wheels and pistons that moved all the rest. The machinery dated from 1913 or thereabouts; it made one think of Eiffel's metallic structures, or of old prints from Jules Verne novels. In spite of this, however, it all seemed to function perfectly. At several stages there were new elements, and innovations were even being planned. We saw the tubular tanks in which the fine white refined sugar was collected. There were mountains, caverns, and stalactites of sugar, as though out of some childhood dream.

We were shown around the factory by the political head of it, and he was attended by a member of the technical staff who had worked there for more than twenty years. The engineer loved his machines; he knew the quirks and workings of every one of them. There were many questions I would have liked to ask him, but the continual presence of the political manager made that hard. We were shown the automatic sacking machine, which looked like it belonged to a recent stage of the factory's evolution, and saw how the rail cars were loaded up, inside huge loading sheds. The trains went from there directly to the port of Matanzas.

After the visit, we were served a mixture of rum, sugar, and mint that Cubans call *mojito* (the Caribbean mint julep), cold cuts, and beer. The political manager and two or three of his co-workers, who also appeared to have political responsibilities, talked to us about the mill: production figures, the harvest season, transportation problems, etc. They told us about the working conditions before the Revolution. No one's job was secure back then. The only lines known on the Island in those days was the one stood in by the cane cutters waiting for work: one peso a day, and hours from five-thirty in the morning until nightfall. After the harvest was in, mass layoffs. If a man had an accident on the job, he'd be thrown out on his ear, without any pay or compensation of any kind.

A different sort of testimony came from the waiter in the hotel dining room, a man apparently with no great political conscience. He told me that the specter of firing haunted all Cuban laborers before the Revolution.

"In the good times we got big tips, ten dollars at a single table sometimes, but we were never free of the worry we might lose our jobs. I worked right here, and we were always, always afraid that tourism would fall off. If tourism fell, you see, we'd be fired. Finding a job, and then keeping it, was all anybody ever thought of. Nobody could ever feel secure. Now, though, even if there's no work, they keep paying your wage."

Of course the moral incentive is not very effective when it comes to serving tables or bringing breakfast up on time, at least to judge by what one sees in the

Habana Riviera. My friendly waiter, who was much more punctual and efficient than the rest, came in one Monday morning completely out of sorts.

"Since everybody went off to cut sugarcane, nobody came to work today. Nobody! Do you understand what that means?"

He's sick of it all. His co-workers' irresponsibility, which all too frequently makes the entire weight of room-service fall on his shoulders, drives him crazy. He studied at the Hotel School; he loves the hotel business; he worked at the best places in pre-Revolutionary Havana. But now he's at the end of his patience; any day now he'll quit and go somewhere else.

His hand does not point toward Havana, it points toward the ocean. His mind, too, like the intellectuals', may be disturbed by pride, the only sin without redemption, as my Jesuit preceptors taught, and as Fidel, their aging disciple, knows very well.

It was not easy to explain the Chilean system of senatorial approval of ambassadors. Why was Gazmuri, Allende's first choice, rejected? I invoked precedent: The Senate had rejected ambassador-designates to Peru, to the United States, without the least intention of insulting those countries. Raúl Roa was an educated, quick-minded man, who knew Chile quite well.

"This is just an argument between the Christian Democrats and the MAPUists," he'd said, and he had been right.[3]

But not all the Foreign Ministry officers were of the same intellectual calibre.

"But now that you guys are in power," one of them commented to me, "can't you shut down the Senate?" The relative weakness of our Executive vis-a-vis the Senate seemed unacceptable, shocking to them all. What kind of Revolution was this? They didn't say anything in the presence of the Chilean chargé d'affaires, but the expression on their faces could not have been more eloquent.

In view of the delay on Chile's part, the Cuban government consulted with the Chilean Ministry of Foreign Relations on the possibility that Mario García

---

[3] The MAPU, *Movimiento de Acción Popular Unitaria* or United Popular Action Movement, was a left-wing splinter group of the Christian Democrat Party.

Incháustegui, who was by now ready to travel, be posted to the Cuban Embassy in Santiago immediately. Chile had no objection, quite the contrary. García Incháustegui, then, called me and invited me to lunch at La Torre restaurant. We would meet there with Duque Estrada, the director of the Americas Section, a section newly created in the Cuban Ministry of Foreign Relations.

Mario García Incháustegui had had a distinguished diplomatic career. He was still relatively young, tall, bony, and bald. He had been ambassador to Uruguay, to the United Nations, and to international organizations in Geneva. He talked to me about his friendship with Hernán Santa Cruz, Ramón Huidobro, many Chilean diplomats. Using his many friendships and acquaintances, he planned to court the media. Immediately after assuming his post he'd give a cocktail party for the press. After all, he'd been a journalist with *Granma*; he was in his element with journalists and reporters. What did I think? I thought all that was fine; his plans and his objectives seemed excellent to me. Duque Estrada, meanwhile, spoke little. He was a short man, strong, and still young, and his beard was trimmed with care. He showed great surprise when I told him I still had no office, nor had so much as been shown a possible house for the residence. He wanted to help me. Since I also complained about the scant information I was given, he started the following morning to send to the hotel all the cables dealing with Chile from all the news agencies. He also lent me a shortwave radio, which allowed me to pick up transmissions from the United States, South America, and Europe. The only country lost in the most hidden recesses of the dial, impossible to pick out, was Chile.

The unfailing gossips and backbiters, who abounded in Havana, as everywhere else, in the most diverse places, later told me stories about García Incháustegui. During the Cuban missile crisis in October 1962, he had headed the Cuban delegation to the United Nations. It was a critical moment for the entire world, and Khrushchev, in order to avoid worldwide conflict, made an agreement directly with Kennedy, without consulting his ally Fidel. Fidel then gave his famous speech in which he summarized in five points the autonomy of the Cuban Revolution. It appears that García Incháustegui, not learning of the Commander-in-Chief's speech in time, aligned himself totally with the argument of the Soviet Union, thereby discrediting the proclamations of independence that were coming out of Havana.

These gossips said that Havana ordered García Incháustegui back virtually within seconds, and that Fidel, in a rage, ordered that he be tried as a traitor.

The sentence, should he be found guilty, was death. The story had it that his friends hid García Incháustegui away until Fidel's anger passed.[4]

I reciprocated the ambassador's invitation, and in the middle of our conversation, when the subject of writers came up, he told me in no uncertain terms that Padilla was an anti-Communist and that his criticism of the Revolution was openly counterrevolutionary. I tried to argue, but García Incháustegui was a blank wall to my arguments. The Revolution had given everything to Padilla, but Padilla, out of ambition, out of the desire to make himself famous in Western Europe by playing the persecuted writer, a kind of Cuban Solzhenitsyn, had become its enemy.

"You've got to be careful," I told Padilla later. "Don't be mad!"

He laughed. He maintained that the regime had an image to protect among leftist intellectuals in Europe. He was convinced that the friendship and solidarity of those intellectuals was an impregnable defense. Had they not been invited to Cuba? Had Fidel and the government not bent over backward in toasts and honors during the Cultural Congress in January of '68?

Padilla himself had told me that the period of the Cultural Congress now lay in the past, but he couldn't seem to reach the appropriate, if extreme, conclusions from this insight. Many of those who had come to Havana in January of '68 were now criticizing Cuba in Europe. K. S. Karol, the essayist and journalist, one of the most active participants in that Congress, had just attacked the pro-Soviet line of the revolution, which had been the clearly defined line taken by the country since Fidel supported the Soviet intervention in Czechoslovakia.

Under those conditions, the honeymoon with the intellectuals of the European Left had to be over. The rupture had to manifest itself at some point; it was inevitable. It is quite possible that my contacts with Padilla and his friends were seized upon and even encouraged in order to bring on that rupture. After all, Padilla made all those critical remarks of his in the presence of the representative of the revolutionary Chilean government. I bore that investiture not only during acts dictated by protocol but every hour of the day and night. In a small city where I was a kind of symbol, there could be no split between private and official life. I was a symbol twenty-four hours a day. I had been invested, without my fully realizing it, with that sacred aura that had once been

---

[4] Mario García Incháustegui died some years later in an air crash.

worn by the ambassadors of old, a reflection of the divine rights of the king or emperor who sent them. When they were in the presence of the anointed one, Padilla and his friends were to some degree committing the ancient crime of *lèse majesté*. Some of the people who were watching us from the shadows must have been rubbing their hands together. In 1968 the publication of Padilla's *Fuera de juego* ("Out of the Game") had caused a scandal. The book had been awarded an international literary prize. The government then published the book, but with a preface by the poet Nicolas Guillen that was strongly critical. Lisandro Otero then commented to someone: "Now we're going to be able to have Padilla's balls," but he was claiming victory too soon. The victory came, unexpectedly even for those who had been "expecting" it, with the arrival in Cuba of the first diplomatic envoy from Cuba's sister country Chile.

Padilla and Belkis Cuza Malé got married during this time. We all gathered in Miguel Barnet's apartment in El Vedado to celebrate the union with a little rum and beer. There was a big wedding cake with white frosting, which was devoured amidst exclamations of amazement and gluttonous delight. Sometime after midnight we all sat on the floor around the last bottle of rum, which was being passed around from hand to hand, and my Cuban friends began singing euphorically, making up the words and beating out the rhythm with whatever object came to hand. Someone, suddenly, called for silence; a capitán or comandante lived next door, and he might complain about the noise. For the man/envoy/symbol of the reestablishment of relations with Chile, the situation might become sticky. But once more I didn't think the higher-ups would concern themselves with such details. I was naive, of course. During this time the anti-vagrancy law had been passed, and a general census was in the works. According to that law, not having a known occupation was a misdemeanor and the offender could be sent to work in a sugarcane field. Was it possible, in circumstances such as those, to tolerate the fact that a bunch of intellectuals, people whose duty lay in "integrating the ideological vanguard of the Revolution," might spend hours banging two pieces of wood together and singing incoherent songs that as often as not bordered on the obscene, and all this under the stimulus of large quantities of rum? This "vagrancy" was something the Cuban ruling elite could not tolerate in the midst of the crisis of the ten-million-ton harvest failure—a crisis that had not been avoided in spite of superhuman efforts. We—my friends and I—were accustomed to the irresponsible marginality offered by the literary life, and we thought we could go on living in the best of all possible worlds. The vagrancy law should have warned us that the government had decided to integrate the "marginal population," by any means it could, into the system. And that would mean that literary impunity was soon to disappear. If we had been able to call upon the experience of Soviet, Czech, or Rumanian writers, we would have been able to read the signs. But it's often been proven that no one profits from other people's experience. After our excesses, which we considered innocent, my Cuban friends had no recourse but to repeat the plea spoken ironically by Apollinaire to the French bourgeoisie at the beginning of this century: "Pitié pour nos erreurs! Pitié pour nos péchés!" ("Forgive us for our errors! Forgive us for our sins!")

For myself, I continued to enjoy Chilean immunity (although there was no lack of desire for my head) but the fate of those who attended the party that night, who sat on the floor around one empty and one half-empty bottle of rum, left me with an anguish, a guilty conscience that few of my compatriots have probably ever experienced, and which I hope they never know. I had hoped that Chile would produce a socialism that would not lose its innocence to the machinery of history. In its favor, I thought, was the inestimable advantage of distance. Cuba was too close to the United States, and Czechoslovakia was a cultural, economic, and strategic corridor between capitalist Germany and the Red East. The two countries, in their different ways, had to pay the price of proximity. (As we can see now, more than twenty years later, distance alone was not enough. The "Chilean road to socialism," socialism through democratic elections, was interrupted by a military dictatorship and then followed by a rather successful market economy. Even Socialist party members, in today's Chile, show great respect for the free market. As for Cuba and Czechoslovakia, they are now in the political antipodes, paying "the price of proximity" in very different ways indeed!)

Padilla had long been requesting that he be allowed to go to a hotel to finish a novel he was writing, since he could not get down to work in his centrally located apartment where visits from friends, a leaking roof, broken plumbing, and the like, and the need to stand in line for even the most basic necessities, kept him from concentrating. After his marriage, he somehow managed to be set up in the Hotel Nacional. From there, within a few days, he moved into a two-room suite in the Habana Riviera, one floor below me. Did the hidden powers, who naturally exercise complete control over the rooms in luxury hotels, want to keep me away from Padilla or did they, on the contrary, want to favor our encounters?

"Nobody will believe you if you tell them you're in disgrace," I said to him. "You're living like a king."

There was another thing: In January he had given a reading at UNEAC to a large audience of young people. The hall had been full, and people had spilled out into adjoining hallways and even into the garden near the windows. Padilla read unpublished poems from a book that he had titled, in order to avoid all possibility of misunderstanding, *Provocaciones*. Since the reading had been organized officially by UNEAC, there was no reason for me not to go. I had a diplomatic engagement, however, and only arrived at the end. The poems, which I could not hear from the hallway, where I stood behind a wall of young people jostling each other and standing on tiptoe just to see the poet, were received with great rounds of applause.

Excited, thrilled by the success, Padilla greeted me by telling me that the first secretary of the Chinese Embassy had come, too, as had the British cultural attaché. I invited him and Belkis and some other friends for drinks at the hotel. With readings at UNEAC, invitations to diplomatic cocktail parties, and a suite in the Habana Riviera, the newlywed poet—whose wife was an important literary personage, to boot—seemed to be at the zenith of success, and of official consecration. Maybe Padilla thought, at the end of his reading, that the enormous audience that had come to hear him, plus the presence of three foreign diplomats, constituted some sort of shield. Such a thought would have been but one more proof that no one learns from other people's experiences.

Meantime, Chileans of all professions and walks of life were passing through Cuba. They wanted to see socialism for themselves, to test their opinions, whether favorable or unfavorable, against actualities. Along with satisfying their curiosity about the Island, they believed they would be able to read the future of Chile in the present of Cuba. These were mainly people of good faith and little political awareness, largely ignorant of the differences between one sort of socialism and another. They came on fact-finding missions for their institutions—church, army, professional associations in the private sector, sports—or to seek aid for their projects, or simply as a way of earning a tacit certificate of good revolutionary behavior to be used in the Chile of the Unidad Popular. Most of them were disposed to see the positive side of things. Aided by the expert guides, they returned to Chile with their desires satisfied and their consciences clear. I saw farmers, glass manufacturers, cellulose technicians, journalists, politicians, priests and bishops, professors, writers, soccer players, folk singers pass through the lobby of the Habana Riviera, all on the same mission.

On the other hand, many members of the Chilean community in Cuba came to my office to ask my help in returning to Chile. In general, from the perspective of their years of living in Cuba, their reflections went the opposite way: Chilean socialism would have to be different, less hard and unyielding, and they wanted to return to their homeland without losing a moment. One had worked for ten years in a financial organization; another, a young man with a fragile and timid look about him, had hijacked a LAN plane to Cuba and the authorities had tried him and sent him off to cut sugarcane; another taught at the university. The hijacker told me that he had been unhappy in Chile, before, because he thought the Left would never come to power with the electoral methods it used, and that he had decided to hijack the plane in order to get to the "first revolutionary territory of the Americas." After two years in Cuba, his desire to return to Chile had become an all-consuming obsession.

Young women also came to see me, women who didn't know where to start telling me their stories: it turned out, after long beating about the bush, that they had married a Cuban, had one or more children, then gotten divorced, and now the ex-husband would not give his permission for the children to be taken out of Cuba. How had they come to Cuba? Some were good militant Communists who had wanted to help out, and at the same time acquire enriching experiences from the Cuban experiment. Some answered me rather vaguely: "I was unhappy in Chile," one young woman, stricken with shyness, told me, "and the Cuban Revolution attracted me." Now she was unhappy in Cuba, too. In Cuba too? She nodded. The Revolution, with all its problems, the sacrifices she had to make for it, was different than she had expected it to be, from a distance. Very different! "The Chilean experiment will necessarily be different," I told her. "Chile has many things in its favor that Cuba didn't have." The young woman looked at me with questioning, intense eyes. I hope so! those eyes seemed to say.

Generally, after the hesitancy and insecurity of the first few moments of their interviews, most of the Chileans living in Cuba who came to see me would grow more trusting and they would reveal an urgent, anguished desire to return to Chile. They would tell me this in a lowered voice, and more than one of them warned me that we might be bugged. I watched three or four of them leave the country, and they did so euphorically, kissing or hugging me with pleasure. I was later told that my successor, the young MAPU ambassador,[5] was not in the least receptive to petitions from Chileans who wished to return to their homeland. I was informed that he let his beard grow and that he enthusiastically joined in the voluntary labor platoons. I was also told (because there was always somebody more than willing to insure that these stories reached my ears) that a group of Chileans, in protest against the deaf ear turned to their requests to return to Chile, had organized a takeover of the embassy, in the best creole tradition. I have no idea how true these tales were; it

---

[5] Because MAPU formed an important part of the coalition that comprised the Unidad Popular that brought Allende to power, it was entitled to a share of the spoils—embassies, ministries, etc.—of Allende's electoral victory.

is true, however, that the bearded young ambassador tried to distinguish himself with the Cuban authorities. Once I had left Cuba, he bestowed upon me the friendly title "bourgeois intellectual." I say friendly because he could have used the more pejorative term "CIA agent," whose use has also proliferated recently. At any rate, the person who heard this accusation was another bourgeois intellectual, who must have thought, quite correctly, that the bourgeois respect for the constitutional system in Chile would not exactly make it easy to condemn bourgeois intellectuals. Furthermore, had that condemnation been possible in Chile, and had it been made, it well might have been made against the person who heard the ambassador pronounce the verdict on me, since the system of accusations and condemnations set in motion with such innocence by the young MAPU member tends, as History has shown, to reproduce itself with deadly speed, so that had the initial accusation become an actual condemnation, not even the unsuspecting ambassador himself would have been safe from the possibility that the machinery that he had set in motion might sooner or later grind him up as well.

But the ambassador, indifferent to these subtleties, cut sugarcane in his spare time, while his beard grew to keep pace with his illusions.

In the midst of the comings and goings of the Chileans who visited me, the embassy received official notice of a visit whose importance surpassed all others. The training ship *Esmeralda*, with a crew of more than three hundred officers, cadets, and sailors, was to arrive for the first time in Havana on its annual training voyage. After the arrival of the first Chilean diplomat, the arrival of the *Esmeralda*, the heir of the long, proud Chilean naval tradition, would be the most tangible, not to mention spectacular, sign of the breaking of the blockade by the Allende government.

I spoke to Foreign Minister Roa immediately and told him that I thought we ought to discuss the arrival of the training ship with the Minister of the Revolutionary Armed Forces. Roa himself offered to arrange my interview with Comandante Raúl Castro, Minister of the Armed Forces, Vice-Prime Minister of Cuba, and brother of the Commander-in-Chief.

During those days at the end of January we traveled to Trinidad, the oldest city in Cuba. Tomás Gutiérrez Alea, the director of the movie *Memories of Underdevelopment*, was shooting a new film there, whose star was the Chilean actress Marés González. I liked the idea of seeing the city and watching Marés work; I had admired her in Chile in several roles, especially in Ibsen and in a Spanish-language production of Bertolt Brecht's *Three-Penny Opera*.

In my notebook I find some notes on that trip.

Trinidad de Cuba, January 30, 1971

Lovely tiled roofs, marvelous ironwork gates and window grilles, stone streets. One of the few cities in the Americas, and the world, where time has stopped. In a way, paradoxically, it is only the Revolution that allows this; the rapid advance of History here has favored timelessness. If this were a historical city in any other Latin American country, it would be full of Yankee tourists with the latest styles in clothes and gadgets. Stands selling Coca-Cola would be set up in front of the cathedral. That is, the merchants, with the blessing of the establishment, foreign and domestic, would have taken over the temple.

Here the quiet of the city is only interrupted from time to time by a passing jeep, or a truck, or a rattling private car. Peeking in the windows of the houses along the narrow streets, one can make out tall, gloomy interiors, at the far end of which are archways with stained-glass panels above and half-walls of bead-and-board panelling or chest-high glass-doored bric-a-brac cabinets below (the ensemble, intended to divide a room visually but not physically, is called a *mediopunto* in the Caribbean) illuminated by light from the patio at the rear. The design of each *mediopunto* is unique, so that every house has a stamp of its own. From the street one can see the gardens and patios filled with green plants, rosebushes, and red flowers that look like plumes of scarlet fire. I am told these flowers are called "six-months" because they last from January to June.

Although one doesn't see it much on the surface, the entire city is turned upside-down with the filming of Tomás Gutiérrez' movie. The first of three episodes of *Lucía*, a Latin American TV soap opera, were filmed here once. I was shown, and immediately recognized, the street on which the first scenes took place. "Trinidad is the Hollywood of the Caribbean," someone says. Though the words are spoken with a touch of irony, as befits a well-informed person of some taste, the phrase strikes me. Our world is full of the Athenses, Switzerlands, Englands, etc. of South America or the Caribbean.

A fiftyish lady with a stern, sallow Spanish face, and wearing the rigorous black of mourning, tells us that Trinidad "is filled with poetry and legend." There still stands the ceiba tree, beside the sea, to which the Spanish settler Diego Velázquez tied his ships, and the place where Bartolomé de las Casas gave his first mass on Cuban soil.

But something brings us back to the present, since the epidemic of transistor radios has arrived even here. At seven-thirty in the morning, while I write in my cabin at the Hotel Las Cuevas, built by the Revolution on a hill outside the city, I hear in the cabin next door the languid, somewhat hoarse voice of a woman singing; the song, the voice must be the favorite of the moment, for I hear its accents everywhere I go in Cuba. In a few seconds I realize that I think I've heard this woman in the flesh, in the bar at the Habana Riviera.

At lunch, a discussion that centers, after some beating about the bush, on the problems of material versus moral incentives. In my own view, it is virtually impossible for the Cubans to emerge from their economic difficulties—low productivity, absenteeism, etc.—without allowing some sort of material incentives. S., my interlocutor, the intellectual son of bourgeois parents, jumps as though someone had shot a dart at him. The process through which the socialist democracies in Europe were passing led directly to capitalist "alienation." S. has had ample opportunity to see that for himself in Czechoslovakia, in Poland, in Hungary. In Eastern Europe there has been created a true consumer society, with all that implies: subjection to work in order to obtain more goods, the appearance of false needs which the market economy must create and constantly renew, etc. According to S., deviation from the system of exclusively moral incentives, the central principle of the Cuban Revolution, would be deviation from the very Revolution itself. What would be the point in having fought the revolution for that? Consumer goods could and should be distributed, but not to the person who has the most money to buy them. Not even to the best worker. Priorities are set on the basis of certain needs: illness, for example, or number of children.

I do not clearly understand the situation of the campesino who simply earns *money* in return for his work: what he has at the end of the day is only paper, to be kept in drawers or shoeboxes and worthless for buying things. Is it worth his while to get up at five o'clock in the morning and work the land until past dark, for a piece of worthless paper? Despite S.'s argument, it seems to me that for this campesino, the collective good—the common weal, as it used to be put— the building of socialism, are, even if he believes in them, ideals that are too abstract. Like mirages, they endlessly retreat as one continues one's hard, arid road.

Absenteeism among the campesinos, their exodus to Havana (where they will live as vagrants, on ruined streets and in empty warehouses), their lack of enthusiasm, their lack of productivity on the job have become a serious drag on the economic and political system. The vagrancy law and the obligatory use, as I understand it, of identification cards are attempts to combat the problem. They are repressive remedies, however, reflections of an unfortunately classic stage in the history of revolutions: the stage of the Comité de Santé Publique, the Committee of Public Safety.

In the midst of all this, according to rumors one hears here and there, the Soviets are requesting that workers be given more consumer goods. I am led to suspect that distribution may take the form of that of Eastern

Europe. My interlocutor, in consequence, will shortly have to moderate his zeal.

He attributes all the recent upheavals in Eastern Europe—the problems on the Polish docks as well as others earlier—to revisionism in economic doctrine. He criticizes the "thaw," the so-called "Prague Spring," bitterly, and almost seems to want to justify, though not in so many words, the entry of the Russian tanks. He talks about Soviet aid to the Eastern-bloc countries and so on. Continuing this discussion, as I would have done in Chile or in a café in the Latin Quarter among friends, and in other circumstances, is not wise, and so I try to change the subject. Someone whispered in my ear in the lobby of the Habana Riviera that S. also worked for State Security. At the moment, I must act like a Chilean diplomat twenty-four hours a day, seven days a week.

We go up into the mountains, to a village named Topes de Collantes. The trip turns into an adventure—brakes failing on S.'s battered Soviet automobile, a wait by the side of the road near a quarry, until we are picked up and carried on by two trucks—and once again I find myself nose-to-nose with the exciting, young face of the Cuban Revolution. The kids leaving school in the little mountain town look healthy, clean, happy. The conversations I stop to eavesdrop on a bit, as I look out over the landscape from the mountaintop, are happy and profoundly *native*. On a gentle slope, boys play baseball. The sound of children singing some hilarious children's song comes from a window in a large hospital. The cold air at this altitude makes people's step springy, their walk quick, their faces bright. People rub their hands together enthusiastically, warmly.

We come to a house in which an experimental theater group has its headquarters. They explain that they work with the campesinos, they do a sort of improvisation based, at the moment, on the stories of Onelio Jorge Cardoso. Often the campesinos get so caught up that after the performance of a story, they stay around and tell their own. The group is warm and friendly, a very nice bunch of people, and the experiment itself is interesting, besides offering a wonderful diversion to the workers in these remote parts.

While we have a cup of coffee, I realize that one of the girls chatting with us, a young woman dressed in old pants that somehow seem to favor her and a very simple wool jacket, is the star of the second part of *Lucía*. I recall the Western world's actresses covered with makeup and wearing false eyelashes, eyecolor, and hair, inexpressive so that the movement of their facial muscles won't bring on wrinkles, alert (though feigning indifference) to the imminent flash of a flashbulb, which must surprise their "good side" and catch their ever-radiant smile—and the comparison, even from the point of view of attractiveness and feminine beauty, absolutely favors the young Cuban woman.

We are in the middle of the area known as Escambray, the region in which the counterrevolutionary guerrilla war took place. The road signs are pockmarked with bullet holes. There have been times when working within and for the Cuban Revolution has meant, did in fact mean back then, risking your neck, and there are times when one becomes aware of that fact, and from then on, one's perspective changes. One must not discard the possibility, on the other hand, that the bugbear of foreign invasion, which, after the missile crisis of October 1962 and the Soviet-American accords that followed it, had become little more than imagined threats, is dredged up by the promoters and guardians of Public Safety for their own purposes.

The stories of José Norberto Fuentes, whose prize I helped decide upon back in 1968, are set in this area, where the signs of battle give witness to the violence of the struggle and to its drama. But Fuentes, who had divided the world into black and white as a chronicler or historian, did not want to repeat this approach as a fiction writer, and so he dared question the dogma of the immaculate purity of the Revolutionary Army and its discipline, one of the untouchable divinities on the altar of Public Safety. All this can be read in the pages of Michelet's history of the French Revolution—Danton's *Comité*, Robespierre, the Revolution, and the guillotine.

There are things about the trip to Trinidad de Cuba that I forgot to note in my notebook, like the visit to that "naive" or "primitive" painter, a black man some eighty years old, retired from the city sanitation service or something of the sort, who took us into his little room, showed us some canvases, and laughed out loud. He laughed with pleasure and at the same time at our frustrated greed and envy, since for several reasons he didn't want to sell his pictures. One, which he considered his masterpiece, he would not part with for anything in the world; he pointed out certain details to us, with great seriousness and self-satisfaction, and then laughed again. Others, still unfinished, had already been sold, commissioned paintings showing the ocean, or leafy trees, or a wide green plain bordered with palm trees and dotted with strolling or tussling little figures. Among his patrons, if one might so put it, were well-known figures from Havana—intellectuals among the governing class who might afford themselves the luxury of traveling around the island and collecting naive painting. As the reader will understand, this word "naive" in no way could be applied to the buyers. And as for the painter, he rubbed his hands together and laughed out loud, opening his mouth and showing what were left of his teeth.

Another detail I made no note of: The driver in the soldier's uniform who brought us down from Topes de Collantes stayed to eat with us in the restaurant of the Hotel Las Cuevas. At the end of dinner he whispered in my ear and asked me to have them bring a cigar for me and one for him. I handed both of them to him, and he lit one up with obvious pleasure, with those mute voluptuous expressions that only Cubans lighting up a *puro* know how to make. When the driver left, our friend the intellectual gave free rein to his disgust. That was the kind of weakness that a revolutionary should never allow himself! Much less in front of foreigners!

"The poor guy was dying for a cigar," I replied. "The sin, if any, is hardly even venial."

S.'s indignation, though, never abated. One morning when I was late coming down—I was not sleeping, but rather writing in my diary—he said to me, only half in jest, that such softness could "cost me my militancy."

S. had one obsessive habit, which seemed to obey some secret desire, or perhaps the deliberate intention, to anger me. He equated the entire Chilean experience with the Cuban Revolution. He would say to me that at this stage I should take the opportunity to buy clothes that would last, to buy a stove, refrigerator, all sorts of home appliances, a solid car, a Volkswagen for example, and a house, if I didn't own one already . . . on and on. "You understand, when the time comes to share things out with the entire population, rationing is inevitable, my friend."

On the way back to Havana we stopped one night in Varadero. We went to the same hotel where my wife and I had spent a weekend a while before. At dinner, in the bar, our friend greeted people at all the surrounding tables. Suddenly he excused himself and went off to talk to someone for several minutes. They were the heads of some service or other, the men responsible for some middle-level functioning of the Revolution. S. would point out someone to us from time to time and give us all the person's vital statistics. He introduced us to two or three. Clearly, he was like a fish in water.

The orchestra, on a platform off to one corner of the cabaret, began to play. Varicolored spotlights lit the stage. The singers' wardrobes were a little out of fashion and their voices warm, cloying, with that unmistakable accent that made me recall the Cuban songs of my adolescence. All this, joined to the greetings my friend was passing out right and left, gave me the strange sensation of being suddenly in the past. But the occupants of many tables were wearing olive-green uniforms and were the officials of a party called the Communist Party of Cuba, words that would never have been spoken in a normal tone of voice, without some hint of scandal or outrage, in the past of that dark cabaret. Nor were the foreigners there the Yankee millionaires of old with their drunken wives or pale platinum-haired prostitutes brought along from Los Angeles, New York, or Miami, but rather stocky Soviet or East German engineers who applauded the musical numbers enthusiastically as they drank rum or beer, or rum perversely mixed with beer or any other available liquor.

I was met by Heberto Padilla, Belkis, and David Buzzi, scared yet at the same time smiling, eager to tell me what had happened to them but frightened by the invisible microphones that might be lurking. They had seen me in the hotel lobby with S. and had kept their distance. Now that S. had left me alone, they came over. They wanted to talk to me, there was no doubt about that, but the coast was hardly clear. In my room, at least, we had some sense of secrecy.

One's natural tendency is to *not* believe that the walls have ears. We pretended, in this case, that we believed they did. For a while we whispered or passed little pieces of paper back and forth. But we really didn't believe it; we never thought there were bugs in the walls, in the light fixtures, in the unsettling mirrors. Within a few minutes, and with the effect of the rum or whisky I had in one of my drawers, we were talking unguardedly, in a "silence" that had become shouting, as though we were all deaf.

On his first day in the Habana Riviera, to the amazement of us all, Heberto and Belkis had been accorded a suite, with a bedroom and living room. The second day they tried to go into the living room and the door had been locked tight. They heard noises on the other side of the door. Buzzi, with his unstoppable curiosity, and emboldened by several drinks of extra-seco on the rocks, went out onto the balcony, climbed over (at the real risk of falling from the seventeenth floor) to the next balcony, and found a man sitting in the living room. From this to deciding that the man was Heberto's own personal spy was but a step. The atmosphere favored that sort of supposition, and Heberto developed the idea with a mocking sort of theatricality, even perhaps flirtatiousness.

That was the way one took things in those days. If we had actually believed in a secret police force, we would have taken more serious precautions. But the State Security apparatus was a thing to warn each other, trade supposedly alarming rumors, and joke about.

The only behavior consistent with a real belief in the possibility of police surveillance would have been that my friends avoid me like the plague. In Czechoslovakia in the fifties, Western writers who were members of the Communist Parties or other progressive movements in their respective countries discovered with shock that Czech writers, old friends of theirs, would cross the street to avoid them when they saw them coming. There was nothing more dangerous for a Czech than contact with foreigners. From such contact, any imaginable accusation could be fabricated. When there is a foreign threat, and when on top of that the government employs the bogeyman of foreign threat as an instrument of discipline and internal solidarity, the most serious thing a private citizen can do is have any relationship with anything or anybody that comes from beyond the country's borders, whether that be books, newspapers, or people. Of course in spite of the blockade and the State Security apparatus (which demonstrated its perfectly real existence as things went on), the situation in Cuba differed greatly from that of Czechoslovakia in the times of the trials, not to mention the period of the great purges in the USSR. There was still some taste left of the Salon de Mai, which had been transported intact from Paris to Havana in 1967, and of the Cultural Congress of January 1968, which all the intellectuals of Europe and the Americas had attended.

The extreme case was that of the French photographer Pierre Gollendorf, who had come to Cuba for the first time to attend the Salon de Mai and had returned for the Cultural Congress. He had stayed in Cuba since then, married a Cuban woman, and now had a two-year-old daughter. Gollendorf insisted on seeing me, and he explained how urgently he wished to live in Chile now that we had a Popular government. Apparently not only could he not bear to live in any country but Chile, but Chile could not do without his inestimable services as photographer, painter, poet, professor of history of art, free-lance intellectual, etc. I was noncommittal, suggesting only that he write to Nemesio Antúnez, the director of our Museum of Fine Arts.

Gollendorf attended two or three of our get-togethers. He was resentful and exasperated in Cuba, but the authorities would not give him the visa to return with his wife and daughter to France, from where he intended to move on to Chile. I vaguely remembered having seen him in Paris, in and around the Place de l'Odéon and the rue Monsieur-le-Prince, with Violeta Parra's circle. "Weren't you a friend of Violeta's?"

It had been him, sure enough, but the almost three years in the close air of the Habana Riviera had aged him. He was attracted by the euphoric atmosphere of the early stages of revolutions, but a bit put off when they moved into their period of hardships and difficulties. But it is a far cry from denouncing that "flaw of revolutionary character" to accusing him of being an enemy agent, as was done not long after, and to throwing him in jail without explanation.

During this time I became aware of Padilla's novel, whose thick manuscript lay on a table in his hotel room. Its title, *Heroes Are Grazing in My Garden*, alluded to the cult of heroes that had developed in the course of the revolution. The heroism of a handful of men had freed Cuba from dependence, chronic poverty, and national humiliation. That, at least, was the official version of history that was accepted and widely trumpeted. Martí, Maceo, Fidel, Ché . . . Their portraits were on every wall, in every magazine; their names were repeated in every speech. If the liberal or leftist parties and unions had taken any part in the Revolution, you couldn't read about it in the history books; the history books preferred to glorify the heroes. One had to acknowledge, on the other hand, that the circumstances within which the struggle against Batista took place favored that interpretation, even when after breaking with imperialism the heroes had not been able to keep themselves in power without organized support from inside and then, immediately, outside the country. But the textbooks, quite significantly, emphasized personality, the men who changed history and led the country to a new destiny.

In our conversations about Chile, Padilla would speak enthusiastically about the possibility of a socialism in which power would be controlled, limited, by some legal mechanism, even if that legal system belonged to the past. In the case of Chile, it was clear that the constitutional system derived directly from the French Revolution; applied in its true sense, it allowed the arbitrary actions and decisions of power to progress while at the same time controlling them. The lack of an equivalent system in Cuba had cost the people of Cuba dearly. The heroes had not been fixed for all time in marble statues, but had stepped down into the street, pulled the gates off their hinges, and trampled the flowers of all those private gardens.

How could anyone have believed that such a novel, whose contents were easy enough to guess from its title, could be published in Barcelona with impunity? To believe that was to show oneself a very bad judge of the moment, for this was one of the most difficult times the Revolution had so far passed through. I didn't think too much about the problem; it was no business of mine. Padilla, on the other hand, miscalculated, and in difficult times miscalculations cost. He might have added some sort of poem along those lines to his well-known and much-objected-to book of poems.

Padilla talked about sending the manuscript off to our publisher friend Carlos Barral. He never asked me to use my diplomatic position to get it out of the country for him, as was later reported in some quarters. Many foreign writers and journalists were entering and leaving Cuba in those days. No one's bags, so far as I know, were ever searched. The fact was that Padilla, haunted by the demon of perfectionism, never could turn the book loose and say it was finished. He would suddenly show one the manuscript and then as quickly pull it out of one's hands, as though he couldn't bear to let it go. I looked at one page and managed to see that there was a conversation between a Czech and a Russian; that might be due to the proliferation of experts from the two countries on the Island, or have something to do with the events of 1968. But Heberto, frantic, tore the manuscript out of my hands before I could see anything else.

During the last few days he had been walking around carrying the manuscript under his arm, as though he thought, or knew, that there were plans to steal it from him. If such were the case, there were only two alternatives for Heberto: get it out of the country immediately, leaving the corrections for the future (or to the exegetes), or else retreat, keep silent, cultivate his garden, even at the risk of finding one morning that the flowers in it had been trampled under the powerful heels of the heroes, who often climbed down off their pedestals, especially at night, and walked the city. But Heberto miscalculated. And besides, it isn't easy to predict what one's own thoughts would have been, how one would have reacted if one had been set down in similar circumstances.

Meanwhile, the day of the arrival of the training ship *Esmeralda* approached, and I had more serious things to worry about than the fate of the manuscript of *Heroes Are Grazing in My Garden*. The real-life heroes had to prepare themselves to receive the visit of the symbol of the glory of the Chilean Navy.[6] One morning I received a call from the public relations director of the Ministry of Armed Services, who told me that the minister, Comandante Raúl Castro, wanted to see me.

Fidel is a man who is late by half-hours and hours. Of course at the same time, a meeting with him that is supposed to last fifteen minutes may wind up lasting an entire afternoon, or two days, depending on the conversation, the enthusiasm, his interest in the person or what the person represents. Fidel is the warm leader full of an inextinguishable curiosity, a man of great imagination, a devourer of histories, chronicles, treatises on natural science, manuals of agriculture, while at the same time surprisingly insensitive to literary or artistic creation. His optimism is contagious, and capable of convincing and mobilizing an entire country, although it may be based on erroneous figures

---

[6] The flagship of the Chilean Navy was always called the *Esmeralda*. Since 1818, when Lord Thomas Cochrane, a Scotsman who was fighting on the Chilean side against the Spaniards, had seized a Spanish ship in Callao harbor and renamed it the *Esmeralda*, that name had stood for Chilean independence and the greatness of the Chilean naval tradition. The second *Esmeralda* had been that of the great Chilean navy hero Arturo Prat, who had fought in the War of the Pacific in 1879, and this training ship now about to visit Cuba was its direct descendant.

and statistics, an inexact apprehension of the realities, as occurred with the 1970 ten-million-ton harvest. He will acknowledge his errors in public immediately, as though they were the product of a collective misfortune, a historical fate whose consequences all must pay, all must assume, and he will be off on a new course with the same enthusiasm, the same optimism.

I had been told that Raúl was the exact opposite of Fidel. One heard how cold he was, and when one was far out of earshot of the bugs, of his cruelty. This cruelty, true or legendary, was the subject of comments even within the socialist countries, where some leaders *supposedly* told others that they had heard from Raúl's own lips the story of how he had eliminated certain enemies. Of the leadership that came down out of the Sierra Maestra, it was he who had had the greatest previous contact with organized communism; he had been a militant in the Communist Party for some time and had traveled to Vienna, Bucharest, and Prague for youth congresses and the like. As the man in charge of the armed forces, which were supplied almost entirely by the Soviets, he had a solid institutional relationship with the USSR. Another significant detail: In 1968, after Fidel had backed the entry of Russian tanks into Czechoslovakia, it was the Army magazine *Verde Olivo* ("Olive Green") which, under Raúl's control, had begun the most concerted and visible attack against Cuban writers. The victims had been José Norberto Fuentes (because of the book I had helped to vote the literary prize to that January), Antón Arrufat, and Heberto Padilla. As it has later been explained to me (since I have never had occasion to read it), Arrufat's book, a play actually, describes two brothers' struggle for political power; it takes place in an unnamed country and at a time in the past. The allusions to Fidel and Raúl are, however, it appears, transparent.

I arrived at the specified time at Armed Services Ministry offices, which are located in one wing of the Palacio de la Revolución, a huge, solid, ugly edifice built during the Batista regime to house the Cuban courts. I have no idea what was behind so much luxury granted Justice in the period of the bloodiest sort of arbitrariness. No doubt Batista felt he needed at some point to ingratiate himself with the judiciary, in order to cover up his crimes.

I arrived punctually on time, as I said, and the comandante in charge of Armed Services public relations, a man named Díaz if I recall correctly, was waiting for me at the door of the building. As I crossed through the lobby, I realized that I was in a privileged place, which no one could enter without authorization. I was entering, without doubt, one of the major centers of power on the Island. Guards, elevator operators, clerks, and orderlies maintained an impeccable, alert seriousness, which did not prevent them from smiling courteously.

I waited for about a minute with Comandante Díaz in the outer office, and then I was taken into the minister's office. Dressed in his usual olive-green uniform, Raúl Castro seemed taller than I had thought he would be. His hair was cut short; he had a neutral, somewhat distant gaze that would light on some random spot on the desk before him; his forearms were hairless, and not particularly muscular, and his body gave the impression of having once been weak but of having been toughened through the course of a vigorous life of intense work and self-discipline. He was not in the least the pleasant subordinate of the Prime Minister, like other members of the government that I had met, but rather a man who, in another style than his brother's, without his contagious enthusiasm or his rapport with the masses and the media, fully shared the burden of political power, though perhaps from the shadows.

We were served a glass of grapefruit juice, offered cigarettes, and after a brief preamble of greetings, we began. Comandante Raúl Castro's manners were courteous and calm. Unlike his brother Fidel, everything about him was measured and controlled; he never "went overboard." No doubt he acted this way in knowledge of my pernicious friendships and my caustic private comments, which had at times out of irony or jest taken on a tone of counterrevolutionary jibing *par excellence,* but I can't be sure.

The minister's eyes were fixed on a file containing all the documents I had sent to the Ministry of Foreign Relations concerning the itinerary of the *Esmeralda.* I figured he had looked over it ten minutes earlier. I explained the importance of the training ship to the Chilean Navy, its popularity, my country's affection for its naval traditions, which were symbolized and distilled in the name of the ship itself. I also explained that the navy had traditionally been the most conservative branch of the Chilean armed services. In our only really bloody revolution, which culminated in the overthrow of the government that had been legally constituted in 1891, the Navy took the side of the oligarchy and of British imperialism against a nationalist president who had attempted to obtain the greatest benefits possible for the country from its nitrate deposits and who had been supported until the end by the Army. The Navy of that period had acted as its British training and its class preoccupations led it to act. But even then, there had been recourse to the sort of judicial pretext that my nation's traditional strict adherence to legal processes demanded: In not waiting for congressional approval of the budget for fiscal year 1891, and in decreeing the budget of 1890 still applicable, President Balmaceda had violated the Constitution. In Balmaceda's time the Navy and the members of Congress, like their British mentors, were parliamentarists. The Army, on the other hand, favored a strong Executive which had, or would have, the power to restrain the forces of the oligarchy, the parliament, and the politicians, who could only think of spending income from the nitrate industries in Paris and the casinos of the Riviera.

Raúl Castro, who had been listening attentively, without moving a muscle, uncrossed his legs and said they had prepared an essentially professional, apolitical schedule of events. Orders would be given to both Cuban officers and private citizens to avoid political subjects in their conversations with the young men of the *Esmeralda*. They would be addressed as "Chilean friends" rather than the more compromising "compañeros." Comandante Raúl Castro was certain (and quite rightly so, as it turned out) that the crew would greatly enjoy the military aspects of the schedule, and that that was the proper course to follow in this visit.

He was not emphatic. He gave the impression that unlike his more expressive brother he was deliberately avoiding any sort of emphasis. The takeoff of the MIGs from their underground hangars would surely impress the Chilean crew, as would the exercises put on by the jets for the guests: "We have few planes, and they are purely defensive in nature, but they are very modern and efficient." He would also like to show them the fishing industry's harbor that had been financed by the Soviets. They would be taken to a baseball game one afternoon, and the Cuban people would applaud them wildly, he was sure of that, and the crew members who did not want to go to the baseball game could go to the movies. "We have made some very good films here in Cuba."

"Comandante, in your plans for the ship, the captain has asked me quite insistently that there be one afternoon free. You recall that they will have been sailing for some thirty days. He has also asked me whether it might not be possible for the young men to sleep ashore one night. Apparently it's a custom on the *Esmeralda*'s voyages around the world that . . ."

The comandante stroked his beard with his long, yellowish hands. He would see what could be done. Of course they would have to understand that the conditions in Havana were not those of a normal city . . .

"Of course! They will understand that. But if you could do something."

They could be given a card so that they could use the facilities of the large hotels, even stay in one if they wished. But whatever the case, one had to foresee the possibility that they would be the object of provocations. Some counterrevolutionary might well take the opportunity to approach them.

The comandante stroked his beard. He promised that he would study the problem, consult with his advisers, and find the best solution.

"The last thing I have been asked, comandante," I said, smiling, "is that thirty or forty young ladies be invited to the dance given by the cadets, which is not the same dance as that given by the captain to the authorities the day after the ship's arrival."

Raúl Castro smiled, too—a little—or rather his features seemed to hint at the beginnings of a smile. One might, he supposed, invite a group of young women from the university, or talk to the Federation of Women. Anyway, he would try to find a solution.

His attitude was straightforward, easy. The captain had asked, in the documents that I had been sent, that thirty or forty "young ladies" be invited. He did not say "young women of society" because that qualification was unnecessary. The detail had reminded me of my childhood vacations in Viña del Mar, when my older sister and her friends would be getting dressed to attend, under the watchful eye of their respective chaperones, the dances on board the *Jeanne d'Arc*, the French training ship that made the hearts of the young women of the spa city flutter for eight or ten days each year. In the office of Comandante Raúl Castro, behind whom, on a shelf, there sat a model of the *Granma*, one became conscious of how long ago that time had been, for Chile, Cuba, the world, and for the Chilean chargé d'affaires, who no longer sat in the speedboat, holding a chaperone's hand and accompanying his sister, as the cutter drew near the dazzling hull of the French cruiser with its fanfares and its bright tricolors, but rather who was representative to the revolutionary government of Cuba from a Chilean government the mere possibility of whose existence, at that remote date, would have given the chaperone a heart attack and sent the young ladies squealing, and which even now filled with anguish and painful uncertainty the heart of the respectable older woman his sister had become and the hearts of her friends, many of whom were youthful grandmothers.

The comandante made it amiably clear that the interview had ended, and the chargé d'affaires, after a few brief words of thanks, stood to leave. In contrast to his brother's hours, the armed services minister's conversation, which had begun within a minute of its scheduled time, had lasted exactly one-half hour. Comandante Díaz accompanied the chargé d'affaires to his car, which pulled away immediately (at full speed) from the heavy, imposing Batista-era Palacio de la Revolución. Between the chargé d'affaires's arrival and his departure exactly thirty-seven minutes had elapsed; they had been used with the utmost efficiency to discuss the details of the training ship's schedule.

My wife Pilar and I found ourselves going out almost every night; when it wasn't to a reception it was to a dinner. The diplomatic corps was greatly curious to meet the new member who on the very night of his arrival had been distinguished by Fidel with literally hours of conversation. *Granma* had published, along with that first interview, my diplomatic and literary *curriculum vitæ*. Chilean politics were followed with interest by real or pretended well-wishers throughout Cuba. Chile was always given a great deal of space in *Granma* and in all other Cuban publications in those days.

It was for that reason that I had the idea of making a complete collection of the 1970 issues of *Granma* for my office. I wanted to know how it had reported the Chilean electoral campaign, the murder of General Schneider,[7] the passing of power from one government to the next, and last, the recognition of Cuba. I soon saw, with no great surprise, that before the September 4 Chilean election the main Latin American news sections were mostly concerned with the revolution in Peru and the Tupamaro movement in Uruguay. A few days before September 4 there was a long complimentary biographical article on Allende, some news about the upcoming elections, but nothing to indicate any confidence in the Left's winning the elections. The government's heart was much closer to the urban guerrillas in Uruguay and to Velasco Alvarado's military revolutionary government in Peru, which had broken all Latin American molds for military governments.

Chile's originality, which lay precisely in our dull, gray sort of respect for constitutionality and in the peacefulness of political coexistence among the factions in the country, did not appear to awaken any great enthusiasm in the Cuban government and its organs of expression before September 4, 1970.

And then on September 5 there suddenly appeared on the front page of *Granma*, which had not adequately prepared its readers for the shock, enormous headlines trumpeting the news of the triumph of the Unidad Popular. From that September 5 issue on (an issue which had probably come off the presses around noon and been distributed sometime after lunch, since the absence of news competition in Cuba gives time for the news to be rounded out and the coverage to be discussed and prepared), the Island news media gave tremendous space to Chile and to Allende.

This, of course, brought all eyes to focus on the first Chilean diplomat to appear, after six and a half years of blockade, at the receptions and official ceremonies of Havana. Every night we went out, my wife in a formal gown and

---

[7] General René Schneider was commander-in-chief of the Chilean armed forces, and in the weeks before the 1970 elections he had made it clear that if Allende won the elections, he (Schneider) would favor the constitutionally sanctioned passing of power. Certain military colleagues saw (probably rightly) in Schneider's attitude a threat to military influence in the government, and a plot was hatched to kidnap him. In the attempt, Schneider tried to defend himself and was killed, and the popular backlash against the perpetrators of the kidnap/murder helped take Allende to the presidency. The military's attempt to influence Chilean electoral politics backfired in its face.

I in a dark suit and tie; we made our way through the hotel lobby, through a crowd of soldiers, shirt-sleeved students, foreign technicians, stunned honeymooners watching every detail of our departure, and old ladies who sat for long hours in the armchairs of the lobby, looking on with contemptuous indifference. We were no doubt viewed as quasi-mythological creatures who slipped out through the spacious lobby as though through some aquarium full of varicolored, multiform species and into our Alfa Romeo that drove us swiftly off to inaccessible towers or the brightly lighted fortresses of Cubanacán, where we would somehow be in contact with dazzling objects, fabulous machines, the brilliance, noise, and madness of the outside world. A bilious soul, given to ill humor and even perhaps to reactionary introversion, would surely have experienced fits of anger and repudiation, incurring thereby the disapproval of his more docile comrades, who better understood the laws of the superstructure, who were more aware of the real problems faced by the Revolution, and who were, therefore, better integrated into the system. The pangs of conscience with which I made my way through that hotel lobby was proof that my own integration into the system, into the "revolutionary process," as the jargon had it, was far from complete, and that this failure of integration led me to "subjectivism" and a correspondingly negative view of the privileges of hierarchy, and reflected the bourgeois-intellectual prejudices that I had inherited from my forebears.

One morning among the ample columns that *Granma* dedicated to Chile, I read that Laura Allende, the president's sister, a member of Congress and of the Central Committee of the Chilean Socialist Party, had arrived in Cuba and was staying at the Hotel Habana Libre. I now think that a good diplomat ought to have known of her arrival, even when his ministry had not informed him of it. I know of many, utterly foreign to the remotest notion of socialism, who would have been waiting for her at the airport, at the foot of the ramp; who would have sent an enormous arrangement of flowers, with a polite visiting card, to her hotel where they would have been placed on a table in her suite; who would have immediately put themselves at her disposal for any desires she might wish to fulfill; who would have sent their wives to go shopping with her or to do anything else that might have come up, such as long stays at the beauty parlor or at work; and who would have joined with vigor and without reservation into the exclamations of delighted praise that the illustrious visitor would utter at every visible achievement of the Revolution.

I recognize, I acknowledge my professional errors. I saw her name in the newspaper and I believe it was not until twenty-four hours later that I knocked at the door of her suite at the Habana Libre. Those were days of intense running about, solving problems, visiting colleagues, going to receptions, and I believed (with inexcusable frivolity) that those things might excuse me to the president's sister. My vain and twisted nature must have been a factor in my neglect, as well, since I would have gone to the hotel sooner (it must be said in all honesty) had I also read in the newspaper of the arrival of Pancho Coloane and Manuel Rojas, two widely read Chilean authors, both good friends of mine. But at any rate, I appeared at the congresswoman's suite twenty-four hours late, an act of negligence which the observers in the shadows must have noted down immediately. But better late than never. Laura Allende's daughter, a sweet-looking girl, and an older friend of hers with a stiff, mistrusting, sharp expression, were seated in the living room of the suite, in silence, in the company of two or three members of the Cuban Federation of Women. There were flowers, boxes of chocolates, and other tokens of greeting from diverse institutions and friends. There was no doubt that in this room one was close to the center of power and what might be called its accoutrements, a phenomenon that Cubans, in spite of their being ruled by a leader who was always in his fatigue uniform, with no sign of gold braid or epaulets, and who was constantly in action, working, concerned with the slightest detail of production and disdaining any show or protocol—a phenomenon, I repeat, that Cubans, in spite of the outward simplicity of their Commander-in-Chief, were quite familiar with. I would say, in fact, that regardless of appearances, Cubans are as familiar with the classical ceremonials and ornamentations of power as any other nation on earth.

Meanwhile, the congresswoman was a virtual whirlwind of activity, answering telephone calls, rushing about the bedroom and sitting room. She asked me to help her classify the many gifts she had brought for the authorities. Who should she send gifts to? Could I tell her which shop sold the lovely ivory things she had seen in somebody's house in Santiago? She had been told they were brought from Havana. This was the first time I had ever heard of such a thing being sold in Havana, and my ignorance was no doubt inexcusable in a professional diplomat.

"Are you sure about that, Laurita?" I asked.

Absolutely sure! Her brother Salvador had brought them to Chile from Cuba in '64 or '65.

Very well, but this was February 1971, and surely all that sort of thing had disappeared from the market.

The congresswoman would hear no objections, and the truth is that another diplomat, more experienced and more committed to his career, would have poked about until he had found some of those yearned-for ivories. When the issue is one of pleasing those who have been touched near or at a distance by the aura of power, a good diplomat ought to be able to glide at a great height of nebulous speech, to speak like a Talleyrand about international politics, to offhandedly quote powerful and illustrious persons whom one calls by their first names, to enter a dining room and see at a glance whether the chairs have been placed correctly, whether the table has been set and the flowers arranged with art, to take charge of the tiniest details and carry out the slightest task with versatility, helpfulness, and efficiency, and to know where to shop. Chateaubriand (whom I do not quote by his first name) said that if people knew the real secrets of diplomacy, instead of being so concerned with diplomats they would find them ludicrous and risible. My stubborn error was in talking to Laura Allende about the political and economic situation of Cuba instead of trying to find ivory trinkets for her and letting the politicians worry about their own affairs. Although politics may be too serious a subject to be left in the hands of politicians.

"Uh-huh," said Laurita, "I hope you and I can talk about this again sometime. I am in total agreement with you that Salvador ought to be informed of all this."

A group of Cubans living in Chile had been naive enough to meet with Salvador Allende about a year before the last elections in order to point out to him that the Cuban model of socialism had serious, basic problems that counterindicated its applicability to Chile. Some members of the group told me about this meeting, and about their disillusionment: The candidate had listened to them, with an all-too-visible lack of interest, and had replied not a word. But really—how could they think that the candidate, an old and experienced politician, a constant traveler to Cuba, was ignorant of Cuba's problems? Telling him a few unpleasant truths, which he was no doubt better aware of than his interlocutors, was not going to alter his intention to use, or not to use, during the campaign and later during his presidency, the Cuban Example. In the 1964 elections the candidate and his party had deliberately kept quiet about Cuba, while his Communist allies, with the inopportune bothersomeness that characterizes them when they get an idea stuck in their brains, hammered at the example of the Revolutionary Isle every ten minutes. In the 1970 campaign things were different: With their continual words of support for Cuba, the Socialists intended to show their credentials as unwavering revolutionaries, their chemically pure revolutionary fervor. This was not in response to a desire to inspire trust, as in 1964, but rather to attract an ungovernable and wayward far-Left that was hostile to the peaceful path of elections (especially since elections had been made to look ridiculous precisely by the lessons that were coming from Havana) but which could, in this particularly tight election, help, without violence and within the channels of democracy which they dismissed, to bring a Marxist into the presidency for the first time.

Fidel had given his pledge to the candidate, promising that Cuba, while skeptical about the matter, had never in principle discarded the possibility of elections in certain countries; and the miracle, which caught not only *Granma* but many revolutionaries of the Americas and the rest of the world off balance, had occurred. The miracle had taken reactionaries by surprise, as well, which made the conquest and control of the government all the easier. But these were but the first steps on a road that promised much rougher going—for the confrontation that had not, in spite of the dire predictions of the most simplistic ideologues, taken place (neither during the elections nor during the passing of the presidential baton nor upon the initial measures taken by the government) was written upon the future with letters of fire; the reactionaries would yet have their day. That was the theory that underlay, and that was often explicitly stated in, all conversations with Cuban officials. This Chilean Revolution of babelike innocence should prepare itself: learn to handle weapons and use the inexhaustible resources of the techniques of mass mobilization, of police surveillance, whose absolute necessity was scorned or ignored only by the liberals, who had joined the Unidad Popular only by a fluke, by virtue of a misunderstanding that the Unidad Popular ought to take advantage of while they could, because the useful boobies would start falling by the wayside or jumping ship sooner or later.

"I have been told," the Yugoslav ambassador said to me in a whisper, out in the center of the lawn where he felt safe from secret ears, natural or electronic, "that your president is not a sectarian."

"Of course not!" I replied, adding that I had even had the privilege of knowing him with some intimacy. "He is not in the least sectarian."

But there were forces that must have been acting outside his control—or perhaps the Cuban style served for certain purposes—because after the recognition of Cuba (which I knew had been arrived at neither so quickly nor so easily as one might have foreseen) the new official class began to talk about voluntary labor, of "compañero" minister or "compañero" ambassador, of setting revolutionary violence against reactionary violence—a reactionary violence that had already shown its fierce face in the murder of General Schneider, a deed performed so as to demonstrate to Chile and the whole world that any peaceful transition to socialism was a dream.

The chargé d'affaires found himself the prey of a most distressing perplexity. Some officialistic pet phrases, some of the initial measures that were taken, the tone and the quality of thought of certain prominent personages in the new government made one fear that the Cuban process was about to be repeated, with but small differences, in Chile. The confidence of the great majority of Chileans of both the Left and Right, who were convinced that the country could avoid the difficulties and deviations of the Cuban Revolution, looked almost foolhardy if seen from the viewpoint of Cuba. There had developed in Chile, with the general complicity of the country, an image of Cuba as an exotic country whose problems could simply not repeat themselves in the "England of South America." But Cuba's problems were the problems of any underdeveloped nation that sets out to begin the complex work of building socialism. After a stage of initial euphoria, perhaps briefer even than Cuba's, Chile would also come up against that hard reality. In the midst of the exaltation over its triumph and the first tastes of power, the Socialist and MIRist[8] factions of the Unidad Popular attempted to "radicalize the process" (to use a phrase in fashion then), announcing with irresponsible complacency (because the prediction was almost one of the commonplaces of the Left) the advent of hard times, which would give people the opportunity to make heroic sacrifices for the nation.

The chargé d'affaires, meanwhile, read in Cuba's present situation the possibility of a gloomy future for his countrymen. The way some "compañeros" of the Unidad Popular erred in their observations, misreading the signs of the situation, or were deliberately blind to certain aspects of it, exasperated him. Their actions revealed them to be taking a dangerously spontaneous course, and to be moved by enthusiasm (which is not always a wise counselor), or by an uncontrolled appetite for power (that passion which in all history has been the single greatest cause of collective tragedies). And to top it all off, the unnecessary repetition of the Cuban phenomenon in Chile would provoke, among those others who also had some appetite for power but who were on the other side of the political spectrum, a fascist reaction of incalculable consequences.

"They've got you pegged for a liberal," Padilla had once said to me. "You're done for!"

I smiled. Only later was I able to derive the true conclusions of that observation. Now, in her suite in the Habana Libre, among baskets of flowers and boxes of chocolates, Laura Allende stopped listening to me. She promised to have a longer talk with me another day. Everything I had told her fascinated her, but . . . She stood up.

"These gifts, then . . ."

---

[8] "MIR" is the *Movimiento de Izquierda Revolucionaria,* or "Movement of the Revolutionary Left," and was, as its name implies, a radical group unlikely to be content with the evolutionary (not, in its view, revolutionary) politics that Chile seemed to be embarked upon.

They had to be wrapped, cards put on them. I assured her that my secretary would handle it all.

"Don't worry, Jorge. The *compañeras* here are so nice, they fix everything for me!"

At that moment the phone rang. Comandante Manuel Piñeiro was calling.

At the time, I simply noted the coincidence: My delicate conversation with Laura Allende came to an end and Piñeiro, ever attentive, ever watching, made his presence felt. Today, with the paranoid suspiciousness that I came to develop later, I believe that as soon as he heard our conversation (directly or recorded) he picked up the telephone. In the Chile, before 1973, people would have called this suspiciousness sick; it would have been argued that suspicions such as these are evidence of mental unbalance. That may be; but I still suspect that Piñeiro picked up the telephone to invite Laura Allende someplace after he learned of our conversation. Just as Piñeiro already knew of my engagement with Lezama and his friends when he invited me to dinner on the same night, putting me to a test which was for him final and decisive. But of course his estimation of me was in all probability already formed, even before my arrival in Cuba—because he had to have "studied" me, and for that study he could call upon the reports from his friends at *Punto Final* and Prensa Latina in Chile as well as upon reports on my previous visit to the Island as a member of the jury for Casa de las Américas; the number of persons reporting on me, perhaps accusing me, had increased dizzyingly, while I remained blissfully unconscious.

I can clearly see now, after more than twenty years, how easy it was for Manuel Piñeiro to manipulate Laura Allende's official visit to Havana. She combined bourgeois tastes and feelings with revolutionary fervor, a blend very typical of the Chilean Left in those days. She obviously didn't want to hear anything negative about the Cuban Revolution. Her end was tragic, and all the sadder when one considers her fragile personality. She was imprisoned after the September 1973 coup in Chile. In 1981, gravely ill, living in Cuba after requesting political asylum there, she sought permission many times to return to Chile, but this was always denied by the Pinochet authorities. In mid-1981 the news came that Laura Allende had committed suicide by jumping from an upper-story window of the Habana Riviera.

As was appropriate in the case of a congresswoman of the governing party (and at the same time the sister of the chief of state), I sent Laura Allende a formal invitation to dinner. I took the opportunity to invite a few other Chileans who were visiting the country at the same time: Mónica Echeverría, the wife of the chancellor of the Catholic University in Santiago; Manuel Rojas and Francisco Coloane, members of the jury for the Casa de las Américas; Cristián Huneeus, a writer and farmer, who was visiting Cuba as a tourist, taking a firsthand look at socialism from the point of view of a Chilean intellectual who had been educated at Cambridge. Cristián was staying with Pablo Armando Fernández, who had been a friend of his since his days in England.

It took some work to get Laura Allende to agree to a definite date for her dinner: Her schedule of visits, volunteer-labor stints, meetings with women and with popular organizations was growing more complicated every minute. Piñeiro had already had lunch with her, by means of the engagement he had made by phone during my visit to her suite, and he had doubtlessly informed her of the government's unhappiness at my fraternization with persons not unconditionally committed to the Revolution. At my insistence, however, the congresswoman at last agreed to a date. I thereupon invited Haydée Santamaría, Comandante Piñeiro himself (who continued to have his doubts about me after the invitation I was unable to accept), the president of the Federation of Women and wife of Raúl Castro, Vilma Espín, Lisandro Otero (who was traveling back and forth to Chile during this time as cultural adviser), Duque Estrada, and perhaps another person, although I am not certain.

Days passed and no Cuban called to accept my invitation. My guests had suddenly vanished off the face of the earth. As for the unpredictable Chileans, on the day of the dinner their full schedules might well take them anywhere on the Island. I ran the serious risk of seating Laura Allende in the midst of twenty empty chairs, a situation the news of which, transmitted to her brother at first hand, would serve as delicious seasoning to the information already sent him by Comandante Piñeiro. The story would run something as follows: The chargé d'affaires lives his life shuttling between the exiles of interior emigration and absolute nothingness.

Haydée Santamaría, meanwhile, was in Oriente Province. The possibility that she would attend the dinner appeared remote. I called her secretary at the Casa de las Américas, who promised to speak with her in Santiago de Cuba and call me back. That afternoon the secretary called: Haydée would come in from Santiago especially to meet Laura Allende Friday at the dinner.

This was Tuesday or Wednesday afternoon. The next morning, Meléndez, with unaccustomed manners, called to ask me how everything was going for my dinner, and whether he might help out in any way.

"Are you coming?"

"Yes, of course!"

Duque Estrada also, of course, was coming. A short while later Lisandro

Otero called to accept my invitation, with pleasure. The Federation of Women telephoned to say that they would be sending their vice president, since Vilma Espín was away. The only person that was still invisible, and that would remain so until the arrival of the *Esmeralda,* was Manuel Piñeiro.

I had the impression that Haydée looked with some sarcasm upon Laura, the Chilean revolutionary with her worldly manners who had warned me that she hadn't brought clothes for a diplomatic dinner but who arrived looking immensely elegant. Haydée, seated on my left, volleyed somewhat brusque replies across my bow to Laura, on my right. Haydée probably saw in the socialist congresswoman an incarnation of the Chilean Revolution, replete with the weaknesses that some Cubans felt a constant temptation to condemn and that at best they kept a discreet silence about, when not insinuating skepticism and contempt.[9]

In the midst of all this, Pancho Coloane took the floor, his voice like that of a hard-drinking sailor in semiretirement, and monopolized the after-dinner conversation. To the barely disguised stupefaction of the government officials and to the attention of Haydée Santamaría, who appeared to enjoy the spectacle, he loudly declared that he, a militant old Communist, had reached the conclusion that in Cuba a person necessarily either became a pure revolutionary or a total and complete hypocrite, adding (of course) that during his visits he had observed a net majority of hypocrites. He went on to toss similar flowers at the feet of the bureaucratic fauna, literary and otherwise, so well represented at the table, and after a few anecdotes which were not, generally speaking, of the edifying sort that would have put Meléndez' and Lisandro Otero's minds at ease about him (anecdotes that placed him, for example, drunk as a lord in a Valparaíso whorehouse, losing a tooth in a bar brawl), the conversation was adjourned.

---

[9] The tragic (or sad) part of all this is that Haydée Santamaría committed suicide in Havana, as Laura Allende did, some ten years after this episode. Some time before her suicide, Haydée had separated from Armando Hart, one of the historic figures of the Revolution. I do not know what her professional relationship with the Casa de las Américas, during the last years of her life, was. At any rate, the cultural policies that she had set in motion during the sixties, with the Casa's invitations to a wide spectrum of intellectuals, its publications of formal and experimental writers, its exhibits of avant-garde painting and sculpture, now belonged to a past buried and forgotten. In mid-1981 there was, however, an attempt to revive those times, and some familiar faces (now looking a bit aged) came to Havana and to the Malecón where the Casa de las Américas building sits, but Haydée, the founder and former director, had passed away.

Haydée and Laura Allende made an engagement to meet again, this time to visit the *Esmeralda* together. Chilean forthrightness allowed me to learn, the next afternoon, that Laura had felt that the dinner was a bit too formal, not the sort of thing, in her opinion, for the climate of life under the Revolution. It may be that Piñeiro's assessment of me as "a person not committed to the Revolution" had somehow, to her mind, been confirmed, precisely by the formal aspect of that dinner and in spite of the fact that Piñeiro accused me of nothing so much as lack of formality. Truth to tell, the diplomatic life in Havana was more rigorous than that of Santiago in 1969 and 1970, where cocktail parties lasted until precisely 11:00 P.M. and the dress code was violated by a motley assortment of intellectuals and eccentric politicians, species that had become extinct in Havana by the time I arrived—unless, under pressure from historical imperatives, they had evolved into the mainstream species that were now encountered.

S. M., a friend I did not ordinarily see much of, though I sometimes ran into him here and there, called me quite insistently during those weeks.

"I want to see you," he would say, and then at last, "There's something I want to talk to you about."

I invited him to have lunch with me at the hotel. We had a drink in my room first, where I think there was someone else as well. S. M. told some stories and jokes, being always sure to talk about things superficially: Anything might have political implications and any joke, therefore, might be condemned as irreverent.

I thought it would be during lunch, when we were alone, that he would broach whatever subject it was, but the pleasantries and light anecdotes continued. It is true that the headwaiter, "the Captain" as we affectionately called him, was looking on, and that microphones might be aimed our way from curtains and candelabra, conceived originally as Hollywood-style elegance but reduced after twelve years of the Revolution to an anachronistic and tattered parody of it.

After coffee, we got up to go for a little walk around the grand lobby of the Habana Riviera, which never failed to remind me of American tourists with chewing gum and cameras. S. M., who was still telling stories, suddenly fell silent. I was tired; I wanted to go up to my room and take a nap, but the sudden silence of my friend alerted me. The conversation that the phone call had prepared me for was coming.

"I want you to know," S. M. said solemnly, "that you have a friend in me, a true friend."

"I have always thought so," I said. "And the friendship is mutual."

He nodded. He continued his walk through the lobby, not speaking for more than a minute.

"I want to tell you something, then."

He went on walking, as though he needed to gather his strength for what he was about to tell me. At that hour there were few people around the hotel. The ocean, which was deep blue and stirred by the wind into countless whitecaps, leapt across the Malecón and wetted the street. I felt an odd, oppressive foreboding, as though my life, which in spite of small ripples had always flowed quietly within its banks, was about to come upon rapids.

"I want to tell you that there are people watching everything you do here. So watch out for yourself."

We walked in silence awhile longer.

"Do you think that my contact with Padilla and that group of people is the problem? The criticism they express in their conversations? All that?"

"No," my friend said. "I don't think so."

"What's the problem, then?"

"Anything having to do with political activity. Do you understand? Anything that's political."

There was probably still time to retreat, but the truth is that I only half understood, or wasn't prepared to understand. Since then, trying to put two and two together (a mental operation I learned to perform very often and very quickly during that diplomatic stretch), I realized that S. M. had mentioned at lunch two or three times one of the highest officials of the government, a personal friend of his. He had said that this person had spoken to him of me sometime or other.

"He respects you, you know?"

Had this, then, been some sort of message? When they talked about political activity were they talking about my reports to the Chilean Ministry of Foreign Relations? Did they want to neutralize the source of direct and objective information to the Allende government that the Chilean Embassy had become? The day of my arrival, Fidel had announced that the minimum essential harvest that year, in order to meet the Island's most pressing financial commitments, was seven million tons. After collecting opinions on all sides, and especially from my diplomatic colleagues, I had informed my government in early January that the harvest would in my opinion barely reach six million tons. In mid-January Fidel lowered the goal announced in his December 7 speech to six and a half million tons. Weeks passed in which the daily quota was not reached. The government railed against absenteeism in the fields; the vagrancy law was discussed, and that meant, in practice, imposing obligatory labor on the entire Island. The alternative would have been to create material incentives, to encourage the populace to work by means of market mechanisms; but in Cuba, according to Fidel's theory, progress would be achieved by advancing simultaneously along the roads of socialism and communism. A return to material incentives would mean the reestablishment of capitalist alienation. In consequence, economic development came to a dead end: One either abandoned the system of moral and ethical incentives, which was what distinguished the Cuban Revolution from all the rest and made it the purest and most advanced model of socialism in the world to date, or by virtue of the implacable irony of events one turned volunteer labor into forced labor.

Did the government want to hint to me, through S. M., that I should keep my mouth shut, in expectation that I would soon be replaced by the young man of the MAPU party who had been chosen by the Chilean government, approved by the Chilean Senate (which had not repeated its earlier rejection of a MAPU candidate), "studied" by the Cubans, and found, to their relief, to be one of their own?

I believe that my friend S. M. wanted to spare me a general mess—which apparently would have made everybody else happy—but I also believe that the high-ranking figure that "respected me" acted deliberately: I would halt all political activity, which was to say suspend my reports to the Chilean government on the Cuban political and economic situation (reports altogether too harsh for readers who were not necessarily politically mature, however well-located they might have been in the hierarchy of the Unidad Popular), and "they" would overlook my private friendships and my dissipations.

If another person's experience served for anything, I would have understood the message, but for experience to count, it must be one's own, and that means that one must live through situations down to their ultimate consequences. I thought about it, and I arrived at the conclusion that none of my activities could be considered political. My diplomatic life was purely formal; the real relations between Cuba and Chile were managed through the intermediary of the Cuban Embassy in Santiago de Chile. My presence on the Island was not only temporary but also entirely symbolic. My conversations with writers belonged to the world of private talk; they were of no significance. I should, however, have thought instead that everything—every sentence I spoke, every meeting, every joke, every official or unofficial trip or movement of any kind, most especially as these things concerned the Chilean chargé d'affaires of the Unidad Popular in this socialist Cuba—was political. But I still had a lot to learn.

And so, like passengers on an ocean liner blindly approaching the immovable iceberg, we cheerfully drank our rum and smoked our cigars from the
Diplomarket, to the accompaniment of Heberto's dramatic bursts of laughter,
Pablo Armando's exaggerated exclamations, Lezama Lima's brilliant mono-
tone monologue as he recited poems and told stories about the euphoric years
when the pseudo-surrealist circles of Paris and all of Europe came *en masse* to
the Hotel Habana Libre, and we sailed toward our fated end.

The wind whistled outside, giving the frequent blackouts caused by power
outages a certain air of drama, and the winter surf sprayed across the Malecón.
Out in the darkness of the Caribbean, its sails spread wide, the ship *Esmeralda*
was sailing toward its port in Havana. All was in readiness for its arrival. The
entrance into the harbor would take place on Monday, February 22, at precisely eight o'clock in the morning. My wife would fly that same day and hour
to Chile, where she would take over the care of our children and make
preparations for our trip to Paris, where I had already been assigned to the
Chilean Embassy with the responsibility of accompanying and working with
the ambassador/poet Pablo Neruda.

Havana, February 21, 1971

The Albanian chargé d'affaires, who speaks very good Spanish, says impas-
sively to me when I ask him how his wife is, that she is "not so good." "Not so
good?" "Yes. Not so good." The shortage of fruits and vegetables has affected
her liver. They have been in Cuba for four years now. "It's too much," he says,
emotionally. He tells me that the roof of his house leaks; rain comes in. He has
called the Services Section of the Foreign Ministry several times. Wearied by
their lack of action, he has written them letters. Weeks have gone by, and
nothing has been done. The roof of his house has collapsed. "What?" I can't
believe I heard right. "Collapsed," the chargé d'affaires repeats, not moving a
muscle. He is a small man, and he sits rigidly on the edge of his chair. He talks
to me about internationalism. When the Chinese become interested in helping
a country, he says, they do so with a commitment to internationalism. They are
the only country that truly practices socialist internationalism.

Suddenly, as though he fears having said too much, the diplomat stands,
says good-bye, and hurriedly begins to walk to the door, stopping every few
feet to try to keep me from accompanying him out. My insistence, which
derives from the rituals of protocol, and the syncopated, brusque gestures that
my colleague makes to stop me all along the hallway, at the door of the
elevator, and through the lobby, create a scene worthy of Chaplin. The idlers
sitting in their armchairs in the lobby, like people taking their ease on park

benches, with nothing apparently to do but kill time, must be startled at our gesticulations, whose total absurdity must strike these people more than it would another sort of person, since idleness and critical thought tend to go hand in hand.

Television gives a dramatized version of what is being called "the Olive affair." As the story told by journalists and the TV movie has it, Olive was a CIA agent who infiltrated the Cuban agricultural establishment and worked there as a high official until 1969. The film portrays the moments when Olive, in Rio de Janeiro and later in Madrid, makes contact with and receives money and instructions from his CIA masters. It also shows the Cuban counter-espionage services in action: The men from State Security get into Olive's office and the place he lives and take photos of all his papers with tiny cameras. In that respect, the movie serves a didactic function: It shows the people of Cuba, in a concrete way, the essential role played by State Security in the safety of the country.

In the middle section of the film, the actor playing Olive reports on the state of Cuban agriculture to his French colleague, René Dumont, who from time to time glances back over his shoulder to symbolize the burden of his guilty conscience. One is put on notice, therefore, that the information contained in Dumont's recent book on the Cuban economy has come directly (through Olive) from the United States Central Intelligence Agency.

The final sequences of the film are given a dramatic and sinister air by the director (or those behind him): In place of the actor who up until then has played Olive, the real person appears before the cameras, sitting at an empty table against a neutral background, in the midst of his full confession. This man is older than the actor who was playing him; his face is fuller, paler, and he speaks slowly, as though his mouth were dry and every word was an effort for him. He says that Dumont always asked him for more information that would allow him to discredit the Cuban Revolution abroad; he, Olive, complied with those requests brazenly and cold-bloodedly, in accord with his orders from his masters at the CIA.

There are rumors that day before yesterday Pierre Gollendorf, the French photographer who has been living here since the Cultural Congress in 1968, was jailed. He was supposed to return to France in two days. He is a friend of Padilla's. Two Germans, likewise friends of Padilla's, were also arrested and jailed a few days before they were to leave the country. In order to be allowed to leave, one of them confessed to being a CIA agent. Unless I am very mistaken, I think, Padilla's situation has become really dangerous. He, meanwhile, oblivious to these alarms, which are the universal topic of conversation and intellectual speculation, goes on as if he were in the best of all possible worlds.

In the reception at the Casa de las Américas at which the year's literary prizes were handed out, Haydée Santamaría told Monsignor Zacchi, Coloane, and me the story of a Batista henchman who was putting a rope around the neck of her brother Aldo, in preparation for sending him to the great beyond. When Aldo for some reason gave his full name, the henchman looked at him in amazement.

"You're Abel's brother?"

"Yes," said Aldo.

"I knew Abel when he was a kid, back at his parents' place. How could you, Abel's brother, become a revolutionary?"

"Because you and those like you, Batista's men, tortured and killed my brother Abel for his part in the assault on the Moncada barracks."

The Batista man, open-mouthed, loosened the knot and let Aldo Santamaría escape. He is now commander-in-chief of the Revolutionary Navy.

"What do you mean, a CIA agent! That's absurd!" These were Padilla's words to me about the television program. "Olive was one of the few people who knew anything about agriculture in Cuba."

Padilla's earlier experience in the Ministry of Foreign Trade, where he worked with Alberto Mora, gave him greater knowledge of the Cuban government than most of his literary colleagues. His comments such as this one on the "Olive affair" were another factor that led to his imprisonment a few weeks later.

"What's it all about, then?"

"Ah!" said Padilla, shrugging his shoulders in a gesture loaded with meaning.

I later realized that these gestures, at once explosive and repressed (since they marked the limits of the possibility of expression), arose each time we touched upon the subject of the responsibility that the country's political leadership, Fidel himself, bore for certain actions. The gesture revealed, in this case, that Olive's crime consisted of not having been in agreement with the Commander-in-Chief's agricultural plans. He had spoken of his reservations to René Dumont, and Dumont had put them in a book, a book that praised the figure of Ché Guevara for his openness to criticism and his constant effort not to lose contact with the people. This attitude, Dumont implied, contrasted with that of the Prime Minister. Later, both in his published letter and in his public act of self-criticism, Padilla would league Dumont with the journalist and essayist K. S. Karol as important agents of the CIA. The evidence, according

to Padilla, was so flagrant that no further proof was necessary. French academics I spoke to later in Paris laughed at these accusations. The accusations,
they said, more seriously discredited the accuser and those who pulled his
strings than the men accused. Those same French academics also recalled
unhappy instances of other self-criticisms, other accusations (which were
known in Chile only among a handful of specialists) whose texts and images
had made a grievous impact in their time on the European Left, an impact
which in retrospect took on great dramatic power when news of Khrushchev's
secret speech on Stalinism to the Twentieth Communist Party Congress began
to leak out. Cuba was repeating the same errors, though with a certain
rudimentary (and perhaps, all things considered, benign) ingenuousness
which revealed not only that one never learns from another person's experience
but also that nobody had stopped to look at and reflect upon that experience.
From the first rigid (though for obvious reasons veiled) anti-Soviet attitudes of
two or three years ago, Cuba had swung without much reflection, and for
purely pragmatic motives, to today's pro-Soviet stance. As for the lessons of
history, they had been ignored—and that meant that no stage of the hard road
would be spared Cuba.

Meanwhile, Laura Allende and her group were, with the most unconditional
sort of enthusiasm, touring the sites of the Revolution's greatest achievements.
One night they attended a session of the Popular Tribunals, and they returned
delighted. That was the authentic justice of the people, destined to replace the
class justice that existed in Chile. And the truth is that attacking the Judiciary
in Chile, with its defects, its slowness, its dusty and moth-eaten files, its
corrupt chambers, its hard line with the chicken-thieves or young rebels and its
leniency with the white collar crimes of the *haute bourgeoisie* was no great
feat.

At a reception at the Chinese Embassy I ran into Ramón Perdomo, the
young assistant editor of *Granma* who had been present the night of my first
conversation with Fidel. Perdomo was the person who had interviewed me
when I confessed, with flagrant shamelessness, my preference for literary over
diplomatic work.

"You still have no house?!" he exclaimed in disbelief. "But I heard Fidel
with my own ears when he gave the order, in front of you yourself, that you be
given the best house."

Perdomo assured me that Fidel had not the slightest idea that I still hadn't
been assigned a house. He would tell Fidel himself, and he promised me that as
soon as Fidel found out, he'd make sure his orders were carried out. We agreed
that I would call Perdomo Monday or Tuesday. We could take the opportunity
at the same time to talk about press coverage of the *Esmeralda*.

My secretary called Perdomo and made an appointment for me at *Granma*. The secretary-consul and I sat down at a round table with a smiling, impassive group of people. Perdomo was only interested in the Chilean training ship's visit. His keenness to find me a house had vanished like magic. The woman journalist who had been there the night of my initial conversation with Fidel was also at the table, with a neutral smile. The secretary-consul (who was, as we all discovered, a specialist in naval matters) gave details on the *Esmeralda* that were scrupulously noted down by our interlocutors. About my house not a word, and I suspected that it would have been inopportune to mention the matter to Perdomo. The whole affair of the house must have allowed the young man to make some progress—useful, even essential in his professional work as a reporter—in the understanding of reality. Assuming that he belonged to that species of person capable of learning from experience.

4

After all the preparations and announcements, the day of the arrival of the *Esmeralda* had come at last. Pilar was to take a plane that same morning for Mexico City, on her way to Chile, but since my responsibilities with the *Esmeralda* kept me from going with her to the airport, we said our good-byes at the hotel. We had agreed that she would not comment on Cuba's internal difficulties while she was in Chile. Everything she said would inevitably be twisted, blown out of proportion, and spread to the four winds.

I departed for the dock with my faithful Tomás, the second of the drivers I had in Havana. We drove at full speed through the cool morning breezes; the sky was clear and the sea a beautiful bright blue. At the hotel, someone had excitedly reported that the outline of the *Esmeralda* had been seen on the horizon. The arrival of the Chilean Navy training ship, flag aloft and crew assembled on the deck, was the most visible (even spectacular) sign of the breaking of the blockade, even more so than my own arrival (and especially as my arrival, because of the error on the part of Protocol, went utterly un-heralded). The closer the Alfa came to the fortress of La Cabaña, where the ship was to dock, the more people we saw running to find a place on the parapets or pouring out onto balconies to watch the ceremony. Sails lowered, the ship had turned its bow down the narrow mouth of the harbor. It had to sail down a long, narrow channel marked off between the outjutting precipice on which La Cabaña was built on the one side and the old city of Havana on the other, before it came to Pier Number One, which opened onto the heart of the old city just at the headquarters building of the Cuban Navy.

The entrance to the ports area of Old Havana is marked by a colonial-period stone bastion and the lions and baroque lamps of the Paseo del Prado,

124

whose heavy wrought-iron frames and standards somehow braved the corro-
sion of the sea air. By the time we reached the curve in the Malecón where
this area begins, the ship was already gliding up the channel. The bare masts
and yardarms of the boat stood out stark against the high, stern gray walls
of La Cabaña. A crowd had gathered on the shore, and people were shouting,
applauding, and waving in enthusiastic greeting. There were fewer people
than I had thought there would be, fewer than the grand sight deserved; on
the other hand, though, one could hardly have asked for more: it was eight
o'clock Monday morning, and there was a harvest going on. Children,
women, and older people predominated. The car, chauffeured by Tomás,
moved slowly through the lines of people, until we drove onto the pier itself.
All the television cameras were right up front. The most famous newscaster
in Cuba (whom I would see racing through the streets of El Vedado or
Miramar in an Alfa Romeo sports model that my drivers, who knew everything there was to be known about cars, said he got through the good offices
of the Prime Minister himself) was narrating the scene, microphone in hand,
even as he waved at me and interrupted himself to tell his listeners that the
Chilean chargé d'affaires had just that moment arrived. A Western reporter
might have added that the chargé d'affaires was wearing a lightweight navy-
blue suit, as the solemnity of the occasion required, with a dark blue tie, and
that he looked serious and a bit pale, which might be attributed to a lack
of sleep and the tensions of the last few weeks, and that he seemed somewhat
nervous—or perhaps it was that after having suffered the pressures and
provocations visited upon him in a foreign land as representative of a country
in the ferment of revolution, his heart was stirred by this long-anticipated
encounter with the symbol of one of the most solid institutions of his own
country, an institution cherished in the deepest depths of his memory and,
for him, going back to the experience of his youth, the years of which had
been spent by him in the foothills of the majestic Mount Santa Lucía, in
the National Forest at Santiago, beside the Río Mapocho, and most memora-
bly on the dusty, sunbaked shore of the bay at Valparaíso whose sparkling
azure waters held the ironclad hull of the *Almirante Latorre* or the legendary white masses of the *Bremen* and the *Queen Mary* or, years later,
the winged presence of this same *Esmeralda*. But most likely the Prime
Minister's favorite newscaster, in spite of a good dose of the necessary
reporter's instinct and imagination, would omit these last pointless touches,
however picturesque, and simply try to paint for his listeners the most
neutral description of the facts, leaving aside the bits concerning the
harsh terrain of recent history and the subtleties of life in society, matters
which his Western colleagues, in their zeal to turn dead facts into

newsworthy attention-grabbers, would probably have been more than happy to put to use.

It was strange to see those familiar, trusting, friendly faces lined up on the deck of the ship I had seen so many times before tied up to the dock in Valparaíso. The psychological pressures of the last three months, which had insensibly become a kind of second nature to me, suddenly seemed to relax; I discovered that a more peaceful sort of human relationship was after all possible, one not based on all-absorbing and omnipresent suspicion. The hierarchical and class-based system, visible, even before the boat berthed, in the difference of uniforms and attitudes worn by officers and sailors, was clearly anachronistic. That anachronism, however, brought me a disconcerting sense of relief, a sense of returning to the familiar aspects of life, a sense that the political commissars would not have hesitated one second in calling by its name and condemning.

The captain saluted me from the bridge, and accompanied the salute with a slight smile of recognition of a fellow-countryman. The white gangway, at the base of which were two little wheels that rolled backward or forward as the ship swayed with the tide, was lowered, and we boarded the ship. With us was the naval commander of the harbor and the aide-de-camp appointed by the Navy. I heard the order, "Present arms!" and then "The chargé d'affaires of Chile!" and I stopped, looking up at the flag, while the officers stood at attention, swords unsheathed, and the band played an excerpt from the moving "Hymn of Yungay," a patriotic anthem composed during the first war against Peru. My generation, which had succumbed to some of the bad habits of surrealism and anarchism, had always looked with mockery upon patriotic shows of this sort; they seemed to us, if not altogether moth-eaten beyond rescue, at the least impregnated with the stale odor of nineteenth-century nationalism. In my youth I had often quoted Neruda's own adolescent lines:

> Homeland, a word as sad
> as thermometer, or elevator . . .

I even mistrusted some of the overly solemn verses of Neruda's *Canto General* ("Universal Song of Chile"), but at this moment the emotion I felt at the honors rendered me by the crew of the *Esmeralda* showed me how terrible had been the psychological pressures I'd been undergoing for these three months.

When the music ended I saluted the captain and three or four of the officers that surrounded him. We (that is, I and the two Cuban officers) were then led into the captain's office. On the wall there was an oil portrait of Admiral Arturo Prat, and on each side of it an antique map of Chile. The captain said that until a short time before, the maps had been reproductions; when Pablo Neruda saw they were fake, he had made a gift to the *Esmeralda* of the originals. The anecdote made me consider the difference in the political habits of Cuba and my own country, where a Communist poet could afford to make such a gift to the most conservative, or at least most tradition-bound, of the armed forces, and the sense of well-being, of relief, that came over me—revealing my recalcitrant bourgeois origins, which merited my being cast into outer darkness—was all the more profound.

Captain Ernesto Jobet Ojeda, who commanded the training ship *Esmeralda*, was a man some fifty years of age. He was tall, athletic, energetic, and invariably good-humored; he loved jokes, and he had a certain youthful ingenuousness about him that in no way excluded intelligence. When the Cuban officers left, we had a fifteen-minute conversation alone. I informed him of the schedule. The captain gave considerable importance to the crew's having an afternoon and evening free and to both the officers' and men's being able to spend a night on shore. After all, they had been at sea for more than thirty days. I explained to the captain that the possibility of entertainment outside the schedule was virtually nil. Arrangements might be made for some of the men to stay at hotels, but there could be no question of showing up at midnight and asking for a room. And as for bars, restaurants, night clubs, and other "places of amusement," things weren't quite the same here in Havana as in the other ports they'd be visiting. The Revolution was experiencing shortages of consumer goods, and therefore strict rationing was in force. But of course they would see all this with their own eyes.

Captain Jobet was not one to beat around the bush. He realized, without making very much of it, that everything anyone said or did would be closely watched and taken note of. He looked at his watch, settled his sword and the other trappings of ceremony that he had on, and we went outside. The harbor master and aide-de-camp were awaiting us on deck.

A crowd shouting "*¡Viva Chile! ¡Viva Allende!*" applauded us as we walked, at the long, quick step set by Captain Jobet, toward the Revolutionary Navy Building. The Cuban commander-in-chief of the Navy, Aldo Santamaría, greeted us in a large reception room next to his office, where we were also met by the flashbulbs of photographers and the TV and newsreel cameras. Among Santamaría's retinue there was an officer whose name and features were Danish; he had lived in Chile and sailed through the southern channels.

After the unfailing daiquiris we were shown the radar and telecommunications rooms, which were doubtlessly much more modern and well-equipped than those of the Chilean Navy. On a wall-map was marked the place the *Esmeralda* had passed the night, waiting for the hour set for her entry into Havana harbor.

"So you had us spotted," said Jobet smiling.

Santamaría answered with a monosyllable. He was a burly, unsociable-looking man of few words. He struck the Chilean sailors as downright unpleasant; I, on the other hand, liked and trusted him. I sensed in him a person who had been beaten down, crushed almost, who had been terribly disillusioned and who, in spite of his position, had no real power. I always thought of him as an innocent, good-natured sort of bear, swept up in the tides of history. The attitude of many of the Chilean officers toward Aldo Santamaría betrayed (to me, at least) their political and social prejudices. I considered it to a certain extent natural, on the other hand, that these officers would sooner or later be distressed and alienated by the deterioration of the city, the shortages of consumer goods, and the environment of suspiciousness and State Security surveillance (this last, especially). The men of power in Cuba would say that we, the Chilean officers and I, lacked a revolutionary conscience, but the men of power, in Cuba as everywhere else, assume that everything can be fixed with a ritual phrase repeated often enough.

That morning's agenda continued with a greeting by the Vice Prime Minister of Cuba, Minister of the Revolutionary Armed Forces, Comandante Raúl Castro. I remember a little mishap that occurred. We stepped into the spacious elevator, "Made in the USA" in the fifties, with our staff; the doors closed, but after a few seconds we realized that the elevator was not moving. After much effort, the Cuban officer, disconsolate, at last resigned himself to pressing the "Door Open" button. The doors did not work, either. Through all this Captain Jobet retained his dead calm and good humor. When the doors at last opened, we were taken to an elevator located in a back hallway, one not used by visitors. There the imposing Armed Forces building showed its tatters: One of the enormous plate-glass windows was broken and had been patched with tape just like any building in the residential areas of Havana might have been.

Raúl Castro told the story of the voyage of the *Granma*.[1] They had had a stormy, dangerous crossing, and everyone (for no one had any experience as a

---

[1] The voyage between Mexico and the coast of Cuba that led to the guerrilla war in the Sierra Maestra and that literally changed the history of Latin America.

sailor) had gotten seasick. But the *Granma* had led to the Revolutionary Navy; the Cuban Revolution had been launched with a naval expedition.

The secretary-consul was quite taken with the personality of Raúl Castro. He declared that this was a "can-do" man, in allusion no doubt to the rumors that the real power in Cuba lay in his hands. But Raúl had quite deliberately avoided discussing any subject in any depth, showing not only the tightly controlled, cold character that contrasted so sharply with that of his brother Fidel but also the talent (which never ceased to surprise me) of carrying on light conversation.

In the office of the mayor of Havana we were also spoken to about history, though history of a period less recent than that of the expedition of the *Granma*. The young city historian was with the mayor, and his knowledge of Havana was prodigious. Jobet, who shared with most of the bourgeoisie and petit-bourgeoisie of Chile an obsession with history, liked him immediately.

The morning, which had been filled with ceremonial activities dictated by protocol, culminated with a luncheon on board ship, where to my delight, after long months in Cuba, I was presented with a wonderful bowl of *chupe de locos*, the conch-and-potato stew that is to Chilean cuisine what *bouillabaisse* is to the French.

As lunch was ending, Captain Jobet told me he had decided to hold the reception that he was to give for the Cuban authorities on the boat itself. He would ask the shipboard orchestra (members of the crew, all) to play for it. It would be the next day, Tuesday, at eight in the evening. That Monday, after lunch, the little office and the Alfa Romeo of the Chilean Embassy were feverishly dedicated to making telephone calls and delivering invitations to the diplomatic corps. Through the Cuban Office of Protocol, Fidel and the entire government hierarchy were invited. Would Fidel come? Would some minister, at least, come? And what about the chiefs of mission? The invitations were going out so soon before the event. Some of the invitations, in fact, could only be delivered on Tuesday morning. Captain Jobet had sent me his schedule, in some detail, by air mail, without taking into account the blockade, and the letter, posted in Valparaíso, had arrived at the same time the boat had. Fortunately a German fellow with Chilean citizenship who was in charge of provisioning the ship, a man named Helmut (who since he was following its itinerary by plane had set up shop in the Habana Riviera forty-eight hours before its arrival), helped us.

Besides making sure Jobet's invitations got out, I had to finish the plans for my own reception, which would be held Wednesday in the rooms on the top floor of the Habana Libre. I felt confident about the headwaiter at the Habana Libre: He belonged to the days of don Emilio, whom he had worked with, as he told me with great pride, on numerous occasions. He assured me that my reception would be a complete success. It was a pleasure for him to work for a relative, a genuine nephew, of the "gentleman" that he had known don Emilio to be. I could rest easy.

I was assured of all this by the headwaiter, with a smile and a slightly old-Spanish accent, in his small office in the hotel. He was sitting under photographs of Ché and Fidel cut out of the newspaper. On a bookshelf were five or six gastronomical volumes in English, French, and Spanish, and a few revolutionary publications. He told me that the Chilean wine, which he was quite familiar with, served at the appropriate moment, would signal the climactic point of the reception. Just let him do his job! he assured me. Not to worry!

About three o'clock that Tuesday afternoon Meléndez called to tell me that they needed to go over the boat for security reasons.

"Security on board will be guaranteed by me," Jobet responded when I managed to contact him by telephone.

"Protocol's telephone call to me," I told Jobet, "makes me think that Fidel will be attending your reception."

Okay. The Prime Minister, as the captain's guest of honor on board the *Esmeralda*, would be assured of the most absolute security. But Jobet insisted on one point that he had made to me the day before: The regulations of the Chilean Navy forbade armed persons on board ship. Jobet was unyielding on this point. No doubt the rule derived from some ancient naval custom intended to prevent surprise takeovers; Jobet was not a person to depart from strict observance of naval tradition.

"I understand all that," Meléndez said, "but the docks can be used to stage an assassination. You can see that!"

Through the noise of the telephone installed on the deck of his ship, the captain responded: "The docks belong to them. They can search them all they want to."

I called Meléndez back.

"All right," he said, grumpily. "But you understand, Edwards, that if the Prime Minister attends the reception . . ."

"I'll try to find some formula to fix things," I said. "Your people can search and guard the accesses to the ship. You can be absolutely sure that there will be no problem whatsoever on board. Quite the contrary! But I have to insist that the rules of the Chilean Navy will not allow an armed escort on a warship."

My sense was that Meléndez, on the other end of the line, was nonplussed. He didn't know how to react to our insistence. For our part, we now knew that Fidel, and in consequence most government officials and the greater part of the diplomatic corps, would be attending the reception.

Captain Jobet's party coincided with an important diplomatic event. Weeks earlier the Soviet Embassy had sent out invitations for a reception to be held that same evening in celebration of the anniversary of the Red Army. In Havana, the Soviet reception was serious competition. But Meléndez' calls had given me some optimism about the success of ours, too.

I arrived at the ship around seven, an hour early. A canopy had been erected on the deck, with pennants flying all along the sides, making a brightly colored wall. The officers were wearing impeccable dress whites. Captain Jobet, with surprising calm and his usual jaunty good humor, was striding about, examining the last details, and rubbing his hands together. The first day, seeing his apparent ingenuousness, I had thought he had been ill-chosen for his mission in Havana. Now I began to suspect exactly the opposite, and I was left with no doubt before the night was over.[2]

The Cuban woman who was the secretary at the embassy appeared in a long flowered dress at the foot of the gangway at about seven-thirty. She came aboard and I introduced her to the captain and two or three officers. She seemed delighted to be on board: She looked at everything with big round eyes, filled with apparent innocence. At ten minutes to eight Sr. Saavedra, the secretary-consul arrived, sputtering with indignation. The authorities had halted him at the gate because he had not brought his invitation; his diplomatic identification card that accredited him as a member of the Chilean Embassy had not been enough for them. After a half hour of arguing he had been

---

[2] In re-reading the manuscript I note that the captain's calm, his indifference to or ignorance of the tensions in the air, were one of the possible forms the "encounter" of the Chilean worldview with the Cuban worldview might take. My personal experience portrayed that encounter in another way, though perhaps not so different after all. The encounter of Chile with Cuba was the encounter of the South with the Caribbean, the encounter, in some sense, of Tradition with Revolution. Chile—a defective though stable democracy, conservative or reform-minded depending upon the observer's point of view, and Cuba—the dazzling and tragic Island that had gone from a dictatorship of the Right to a dictatorship of the extreme Left. This book, more than a "testimonio" on the Cuban Revolution, is a story, at various levels, of the encounter of two worldviews at a critical time for both countries. Before, it had been specialists, experts, leftist militants, intellectuals, professional politicians who had traveled to Cuba. Now the encounter was going on at all levels, and the clash, or collision, or simply "meeting," had its dramatic aspects, as it had, too, moving and burlesque aspects. It was the "encounter of two worlds," two different versions of Latin-American history.

allowed to enter, but just to get an invitation; his wife was being held hostage outside for his return. The indignation of the consul, who considered the distinction of his post as representative of his country to have been insulted, was vented in the presence of the Cuban aide-de-camp, who put on a most innocent and noncommittal face; I myself tried hard not to laugh. Later I learned that others of our invited guests had been retained at the gate to the pier, so I sent down invitations. Due to the pressure of time, many invitations had been made by telephone by my secretary. Some of the guests, among them the secretary of the Swedish Embassy, were unable to get word to me, so in the face of the guards' obstinacy there was nothing for them to do but turn around and go home again.

At precisely eight o'clock an avalanche of guests came rolling down the pier in closed formation. Leading the platoon were President of the Republic Osvaldo Dorticós and Minister of Foreign Relations Raúl Roa. I sent word to Jobet, who immediately gave a series of naval protocol orders that went straight over my head. Dorticós and Roa came up the gangway followed by other ministers, military authorities, and members of the diplomatic corps, while for Jobet and me there began the round of greetings and handshakes. People were introduced first, in a loud voice, to Jobet, and then it fell my turn to shake their hands. Even the Soviet ambassador came, explaining that he had to return to his embassy in five minutes, since he was the host of the Red Army reception, but that he hadn't wanted to miss the Chilean naval reception. The person who arrived neither then nor ever was Jobet's own Cuban host, Raúl Castro, though he did attend the Soviet gathering.

The greetings at the head of the gangway must have lasted some twenty minutes—interminable minutes, which left my right hand numb. At last the pier was deserted. Strains of music were heard on the deck.

"Well!" smiled Captain Jobet. "Let's go up and see to our guests."

"Wait!" I blurted out.

Along the empty pier three or four Alfa Romeos were approaching the ship at breakneck speed.

The cars stopped abruptly at the foot of the gangway. Their doors all opened at once and military men with large revolvers strapped to their waists began pouring out. I recognized the red beard of Manuel Piñeiro Losada, Vice Minister of the Interior and head of State Security. From another car Fidel Castro had meanwhile emerged; followed by six or seven men, he strode purposefully toward the gangway and came aboard. He greeted Jobet very cordially and with great courtesy. Then, icily, he offered me his hand. Behind him, in spite of the warnings from Jobet that I in turn had communicated with absolute clarity to Protocol, eight or ten armed men were coming aboard, and there was nothing that the captain of the *Esmeralda*, in those circumstances and in the confusion of the moment, could do to stop them.

The young officer in charge of the cloakroom saw what was going on, and made a small act of challenge to the Prime Minister: "Your cap!" he said.

Somewhat disconcerted, Fidel, who was carrying his cap in his hand, extended it to the officer, who took it and gave Fidel a numbered ticket in return, as though Fidel were an ordinary visitor.

Fidel looked at his ticket a moment and then said, with admirable levity, "I got number eighty-three."

Followed by his praetorian guard, he immediately went up to the main deck, where the orchestra was by now filling the night air with music. The officers of the *Esmeralda*, in their sparkling white uniforms, stood in a hostile double rank looking with obvious displeasure at the Commander-in-Chief's personal escort with their big revolvers at their waists. Fidel went straight up to one of the officers and shook his hand, then to another, and soon the ice began to break. I had to deal with Dorticós and Roa: While Fidel was greeting officialdom, the two men had been left standing completely alone at the rail.

The foreign diplomats were delighted to have seen Fidel; some, after months or years on the Island, were meeting him for the first time. Many of them came up to me to thank me for the chance to meet him, as though I possessed the keys to open any door. Captain Jobet, meanwhile, accompanied by Fidel and Laura Allende, performed his role as host with perfect naturalness. The problem of the praetorian guard, which save for the incident with Fidel's cap and the initial coldness of the ship's officers, seemed to have passed completely.

Fidel chatted with the members of the orchestra, exclaimed over the pisco sours and the empanadas, and, as was his custom, told jokes—which were greeted with noisy laughter. After about an hour of this, Captain Jobet asked me to invite the Prime Minister to his private office. I was to take charge of Dorticós and Roa.

Prime Minister Fidel Castro and Captain Ernesto Jobet went down the ladder, and immediately after them went the President of the Republic Osvaldo Dorticós, Chancellor Raúl Roa, and last the Chilean chargé d'affaires, who had been warned by the iciness of the Prime Minister's handshake that his debauchery with dissident poets and writers was not to be overlooked. The little group entered the captain's private office, and after them, with no advance warning, the muscular and well-armed members of the Commander-in-Chief's personal guard elbowed their way in as well.

Captain Jobet opened his arms to hold back the escort.

"Gentlemen!" he said. "I must ask you to remain outside this office."

In his voice there was but the slightest tremor of rage. The soldiers, headed by Manuel Piñeiro, did not budge an inch; they looked stolidly straight ahead. I noted that Fidel, extremely uncomfortable, pretended that his entire attention was consumed by the objects that decorated the office. Raúl Roa and Dorticós stood as stiff and inexpressive as statues.

"Gentlemen!" Jobet insisted even more strongly than at first. "This is *my* office, my *private* office. *I* choose whom to invite into it. So I must ask you to leave."

The soldiers still did not budge, and their faces remained neutral. Captain Jobet, at that, turned toward Fidel, who was still examining the objects that decorated the room.

"Prime Minister," he said, gesturing toward the guard, "please."

Fidel stepped toward his guard and made a gesture that he was to be left alone. Piñeiro gave a half-turn and the soldiers stepped outside into the hallway, where they took up positions that enabled them to see inside the office.

With astounding composure, as though the incident had been of not the slightest importance, Captain Jobet immediately was transformed into the perfect host. The Prime Minister had no doubt heard of the pisco sour, one of Chile's favorite drinks? Of course! The Prime Minister declared that he was an old admirer of the pisco sour; his Chilean friends always brought him bottles of pisco. The bottle offered by the captain of the *Esmeralda* was an excellent one. "Excellent!" echoed Dorticós and Roa, who had taken seats together off to one side, facing Fidel and Jobet. Jobet came up to me and whispered in my ear: "Go ask Laurita Allende and Haydée Santamaría to come down if they'd like."

Laurita asked me to wait a moment. Before she came down she wanted to talk to the sailors. Haydée was also chatting with the crew; she told me that she'd be down in a few seconds. After a few words with some of the sailors and the cook's helper, Laura Allende joined me and we went down to the captain's office. Haydée remained on deck, saying she'd be down later.

Laura Allende sat to the right and in front of Fidel, to one side of the portrait of Arturo Prat that commanded the room. Served in abundance, the pisco sours had begun to loosen tongues and lighten the atmosphere of the first uncomfortable moments. Jobet described the winds the ship had had for the last few days of their trip. There was some talk of Arturo Prat and the Battle of Iquique at which the second *Esmeralda* had been sunk. Fidel said he was reading Gonzalo Bulnes' *Historia de la guerra del Pacífico* ("History of the War of the Pacific"), a copy of which he'd been given by a Christian Democratic senator who had visited the Island. He gave some details that indicated a pretty thorough familiarity with the book. Then he turned the subject to the uniforms of the Chilean and Cuban navies.

"You see, Prime Minister," said Jobet with good-natured kidding, "you may give no importance to naval traditions. But the stripes and the silver and gold bars have very precise significance. They indicate the number of masts and the grade of ship the officer captains. That is why the captain of a frigate wears three stripes and three bars, corresponding to the three masts of his ship, while the captain of a warship wears four. If I may say so, the insignia of the Cuban officers symbolize nothing specific."

Fidel put on one of those expressions of interest and curiosity so typical of him, especially when he wants to disarm an angry interlocutor with his apparent ingenuousness. He said the uniforms had been copied, not so long ago, from the Soviet Navy, from whom because of the blockade Cuba received all its military matériel, but he had to admit that the emblems had been adopted more or less at random.

There was a moment of silence and then Fidel suddenly, with a serious expression, stood and began to pace back and forth before Jobet.

"Captain," he said, "I want to apologize. I have felt absolutely safe on your ship, and I am very happy, very pleased to be on it. However, the peculiar situation of the Cuban Revolution—the blockade, the foreign threat to our national security—gives my life a political importance. My life is linked to the survival of the revolutionary process that we have undertaken. These men you see with me are responsible for protecting my life under any and all circumstances. I confess to you that this causes me great personal inconvenience in many ways. Many times I'd like to get rid of them and go places by myself. But they do their duty, and they follow me everywhere. So I ask your understanding, and that you forgive the incident a few minutes ago. I repeat to you that I have felt very much at home, very comfortable, and very safe here."

Jobet replied in a most friendly and understanding way. Laura Allende, who had not been present when the guard burst into the office, spoke up: "Salvador goes everywhere with his personal guard too. I don't see why that should surprise the captain."

The conversation that night, in that sanctuary of Chilean naval tradition anchored at Pier Number One in the harbor of Havana, Cuba, "first free territory of the Americas," was animated and somewhat disconnected. The rivers of pisco sours, worthy of the famously generous hospitality of the Chilean people, helped to loosen inhibitions. Later Jobet told me that when

Allende had come to the dock to see the *Esmeralda* off, he had indeed, as his sister had said, come aboard with the Group of Personal Friends (or GAP, by its Spanish-language initials) that, seen from the viewpoint of the dock in Havana, looked to be a more or less faithful imitation of the group that protected the Maximum Leader of Cuba. When the time came to offer Allende a drink, Jobet went on, one of these personal friends opened a briefcase and took out a bottle of whisky and a glass that was taken along everywhere for the president. No one else could have a hand in preparing his drink. It was clear that Jobet was making a discreet allusion to the introduction of Cuban habits into the political life of Chile.

These two details—Fidel's guard and Allende's bottle of whisky—showed how security measures could pervert the political objectives a country seeks. Means do influence ends. The courtesy shown to the Chilean Navy, as symbolized by the visit to the *Esmeralda* of Fidel in Havana and of Allende in Valparaíso, was contradicted and discredited in each case by an obsession with security, one of the diseases of modern life.

Afterward, in a revelation that struck me as indiscreet, Fidel said that Allende had called him to ask that he greet the *Esmeralda* personally. Fidel assured Jobet that he had put all his other activities aside so that he might comply with his friend Salvador Allende's request. What thoughts might this little revelation have produced in Jobet? Behind his courteous and good-humored manner was a man of great reserve. The longer I knew him, the more enigmatic he became to me—like one of those ship's captains, simple and frank in appearance but inwardly very complex, that figure in the novels of Joseph Conrad.

There was a moment when the training ship's gold-embossed visitors' book was opened on the dining table and Dorticós and Fidel signed long messages of good wishes. Fidel's spoke of the Cuban and Chilean revolutions.

"You've got me mixed up in the Revolution now!" Jobet exclaimed.

"Do you mean you haven't realized, captain," Fidel quickly riposted, "that the Chilean naval traditions that you admire so greatly are revolutionary traditions?"

Fidel's point was well taken. I intervened to remind everyone that the first *Esmeralda* was a ship that had been seized by Cochrane, in the midst of the War of Liberation, from the Spanish imperial fleet anchored in the harbor at Callao.

We all sat down again and continued our conversation, with witty remarks from both Fidel and Jobet. The pisco sours had given way now to *hors d'oeuvres* and glasses of Chilean wine. Off in their own corner, Dorticós and Roa laughed on cue, but otherwise said not a word. It was strange to see a president of the republic and a minister of foreign relations taking such an obvious back seat. Laurita talked about the tremendous amount of work she had done during her visit to the Island.

"And you, sir," said Fidel, turning toward Jobet, "what would you like to do during your stay in Havana?"

"You know something, Prime Minister?" said the dauntless Jobet serenely, "I'd very much like to play a round of golf."

"Golf!" Laurita Allende exclaimed in dismay. "How can you think of playing golf in Cuba, captain? Why all I've done is work. I've done volunteer work in the country, even on Sunday at the crack of dawn. I've visited factories, schools, women's organizations, people's tribunals—I haven't rested for a second."

"I do volunteer work all the time," Jobet replied, his coolly pleasant attitude never wavering. "Being captain of a training ship, where discipline has to be maintained and two hundred youngsters have to be taught to be sailors, is not an eight-hour-a-day job. I have to work night and day—and Sundays, too. That's why when we reach port, my favorite way to rest is to play a round of golf. Golf courses always have trees and grass and clean air. They are beautifully landscaped. And as you know, all men have something of the boy about them; we like hitting and chasing balls. If you can do that in a beautiful natural setting as well, why then."

The congresswoman never relented, however, in her protests. Fidel, who was listening to all this attentively, suddenly stood up and put a hand on Laurita Allende's shoulder.

"Laurita!" he jokingly said to her. "You'll never win over the Chilean sailors with all that talk of work!"

"And besides," Jobet went on, "everyone knows that the Prime Minister is a great lover of sports."

"We'll get a golf game together for you," said Fidel. "Your aide-de-camp will be notifying you."

I don't remember whether Laura's protests continued. Meanwhile, my friend and fellow Chilean Cristián Huneeus, who had been invited to the reception by the captain, was making signs to us from the hallway, behind the double line of bodyguards sitting on the floor or leaning against the wall in boredom. Jobet signaled him enthusiastically to come in, and greeted him with a great hug.

"And what is it you do?" Fidel asked Huneeus after Jobet had introduced the two men.

"I am a writer and a professor of literature at the University of Chile," Huneeus replied.

If he had announced his parallel profession as apple and lemon grower, he'd have had a better chance to favorably impress Fidel. But Cristián Huneeus thought, as many of our friends still think, that literature is a passport to the world, or at least a shield against it.

"Another writer!" exclaimed Fidel.

A while later, Fidel was looking at a calendar printed in Chile that bore a fragment of poetry for each month. His very limited liking for writers was manifested in the mocking or sarcastic remarks he made about each fragment. One by Nicanor Parra inspired great hilarity in him. Another, in which with terse, harsh, and well-crafted lines, Gabriela Mistral described a sea urchin, provoked Fidel to say, shrugging his shoulders and flipping the page, "I don't see what this has to do with a sea urchin." But then he bumped face-to-face into a poem by Neruda, two somber, solemn lines. I was looking over Fidel's shoulder, and he could not but have been aware of my friendship for the poet. There was the added fact that Neruda was one of the most important members of the Unidad Popular, and that he had been attacked from Cuba by all and sundry, with an enormous outpouring of propaganda, during the period when Fidel's relations with the Chilean Communist party were in decline. Fidel read the quotation from Neruda and turned the page without a word.

As was customary those days in conversations with Chileans in Cuba, there was talk of the wines sold by Baltazar Castro. Several of us made jokes about its quality. The wine Castro exported was a light wine, without great body, and though it wasn't bad for the tropics, criticizing it had become a party game for my compatriots. Someone added the fact that don Baltazar, in spite of his friendship with Fidel, had broken away from many militants on the Left in Chile to support the Christian Democrat government of Frei.

"These Chileans are a strange lot," Fidel observed. "They disagree about everything but the quality of Baltazar's wine. Although he sells it at blockade prices, I'll tell you!" He laughed as he paced the room with great strides, as though he were stepping off its dimensions for some measurement he was taking.

"As chargé d'affaires," I said, "and after conversing with the Chilean agricultural mission here, I am authorized to offer, at the same price, a wine of considerably better quality."

Fidel stopped pacing and looked at me fixedly.

"You are chargé d'affaires," he said, after a few seconds of silence, and switching from the formal *usted* to the familiar (and possibly somewhat aggressive) *tu* form of the personal pronoun with me, "but you don't know anything about *business* affairs! Aren't you a writer?" This last word was not spoken as a compliment.

"I do know something about business affairs, though," I replied. "And didn't you know that Baltazar is a writer too? He's written several novels." I, too, used the familiar pronoun with Fidel.

"That's right!" Fidel exclaimed, in apparent euphoria. "These Chilean writers are a force to be reckoned with!"

The conversation was growing more and more animated. One witty (or barbed) remark followed another, and we Chileans (Laurita Allende, Jobet, Cristián Huneeus, and I) and Fidel tried to outdo one another. The only people who remained silent and inexpressive, withdrawn into their corner, laughing when it seemed necessary to do so, but otherwise never taking part in the repartee, were Dorticós and Roa. Piñeiro had entered the room behind Huneeus, and he did not take his eyes off him; he kept his hand near the butt of his pistol, as though he feared that Huneeus, who was but an inoffensive writer and professor, but whose presence had not been foreseen, might make an attempt on the life of Fidel. This detail, which in the midst of the witty conversation and the pisco sours and the general hilarity had escaped me, was brought to my attention later by Huneeus.

In the middle of the party, Dorticós and Roa, as though obeying a sign from the Commander-in-Chief or some unwritten order, rose to their feet, said good night to everyone present, and left.

Castro kept calling Huneeus "poet," with slightly mocking familiarity. Jokes were traded back and forth between the Chileans and the Prime Minister. Fidel carefully examined the portrait of Arturo Prat and then looked at Jobet's bald head, and said: "Are all captains of the *Esmeralda* required to have the same 'haircut'? Is there some regulation in the Chilean Navy that we don't know about?"

It was true—Ernesto Jobet's bald head was identical to Arturo Prat's. No one had noticed this, and when Fidel pointed it out, we all burst out laughing. Jokes about bald-headedness continued, and at one point Fidel laid his hand on my bald spot like a priest protectively and gently bringing a novice into the order. Who knows how many things he was trying to tell me with that gesture! Later I learned from Fidel himself that his coolness when he greeted me at the head of the gangway was intentional: He had received extensive reports about my "dissipations" and my conversations with malcontent intellectuals. He thought that my contact with those groups was proof of hostility toward the Cuban Revolution, and to the Chilean Revolution as well. He did not think that a better, more humane sort of socialism could arise out of criticism; I suspect, in that regard, that his thinking was not dialectical. Writers, on the other hand, with the exception of the fierce bureaucrats of literature, the untouchable Fernández Retamar and Lisandro Otero, the courtly and orotund Nicolás Guillén who rested on his faded laurels as a revolutionary in the Latin Quarter in Paris many years ago in the accommodating *hôtel* of Mme. Salvage—with the exception of these men, I repeat, most writers in Cuba had encastled themselves behind a rigid, resentful dissidence that also excluded openness, and save in scattered moments of lucidity refused to consider points of view that might have led to a dialectical process in the Revolution. I confess myself guilty of having, frivolously and naively, committed that same act of willful blindness. I might have helped them to see beyond the dark side of things, but I didn't, and it may be that because of that lapse I have caused them very grave harm. Our bloodthirsty critics should acknowledge, however, that in such situations as that which presented itself to me, it is very easy to cast blame *a posteriori*. The person that comes out on top, the person that winds up receiving the hero's praises, will always be the one that was right all along. And those that don't think like that person will be ground up and spat out by the machinery of the Revolution, to the applause of the opportunistic writers that come out of the woodwork, that seize upon the sophistries of the moment without the slightest scruple, and that with all the paraphernalia of the farce that is "intellectualism" discredit and destroy those who have been chosen by the all-powerful index finger of Writer Número Uno to be the victim sacrificed to undeniable and indisputable Truth.

But these, too, are *a posteriori* lucubrations. That night, on the *Esmeralda,* Fidel and we were in Utopia, Cockaigne, "the best of all possible worlds." We had forgotten all about Piñeiro, who was watching the proceedings from behind a column with his hand on his pistol, while his henchmen in double file sat or lay on the floor or slouched against the wall outside in the hallway. Up on deck the orchestra was still playing. When Laurita Allende and later Fidel retired (Haydée Santamaría, strangely, had not accepted the invitation to come down), Captain Jobet, Huneeus, and I went from pisco sours and Chilean wines to a noble bottle of Scotch whisky. The secretary of my small mission, in her flowered dress and best smile, put her head in the door, now that Fidel's bodyguards, after his departure, had left it unoccupied. Had she come down to take mental notes on our after-party remarks? And if that were her objective, who did she plan to report them to? The fact is that all Jobet, Huneeus, and I talked about was the wonders of sailing a tall ship and the pleasures of Scotch whisky. Jobet, at any rate, maintained the perfect bearing and impassivity that befitted the captain of a warship. I, on the other hand, with the uninhibitedness that some diplomats give in to at four o'clock in the morning, took my secretary by the waist and began to dance.

I confessed to her that her continual presence in the hotel room that served as our office, her thin tropical dresses and her tanned legs, all caused me constant perturbations of the spirit. She listened to these declarations with the most open of smiles. If she did so with the thought of hearing intelligent political commentary on Fidel, or of being in attendance when conspiratorial whispering, fueled by alcohol, took place between a naval officer and a sometime literary man and current chargé d'affaires, she must have been terribly disappointed. Never in the gaiety of a party had such perfect composure been maintained by man or woman as was hers. I whirled her around like a top while Captain Jobet looked on in hilarity, but the stern and unwavering expression of the hero of the Battle of Iquique, from his place of honor on the wall, seemed to impose on the gathering the air of strictest discretion that the circumstances demanded.

The party that I gave the following day as head of the Chilean Embassy, up on the top floor of the Hotel Habana Libre, was better attended (since most of the government and the diplomatic corps, and all of the Chilean community, had been invited with sufficient notice) but less interesting. Fidel, who had met his obligations to Captain Jobet the night before and now no doubt wished to underscore his displeasure with myself, did not come. Of course it was very seldom that he attended diplomatic receptions or other social events. All or almost all the ambassadors came, however, as did many ministers of the government, including Raúl Roa, Carlos Rafael Rodríguez (whose rise on the rungs of power was the talk of the town among the self-styled "well-informed"), Jesús Montané, and others. I had made the decision to invite only the official heads of cultural organizations and to exclude the difficult ranks of writers and artists. With this, I hoped to make clear that my friendship with them was purely personal and private. The hope was stillborn: There was nothing that could avoid the political, there was nothing that could be held strictly private or personal in the circumstances of the moment. I might as well have invited my literary colleagues; my problems would not have been any more serious.

I was sitting for a moment at the table of Raúl Roa, Carlos Rafael Rodríguez, and Jesús Montané, making small talk about the quality of Chilean wine and other such burning issues, when suddenly I was told that Regis Debray, who had been released from prison in Bolivia recently and who had arrived from Chile two days ago, wanted to say hello. Debray was at a table where he was surrounded by the major figures of *Juventud Rebelde,* the young hardliners of the Cuban Revolution, and good friends on the Chilean team that produced the magazine *Punto Final.* I had been invited to the editorial offices of *Juventud Rebelde* once, and I had the impression they were watching me as they would an insect, with condescending smiles but ready to pin me to the specimen-tray with the other prehistoric examples of bourgeois intellectuals, mild *Allendistas* and friends of the "revisionist" Pablo Neruda. Debray stood and with a tired, melancholy smile shook my hand and said he'd like to talk with me. We agreed that there would be time to talk after the departure of the *Esmeralda*.

Meanwhile, the young Chilean officers, in their impeccable white uniforms, were mixing with the crowd, carrying on conversations with that freedom and animation that are fairly typical of my fellow-countrymen but that were a constant source of surprise in the stiffer and more repressed air of diplomatic Cuba. Comandante Piñeiro, in a guayabera, was chatting in a corner with someone, and did not show much interest in joining the rest of the party. Monsignor Zacchi, the ever-active papal nuncio, was moving from group to group with his usual vivacity. The Yugoslav ambassador, tall and elegant, was chatting and above all listening, with an expression of only apparent distraction.

The French ambassador, a dry, slightly ironic, taciturn man who walked with a slight limp, thanked me very much for the invitation. Three or four days later, running into each other at a reception at another embassy, he said: *"La tenue de vos marins doit avoir fait beaucoup d'impression sur les autorités cubaines."* ("The *tenue* of your sailors should have very favorably impressed the Cuban authorities.")

I looked up the word *tenue* in the dictionary and found that it meant, among other things, "politeness, behavior in society, from the point of view of manners; way of dressing; bearing." A lack of *tenue* would be impoliteness, carelessness in dress and in gestures and movements. The French ambassador's comment presumed that we shared the old values upheld by traditional military discipline, and that such values might have slipped a bit in Cuba. Ambassador Bayle, who told me he'd been appointed to Havana by General de Gaulle with precise instructions to maintain good relations with Cuba, appreciated those traditional military virtues, which in his view (and perhaps mine as well) were better observed and respected in Chile than in any other country of Latin America.

It is well known that Chilean women are enterprising. Some young women of the Chilean community in Cuba came up to me, as the party went on, to ask me if they couldn't take the sailors out somewhere dancing. It was Wednesday, and the nightclubs of Havana only opened from Thursday to Sunday. Cristián Huneeus had the brilliant idea of handing off the problem to Manuel Piñeiro, who was still standing in a corner talking.

"Couldn't you get somebody to open up a nightclub for them?" Huneeus asked him.

"I'll see what I can do," Piñeiro said. "Wait while I go see."

He disappeared from the party, never to return. We thought, with Huneeus, that our outrageous proposition had forced him to make himself scarce. This, however, showed our ignorance of the inexhaustible resources of the vice minister of the interior. Piñeiro organized a very nice dance to be held at the Tropicana, the best nightclub in the city, the next evening. There would be some thirty young women, dressed for the occasion. But the next day was to be a new chapter in the saga. Plans were that there would be a breakfast on the ship at eight-thirty the next morning, followed, at Jobet's request to the Prime Minister, by a round of golf.

Now the party at the Habana Libre began to break up. The only people left were the members of the Chilean community, who will generally stay as long as there's liquor left in the bottles. I gave orders to the headwaiter to cut off the drinks, and the last of the Chileans, faced with the absence of any further incentive to stay, began to make their more or less zigzagging exits, showering me with protestations of their somewhat excessive esteem for me and thanks for the lovely evening.

Captain Ernesto Jobet Ojeda was one of those perfect golfers one sees in English movies and reads about in detective novels: white-and-brown saddle oxfords with cleats, a golf cap to protect him from the sun, a sky-blue polo shirt, and a little bag at his belt to hold the tees. He handed over his golf bag to his aide, who had worked with his chief before, and we set off in high spirits. The morning was sunny but not too hot. On the pier there was a long line of people, the residents of Havana, waiting their turn to go aboard the *Esmeralda*. They watched us walk by them as though we were visitors from another planet. Jobet strode along vigorously, while I, out of shape from the diplomatic life and from lack of exercise, and in spite of the fact that I was younger than he, had to struggle to keep up. I had the unpleasant feeling that I would make myself totally ridiculous on the golf course; but a mature man must overcome those emotions, must realize that ridicule is unimportant, and try to play as well as he can.

At the entrance to the pier, the wife of the correspondent from *Unitá*, the Rome Communist daily, was standing with a group of her students. She was a young, attractive woman, who had told us at my party the night before that her father was an Italian navy officer, which made her especially enthusiastic to see the *Esmeralda*. Jobet gallantly ordered his aide to take her directly to the ship and have the lady and her group given a tour. After this, to a general air of expectancy, we all got into an Alfa Romeo and speeded off to the golf course a few miles from the city, a small English-style country club now used by diplomats and foreign experts and technicians.

I only managed to hit the ball on the eighth or tenth try. Jobet sent his flying through the air, with the solid *thwack* and the swift ascent only achieved by experienced players. To my personal consternation, there was a photographer. (*That* is the true national pastime of Cuba.) I vigorously waved him off, telling him I would not allow my absurdities to be made fodder for international ridicule, but the photographer was unyielding and impassive; he smiled with equine teeth, and when I made my approach to the tee (hoping with furious hope that this time I would be able to hit the ball) he raised his own demonic device and shot.

By the third or fourth hole things were going a bit better. There was not another soul on the little course, whose grass had ceased to exist on the fairways quite some time ago, though it still survived (albeit somewhat fadedly, and more like a sample than the real thing) on the greens. The club manager, a young man who'd been a professional golfer (a relic of the past, indeed), had joined us. Suddenly we saw, advancing toward us over a little hillock, three figures—Fidel Castro, Aldo Santamaría, and Jobet's Cuban aide-de-camp. "Fidel!" I remember Jobet's aide exclaiming, unable to believe his own eyes; he went on babbling excitedly, forgetting altogether about finding a ball that I'd lost. Jobet, on the other hand, awaited the visit with imperturbable calm.

After the greetings had been dispensed with, Jobet continued his round of golf as though nothing had happened. Golf was important to him when he made landfall; that had been explained to Fidel the other night, and Fidel, unlike Laurita Allende, had immediately understood. I thought Jobet would break off the game at the sixth or seventh hole, but the perverse rules of diplomacy led me into error there. The fact that Jobet would continue his game to the end, with perfect ease and good humor, even though his game was taking up the time of the prime minister of Cuba, must have made Fidel reflect at least a moment about the nature of power in Chile, far beyond any formulaic idea about "bourgeois respect for constitutional government" or the necessity of moving from the victory of government to the victory of revolutionary power. The moment was revelatory of the essence of political life in Chile, and Fidel probably "got it"; and I say this in spite of the fact that Fidel would later show, in diverse aspects of his relationship with Chile and, as it goes without saying, his personal relations with me, a much more partial understanding of what was being called "the Chilean experience." The Manicheanism that led Meléndez, the director of Protocol, to talk to me about the "good guys and the bad guys" was not a particularly sharp instrument of thought when applied to the politics of my own country.

"But Meléndez is a nobody," my friends would say to me. "Meléndez was a tie salesman in El Encanto," which as we all knew was a large pre-Revolutionary department store that had been destroyed in a counterrevolutionary attack. Meléndez may have been a nobody, but he had sat in his office in Protocol and decided that not one soul would be waiting for me at the airport; that I would spend six days in the hotel without transportation, while the "bad guys" of the Cuban literary community surrounded me and subjected me (with affability of the most criminal sort) to their treacherous blandishments; that after weeks of insistence I would at last be shown a house in ruins for the use of the Chilean Embassy. Raúl Roa offered me all manner of facilities; he would ring a bell and give Meléndez orders in my presence, just as Fidel had done that first night: "Find this man a good house for a residence and another one for the embassy." Still, to judge by the results, it appeared that while men of some calibre, such as Roa, occupied the seats of government, the tie salesmen controlled ever widening spheres of real practical power.

Fidel listened to Jobet's explanations about golf very attentively, with that humble, youthful attitude he often adopts as he strokes his beard, but he refused to try a shot—he had injured a finger in a visit to a mine a few days earlier, he said. (The story was that he had dislocated it as he was examining or trying to move one of the cars for transporting minerals—I had read about the visit in *Granma*.) But finally, in spite of the dislocation, Fidel picked up a putter. As virtually everyone knows, the putter is a delicate instrument, and is to be used gently; it does not require great force from the fingers. It does, however, require control and precision. Fidel was standing at a point from which the champions of the game would have needed two shots to reach the green. Fidel, though, considered a second and then swung; the ball flew through the air—and fell straight into the hole! Fidel had taken a putter and made a hole-in-one with the same unerring aim that, as history (or legend) tells, he sank a ship with one cannon shot during the Bay of Pigs invasion. I hereby testify to Fidel's shot.

The club pro explained to Fidel the concept of par. Fidel was in excellent spirits. The coldness he had made so much of in greeting me at the *Esmeralda* two nights ago had given way to a bantering, subtly needling sort of cordiality. Par on the next hole was four.

"I'll give you six," Fidel, who had already seen me whacking blindly at the ball, and raising divots right and left, said. "If it takes you more than six, I win."

"Agreed," I said.

I was on the green in four, though pretty far from the hole.

"I'd advise conservatism," Fidel then said. "Don't try to get it in with one stroke. Just try to get closer with the first stroke, and then with the second one you can sink it."

"Slowly but surely wins the race?" I replied, quoting once again from his speech on December 7, 1970, at the Congress of Basic Industry. Fidel shot me a look out of the corner of his eye. My ball, meanwhile, missed both the first and second time, and I lost the bet.

Par on the next hole was four, too, but the distance between the tee and the green was greater. It should almost have been a par-five. Fidel gave me seven strokes, and paid not the slightest attention to my protests. "All right," I finally said, half resigned to losing a second time, though not actually giving up beforehand. I was near the green in four, but behind a tree, in a terrible lie. The aide gave me some advice about how to hit the ball. I determined to follow the popular wisdom to the letter. I concentrated, blocking out the rest of the world, and I swung. The ball arced lightly, landed on a lip of the green, and rolled softly, perfectly, into the hole, although it was prevented from falling in by the flag, which no one had had the foresight to take out—no one thought there was the remotest possibility that I could hit the hole from so far away. As this was the last hole and we were near the clubhouse, there was a group of spectators—workers from the club and other nearby places and a phlegmatic group seated around a table, vaguely smiling at the presence of Castro. Their general comportment gave the distinct impression that they were members of the embassy of Her Britannic Majesty. My shot inspired cheers and applause. Fidel gave a genuine start.

"After this," he said, "what can I say!" He acknowledged my triumph with a hearty handshake, to general laughter and joking.

Afterward, in the club's little bar, under the coat of arms of the United Kingdom and the portraits of the Queen and the Duke of Edinburgh, Fidel asked the aide-de-camp to send the course manager some sacks of compost and some watering equipment for the fairways and greens. He made the following observation: Since foreign diplomats and experts used the golf course a great deal, it made sense to be sure the fairways did not give them a bad impression of Cuba. There was not enough attention, Castro said, paid to that sort of detail. It occurred to me that Fidel's order to the aide-de-camp probably would have the same effect as the order he gave Meléndez the night of my arrival in Havana, to the effect that a house be immediately found for me. Months later, however, I was told by a diplomat in Paris that his golf-playing colleagues stationed in Havana remembered my passing through with gratitude every time they played a round. They thought it had been at my urging that the

Prime Minister had been persuaded to go to the golf course, and that it was from that visit that the grounds had later received attention diametrically opposite that visited upon barbarous Europe by Attila the Hun. Fidel had made the grass green again.

After this most unusual round of golf, which was played by a professional ship's captain and a chargé d'affaires/novelist (both in a sense envoys of that Chile just beginning to be led by its Unidad Popular government), and whose spectators included the Prime Minister and the commander-in-chief of the Cuban Revolutionary Navy, the heterogeneous group, refreshed with a glass of beer drunk under the awning of the British Lion, got into a jeep in the following order: in the front seats, the driver and the commander of the Navy; behind, at the left window, Jobet; in the middle, the Prime Minister; on the right, the chargé d'affaires. At no time did the Prime Minister's escort appear, a detail that I took to be a gesture of politeness toward the Chilean captain after the incident of two nights ago on the *Esmeralda*. We did once see, three or four hundred yards away, another jeep, but it disappeared immediately. Jobet commented to me later, on the way back to the *Esmeralda*, that we had been under surveillance the entire time, but from a distance, so that it would be unnoticed.

We drove through some small towns on the outskirts of Havana and the people, seeing Fidel without an escort, in a solitary jeep, were first dumbstruck with amazement and then broke out in cheers and applause. I guessed from one old man's expression that Fidel was not his favorite person, but he too applauded, though he did so with stiff, mechanical motions that probably cost him considerable psychological effort.

Fidel took us to the Parque Lenin—six hundred hectares, some fifteen hundred acres, near Havana, where there were plants and trees of virtually every species imaginable. He showed us where an artificial lake was being created. There was a theater on the lake. Then he led us to some riding stables; there would be two hundred ponies available there for the children of workers and campesinos to ride. We went then to an amusement park for children. There was a little train to take the kids all around the park, with a wonderful miniature locomotive engine like those one sees in the Westerns. We got out of the jeep to stretch our legs. Men with indifferent expressions were working the land with picks and shovels, or resting against a boulder, their hands crossed over the handles of their tools. Their eyes were fixed on some invisible point in the distance, or would follow us as though we were part of the landscape. The presence of Fidel, which in the neighboring towns and villages had caused a great stir among the few people who had become aware of it, produced in these men, who appeared to work and to rest as their whims dictated, not the slightest reaction.

"They are madmen," Fidel said. "They're brought in from the insane asylum, which is right nearby, to work in the fields. Apparently working the land is tremendous therapy for the mentally ill."

And so it was: The modern insane asylum, located near Rancho Boyeros, was one of the Revolution's indisputable achievements. Later, in Paris, an intellectual to whom I recounted this anecdote commented that the madmen who hadn't applauded Fidel were the ones who were really sane, and the people applauding in the streets were the real madmen. The thought was worthy of a European liberal, the enemy of any form of totalitarianism; despite its bias, and even in the case of Cuba, this observation did not lack all validity: Those men, though ill in spirit, were the anonymous men and women that worked the land; their sanity consisted in contemplating with indifference the comings and goings of eminent persons. And yet who more than these madmen had benefited from the Revolution? The mental hospitals of the past were reported to be hells, ruled by venal and no doubt sadistic administrators. And in remembering these placid and well-cared-for madmen of Havana, I remembered as well a sinister true story that had taken place a few years before in Lima: A Lima businessman bought madmen and made them work in a garbage dump outside the city collecting and washing bottles and jars for resale.

All the problems, the achievements, and the contradictions of the Cuban Revolution emerged in this visit I made in the company of Fidel and Captain Jobet to the Parque Lenin. The park might be a wondrous marvel of public works, open to the people of Cuba, but the gigantism typical of Fidel's projects was immediately visible. While a fifteen-hundred-acre park was being constructed outside the city, the city itself was peeling and falling slowly apart. The huge investment in the park also meant there had to be a sacrifice in other places, a sacrifice suffered directly by the people in the form of scarcity of essential consumer goods. In their hermetic, majestic indifference, the madmen were at least partly right.

After this visit, we went to a restaurant that also served as a school, and that gave a preview of the architecture to be employed in the park. Fidel told us that dozens of similar buildings were to be built throughout the park's fifteen hundred acres. Here, there was no doubt that people had been forewarned of our visit. Fidel's presence produced wild excitement: Girls and young women jumped up and down around him and clutched at his hands. We went into a schoolroom and the students leapt to their feet without a second's hesitation. Fidel asked several questions, then introduced Jobet. Then at last, keeping up the tone of bantering that he had adopted with me from practically the first moment of the day, he asked them what country they thought I was from. There was silence, and then a thin girl's voice said: "Italy."

"Italy!" Fidel, Jobet, and I burst out laughing. "Why Italy?" Fidel asked, leaning over in one of his characteristic interrogative poses.

"Because he looks like an Italian movie star," the little girl said.

"Ah!" exclaimed Fidel, looking at me over his shoulder. "That's a good answer!"

We also visited an agricultural research and planning center, where there were maps and models of the entire Havana region. The only people working there were experts under thirty; they seemed to know their jobs and to be passionately dedicated to them, and they listened to Fidel intently, soberly, though with an attitude much more natural and egalitarian than that we had observed in the prior encounters.

When we left, Fidel told us with some feeling that the Spaniards were totally mistaken in their plans for sugar-beet production. From the point of view of the international division of labor, it was an aberration. Cuba had the best natural conditions in the world for sugar production. The rational thing to do would be to have Spain sell Cuba trucks and let Cuba supply the sugar needs of the Spanish market. It was curious that Castro would expect that sort of rationality from a capitalist economy. His idea, oddly enough, was similar to the concept of comparative advantages that began to be fashionable in Pinochet's Chile. But that incurable optimism, linked to an insufficiently thorough analysis of economic and political circumstances, to a habit of transforming desires into realities, was perhaps the origin of many of Cuba's errors. Meanwhile, to bring our tour to an end, Fidel Castro took us to his favorite place: the dairy farm where he carried out his experiments in the hybridization of cattle and various kinds of grasses, in an attempt to find the best cow for the country and the best fodder for that cow.

Many books on the Cuban economy have described the famous model farm on which Fidel Castro carries out his hybridization projects. For my part, I am but a layman in this subject. I only know that Fidel has attempted to cross-breed cattle in such a way as to produce stock that will maximize the production of meat, the yield of milk, and tolerance for the climate of Cuba. It is my understanding that he has cross-bred Zebus, which adapt well to tropical climates such as that of Brazil or India, with high-milk-producing Holsteins, which produce less meat than the Zebu and tolerate the climate less well. I reiterate that the subject is much more complex than this sketch, and I refer the reader to specialists for more information.

What I have seen in those books is a true and faithful description of the Swiss Family Robinson-style cabin that Fidel took us to. It was a one-story building, rectangular, built of good wood, and measuring some forty to fifty feet long by eighteen to twenty feet wide. In the front half of the building there was a single room partitioned off at one side by a bookcase and a refrigerator, with what appeared to be a kitchen on the other side. In the bookcase I saw works by José Martí, treatises on the history of Cuba, economics, natural science, and, the great majority, agronomy. The room was furnished with rustic wood furniture of a very sober aspect. I cannot recall whether there was any decoration on the walls, but nowhere did I see the bright, vibrant colors of Portocarrero or Amelia Peláez that one saw so frequently in public buildings and the homes of the well placed. This interior, on the contrary, was austere, and the austerity seemed to fit that of a man of the country, a man of action. It may have been a decor, but one would hazard that the decor suited the person's true self. I glimpsed through an open door an almost monastic room beyond. This appeared to be one of the mysterious sleeping quarters inhabited from time to time by Fidel Castro, whose residences comprise a part of the secrecy that surrounds his movements, for reasons of security, and a part of the legend that has been woven about him. What I managed to see were a pair of boots in a corner, a large modern book, with pictures, about plants or fish, published in England or the United States, and a contemporary-style reading lamp on the night table. On the training ship Fidel's extensive knowledge of Chilean history had surprised me. Someone told me that after his interminable and exhausting days, the Prime Minister stayed up reading for three or four hours, leaving a maximum of four or five hours a day for sleep. After coming to know him a little, it's my impression that this report is perfectly correct.

Our lunch in the cabin was aimed first of all at simple nourishment, since Fidel seemed to disdain all gastronomic subtlety, but then second at a demonstration of the products of the model farm. A soldier who appeared to be a man of the Comandante's trust set on the table plates of assorted cold cuts and sausages and large pottery pitchers similar to the ones in German beer halls. But instead of beer, the pitchers were filled with milk, and had labels on them to differentiate one from another. Fidel asked what cow each milk had come from—the cows had delicate feminine names like María Rosa, Clarissa, María Gracia—but he claimed to be able to tell the difference between the various milks by their taste.

"Ah! This one!" he would exclaim. "This one tastes like almonds!" And he would pass the pitchers along for us to taste. By the end, total confusion had resulted; it was impossible to tell what cow (Clarissa, Florinda, María Gloria) went with what pitcher, and in some of them the milk had been "blended," to boot.

Never in all my life as a drinker of the fine red wine of Chile had I been subjected to such euphoria, such drunkenness, produced by milk. We made clumsy jokes about it. Then, at Fidel's request, the soldier brought in a large round plate of cheeses. These, too, were products of the model farm. We tasted a Cuban Camembert. There was no denying that it was excellent, even though it was softer and creamier, and with a less insistent taste, than the Camembert of Normandie.

"We are going to achieve a Camembert better than France's," said Fidel.

"Ah!" I exclaimed. "That will be hard. It's like telling me that the Rumanians will make a better daiquiri than the Cubans."

The milk must have gone to my head. But Fidel was in a wonderful mood.

"I once brought a French expert here," he said, "and I told him what our plans were. Do you know what his reply was? 'That is not possible, Prime Minister!' he said. Those French are such chauvinists!" Fidel laughed.

I then told a story about my father, who, as a hard-working bourgeois, and something of an expert in the grain business, barley included, once tried to set up a whisky factory in Chile. It had been his contention that the quality of Chilean barley combined with the climate of certain coastal regions, the wood that the barrels would be built of, and the water from certain springs, would create the perfect conditions for making a whisky in Chile that would be in every way the equal of Scotland's. He lacked the capital to carry out his plans, but his little company managed to produce a liquor very similar to whisky.

Fidel was delighted with the anecdote.

"Your father was absolutely right!" he exclaimed. He went on to note that the origin of Chilean wine, whose quality was now recognized worldwide, must have been very similar to my father's whisky enterprise.

I was amused (although I remained silent about it) to think that Fidel would have gotten along much better with my father, a confirmed member of the old Liberal Party, staunch Alessandrist, and all-out enemy of anything that smelled even slightly of socialism, than with me. Fidel would have seen eye to eye with him on economic progress, on industry, while he surely looked upon me as some sort of recalcitrant lunatic. The paradoxical thing about the case was that I had had bitter arguments with my father over my leftist ideas and my defense of the Cuban Revolution.

The paradox was only apparent. It is quite probable that Mao, deep down, got along better with Nixon than with the long-haired intellectuals who paraded through Washington protesting against the bombing of Vietnam. In today's world there is a sort of Power International: a metaestablishment of great initiates, from which poets and intellectuals are scrupulously excluded because they are in essence intransigent and malcontent. It is one thing that those intellectuals may be useful to any given policy during a particular stage of it, as Mario Vargas Llosa or Jean-Paul Sartre were useful at one stage of Fidel's politics, although they soon cease to be so, and another thing that they actually share power.

"It's monstrous!" someone cried when I told the story of my morning spent with Fidel. "Fidel has a milk-tasting with his friends—Château María Luisa, María Rosa Reserve—while there's no milk in Cuba. Children have a strict quota until they are seven, and adults have to prove they have an ulcer or worse—and even then, milk is hard to find. Don't you see? It's monstrous!"

But my friend, who was walking through the hotel lobby when I came downstairs a moment for some fresh air, as they say, to stretch my legs, may have been there by accident, or may have been sent by State Security to plumb my fresh, immediate impressions, and those that Jobet might have shared with me as well. Even if he hadn't been sent by State Security it was likely that they would interrogate him later, in order to find out, through him, what I had thought, and through me, what Jobet had thought. In summary, the hellish circle always closed, somewhere along the line, and sooner or later they would catch you off guard. Unless even as a foreigner you agreed, as often happened and continues happening, to join the machinery, offer your services, and suffer the consequent mental deformity.

I sometimes think that so far as the Cuban government and its officials were concerned, in order for a man (even the Chilean chargé d'affaires) to be saved, there was no alternative but to become a tool of the State Security system. The chargé d'affaires might have given inestimable service to Cuba, and left Cuba covered with glory, well advanced on his diplomatic career. The fact that the chargé d'affaires was not a "careerist," a climber on the rungs of the bureau-cracy, as might have been expected of a counselor with more than ten years' service behind him, disconcerted the men of power in Cuba; and the fact that the pressures they brought to bear later on the government of Chile to strike him from the rolls, erase him from the lists, had absolutely no effect within the Foreign Ministry or upon the highest officials of the Chilean government, while provoking from other circles a temperamental response that was not translated into concrete results, must have made them think. Another man's experience—not to exclude by this phrase another *country's* political experience—is not easy to assimilate. With the inevitable slowness which this mental process implies, if it is to be carried out in a serious way, Fidel has shown that he is able to think and to profit by experience.

The problem was that that team of tie salesmen who had managed to get into positions close to, and surrounding, Fidel *were* impregnable to all thought and experience. When they ran into the sanctum of the Unidad Popular government waving my file, demanding my head, the wall of inertia that rose up against them (in spite of the few predictable sparks that of course were struck) seemed to them tantamount to betrayal. They retreated to their laboratories for feverish consultations, and no doubt reached the conclusion that this nonreaction—my apparent impunity, insured by the solid and imperturbable presence of Neruda, the serene reply from Clodomiro Almeyda, even by the recognition by the navy of my unwearying labor during their visit to Cuba—was one more proof that the Chilean revolution was no distilled and unadulterated Revolution that might please the demanding palate of the consummate tie salesman. We had to be studied well, then, and there must not be too great a hurry to issue us the certificate of good revolutionary conduct. The final and definitive confrontation had to be achieved first, at which time the lukewarm, the "deliberative," the bourgeois intellectuals (as I and my kind had been called) would be eliminated, and the field would be once and for all, and perfectly clearly, divided: On one side, the right hand of God, would stand the Good, while on the other side of the line, to the relief of the spirit of the ineffable Meléndez and that of his henchmen, the Evil.

Out on the terrace of the Habana Riviera, my friend spoke with great indignation, as though my description of the milk-tasting session had aroused an unquenchable fury in him. But Fidel's plan was not to keep, as though for his private garden, a little model farm. From that farm there would grow an industry that would supply milk and meat to the country and even allow it to export meat and fine cheese. For the moment there was no question of widespread distribution, in a market where money was no object, of an inevitably scarce commodity. What was perfectly likely, however, was that a great deal of dreaming had entered the grand plans for hybridization; the production of Camembert, traditionally considered a winter cheese in France, was probably a futile and costly luxury for the agricultural industry of a tropical island. The idea of producing a Camembert better than the Camembert produced for centuries in Normandy, where ancestral Norman cattle grazed upon the most lovely pastures on earth to produce a milk of unrivalled quality, sprang from the ambitions of a man who had no patience for the immutable laws of Nature, a man who had once turned the course of History and who now, less successfully it seemed, was attempting to violate inviolable Nature. His willfulness was closer to Nietzsche than to Marx, but as confirmation that the protagonist of this unequal match between Man and Nature, himself the heir of such Spanish men of action as Loyola, don Quixote, and the caudillos of the

Carlist wars, was not always lucid about his true relationship with Marxism (in spite of the fact that he had stood in the middle of the Plaza de la Revolución and made an historic speech in which he declared himself a follower of Marx's philosophy), he did not seem to be able to admit that his willfulness, his Nietzchean plans for mastering Nature, found in the world a resistance that confirmed Marx's observations more than those of Nietzsche. After forcibly wrenching this child of his, the Cuban Revolution, from History's womb, he stubbornly proposed to do the same with Nature. It is likely that Fidel, in his heart of hearts, saw Nature as History, and History as a field in which he might introduce new crops, try out new hybrids, new breeds—History as, in a word, Nature. But I always thought that Fidel, in spite of appearances, was sensitive to the silent answers that History and Nature made him.

We found one of Nature's mute and incontestable answers awaiting us as we returned to Havana in our jeep: fields of scrawny, abandoned coffee plants, what had been the great experiment, the great hope, the Havana Cordon that young volunteers had planted at the time of my first trip. Someone had told me that this belt around the city had formerly been occupied by small Chinese landowners who grew the lettuce and other vegetables that supplied the city. In one fell political swoop, the government had expropriated all these parcels of land that constituted a "capitalistic" enclave and whose activities obeyed dark material urgings. From that time onward, lettuce was a luxury item, for the consumption of diplomats and other privileged men and women.

That is just one version of what happened, and I cannot vouch for it—although I would be surprised if there weren't some grain of truth there. Only the most simplistic Marxism would allow one to maintain that commenting upon this phenomenon, which is a perfectly understandable sort of mistake, is counterrevolutionary.

Counterrevolutionary, though, is the only word for a Czech gentleman who in order to escape the communism of his country fled to Batista's Cuba. One day he woke up and found himself in Fidel's Cuba, where experts brought over from Czechoslovakia began to help with the organization of the economy. The Czech gentleman, finding the devil hot upon his heels and driven by that vision to the verge of despair, made up a long and careful list of all the Cuban grasses and weeds that possessed any nutritional value, and before fleeing once again, this time to Miami, he left the list to a friend. So that his friend might survive what was coming . . .

Fidel ignored the dry, dusty coffee fields, and Jobet seemed tired. The kids on the boat were going to have a party at the Tropicana: Piñeiro, showing himself at last sensible to Huneeus' and my own pleas at the reception in the Habana Libre, had organized it for them.

That night I went over to the ship, which was to depart the next day, and the young officers told me about their party. Piñeiro had been there, along with some members of his staff, and about thirty young women of university age. The Chilean officers said they had surprised two girls looking at themselves in their new dresses and marveling. Nothing escaped Piñeiro! The young women were charming, simple, correct. Naturally, they asked how the sailors had liked Cuba, whether they'd enjoyed themselves. The question was asked insistently, but the young officers, aware that they were being interrogated, thought they had evaded the girls' questions pretty well.

But the truth is that the young women sent by Piñeiro were cleverer and better trained for their job than the officers were. Sometime later, a Cuban sociologist asked a Chilean visitor to Cuba how it was possible that the sailors hadn't been prepared before their trip; they had arrived in Havana as though for a vacation—all they wanted was bars, nightclubs, women. They could find those things in the capitalist "paradises," but no one had bothered to explain to them what a socialist revolution was. The students from the department of sociology who had made up the party contingent sent by Piñeiro had done a scientific study of the opinions they had heard. The result of the study, according to the sociologist, was sad.

The sociologist was right. It is one thing to observe and try to prevent the economic errors that led to a situation from being repeated somewhere else; and it is another thing entirely to explain to kids from good bourgeois or petit-bourgeois families, kids just being untied from their mothers' apron-strings, the realities and difficulties of a country eighty miles off the coast of the United States that had just broken away from Yankee imperialism.

Piñeiro didn't need sociological surveys. He saw the sailors' reactions immediately.

"What social class does the navy largely come from?" he asked a Chilean politician he had some trust in.

"It's small-town boys mostly," was the reply.

"There's no problem with them, then," Piñeiro observed. "And what about the officers?"

"The bourgeoisie and petit-bourgeoisie."

"Well," said Piñeiro, "we'll have to assign a political commissar to *them.*"

The following conversation, which transpired in the middle of a party and so reflected the swaggering that parties sometimes inspire, was witnessed by Chileans who were not great believers in State Security discretion. Comment by an unhappy Cuban: "There's no problem with the sailors. They can be twisted around your little finger. The officers, though, have got to have a hangman put in with them."

The night before the ship's departure there was an odd atmosphere on board. The youngsters had been bruised, battered, shocked by the experience, as though they had glimpsed in Cuba the gloomy future that inevitably awaited Chile.

I had advised the chaplain to have a talk with Monsignor Zacchi, the papal nuncio, who took a positive view of the Cuban situation and its possibilities. The chaplain had had his talk, but he seemed none too happy with the outcome.

For the young sailors and officers, the coup de grace had been the inquisitorial attitude of the young women brought by Piñeiro, in their new dresses, to the Tropicana. An excess of police zeal, like excess of diplomatic zeal, always produces results opposite those sought.

There was a Cuban woman I knew, X., who had fallen, one might say, for one of the officers; the feeling appeared to be mutual. She had brought her months-old daughter to the ship. Suddenly she came up to me and said in that thick Cuban accent: "I want to ask a big favor of you. Will you witness my daughter's baptism?"

The request took me by surprise, but it seemed sincere to me, and I couldn't refuse. I felt myself suddenly transported back to my youth. The ceremony took place in a small cabin on the *Esmeralda*, in the presence of the chaplain, the officer who was the woman's newfound friend, the second-in-command of the ship, and me. The heat was unbearable. The words of the baptism ceremony, whose meaning I understood for the first time, produced in me a strange emotion; there was a knot in my throat. I discovered in the rite of baptism the first initiation rite of the old Christian tribes, a meaning beyond the narrow element of dogma that had been taught me by the Jesuits. I realized that after that initiation comes confirmation, with its significant applause, and then communion, with its symbolic anthropophagy.

I played my role as witness conscientiously. I had met X. on the Rambla, near the Habana Libre, in 1968.

"What are you guys doing?" she had asked.

"We're writers."

"Writers! I like novels, but romantic novels."

"What romantic novel do you like?"

"*La amada inmóvil.*"

"Have you read that 'novel'?"

"No," the girl had answered, with the most charming and disarming of smiles, "but I saw the movie."

She had an ugly scar on her left hand.

"After the Alegría del Pío battle," she had said (and I can still hear the warmth of her voice), "the Batista troops came and carried off my father. My father was a Spaniard, a Communist, and since we lived near where the battle took place he had helped the revolutionaries by carrying food to them. I stood in front of my father, to try to defend him from the soldiers, and they gave me this . . . with a machete," she ended.

"What happened to your father?"

"We never saw him again. The Batista troops killed him," she had said, as though it were the most natural thing in the world.

"What about you? Are you a Communist?"

"I am a Catholic," the young woman had said, raising her head proudly. "My mother brought me up to be a strict Catholic. I don't like communism. That's why I'm trying to leave. I've already requested a visa."

In the three years since, she had aged. Her fancy for romantic novels[3] had led her to experience suffering in real life. She was proud to have managed, after long insistence, to speak personally with Fidel Castro, who had ordered that she be given her own place to live in.

"I congratulate you on your attitude during the baptism," one of the officers said to me.

"Why?"

"Marvelous," he insisted, with a look of tacit complicity.

I didn't quite understand what he was getting at. Afterward I was told that the German ship's purveyor had snatched a pin away from X. and had a look at it. "It's not a microphone!" X. had exclaimed, giving herself away.

"And she had the brass to baptize her daughter!" the officers muttered.

There was wine to drink, and everyone was tired, sweaty, put out. For my own part, I had suspected for quite a while that X. had some connection to State Security. Later she insisted on taking us along with the consul to dinner at the house of a purported uncle of hers. I couldn't go, but the consul assured me that the man was no uncle of X.'s and that he had offered to organize parties with little girls. The "uncle" declared himself quite given to little girls, and an expert in the subject. It was easy, he said; it was all a question of giving them

---

[3] She was, of course, a bit confused about her genres: The "romantic novel" she was only familiar with through the movies was actually the famous poem by Amado Nervo.

some little gift. X. seemed very disappointed that I hadn't gone to her "uncle's" house. Doubtlessly the bait of little girls was to be dangled before me too. State Security had long ago come to the conclusion that I was not altogether indifferent to the female sex. But to suppose that I, at the ripe age of forty, had such an exaggerated and exclusive taste was just another example of their own infantilism. The only thing the astute Piñeiro didn't do was the most effective thing he might have done: ask me my opinions and discuss them calmly, over a glass of rum, after a long day in the office. It's likely that Piñeiro didn't know that I had not the least idea who he was when we were introduced that first night in Havana. It's likely, therefore, that he had made up for himself some complicated explanation for my relative indifference.

As for the love-stricken officer of the *Esmeralda*, I think he was unaware of the possibility that X. might be a Castro security agent, or that she might be manipulating him in some way for the State Security apparatus, and be a good Catholic at the same time. My impression of X. is just that. Unless X.'s cynicism passes all the limits of my imagination, which would mean that the officer was right. But I frankly believe that X. still admired *La amada inmóvil*, venerated the memory of her father, an anonymous hero of the revolution, and followed to the letter the religious teachings her widowed mother had given her. It was entirely possible, too, that State Security had promised to reward her with that trip to Canada she had been talking about in 1968 if she provided them some service first. She'd have gotten small privileges later on, and would have become habituated, within her modest ambitions, to being a State Security collaborator.

After the baptism I went to the captain's cabin in order to apprise myself of the details of the next morning's departure. Jobet received me very laconically and said he had work to do at his desk. I presumed he was going to draft his report on the voyage for the Chilean naval authorities, and I could well imagine the political tack, probably not explicit, the report would take.

The officer that had been with me at the baptism invited me, therefore, to go have a chat with him in one of the other cabins. The heat in the small dark rooms of the ship was suffocating. The officer, in shirtsleeves, sat at what appeared to be his worktable and looked at me with a serious expression. Behind his head, through the porthole, one could see the rooflines of the warehouses along the docks. It occurred to me that I ought to consider the possibility of bugs in the stateroom, but I immediately discarded the idea; it seemed too dramatic and outrageous. Those days I was very much troubled by a sense that I was under constant State Security surveillance; I was having insomnia night after night; I had difficulty breathing, accompanied by chest pains and the sense that I was about to have a heart attack. I confess that the ship, filled with those slightly spoiled kids from Valparaíso and that innocent, smiling crew of sailors, seemed a perfect oasis to me. My greatest happiness would have been to weigh anchor and sail off with them at that very moment, cast off onto the open sea and forget about diplomats and intelligence agents.

"I would be entirely in favor of making profound changes in Chile, along Peruvian lines, for example. I think they're needed," the officer said. "But not like this. For me, this is unthinkable!"

He looked at me with intensity, his eyes gleaming darkly. The porthole sank slowly and revealed the wrinkled walls of the warehouses.

"We are taking another road," I said.

"Don't be so sure!" the officer replied, his eyes glittering. "You don't know! You left Chile early on, and you don't know!"

Recalling my readings on the Chilean civil war of 1891, in which the parliamentary leaders of the "establishment" of the time, with the aid of the Navy, rose up in revolt against the constitutional president José Manuel Balmaceda, the thought struck me that the atmosphere within the fleet, when the rebels took refuge in it in early January 1891, must have been something like this. And yet the rebellion of the parliament and the fleet nipped in the bud one of Chile's greatest chances to achieve its economic independence and to develop itself into a modern state. The parliamentary bigwigs who formed a junta on board the ships in the fleet did not know that in setting in motion that revolution supposedly in support of the constitutional system of Chile (which was in essence a counterrevolution) they were committing an act of long-term suicide as a national bourgeoisie—that is, as a ruling class that at one point in our history was legitimate. Balmaceda had wanted to use the wealth of the nitrate deposits to stimulate the nation's autonomous development. His opponents, those who under the aegis of the fleet's parliamentary leanings had rebelled against him, had been manipulated like puppets by English imperialist masters and had frustrated Balmaceda's great plan for the nation. The almost idyllic atmosphere that I felt in the ship fueled these long reflections.

The next morning, the day of the ship's departure, I was to have breakfast at eight in the captain's cabin. I warned Tomás, my driver, that we would be leaving at seven-thirty.

Something odd was going on with Tomás those days. A few days before my wife Pilar went back to Chile, she was waiting for me in the car at the Ministry of Foreign Relations and she saw somebody who looked like Tomás' boss call Tomás over. A whispered argument, which neither of the two parties had been able to dissimulate very well, had taken place, and Tomás had come back to the car visibly upset. Later he told us that he was going to be replaced because he had been called away to do other, more responsible, work.

It never occurred to me that the replacement would be made precisely during the time the *Esmeralda* was in Havana; one would naturally presume that the sabotage of my mission, which was already hobbled by lack of offices and official residence, would be entirely too flagrant. Lack of residence had already made my life not only difficult, but also dear: The reception for the sailors at the Habana Libre had cost me fifteen hundred dollars, which I paid in cash in U.S. currency, and that did not include the whisky and Chilean wine that I also supplied. The director of Banquets, however, had told me that the cost had been much higher and that he had lowered it, for me, to that nice round figure—much higher in Cuban pesos, that is, but Banquets maintained the fiction of parity between the dollar and the peso. Had I had a residence, and consequently been able to purchase food and liquor in the Diplomarket or import it directly, the cost, according to all my colleagues I consulted, would have been a third.

Transportation was another of the calculated difficulties that I, as a friend of certain persons who were not unconditionally pro-Fidel, was forced to face. My first driver, Agustín, had overslept the morning I was supposed to go to the airport to see Mario García Incháustegui off on his first trip as Cuban ambassador to Chile. But recently the disciplined and warm-hearted Tomás had looked after Pilar and me with real affection. He was always at his post early, rubbing down the Alfa until it shined or reading *Granma,* waiting to take us wherever we needed to go, and to do so efficiently. But the morning of the *Esmeralda*'s departure, Tomás was nowhere to be seen. Apparently, somebody was trying to make me miss every departure I was scheduled for.

I called Tomás' room. I looked for him in the lobby. He was nowhere. One of the doormen or busboys thought he had seen him leave with the consul and the German ship's purveyor for the airport.

"But Tomás should have told the consul that he had an important commitment with me this morning!"

At the door and in the lobby, no one knew a thing. As for Tomás, he had obeyed the consul's orders without a word, so this whole mix-up was really the embassy's own fault. And it was seven minutes till eight. The ship must already be getting ready to cast off.

Suddenly I saw an old man cleaning a rusty old Chevrolet or Oldsmobile, a relic of the prosperous fifties.

"That wouldn't be a taxi?"

"Yes," one of the doormen told me. "That's a taxi."

I ran over to the old man.

"Can you take me to Pier Number One, immediately?"

The old man, after the effort of wiping down his ancient rattletrap, not to mention the surprise my request (which I admit was quite brusque) gave him, had to catch his breath.

"Let's go," he finally said.

He opened the back door for me with great deliberation, then got into the front seat and made himself comfortable, in obedience to some old ritual. I decided it was best not to make him nervous.

"Pier Number One?"

"Pier Number One," I nodded. "Where the Chilean ship is docked."

The old man turned the key and the rickety old car, by some mechanical miracle, started. When we'd gone about two blocks down the Malecón, beside a sea whose brilliant blue heralded a day of glorious sun, I said to the old taxi-driver:

"Compañero, could you hurry a bit? I'm running a little late."

He nodded, and the noise of the engine, which was loud to begin with, grew louder yet, though I could detect no acceleration worthy of the increased volume. But I soon saw that his taciturn shell and gruff voice covered a heart that was at least in the right place. As the blocks passed, the car picked up speed, and the noise of valves, pistons, and rattly fenders was now almost deafening.

When we began to approach Pier Number One, we saw two or three soldiers stopping traffic.

"Straight ahead!" I cried, and the old man went straight ahead. I showed the soldiers my credentials and told them I was the Chilean chargé d'affaires. I had to give the same explanation at the entrance to the pier itself.

Although the broken-down old Chevy, covered with dents and scratches that hardly befitted the usually dignified gestures of diplomacy, raised some eyebrows, we made, the taxi-driver and I, a quick and triumphant entrance onto Pier Number One. I managed to board the ship, and immediately the gangway was pulled up. The ship's band was already playing. I arrived just in time to station myself between Fidel and Aldo Santamaría as the first chords of the Chilean national anthem were played.

"In these countries of ours," Fidel said to me, "there's always been a poet that had nothing to do with the Revolution but who shows up and jumps on the bandwagon and composes the national anthem."

This comment revealed that Fidel had a singular notion of the role of poets. He may have been thinking about some of his own official poets, of course, who had flown in from U.S. universities and other equally comfortable exiles to take over the directorship of the bureaus of culture. Once there, at the slightest suggestion that wafted down to them from Above, they would write letters filled with irate revolutionary fanaticism denouncing colleagues that the Power had decided to condemn to purgatory, or the inferno itself. It looked to me, however, as though Fidel's scorn extended to official and nonofficial (or antiofficial) poet alike, even though his regime rewarded the former's unconditional support with some crumbs of privilege, and corralled the latter in sordid rooms with faded and tattered wallpaper, where they were reduced to nervous muddling, or sterile grumbling.

At any rate, even if only as a symbolic salute to the flag of poetry, I answered Fidel's remark with a piece of information: "The man who wrote the words to the national anthem of Chile was Eusebio Lillo, an important poet *and* political figure of the nineteenth century. He was one of the ministers in the Balmaceda government, and José Manuel Balmaceda, as you know, was our great president at the end of the century."

Fidel, whose relative isolation on the Island produced an inevitable loss of perspective, often made somewhat rough-and-ready comparisons of Chile and Cuba, in spite of the fact that on many occasions he seemed aware of their differences, and sometimes became almost angry when some of his Chilean friends couldn't see those differences and suit their actions to the real particularities of the Chilean situation. But while Fidel criticized this error, he also fell into it himself, especially when it came to problems concerning literature and literary men and women, a point upon which he showed an odd lack of serenity. I finally came to wonder whether some sort of literary frustration might not help explain Fidel's curious attitude.

Fidel thought that if Cuban poets had not been central to the revolutionary process in Cuba then Chilean poets couldn't have any very great role in their own. When one considered the Maximum Leader's prejudices in this regard, the fact that he was ignorant of the true situation in Chile was not so surprising; what was surprising was his deliberate "forgetting" of *Cuba's* great poet and man of action, José Martí, a man whose image was everywhere, on posters and in official publications, and whose words were repeated, virtually like mottos, constantly. It seemed, in fact, that Martí had begun to suffer the fate of so many Latin American heroes, whose marmoreal proliferation in statues, names of streets and plazas, and chapters of textbooks, winds up obscuring the vital and, in the best sense of the word, didactic significance of the exemplar.

After the ceremony, while we had breakfast, Fidel talked about the gifts he had given the ship: sacks of oranges and tamarinds, hundreds of giant shrimp. He had also brought immense cheeses from the farm we had visited the previous day. Captain Jobet, under his cheerful and gracious demeanor, maintained his habitual reserve. But I discovered that the sailors later commented upon these gifts, and saw them as expressions of power gone excessive, especially in a country whose shortages they had seen with their own eyes in the city's streets and public places—the empty stores, the people formed up in lines for two hours in the midsummer tropical sun to buy an ice cream cone at Copelia. It was likely, too, that characteristic Chilean austerity, the tight-fistedness of that ministry in Chile that corresponds to the U.S. Management and Budget Office, and which still works under a system of controls inherited from the colonial tributary offices, may have contributed to give a false sense of profligacy to the Cuban leader's gesture of good will. Chile's opening of relations with the blockaded island of Cuba surely was worth a few magnificent shrimps. When they were presented they were cause for criticism and backbiting (our national pastime), but there could be no doubt that once served up on the table, in the midst of the monotony of a high-seas voyage, the rich delicacy of the shrimp and the tart sweetness of the tamarinds would make the gesture better understood, not to mention better appreciated.

The problem was that certain events of the last two days had obscured and diminished the political significance of the voyage. The incident with Fidel's bodyguards had been brilliantly repaired by Fidel himself. But at least one of the visitors to the ship, during the tours that the residents of the city were given, had slipped a pencilled note, in handwriting that showed limited education, to one of the crew: "Be careful in Chile . . . We are starving here . . . The first thing the Revolution done here was do away with navel and military careers. All the career officers was fired . . . Watch out so the same thing don't happen to you."

A message dictated by the CIA? By some Cuban counterrevolutionary group? When it comes to this sort of message, all things are possible. The sailors told me there were many such messages, but this is the only one I saw. However that may be, the spelling and the handwriting seemed authentic; they showed what one might call counterrevolutionary spontaneity, and the note had its effect on those who read it.

There had been another sort of incident, as well, which had contributed to the deterioration of the climate of the visit. Far from obeying the guidelines for neutrality agreed upon in our preparatory meeting and sent out to commanders by the Ministry of the Revolutionary Armed Forces and its commander Raúl Castro, one Cuban officer giving a speech to a group of Chilean sailors during their tour of military installations told them that the common task of the Cuban and Chilean armies was to battle Yankee imperialism, which was the foremost enemy of the nations of Latin America and the world. Irritated, the officer in charge of the Chilean group broke off the ceremony, refused to thank his hosts or give his speech in return, and ordered his men to fall in and march back to their bus.

One detail, apparently trivial, had greatly disturbed the young men of the *Esmeralda*. At first I didn't understand very well. The Chilean Army, Navy, and Air Force are masters of the parade. Everyone in Chile turns out on holidays to see the spectacle. In Havana, one of the sailors' activities was laying flowers at the monument to José Martí. The band played as they laid their wreath and then marched in formal honors through the center of the vast (and empty) Plaza de la Revolución. In Chile, people would have turned out instantly. Idlers and strollers along Alameda Boulevard would have stopped to watch, and the office workers of the city would have hung out their windows. But the parade through the Plaza de la Revolución had only three or four distant spectators. The sailors didn't say anything to me after their maneuvers in the desert of cement, but from scattered phrases later I gathered that the incident had been most unpleasant for them. No one could convince them that the absence of an audience, during their homage to the hero of Cuban independence, had not been calculated and intentional.

The other frankly negative element (an element much more serious, given that it reflected the hard times of the Island after twelve years of the Revolution) was the sailors' experience of the streets during their time on shore: store shelves and windows empty, long lines at the cafés, the rank smell and obvious deterioration of Old Havana, whose colonial architectural charms did not offset the impression of decay received by the sailors. They made the simplistic comparison with the streets of Valparaíso or Viña del Mar, and reminding them of the blockade did little good. Was this the model that the Unidad Popular was offering the country? Eighty percent of the common sailors, perhaps more, missed the shop windows of the consumer society they came from, however inaccessible the goods in those windows might be to them. A Cuban doctor had come upon a group of them looking for a bar where they might get a drink. He took them home with him and shared his ration of coffee with them, plus a glass of water. "If a doctor lives like that in Cuba," one of them later remarked, "what must everybody else live like!" A sailor or a plumber in Chile might live like that, but a doctor! And even they, the sailors, plumbers, carpenters, might splurge and offer a guest something more than a cup of black coffee and a glass of water. And if you were a little short that week, you could always get some credit from the corner store, or borrow a few pesos from your brother-in-law. Even if their daughters, oppressed by need, couldn't finish their studies and were forced to become laundresses or maids, things were never quite this bad.

"Compañero Allende's strategy backfired on him," one of the ship's stokers said. I didn't hear this, but several officers assured me that those were his words, and it wouldn't surprise me, given the atmosphere I saw all over the ship that last day, if they were.

What the sailor was referring to was that Allende had boarded the *Esmeralda* in Valparaíso harbor to see them off, and he had talked to them about the significance of their trip to Cuba as a symbol of the reestablishment of relations between the two countries. Who had planned the trip—Allende, in order to strengthen contact with Cuba, or the naval authorities, for purposes of information or even perhaps to provoke such reactions as the sailors were experiencing now? There was ample food for thought in this. One thing was obvious: After five days in Cuba, the sailors, who came from a country starting out on the road to socialism, were not going to carry away an image of socialism that might be expected to seduce them. That was one of the few unquestionable consequences of the visit.

I told one and another officer that Chile's road would be different, but such an observation, rational and *a priori,* could not wipe away the emotional impact of what they had witnessed with their own eyes. Besides, I myself felt that impact. And some details, some statements, certain economic measures, the general attitude in Chile toward the problems of work and productivity (problems wherein ideas put forth by moderates seemed to meet with contempt in the rest of the Unidad Popular), the much-celebrated sending of brigades of Chilean young people off, that first summer vacation under the new government, to do volunteer work in the southern part of the country—all these things added up to give me more than enough reason to fear that the lessons of Cuba were not being sufficiently attended to in my country. The unconditional and perfervid loyalty that had been necessary when the Unidad Popular was a force in the opposition could not be done away with, or even very greatly toned down, within the few months that the party had now been in power. And the desolate streets of Old Havana, with its dank smell of sewage, held up to the crew of the *Esmeralda*, both officers and men, a none-too-encouraging mirror of what the socialist Chile proposed by compañero Allende might become. If he had hoped that this voyage would win over supporters, the strategy, as the stoker said, had backfired on him. Unless Allende, as I sometimes suspected, knew more than he let on, and the strategy had had other origins—in which case Allende's visit to the ship in the Valparaíso harbor, his telephone call to Fidel the night before the ship's arrival in Havana were attempts to neutralize the strategy, since the sailors' reaction, the impact on their imagination of the ruined and smelly streets around the docks, were (for Allende, a seasoned politician who had known Havana for many years) perfectly foreseeable.

One last revealing incident: The sailors of an East German ship that was anchored during that same time in the harbor near the *Esmeralda* foresaw the Chilean youngsters' reaction. The first day of the visit, they rowed over and raised their oars in salute. The German captain and a group of sailors were received on board the *Esmeralda* with all honors.

"This is not the kind of socialism we like," the Germans said as soon as they were free to talk (and their tongues no doubt loosened with a few rounds of pisco sours). "Don't fool yourselves into thinking that."

Later the Chilean officers were emphatic when they told me this anecdote; we were pacing the deck of the *Esmeralda* as a German boat rowed nearby, raising its oars from time to time in greeting.

The *Esmeralda*'s engines powered us down the narrow channel, about a half-mile long, that leads out of Havana harbor. Then the engines stopped, and there fell the silence that preceded raising sail. Comandante Piñeiro had stayed on the ship with Fidel, as had Miyar, chancellor of the university (and semi-official photographer of the occasion), Aldo Santamaría, and a few soldiers, most of whom had brought their cameras. A fleet of Cuban Navy destroyers was to join us as soon as we cleared the harbor.

Suddenly we heard whistles all over the ship and we watched as cadets and sailors alike, with amazing agility, scaled the cordage up into the highest tops of the masts. Jobet explained that the different whistles represented different orders. When he saw Fidel's look of skepticism, he called over one of the deck officers. The young officer whistled to show us that one blast meant climb, another, unfurl the sails, another, halt, etc.

"So," Fidel said, walking along the bridge and bowing his head, "in order to do this work you have to be one part sailor, another part acrobat, and another part musician."

"Absolutely!" Jobet smiled.

"And what about you, captain?" asked Fidel. "Do you know the signals?"

"Everyone on board this ship must know them," Jobet replied, and the young officer who had given us the demonstration nodded, smiling broadly.

Fidel went on to ask, still somewhat skeptical: "And when you were starting out, did you climb the masts, too, captain?"

The sailors stood on lines as they supported themselves with their legs and torsos against the high yardarms and used their hands to loose the sails. The sails began to drop and unfurl, and the ship slowly and noiselessly began to slip past two Soviet cargo ships, beginning its trip through the neck of water that led onto the high seas.

"Of course!" Jobet replied, as at the same time he kept his eyes fixed on the work going on before and aft the bridge.

"You climbed all the way up there?" Fidel insisted, pointing up to the highest yardarms as though he suspected that the class-bound, or at least hierarchical, nature of the Chilean Navy, so visible in the types of uniforms and other details of the officers and men, would have exempted the officers, sons of the bourgeois that they were, from the dangerous maneuvers performed by sons of the working class.

"All my officers," said Jobet, who had caught the political implications of the question, "have gone through this same training."

Fidel didn't say a word. Perhaps he thought that the force of Chilean naval tradition lay precisely in this all-encompassing knowledge of the craft. Beyond the class origins of the officers, one saw in them an identification with the ship that indicated a new aspect of the phenomenon of hierarchy, an aspect probably theretofore unknown to Fidel, if not scorned by him. It was a state of command very different from command in the army of Batista, which Fidel had defeated relatively easily, more easily than foreign journalists could have imagined. One must admit that Fidel, in his first conversation with Jobet, said that the Batista navy was the only adversary that put up any serious resistance, and therefore the only adversary worthy of respect, during the entire revolutionary conflict. At any rate, one imagines that the attitude of Jobet and his officers must have inspired in Fidel some reflections about the Chilean political picture. He was already aware, of course, of the opinion of Cuba that the sailors and officers of the *Esmeralda* had formed. Now, seeing the efficiency and perfect discipline of the boat as it sailed through the narrow channel out to sea, he was completing his education. The sails were now fully spread, while the sailors kept their places up on the lines and yardarms, and the ship sailed slowly, silently out, leaving behind the colonial stone walls, now lit by the morning sun, of the fortress of La Cabaña.

When we reached the open sea, the sailors descended from the masts. The operation had been performed impeccably. There could be no question, then, of sending off adolescent guerrillas to fight this force, as Fidel, with the narrow perspective given him by his life on the Island, might have thought of doing sometime in the past. Piñeiro, the great inciter of extreme left-wing Chilean groups through his writings in the magazine *Punto Final* (which some ironists claimed was directed by Piñeiro from a distance), had apparently come to the same realization very quickly. Mixing among the cadets, he was trying indefatigably to strike friendly sparks among the crew. His jokes and witticisms had tremendous success with his beardless audience; the laughter of the sailors could be heard all the way up on the bridge. He had himself photographed with them, in the center of the groups, putting his arm over their shoulders, and clearly savoring his own skill at keeping them hanging on his slightest words.

About a year later, a Chilean who had lived for a long time in Cuba told me his version of the history of Manuel Piñeiro, who was also known as Red Beard, the First Vice Minister of the Interior, in charge of State Security.[4] He told me, to my great surprise, that Piñeiro had studied "security" (a subject of great interest to the Americans) at West Point. When he returned to Cuba, still during the Batista years, he had joined the guerrillas in the Sierra Maestra. In the United States at the time there was considerable sympathy for Castro's guerrillas, though these were viewed with mistrust by the Cuban Communist party. Herbert Matthews did a series of interviews with Castro in the Sierra Maestra, and his reports were published by *The New York Times*. In the columns of American newspapers, Castro's adventure was what was called a "story": It was romantic, and it seemed no threat whatever to Yankee imperialism. One "liberal" millionaire or another seemed always disposed to aid the exiles who sailed from the Florida peninsula to carry contraband weapons and other supplies to the Sierra. In the early pages of this book, I talked about my brief contact with the Revolution at Princeton. I had seen with my own eyes, in late 1958, the clandestine organization of this aid from exile.

In 1961, after the Bay of Pigs invasion, Piñeiro had invoked the special training and education he had received at West Point, and he was immediately appointed to organize Fidel's personal security. Until that moment Fidel had traveled throughout Cuba freely. It was not unusual to see him late at night in a restaurant in Havana. But from the moment Fidel's personal protection became a serious political problem, Piñeiro's power began to grow. Over the years, his job made him the intermediary between Fidel and the outside world. As experience well shows, security agents start out surrounding their charges for their own safety, and wind up turning their lives into a gilded cage for them. From that point to the point at which the chief of state's power is supplanted, or at least decisively influenced, by that of the chief of State Security, is a short distance indeed.

I wouldn't have been surprised to learn that Piñeiro, before going to West Point, had been educated, like Fidel, by the Jesuits. He possessed a mixture of informality (like the Americans) and sporty, hail-fellow-well-met demagoguery (like the modern generation of Jesuits), and this combination made him enormously effective at anything involving manipulation and proselytizing.

---

[4] My Chilean friend's references to Piñeiro's West Point education and his organization of Fidel's security apparatus were stricken from previous editions, out of prudence. I have not been able to corroborate this information, but I leave it in now for what it may be worth.

When I saw him giving great bear hugs to the sailors, talking to them in their own language, in the midst of a noisy crowd of them, I involuntarily recalled the Chilean Jesuits of the Colegio de San Ignacio. The Chilean priests, unlike that hard and implacable generation of Spanish Jesuits that they succeeded at San Ignacio, organized soccer tournaments in the school stadium (for physical exercise contributed to the health and discipline of the student), and they behaved toward the students with a familiarity and informality which I, as a poor athlete and recalcitrant intellectual, never fully shared in.

After graduating, I found that the familiarity was repeated at annual dinners and other commemorative rites—palpable demonstration of the fact that the ultimate goal of keeping the sheep inside the pen had been fully achieved. There were desertions, like mine, and even some among the priests, who in being so modern, in abandoning the ancient rigidities, came at last to hang up their cassocks and marry. But each case served to underscore the proof that there is no health possible outside the Church.

And what about Cuba? Was not self-criticism a process similar to confession, which cleanses away sin and gives access to the communion of the righteous? Piñeiro had found himself not many weeks before face to face with one of the dissident writers, or impenitent sinners, and had said: "You've aged so! You've even got gray hair!"

"It's you, Manuel Piñeiro, who's aged me," his interlocutor replied.

To which Piñeiro might have responded: Repent of your sins, make a confession, my son, take communion, and you will see that the stray sheep is welcomed back into the fold with redoubled joy. So long as your repentance is sincere, that is!

From the bridge, one of the officers was observing Piñeiro's youthful effusions; his success among the crew was obvious, and the officer's irritation was ill-concealed. The officer belonged to a more rigid type, brought up perhaps on the old Hispanic principles. In fact, when I saw him again in Toulon, a month later—since my first mission as minister-counselor in Paris was to accompany Pablo Neruda to Toulon to greet the *Esmeralda*, which had crossed the Atlantic after leaving Cuba—I saw at once that he was delighted with what he had seen of the Franco regime when the *Esmeralda* had come through Barcelona.[5] If that navy officer had been in power, he probably would

---

[5] This paragraph was only retained in the 1982 edition. In the censorship I imposed on myself in late 1973, as I corrected the drafts of 1971 and 1972, I felt the pressure not only of events that had taken place in Chile and of my own personal situation within the Chilean drama, I also had to submit the text to the real censorship that existed in the last stage of Francoism.

have been very much like those military men who censored indecent movies and plays in Franco's Spain. But I must admit that at that moment, while the officer looked down on the festive group that surrounded Piñeiro and shook his head in barely controlled indignation, I shared his feelings. The pressures of all kinds and the tensions of the moment made me lose my perspective. And it is only fair to admit that the same thing may have happened to the officer, who arrived in Spain straight from Cuba and had the paradoxical experience of breathing the libertarian air of Europe, comforting in almost any situation, on the soil of Generalísimo Franco.

While we are on the subject of ecclesiastical or religious metaphors, there was one that was contributed by one of the lowliest sailors on the ship. Fidel had gone over all the installations, talking at length with sailors and cooks alike. As he returned to the deck, he walked up toward the bow and climbed about halfway out the bowsprit, supporting himself on the lines. In that position, turned toward the deck and not out toward the ocean, he posed for the many olive-drab-garbed photographers, amateur and professional, who made up his retinue. With his beard and his imposing height, and as the ship rose and fell, setting him first against the blue sea and then the blue sky, he seemed some Neptune risen from the waves.

"They don't believe in God," the sailor said, watching the show out of the corner of his eye, with the look of one none too taken with this Fidel/Neptune who sat astride the bowsprit among the cordage, "but they treat him like he was God, so they've just traded one God for another. What's the big difference, then?"

We were on the open sea, the sails were full, the skyline of Havana had sunk beneath the horizon behind us. Captain Jobet looked at his watch with visible impatience. It was time for lunch, and his men couldn't go on forever with the Prime Minister. The rest of the officers were also beginning to show signs of uneasiness.

Months later, in his official visit to Chile, Fidel showed the same inability to end things, the same lack of moderation, and on that occasion within a much more risky political context, since he was facing a stormy Chilean opposition that was fired up by his very presence.

Someone, at last, pointed out the Cuban destroyers in the distance, and the Chilean officers breathed a sigh of relief. The *Esmeralda* lowered its sails and lay dead in the water. The Chileans saw me off with firm, warm handshakes and expressions of kindness and understanding. I think they felt sorry for me, and the truth is that I would have been happy to go on sailing with them, all the way to Europe. On the ship I had felt myself on native soil, and had had the almost literal sensation of being able to breathe.

A Western diplomat, taking advantage of the noise of a party to muffle our conversation, remarked to me some while later that the fascism of military governments might well be less oppressive than police-state socialism. The diplomat had conceived this idea by imagining a hypothetical government by those sailors, whom he had observed at the *Esmeralda*'s reception and my own in the Habana Libre. But the comparison was misplaced. The Chilean officers were not in power, and one would have to know how power might change them. My diplomat colleague maintained that right-wing military men only repress the opposition, while within the Cuban regime, control appeared to be spreading little by little into every aspect of daily life. My colleague cited the case of the Spain of the moment, and deliberately overlooked other, worse, examples of fascist dictatorships, among which one might include the Spain of Franco in its worst years. But I do think it unquestionable that the Left, locked into the blinders of Manicheanism, has not carried to their ultimate conclusions their thoughts about police-state socialism: Stalinism in its diverse and subtle manifestations. In old, democratic Chile, the balance of various powers, including that power represented by the *Esmeralda*, prevented sectarianism from having any greater impact than it did on the life of the ordinary person. That is why I looked at the *Esmeralda*, swaying motionless on the waters of the Caribbean, and thought to myself the unconfessable thought that it was a good thing that that force, which played a moderating role in the complex Chilean situation of the moment, existed. The thought, however, was far from implying the desire that that force assume total power. The measured and reasonable cordiality of the officers and men of the *Esmeralda* came in large part, indeed, from the fact that they did *not* possess great power. (Of course, this balance of power changed drastically and tragically with the ascension of Pinochet in Chile.)

"Take care of yourself!" the officer who had watched Piñeiro from the bridge told me, just as we were saying good-bye. "If anything happens to you, we'll have our eyes open."

Those were not encouraging words, especially if one considers that the end of my mission in Cuba was not yet in sight; they might mean that if word came of my death by accident or suicide, the Chilean Navy would have another explanation of the matter. That seemed very little in the way of guarantee of my well-being!

When I boarded the destroyer alongside Fidel, my spirits were at low ebb; I was saying good-bye to the security, the familiarity, that the *Esmeralda* had represented for me all these days, and entering a world unfamiliar and, given the formalities of protocol that were still so firmly in place, somehow sinister.

Fidel insisted that I go up to the bridge, where the rolling of the ship was dreadful. The destroyers then passed at full speed alongside the *Esmeralda*, whose crew, lined up on the deck, saluted the Head of State of Cuba. As soon as we turned and headed back to Havana, I noted that Fidel drew away, avoiding the conversations with me that had been so frequent and apparently open and free of tension during the visit of the ship.

With that inexhaustible restlessness of his, Fidel roamed the ship, examining it and conversing with its crew. Suddenly, looking into a round hole that led to the rocket storage compartment, he lost his footing and disappeared from our view. Piñeiro and the others ran to help him, but Fidel had already gotten up and was climbing the ladder under his own steam, poking his head out, a little angrily, above the steel plates of the deck. I now remember the story of the finger he had dislocated a few days earlier when he was pushing around rail cars during a visit to a mine, and recall too the strange photograph that the news agencies broadcast, months later, from Chile: Fidel about to fall off a boat, caught by the quick hands of the crew, with one foot on the boat and the rest of his body off it, head downward.

Once again the elements (which the Maximum Leader wished to dominate at all costs) showed that they could betray him. But Fidel, too, was under the lucky star of the great, who are saved by that star over and over again from those very elements!

The Commander-in-Chief's coolness toward me continued throughout the return voyage, which in spite of the speed of the boat seemed interminable to me. In my presence he ordered up a lunch, which would be served the minute land was reached, for the principal persons there—the chancellor, Piñeiro, and some others—but made not the slightest move to invite me. My exclusion from the circle of the chosen few became thus all the more clear. After ordering this lunch, Fidel sat down on a steel bulkhead on the bridge and started chatting with the youngest crew members. The noise and the wind prevented me from catching his words, nor did I think it my place, given the marginal standing that I had just been assigned by the lunch order, to make any attempt to hear them.

On Pier Number One, which we stepped onto a bit dizzily after the rolling of the destroyer, our leavetaking was brief and glacial. The blue Alfa Romeo now awaited me, and was still being driven by my friend Tomás, although two or three days later he would be replaced, as though his caring treatment of me had become a serious inconvenience. The car started and it slowly drove toward me to pick me up. We returned to the Habana Riviera at full speed, driving down the sunny Malecón beside an ocean from which the four masts of the *Esmeralda* had disappeared, and whose empty horizon I gazed upon now with dismayed and apprehensive melancholy.

Havana, March 6, 1971

Conversation last night with Regis Debray. After his four years in prison in Camiri, in the interior of Bolivia, he went to Chile, where he often saw Salvador Allende and Neruda. He admits that in spite of a certain prejudice on his part against Neruda, Neruda's personality won him over. Neruda spoke to him of me, which is why he has asked Paz Espejo, a Chilean woman who teaches philosophy at the University of Havana, to set up a meeting with me.

Debray speaks little, slowly, watching me. He has no doubt been warned about me by his Cuban friends. He asks me about the *Esmeralda*'s visit. What do I think? As I reply, his questions become more pointed. This takes on the air of an interrogation.

"I believe," I say, "that the visit has been good for Fidel, because it has shown in a tangible way that the blockade is broken and because it has shown the captain of the ship that Fidel is an honest and honorable leader, concerned night and day about improving the Island's economy. On the other hand, I'm not sure the visit was so good for Salvador Allende."

"Why not?" shoots back Debray, pricking up his ears, abandoning for the moment his impassivity and revealing a hint of aggressiveness.

"Because the sailors arrived at a very critical juncture for Cuba, after the failure of the ten-million-ton harvest, and while they are obviously aware of the difficulties faced by the Island they took away the impression that Allende, for purely political reasons, has been painting an idyllic picture of Cuba which in no way corresponds to reality. The sailors' general impression, which they share with many Chileans, is that Allende wants to do an experiment very similar to Cuba's in Chile, with differences that are intended to calm public opinion but that are definitely of secondary importance. Therefore, seeing the situation in Cuba up close traumatized them, it made a violent impression on them, and one that is not in the interest of the Allende government. Do you see?"

Debray makes a stubborn gesture to indicate that he does, although he is far from sharing the sailors' opinion—or my own as he thinks he sees it. Everything about him, though—his deliberate slowness, his reserve (in spite of which he utters quite a few revealing remarks)—corresponds to the end of innocence, the end of illusions, the end of the romantic revolutionary stage. When he first came to Havana, *Juventud Rebelde* announced a long program with Regis Debray on television. That program has never been mentioned again. Rumors abound that Fidel had not wanted the program aired; according to this story, Fidel's relations with Debray were now not nearly so good as they had been in the past.

I ask him about his impression of Cuba today, after the years and the events that have transpired since his last visit. Debray runs his hand through his thick silky blond hair; he tries to describe the neck of a bottle, pointing at the bottle of whisky I have brought him and asking if such an expression exists in Spanish. I tell him that exactly the same expression is used in Spanish: bottleneck. And so then I in turn ask him: When does he think the Cuban Revolution will emerge from this "jam"?

"History is slow," Regis Debray says.

We decide to go visit another Chilean friend of ours, a woman, but first we separate: He has to meet somebody else for a second. Debray reappears at our Chilean friend's house almost two hours later, in the company of the famous Antonio Arguedas. Debray hadn't said a word about bringing along the former Bolivian minister of the interior, a man who had confessed to being recruited and paid by the CIA, and the person who had turned over Ché Guevara's Bolivian diary to the Cuban revolutionary government.

In terms that strike me as unreal, though which probably contain a considerable amount of truth, Arguedas talks about the power of the CIA in Chile. He names a high-ranking official in the Frei administration and says that he was the CIA man in the Christian Democratic government. Arguedas equates the Chilean and Bolivian governments entirely too schematically and ignores the considerable differences between the two. He also gives the impression that he is attempting to justify himself by seeing the CIA around every corner.

He says after secretly fleeing Bolivia in the wake of the Ché Guevara diary incident, he was arrested in Chile, and that he asked to be allowed to make a statement to the press. The man conducting the interrogations at the time was that man in the Frei administration. The official offered to arrange a press conference, on the condition that Arguedas not discuss certain very delicate matters concerning the role of the CIA in Latin America. The hour of the press conference arrived, and Arguedas was led to a room in the Investigations Building, in the center of Santiago. There he found reporters, photographers, television cameras waiting for him. The next morning he asked to see the newspapers; there was not one line, one word, about his press conference. Nor was there any in the afternoon papers. During his next interrogation he railed against the official for having played such a dirty trick on him and put on such a farce.

"But you didn't keep your end of the bargain," the government official said. "You talked about matters that you had given your word not to talk about."

Arguedas reminds me of the Dominican journalist who stood up at the

Congress of the International Organization of Journalists in early January and declared himself a double agent. State Security specializes in these situations; they create a climate that justifies the existence of State Security and its growth. The paradox lies in the fact that the CIA actually exists; if it has not managed to bring down the Revolution, thanks for that probably go to the efficiency of the State Security system. It is said that State Security found out about the plans for the Bay of Pigs invasion before it happened. It is also said to have deflected various attempts on the life of Fidel Castro. But State Security's excess of zeal, its autonomous growth, have become a danger of another sort; they erode and undermine the Revolution in another way. Given the cancerous growth of the State Security apparatus, it would seem that the only remedy is the erosion of power that comes with time.

Chile, in the meantime, tries to carry out its Revolution without the need for a police-state apparatus—with no more police presence than in any normal state. I acknowledge, of course, that the phrase "normal state" is meaningless, and that if it were within their power to do so, many militants of the Unidad Popular would set up a secret police apparatus, and that it would be as sinister as any other. The seeds of that police apparatus are no doubt already beginning to germinate and send out tendrils in Chile, but in absolute contrast with what has occurred under the Stalinist terror-state, the Chilean apparatus will only have the power of surveillance, not the power of repression, much less the power to physically destroy their imaginary or real enemies.[6]

Was this peaceful, non-repressive revolutionary process possible in Chile? The antibodies triggered by right-wing fascism were, no doubt about it, inevitable. Every morning at the same hour and following the same route, General Schneider traveled without escort to his offices in the Ministry of Defense building. It was more than likely that his successor would have an escort, would travel at no fixed time or along any fixed route. After those days, Chilean politics were not a secure activity any more. Meanwhile, the "police" on both sides, the double and triple agents, multiply at will. Is a revolution conceivable without a State Security system, without the Comité de Santé

---

[6] These musings from my journal can now be seen to be at once optimistic and filled with dread. The experiment was worth trying, but it was stamped out before it could bear fruit.

Publique looming in the shadow of the guillotine? And was this a valid reason to wish to put it off for another day?

I wondered in those days if the experiment of the Chilean revolution was worth trying: a revolution taking place within a pluralism of political parties and respecting the freedom of expression. But going back to Debray, he had many friends, in both Cuba and Chile, who were watching the Unidad Popular's current experiment with secret scorn, seeing in it a simple transition to an inevitable confrontation whose violence, whatever the outcome might be, would invalidate the peaceful principles that were invoked by the Allende government.

A conversation upon my arrival late that night at the hotel:

"Is there any fresh milk?"

"What room, sir?"

"1813."

"Yes, sir, there's fresh milk."

The eighteenth, nineteenth, and twentieth floors of the hotel were reserved for official guests of the greatest importance.

Padilla had been living in another hotel, but then he had been sent back for a few days to the Habana Riviera. For my own part, I felt that after the visit of the *Esmeralda* and the tense, even curt last minutes I had spent with Fidel as we returned to land and parted on the pier, I was in serious trouble. My mission in Havana might mark both the zenith and the abrupt end of my diplomatic career. The thought of this possibility, even if no government official or diplomat in the world would believe it, brought a sense of real relief to me. At last I could devote myself to writing, I could make my living with work connected with literature. I didn't realize that a personal conflict with the Cuban regime could have much more serious consequences than I had imagined—not just the end of my career and being freed so that I could devote myself calmly to writing and cultivating my garden (or the moon, if I wanted to!), but consequences that would pursue me for a very long time, and in any activity I undertook, not just my writing. Writing, it turns out, is a political activity *par excellence,* and however much writers would like to shield themselves behind the banner of professional neutrality (or neutral professionalism?), it is a very hypothetical banner to shield yourself behind.

Padilla was overwrought, insane, and Belkis on occasion seemed to add fuel to the flame. Padilla would start screaming, for example, when the waiter didn't bring his salad fast enough, or he would bluster in indignation over at his table when somebody at my table didn't ask for the cigar he was entitled to, and so wasted the chance to give it to someone else. On one occasion, at the end of a conversation in my room during the course of which Padilla had been drinking pretty heavily, he started yelling toward the supposed bugs planted in every corner of the room.

"Did you hear that, Piñeiro?" he would scream. "And you ought to know that X. was here, too, and although he didn't say anything he didn't disagree with what we were saying, either. Do you hear me?"

I took Padilla by the arm and gently pulled him out of my room, while X., who was terribly concerned, shook his head, no doubt saying to himself in his heart of hearts that my goose was cooked, it was best not to see me anymore.

Padilla's indiscretion and egocentrism had become frankly dangerous.

"This is going to come out badly for Padilla," X. told me. But that meant it would come out badly for all of us.

"It would be interesting for you to meet Y.," I said to Cristián Huneeus one rainy day during his literary/sightseeing tour. We met at a friend's house, and I took along two bottles of whisky: one to drink during our conversation and another for our host. Y. had been a revolutionary from the very beginning, and had held high offices in the government. My idea was that Huneeus should not just meet writers. Writers, save some who could claim greater maturity or experience, as in the cases of José Lezama Lima or Enrique Labrador Ruiz, always came back to the same subjects, the same stories, the same old tired gossip.

We drank the first bottle voraciously, and within forty-five minutes, as usual, tongues had loosened. Y., who drank right along with the rest of us, listened with pleasure as Huneeus and I talked about the *Esmeralda*'s visit, speculated on the future of Chile, and wondered about the influence that the Cuban government might have in Chile. At eleven that night I left; I had an appointment early the next morning.

Three or four days later, I was told how Y. had reacted. He had wound up getting quite drunk and telling Padilla, as he drove him home, that if Huneeus and I were not already CIA agents, we'd wind up being ones sooner or later. When the revolutionary process got tougher in Chile, he said, we'd come out against the revolution. Weren't those two bottles of whisky I'd brought along suspicious? Couldn't one smell a whiff of bribery in that gesture of mine? At the high point of his drunkenness, Y. declared somebody ought to formally accuse Huneeus and me. Padilla, alarmed, had told him not to do anything until he sobered up and talked to him again the next day.

That, at least, was the version of the evening's dénouement that we were given. Did Y. make his accusation? Did his drunken aggressiveness take exactly the form we were told it did? Had certain details been omitted from the version that reached our ears? I have already said that in the process of writing this book I discover truths that I had not perceived before. I also come up against mysteries which I had not, and have still not, achieved an entirely lucid grasp of.[7]

Through all this, Padilla continued to maintain that his international prestige, which he was a master at magnifying out of all proportion to reality, would protect him from any unpleasant surprises that might be sprung at him out of the State Security machinery. My own nervous tension grew, as did my insomnia, and with ever-increasing anxiety I began to fear that I would be trapped on this Island, that I would never be able to recover the kind of life that I had once possessed and that now I saw as the most desirable, yet least attainable, life imaginable.

Several "friends," both men and women, approached me under one pretext or other, through all of which it was easy to see that they were attempting to obtain any information I might have about the visit of the *Esmeralda*. This odd insistence revealed that my situation, and that of some of my friends, had, after the visit of the *Esmeralda*, turned critical.

The only moments of calm were given me by P., with whom I went to the beach on Sunday mornings to have a swim and take a walk along the ocean. P. was an older man, and he had had a full life. He looked with a degree of distrust upon the intellectualism, or mental overexcitement, of Padilla, especially as it alternated with bouts of terrible depression. P. did not fool himself that the economic situation of Cuba was good, but his view of the Revolution took a wider perspective, and he did not employ oversubtle arguments in discussing

---

[7] Y., in truth Alberto Mora, was the son of Menelao Mora, who was one of the organizers of the assault on Batista's Palace of Government in 1957, and who died in the attempt. Alberto disembarked in the Escambray mountains, the second front in the struggle against Batista, early the next year. In the first stage of the Revolution, he was minister of foreign trade. Heberto Padilla was director of one of the offices within that ministry, the office concerned with the trade of books and art objects with foreign countries. In the days that I was living in Havana as chargé d'affaires, Alberto Mora, who had been removed from power some time before, dreamed of starting a new life as a film director. Some time after I left Cuba, and after Padilla's brief imprisonment and the famous self-criticism, I learned that Alberto Mora had committed suicide.

it. He belonged to a family of pre-Revolutionary sugar-industry millionaires. He recalled that in the old days he would drive to this same beach, where he had opened a bar, in a block-long automobile. The last yearly dividend he had received from his family sugar-processing plants had been a check for a hundred thousand dollars, and he had spent it on a ten-month vacation in Europe. His family had emigrated to Miami and New York; he had become the sheep that strayed from the fold into the clutches of Castroism, and his family bitterly reproached him for it.

During our walks along the endless beach of white sand, pine trees, and clear blue water, he would tell me stories of his role in the early literacy campaigns. He had never before had any real contact with the Cuban campesino. During his stint with the campaign he had realized how appalling the poverty of the countrypeople was, and what the medical assistance, teachers, and other forms of social and legal justice brought to them by the Revolution meant to their lives. P. had seen a child with maggots crawling from his ears and mouth; he had seen the child die from a plague that in a very short time the Revolution's medical and sanitary initiatives would totally eradicate from the Island. The vision of that maggot-eaten child had finished the education of my friend's conscience. At the same time, the abundance that he had known before the Revolution had led him, with the passing of time and in virtue of a process of saturation or satiation, to an attitude tantamount to asceticism. He had grown accustomed to a life of poverty, of doing without many things, and rationing hardly affected him. He had come to appreciate the simplest gifts of life: the ocean, the sun, an orange, a new razor blade, a cup of thick rich black coffee. In his mature years he had discovered Balzac, the great monster of the European novel. As P. was nearsighted, his greatest desire was to own a copy of *The Human Comedy* in large letters. Sometime afterward, from Barcelona, I sent him the edition he needed, along with a special magnifying glass to help his reading.

At Padilla's public self-criticism, chaired by José Antonio Portuondo less than two months later, P. was the only one of the people who had been members of the "Padilla gang" that was not subpoenaed. I now think that his exclusion from the self-criticism, decided at who knows what level of the hierarchy, was an act of good judgment, though his exclusion might cause the evil-minded to raise their eyebrows and venture conjectures as to the nature of the role played by P. in the events that preceded the self-criticism. This generalized mistrust, which is capable of poisoning any human relations, is one of the vices that are typically engendered by State Police apparatus. But it is important to rise above these suspicions, this distrust, especially in a situation as tense as ours was during those days, for if not, the absolute predominance of distrust winds up perpetuating the power of the security apparatus. And modern history has shown how strong and fearsome such power is, and how rich with ramifications and subtleties that surpass the imagination of simple citizens. But history has demonstrated, too, that in spite of the appearance of indestructibility, the State Security apparatus, whatever its name, has feet of clay. It moves in, and with incredible quickness it spreads its nets, stretches its tentacles everywhere, like the cells of some malignant tumor, but through phenomena as simple as trust between one person and another, phenomena by definition incomprehensible to a secret police agent, human nature in the long run checks its progress.

I will pay no mind, then, to the evil-minded, but rather go on thinking that the authorities acted rightly in saving P. his own self-criticism. In our blurriest and most alcoholic conversations he would keep his own confidence, and later, when we were alone, he would give me a balanced view of things, without any sort of demagogy or the rhetorical excesses of negativism or "subjectivism."

I had other wonderful friends, whose cases would also merit an effort of understanding and sympathy on the part of the Powers That Be, in spite of the fact that the Powers That Be, wrapped in their cloaks of self-satisfaction and with their backs covered by international "understandings," don't seem inclined to make such efforts. M., for example, made me think of one of those great women of the old Hispano-American tradition: self-denying, strong-willed, straight-talking, concerned with the slightest detail of the house, the children, the husband, and at the same time gracious and good-humored. Even her pale, broad face, lined with work, embodied the Cuban heritage in its noblest aspect.

Others were fearful, frightened, crushed by the situation. Since they had no fixed work, nothing to keep them constantly occupied, their minds became hyperactive. The ghosts of the imagination, wakened and roused by the surveillance, the noises on the telephone, the occasional visits from acquaintances who came to look around and take notes on the conversations, the books that were lying on the table, the undesirable company—all this transformed idleness into nightmare. They killed time by standing in line at the stores or by puttering around the house. Bewilderment and anxiety made them talk too much, and perhaps count too much on the changes their friends from Chile might make when they came. How could our coming improve the situation? If they had had some experience, they might have foreseen the danger and kept a prudent distance. Some of them were led later to the stage at UNEAC by the first violin Padilla, at the behest of the implacable baton of *maestro* Portuondo, the conductor of all this, and their unconnected and raggedy confessions marked the most painful moment of that collective self-criticism. Borrowing a phrase someone used to say good-bye to me, I might say that I hope to live long enough to return someday and sit down with a bottle of Chilean wine over a plate of black beans and rice, and talk, in socialist Cuba, with these friends again.

Mónica Echeverría, the wife of the chancellor of the Catholic University in Chile, had said to me with the perfect candor, the perfect innocence of a woman who had been invited to come for a short time to Cuba, and who was perfectly unaware of the internal tensions of the Revolution: "Miyar, the chancellor of the University of Havana, told me you spend too much time with Padilla and his friends, and that you ought to visit the University and see another side of things."

"Well," I said, "diplomatic work hasn't left me much free time. I like to see my writer friends when I have some time to relax. And as for Heberto Padilla, for some time he's been living in the same hotel I do, one floor away from me, so I could hardly stop seeing him even if I wanted to."

Mónica looked at me in surprise, although with no pretense of drawing any great conclusions from the detail I had just revealed to her.

"Still," I added, "tell the chancellor that I'll call him as soon as the *Esmeralda*'s visit is over."

Mónica Echeverría's innocent and well-intentioned warning came on the eve of the training ship's arrival. I had invited the chancellor and his wife to the Laura Allende dinner, which Mónica also attended, but he excused himself. He had then, as part of Fidel's retinue and designated photographer, gone out to see the ship off. I knew that Miyar had talked with Padilla several times, on Fidel Castro's behalf, about a year after the storied publication of *Fuera de juego*, the book of poems that had won Padilla the Casa de las Américas poetry prize, given by an international jury, and which had then been published with a strongly critical introduction written by the Cuban literary authorities. Through the offices of the widow of a guerrilla killed with Ché Guevara in Bolivia, Padilla, who had spent a year without occupation after the *Fuera de juego* incident, sent a letter to Fidel asking for work. It was then that the chancellor had called him and had more than one meeting with him.

Padilla said that on that occasion, through the intervention of Fidel and the chancellor of the university, his political problems had come to an end. He insinuated with some bravado that Fidel had, on account of that letter, defended him to the most hardline sectors of the government: State Security and the Army, Manuel Piñeiro and Raúl Castro. Fidel's presence, according to Padilla, was a guarantee against sectarianism, which without that moderating influence would already have invaded Cuban life in every aspect and made it thoroughly militant, in the best manner of Stalin.

In early 1971, as I have said, insistent rumors of a change of command circulated through the diplomatic corps. Padilla had nothing but contempt for such gossip. Fidel would never agree to share power, much less with a man like Carlos Rafael Rodríguez! He was capable, by temperament, of bringing the country to the verge of apocalypse, but he would never willingly give in or give up. His reactions during the October 1962 missile crisis, when Khrushchev was said to have withdrawn the nuclear warheads from the island without consulting Fidel, had been sufficiently revealing. The Soviets knew these reactions of his by now, and took the necessary precautions. A delegation from the Chilean Communist Party reproached Khrushchev at the time for not having consulted Fidel before pulling out the missiles, and Khrushchev gave them a simple, crude answer: "And what if Fidel said no?"

But let's go back to those days in February and March 1971, when another grave crisis was developing. This one, however, was not so spectacular as the 1962 missile crisis, and was, in consequence, overlooked by the international press. What happened was this: Fidel believed that if the country could produce a bumper sugarcane crop in 1970 and every year subsequently, the country's economic problems would be solved: Sugar could be sold on the world market for all the goods and services that Cuba needed. In order to achieve this record crop, every resource, both material and human, of the Revolution was put at its service. Men and women (and children, sometimes) who worked in the city were encouraged to go into the fields for periods of volunteer labor; Saturdays and Sundays became days of work. Great areas of land were planted in sugarcane, and other crops, especially of foodstuffs, were relatively neglected; the vegetable farms of the past may not have been converted into sugarcane fields, but their workers were "borrowed" for the sugarcane. Because the entire country was enlisted in the work of the crop, the entire country dreamed of the economic independence they were winning, and so when the crop "failed" (that is, when the goal of ten million tons was not reached), the entire country was emotionally devastated. And economically devastated as well, since the agricultural infrastructure had to a great degree been damaged. The shock to Cuba cannot be overstated; the fact that there was little drama in the failure (it was not a military defeat or a plague) and the fact that its effects were delayed, and not to be felt except over a period of time, made the Western press overlook it. But the failure of the "ten-million-ton harvest" became a turning point in the Revolution, a failure that must not be repeated, a bogeyman, a nightmare to those, like the writers and poets, conscripted against their will (and for naught, as it turned out)—but never the object lesson in planning and listening to expert advice that it might have been.

The delayed effects of the failure of the ten-million-ton harvest, whose terrible impact on every sector of the economy had been revealed by Fidel himself in that dramatic televised self-criticism in mid-1970, were making themselves felt now in February and March of 1971. Heberto Padilla was no more than a small irritation in the midst of this crisis, a supporting actor, but he had unexpectedly become dangerous, as well as usable in some sense, because of his contact with the diplomatic representative of the Chilean Unidad Popular.

Meanwhile, Padilla, who apparently lived in a state of intellectual fever, quite often contradicted himself. Sometimes he would say that he was kept afloat by the conflicting pulls of the currents within the government, which the internal crisis had aggravated. He could even enjoy certain privileges, such as his room in the Habana Riviera, thanks to the help of well-placed friends in the halls of power. One day at the front desk, after I had been staying there for a couple of weeks, he was told, in my presence, that he could stay fifteen more days, at a time when newlyweds with many political brownie-points were only allowed to stay five or six days.[8] Padilla had received the news with a vain, enigmatic smile, as though to suggest that a powerful invisible hand carried out his wishes. If that invisible hand existed, it was more than likely playing with the poet, for as we all know, those whom the gods would kill they first make mad. And that neurasthenic figure Y., who had found my gift of two bottles of whisky suspicious, had given me, in Padilla's presence, a piece of advice that no one had asked for and that therefore could apply to any of us present: "Forget any political ambition. If you get involved in politics there'll always be somebody colder and shrewder who'll play with you, who'll lead you on and pull your strings and generally use you for their own ends. If you feel that as a writer you can do something worthwhile, then do *that*, and take advantage of favorable situations. Keep your relations to politics, diplomacy, and literature, as well. The example of Stendhal."

The example that Stendhal gave, he might have added, after a long hard period of learning, and of wracking disillusionments, the same sort of learning and disillusionments that I myself was going through those days at a dizzying pace—so dizzying, in fact, that there were times when I felt that my head was about to explode or that I was going to stop breathing and die of asphyxia.

I called the chancellor of the university, then, after we parted from the *Esmeralda* with its wind-filled white sails headed out to the open sea, and he immediately gave me an appointment for the next day (or perhaps it was the day after that, I'm not certain).

---

[8] The Revolution dedicated the Habana Riviera to newlyweds and VIPs. You didn't walk in and ask for a room.

Accompanied by one of his staff, the chancellor greeted me in the Council Chamber of the old university, the same room that can be seen as a backdrop in the photographs of the young Fidel Castro when he was the leader of student demonstrations. Miyar was a man of about the same age as Castro, and had probably been alongside Fidel, literally or figuratively, in those student struggles as well as in the guerrilla war in the Sierra Maestra. Within the revolutionary hierarchy, Miyar's post was considered to have considerable strategic importance, as his job was to guide and oversee the education of the future leaders and technical talent of the Cuban Revolution. Miyar had the Prime Minister's absolute confidence.

The chancellors of the principal Chilean universities had visited Cuba not long ago, at the invitation of the University of Havana. Miyar spoke with pleasure of that visit. He made it clear, however, that the concerns of his Chilean counterparts were still far removed from the concept of the role of the university that Cuba now espoused. The university, according to Miyar, must be closely linked to the revolutionary task of creating a new society.

"You understand, S. Edwards—this was not a country. We are the ones who have been given the job of creating it."

The university could not afford to devote itself to purely academic exercises or purely academic research. On the contrary, it had to be an instrument in the development of the nation's economy. Miyar, who suggested but very diplomatically left unspoken the contrast he saw with Chilean universities, talked to me about the work that was being done to determine the best varieties of sugarcane for the soils and climate of the Island, the experimental farms the students were working on, the systematic research into pineapple and citrus farming, into artificial insemination. I listened attentively and with real interest. For my own part, I didn't doubt that Chilean universities had to reform and renew themselves. As a young man I had been the victim of a purely book-oriented law school, and was never taught what a real defense of a just cause might consist of. This was the dense and intransigent mediocrity of the González Videla presidency. The profound dissatisfaction and discontent I had experienced, and which my generation manifested in anarchic rebelliousness, was the herald of a different historical stage to come. From the standpoint of today, though, I think that those years I spent in the University of Chile Law School between 1949 and 1953 taught me more than a little. The arguments that Miyar used to support his points of view were excellent, but he overlooked the fact that his arguments might not be entirely applicable to a university older than his, and that I, as a diplomatic representative, might not be the proper person to point that out to him. In a backward country, more than in any other, the university ought to teach men and women how to think, since underdevelopment and mental confusion (which is always encouraged by imperialism's untiring propaganda machine) always go hand in hand. Teaching people to think is a more complex and perhaps more important work than selecting seeds or perfecting ways to cut sugarcane. But in our conversation, Miyar was unequivocal, categorical, definitive, in a clear allusion to other sorts of conversations, which apparently were the worst kind of crime:

"In Cuba we don't need critics," he said. "Criticizing is easy. You can criticize anything. What's hard is doing something, working, creating a country. That is what we need: doers, builders of society."

In those days one heard it said that certain sectors of the government had begun a campaign against a magazine whose name was suddenly to take on strongly subversive connotations: *Pensamiento Crítico*, "Critical Thinking." This was a journal of Marxist studies published by the Department of Philosophy at the University of Havana. Both Chileans and Cubans with ties to the university whispered in my ear that Raúl Castro was in favor of suppressing it and putting all Marxist theoretical studies under the control of the Army. I had run into Jesús Díaz, who had been awarded a prize by the Casa de las Américas for a book of short stories, and other contributors to *Pensamiento Crítico* in the home of Paz Espejo, a colleague of theirs at the university. They asked me many questions about Peru and Chile. I talked to them about the originality of the Peruvian Revolution, its unquestionably progressive aspects, agrarian reform and the Industrial Law, the systems of worker participation (something like capitalistic profit-sharing plans) and control of foreign capital that had been worked out by the military men now in power. Change came, I said, to Latin America in unforeseen ways, and caught American imperialism with its guard down.

(At the time, I still had some hopes for the so-called military revolution in Peru. I have since seen it as a military dictatorship of a populist ideology, but one which was not exempt from the basic evils of all dictatorships: a press muzzled, thought in chains, universities crushed. And to top it all off, the conduct of the economy was a crashing failure, brought on by demagogy and the impossibility of critical control of the acts of the government. I now believe that in spite of the inevitable problems that the Belaúnde government would face, when the citizens of Peru elected Fernando Belaúnde as an escape from dictatorship they gave a stirring example of good political judgment.)

Paz Espejo later told me that my explanations and replies had satisfied my interlocutors very well, but that she had gotten the impression that they had been disappointed by the fact that I had not asked them questions in return. This comment puzzled me. They had wanted to meet with me to talk about

Chile and Peru. Was I supposed to ask young people I was meeting for the very first time questions about Cuba?

"Apparently they wanted to talk to you," said Paz.

"Then why didn't they?" I replied.

But speaking out under their own initiative, without waiting for questions from me, would have put them in a compromising position. And putting questions about Cuba, right off the bat, to a circle of totally new faces would have been more than compromising for me, so Chile and Peru, even though they were similar because both had broken the blockade of Cuba, were still immeasurably far apart. I might give myself the luxury of describing them the way the astronauts did when they described the surface of the moon.

After I left Cuba I was told that *Pensamiento Crítico* had been shut down once and for all. Criticizing, as the chancellor of the university had told me, was easy; what was hard was building. Meanwhile, Jesús Díaz had had a chance to visit Chile, and in a meeting of the Institute of Chilean Literature in Santiago he had been introduced in the following way: "Capitán Jesús Díaz, director of the Department of Philosophy at the University of Havana."

In that meeting, somebody asked his opinion of the work of Severo Sarduy and Guillermo Cabrera Infante, famous expatriate Cuban novelists.

Jesús Díaz: "What are we here for—to talk about literature or about *gusanos*?" He explained that he was willing to discuss the work of friends of the Revolution, but that the creations of its enemies should be dismissed and, in the words of a Díaz emulator, in a private but nonetheless famous letter to an English critic, "struck from the annals of human culture."

When the meeting at the Institute of Chilean Literature was over, Jesús Díaz asked a small group of like-minded people, as might have been predicted, about the political tendencies of the person who had mentioned the two forbidden names. Some of the Chileans present, in spite of belonging to that inner circle, came away with a queasy feeling about Díaz' question. And as for Capitán Jesús Díaz, he must have thought that in order to avoid any unpleasant surprises the future might hold, the neophyte revolutionaries of Chile needed to be brought smartly into line. It came as a great surprise for me to learn in Madrid last year that Jesús Diaz doesn't think that way anymore. He has decided to stay in Europe, and so he has turned into a *gusano* himself.

The chancellor invited me to walk with him through some of the buildings of the university. We visited an important research institute where biological, botanical, and other experiments were underway. To the eyes of an outsider, it all looked like the most modern technology. We walked endlessly through rooms filled with machines and equipment incomprehensible to me, all attended by young men and women in white smocks and aprons who smiled at us as we passed. There, hidden behind the crumbling façades of Havana, the seeds of the future country, the nucleus of creation of the Revolution, seemed to be germinating. If instead of refusing me entrance to the Protocol reception area at the airport, while the twine on the box of wine cut into my fingers, and leaving me stranded several days without transportation in my un-air-conditioned rooms at the Habana Riviera, they had taken me that first week to tour these laboratories which swarmed with busy, healthy-looking, happy-looking young men and women, my entire experience on the Island might have been different. But now, perhaps, by the time the chancellor had invited me on this walk, it was too late. My rooms in the Habana Riviera had been peopled with muttering, cursing, grumbling ghosts that had set up their bazaars in my quarters.

The chancellor also took me to the huge Engineering School, whose buildings had not yet been completed. Among the throngs of students that passed through the open, airy spaces of the first floor, dodging the great cement columns, I saw many Vietnamese faces. In the electrical engineering laboratories I got a distant sense of what they were studying. I observed that the upper-level students took an active part in the teaching of the newer students. In that way, they helped to address the problem of teacher shortage.

The projects that Miyar showed me were like islands of progress in a sea of deterioration and backwardness.

The Cuban Revolution had started at a very primitive economic level: these projects were brilliant images of the future, but they were still very small and very limited in scope. The secretary-consul, who was always depressed by the discomforts that haunted our hotel, looked at me now, as we toured all these laboratories, with eyes of frank enthusiasm. Here's what we've been looking for! he seemed to say to me.

Our lunch came from a university farm, excellent food, and then we set off to visit some of the agricultural facilities. We saw one area where different varieties of pineapple were being tested. In a little field hut we were given slices of pineapple to taste, the most delicious pineapple I have ever tasted; the flesh melted into sweetness and perfume, as though the entire essence of the tropics had been distilled there.

We went through a huge field of sugarcane. This cane looked greener, straighter and more erect, fuller and more regular than any I'd seen elsewhere. The young people walking about near the administration huts looked healthy and optimistic, too, and this look was not what one saw in the streets of Old Havana or the lobbies of luxury hotels. There could be no doubt that the Revolution had been fought and won and was now being carried on for these young men and women; they embodied the destiny of the country in its finest expression. And yet—how was one going to get the same degree of perfection in pineapples and sugarcane all across the Island? Could it be grown like this? Within the university farms everything seemed to work beautifully, but outside them, everything had fallen into erosion, decay, discouragement, absenteeism. How was the entire Island to be converted into a university project, a young people's experiment?

I suspected that Fidel had more than once been tempted to seek out this Utopia. On Isla de Pinos, the Isle of Pines, that lay off the coast of Cuba, and that I had visited in 1968, he had probably tried to realize this ambition: The Isla de Pinos was governed by young people, and socialism and communism were being tried in parallel. But it was very likely that the problems on the much larger Island of Cuba, which were the result of the clash of generous aspirations and pig-headed reality, would, after the three years that had passed since my visit, have by now begun to plague the Isle of Pines as well.

That afternoon Miyar and I got on a tractor and rode through a university citrus farm. Miyar was sitting on the right fender, straddling the headlight, and I on the left. We tasted some of the most delicious oranges, mandarin oranges, and grapefruit I have ever eaten. The neatness of the groves and the orderliness of the irrigation system were perfect. In a clearing, surrounded by the dense dark green of the trees, as the shadows of evening began to gather around us, I caught sight of a mound of fresh, shining fruit. I imagined the riot those oranges would have caused if they had been in a store in Old Havana or El Vedado. There was a shocking contradiction between the deserted abundance of that mound of oranges suddenly come upon in this clearing and those sad stores, which lacked the bright spots of color that would have been lent them by fruits and vegetables, and where people stood in line to hand over their ration coupons to buy a little coffee, some matches, a ration of rice and sugar, plus the unfailing head of cabbage, which sometimes, too, had to be bought with ration coupons.

On my return, Heberto Padilla was still in the Habana Riviera, where he still, against all the normal rules, was in possession of his rooms. His emotional state had reached the stage of paroxysm by this time; he was almost completely out of control. I talked to him about the wonderful projects I had just visited.

"They're microwonderful projects! They're microgreat projects! Do you understand?" he raged at me. "They're micro-big-deal projects!"

I did understand. The economy of socialism might concentrate its efforts on one small sector and obtain visible, exciting results, results that were also good for impressing the foreign visitor, but their significance for the general economic development of the nation should not be overestimated. Still, in those "microgreat projects" one might discover the seeds of a future abundance, an abundance that in itself would relieve the tensions of the country and allow poets to wander about and breathe freely. As people have been saying since Plato, poets are the vehicles of criticism, the spokesmen of our discontent. It's virtually impossible that the world work any other way. Therefore, not tolerating criticism inevitably means putting a gag on writers. Padilla was not muzzled yet, but I think that at the height of his agitation he sensed that the gag was near. Almost in spite of himself, his criticism turned quickly to bitterness and venom. In spite of his lucidity, the impression he gave was that the pressures he was under had in some way driven him over the edge. During those days he started taking his manuscript with him everywhere he went, sharing the responsibility of guarding it with his wife Belkis.[9] He kept Belkis informed in detail of his itinerary for each day, and she would telephone him periodically to make sure that he was all right. Had they had some sign, some concrete warning that State Security was about to switch from surveillance to action, or were they simply interpreting that cloak-and-dagger, secret police atmosphere that enveloped them, and all of us? How had that scene with Y. and his drunken revelations, his threats of accusation, really gone? I refused to ask too many questions, in spite of the show Padilla made about protecting his manuscript; that ostentation seemed designed to invite questions, but it never really disturbed me too much because it was characteristic of Heberto's style, his persona of the moment.

As all this was going on, the term of my mission was coming to an end. The ambassador was supposed to arrive soon. The Unidad Popular in Chile was a coalition of political groups, and so the Chilean foreign embassies were shared out among the member-groups. As the dividing-up took place, it was agreed that the Cuban mission would fall to MAPU, which was a group that had arisen in 1969 out of a breakaway leftist sector of the Christian Democrats. By late 1970 it was dominated by its youngest militants, who had pushed aside the parliamentarists and former high officials of the Frei administration such as Alberto Jerez, Jacques Chonchol, and Julio Silva Solar, and given the party a Marxist-Leninist direction pretty far removed from the Christian-reformist

---

[9] The manuscript of the novel *En mi jardín pastan los héroes* (*Heroes Are Grazing in My Garden*, trans. A. Hurley, New York: Farrar Straus & Giroux, 1984) was published in Spain (Argos Vergara, 1981) after Heberto left Cuba.

tendencies of its origins. The group's definition, however courageous it may have been, had one great drawback: MAPU lost the chance to act as a bridge between the Catholic middle class, at the time largely disillusioned with the Frei government, and the Unidad Popular, which began with a minority in Parliament and so had an urgent need for support of that kind. There were already two large Marxist groups in the coalition supporting Allende. Was it really necessary to add a third, ultra-Marxist, party or was it more important to maintain links with the Christian petit-bourgeoisie? The answer now belongs to the realm of historical speculation. I had seen Alberto Jerez before I went to Cuba, and he had told me that "there was nothing to be done," that they, the "old men" of the group, none of whom was more than fifty years old, had lost the internal power struggle.

After the Senate's rejection of Jaime Gazmuri, who was the first MAPU candidate for the ambassador's job proposed by the Executive, Allende presented another name, and the Senate had gone along. The ambassador, Juan Enrique Vega, another of the young men who had taken over the MAPU leadership a year after its break with the Christian Democrats, was due to arrive in Cuba any time now. Meanwhile, the Foreign Ministry had informed me of the arrival of a career diplomat who would be replacing me as chargé d'affaires; this man would stay on after the arrival of the ambassador as minister-counselor to the embassy. I had been instructed that I would soon be transferred to Paris, where I would work with Pablo Neruda as his minister-counselor. From both the Cubans and myself, the Chilean Foreign Ministry had at least a partial version of the story of my difficulties, and they wanted to get me out of Havana.

At this time I had been in Havana for three months. I still had no house for the chief of mission, no offices for the embassy. I was leaving constant messages for Meléndez, but it was harder to get through to him than it was to Raúl Roa, the minister. Capitán Duque Estrada, director of the Americas Section of the Cuban Foreign Ministry, tried to help me find offices and a residence. He had seen a good house for the embassy in El Vedado, but it was currently occupied by some offices of the Academy of Sciences. Those particular offices seemed neither very important nor very necessary: There were pamphlets, old books, a few tables, and some typewriters, none in particularly mint condition. The first time I saw the house, at the beginning of my mission, I was promised that the house would be vacated soon. Weeks passed, however, and then months, and no one showed the slightest rush to move out, as though words spoken inside that house had a meaning exactly opposite that found in the dictionary. The young scientists smiled their virtually Oriental smiles, showed me around the rooms (where one saw no very great activity going on), and made imprecise references to an impending relocation. It was a house of mixed architectural style, built in the twenties; it was dark and cool, well-cared-for, and it had a large stained-glass window, yellow and green and red, in the vestibule, above the wrought-iron and marble staircase. The window portrayed a scene from *Don Quixote* with the face of Cervantes down in one corner. The house was on a quiet street of beautiful leafy trees, and opposite it stood a lovely colonial mansion that had belonged to José Martí. His elderly daughter lived there now.

The atmosphere of the Academy of Sciences offices somehow made me think of a Latin American biologist who often came to my office. Every visit left me exhausted. The man radiated indignation and bitterness. He had been a militant in left-wing organizations, and so had been persecuted by the reactionary governments of his country. For ideological reasons he had turned down offers of jobs in Europe and Mexico and had come to Cuba, where he thought he would be able to help from the scientific side in the forging of the Revolution. Only after long months had he managed to obtain a few rats for his experiments. And since he had no cages, he had had to keep the rats in an old iron bathtub, where they were still kept to this day. His greatest concern was his children's education. In his view, the situation in the Cuban schools had become disastrous. The biologist showed me his publications in international scientific journals. His only wish, now, was to go to Chile, where he thought scientific research might be carried on at a higher level.

Meanwhile, I had been shown a place the authorities wanted me to believe was the only possible residence for the ambassador: a sort of fake Renaissance palazzo in the Cubanacán section of Havana. It had been, several years ago, the site of the Chinese Embassy, but the Chinese, perhaps because of the proximity of the Soviets who were directly next door, had moved to another section of Havana. The enormous house, with its marble floors in black-and-white domino, its hand-carved cedar ceilings, its crystal, its columns, made one feel that one had stepped into the neurotic atmosphere of the films of Luis Buñuel. Its twisted luxury had a deranged, sickly look to it. And both the interior and the gardens of the house were in shambles; everything was covered with dust and cobwebs, broken shards of glass, and in the garden weeds grew wild. There was no alternative, though. The house would be fine after a month or two of repairs, and so I agreed, not without a twinge of compassion for the future Chilean ambassador to Cuba, who was after all the person who would have to live in it.

My own offices, then, continued to be in a suite on the eighteenth floor of the Hotel Habana Riviera. The only progress I had made was in managing to persuade the Powers That Be to give me offices separate from my private quarters. Every time I went to the Ministry of Foreign Relations I insisted that I be assigned the house in El Vedado that was to be used for the embassy; every time, I received the same charming smile and the same promises, which never came to any concrete end. We worked in Room 1819 with my portable typewriter and a kerosene lamp, which we used when the lights went out (as they did every afternoon). There we attended to the endless procession of Chileans who would come in, as Chileans did at embassies around the world, to say hello, ask for news from home, pick up mail, read the newspapers, and often ask for help in traveling to Chile. More than one young woman came in to plead for work at the embassy. She would have problems, for example, because her Cuban ex-husband wouldn't let her take their children out of the country.

These were for the most part problems that I could not solve. On one visit to Carlos Rafael Rodríguez I managed to get him to authorize a visa for the Cuban wife and children of a Chilean kid who had worked for Rodríguez for years. I obtained visas by similar means for others, as well, but the case of Chilean women with children of Cuban husbands had no visible solution.

The modest staff at the embassy consisted of the secretary-consul, who was a career officer in the Chilean Foreign Service; the Cuban woman who was our typist, and who had had some prior experience in embassies; my driver, who was assigned by Protocol; and me. Documents, newspapers, papers, and files (which accumulated at an unearthly rate) were piled on beds, tables, and in the closets. In the bathroom there were a couple of empty briefcases for use as diplomatic pouches. In the little safe that Protocol had lent us we kept the rubber stamps, the cables, and the "confidential" documents. The safe was fickle: Sometimes it opened as though of its own accord, and other times, even with the combination, it would remain hermetically sealed.

"The only solution," the secretary-consul would say, "is not to have secrets."

"What secrets are we going to have?" I would reply. "The only real secret this embassy has is that it doesn't have any secrets. But we must prevent that from leaking out, at all costs."

Almost every morning we were visited by a young man from the Cuban Foreign Ministry who would bring us two, three, or sometimes even more diplomatic or foreign service passports to be stamped. Many of these belonged to the support or domestic staff at the Cuban Embassy in Santiago. Some of the faces in the photos, which did not always look as though they were the best faces one could find for the salons of the diplomatic corps, were familiar to me. I later discovered that I had been seeing them wander about the lobbies, bars, and dining rooms of the Habana Riviera for weeks and weeks, rubbing up against the diplomats, the foreign visitors, and the Cubans of the embassy or hotel staffs.

Gossips in Chile told me that the Cuban Embassy in Santiago already occupied several floors of a building. The personnel had several houses. In Cuba, however, time passed and the Chilean Embassy in Havana, composed of two Chilean diplomats, a Cuban secretary, and a driver assigned to the embassy by the Office of Protocol, was still housed in Room 1819, still had no air conditioning as the months drew on and the weather grew hotter and hotter, was still using a portable typewriter for its official correspondence and a lantern for power outages, and had a safe that opened and closed as the demon inside saw fit.

It was natural that Cuba's only embassy in South America, after so many years of pan-American blockade, would be important. But Chilean gossips, egged on by the smiles of complicity of some Cubans, were beginning to whisper. One heard that certain diplomats had traveled to Chile for the purpose of organizing a State Security system similar to Cuba's for the Allende regime. I didn't think our highest priority was creating a secret police apparatus. Under the pretext of thwarting opposition conspiracies, all it was going to do was goad the opposition, furnish it with its own pretexts and give it ammunition for its own arguments, push people into the enemy fold. But state police forces (and when I say police here, I am always referring to large state secret-police-type organisms) thrive on the existence of enemies, visible or clandestine, and the perverseness of the whole situation is that they invent enemies in order to justify and increase their own power. The police bring about a polarization of political forces; they create a state-universe of Manicheanism. Their *modus operandi* is to exclude and simplify. That is why the state police, no matter how concrete their methods, are abstract and inhuman in their motives. Their raison d'être is the enemy within, and especially the enemy that is hidden, and that acts without scruple. Who can refute that raison d'être? The revelations from a U.S. source about the attempts to topple Chile's government were overwhelming arguments in their own right. But how was one to prevent the tentacular growth of the State Security apparatus? How was one to defend the Revolution without falling into the rarefied alter-universe of generalized suspicion and distrust? The experience of freedom and law was one reply, but a reply that found little credit or sympathy in the circles of power in Cuba.

Another of the gossips' hypotheses was that Cubans traveled to Chile to help in the armed confrontation that was considered now inevitable. Cubans, guerrilla fighters from Brazil, Bolivia, and Colombia, revolutionaries from everywhere were flocking to Chile. Since the imperialists, for their part, did not sleep, Chile was fated to be the stage for a modern Spanish Civil War, in which International Fascism and International Revolution would try their arms. The most likely scenario was that the country would be host to a bloodbath, and this prospect seemed to excite some would-be guerrillas. Had not Ché Guevara said that two, three, many Vietnams had to be created in Latin America? My reservations about such a brilliant future for my country, which had lived in perfect peace since Allende's inauguration in 1970, were in themselves suspect. One had to joyously embrace Chile's privilege to be the country where the continent's first revolutionary battles would be fought, where the first South American Vietnam would occur.

This hypothesis, of course, never found official expression. No member of the government had ever so much as hinted it to me. And yet it did float about through certain official circles, especially among the bureaucratic intellectuals who had fought their own bloody pen-and-ink wars, and it did come up in conversations. There was talk of contacts with MIR and other extreme left-wing groups in Chile. Piñeiro had posted some of his most trusted lieutenants to the Cuban Embassy in Santiago. The Cuban undercover presence in Chile during the Allende days didn't grow enough to have any real military significance, but it served as a very good pretext for the Armed Forces coup and even for the repression that came after. They were the external enemy that Pinochet and his men needed in order to go into action. If one got upset about this, one gave clear signs, so far as Piñeiro and his friends were concerned, that one was either a bourgeois intellectual or a closet counterrevolutionary.

I now think that on the basis of information that was gathered and studied after the announcement of my appointment to Cuba, a sentence had been handed down against me even before I arrived. All one had to consider was what sort of person I was and who my friends were. All the inconveniences, all the obstacles that I encountered, from the time I set foot off the plane, stemmed directly from that State Security examination of my family, my forebears, my roots, and obeyed a decision made somewhere within the administration. That is why my stay in Havana has often made me think of the novels of Kafka: One was plunged into a trial whose gears had begun to turn without one's knowledge, and in which the sentence had been passed against the unsuspecting defendant long before, by an authority that was invisible and unknown.

5

The date for my departure to Paris had now been set. I was to take an Iberian Airlines flight to Madrid in the early morning of Monday, March 22. Since my mission had been quite brief by the usual diplomatic standards, only a few informal farewells were to be given me. My writer friends had made plans to have dinner with me the night before my departure. At the embassy dinners, each respective ambassador made a little toast to wish me success in Paris, and many of them expressed their cordial envy of me in my new posting.

At one particular dinner at an Eastern European embassy, a socialist ambassador took me out into the middle of the enormous garden.

"I had an interesting conversation with the Soviet ambassador," he said to me, his face a mask of distant irony. "He said socialism had triumphed all along the line: in education, in medicine, in the sciences, in sports, in the exploration of space, and in international affairs. The only area it had failed in, so far, was the organization of the economy. 'But Ambassador,' I replied to him, 'that's why we fought the Revolution!' "

My diplomatic friend spoke softly, in the most open area of the garden. The embassy was located in a modern house that had belonged in the past to a United States military attaché. My friend, watching me closely out of the corner of his eye, went on: "You people in Chile ought to think about that. You ought to consider that none of the present models of socialism is valid for you."

"We have no plans to follow any particular model," I replied. "We've tried to find our own way, a plan to fit our own situation."

"Just think," the ambassador insisted, "Czechoslovakia had started down the right economic path. But its experiment was interrupted. And now we too, after some time, are beginning to work well, but we are a poor country, and we have to start at a very low rung on the ladder. If Chile's experiment turns out to be attractive, the rest of Latin America will follow suit. If not, there could be a serious reaction throughout the region. Some of our leaders have spoken with Allende. They have come away with the impression that Allende is not sectarian. That has been the information received by my government and my party."

But this private conversation was growing imprudently long, so we returned to the terrace where there was much drinking of whisky and smoking of Havanas.

"Your country's experiment is decisive," said another Eastern European diplomat as he found a place at my side. "We are following it with the greatest attention. One must help your country at all costs. The Chilean experiment *cannot* fail."[1]

Three or four days before my departure, the minister-counselor who was to replace me arrived. I had met him several years earlier in Chile; in Havana, he seemed to have been sent from some other world: his punctilious habits, his way of dressing, his mental set had not changed in the slightest, and the contrast with the Cuban surroundings was therefore doubly striking. The new minister-counselor had entered the diplomatic service during the years of the Popular Front, sometime around 1940, and he was typical, in the good sense of the word, of the old Chilean centrist *Partido Radical*.

A short while after getting off the plane he told me he had to talk to me about something that was a bit delicate. During his flight from Washington to Mexico, the person sitting beside him, a man of medium height, had spoken to him. He had said he represented an American "consulting" firm. When the man learned what post his seatmate was about to occupy in Havana, he had shown great interest. They—his firm, that is—needed a person to send them periodic reports on the economic situation in Cuba. "Someone like you: intelligent, well-informed, educated. We would be willing to pay an 'interesting' amount of money, in dollars of course, for those reports."

I discussed all this with my colleague on the Malecón as the evening grew darker and the waves crashed against the seawall and surged up onto the

---

[1] It is pretty clear (nor do I see any reason, after so many years, to hide it) that the man speaking was the Yugoslav ambassador. The conversation took place in the East German Embassy gardens.

cracked and broken sidewalk. We reached the conclusion that our own Minister of Foreign Relations had to be informed at once, via a diplomatic note for his eyes only. My colleague was making his debut in Cuba with the tangible discovery of one of the sinister realities of today's world—the CIA. The little scene on the plane would provide him some insight into the defensiveness shown by the Cubans in many situations.

As for me, the round of farewells had begun, and a week before my departure I had gone, in the company of my good friend P., to bid my own adieu to the beautiful sand, the pine trees, and the blue ocean of the beach at Santa María. I still feel nostalgia for that beach: the only place in Cuba where I could forget gossip, bugs, political rumors, diplomatic and social commitments. The beach runs as far as the eye can see, with its fringe of pine woods and its white ribbon of sand. One breathes a dense atmosphere there, fragrant with the ocean and the pines, and one's lungs expand.

"So long as we have this sun and this beach, there's not a whole lot more we need," P. said.

The petit-bourgeoisie, or at least the older members of it, had not lost their avidity for the consumer goods of the Americans. Before the Revolution, all Cuba produced was sugar; everything else, even tomatoes, soap, and toothpaste, was bought from the United States. Still, the general scarcity of "things" had turned P. into a philosopher.

As we returned to the Alfa, which we had left near a Party-occupied house where we were always allowed to shower after our swim and were offered a cup of coffee (a house which, to judge by its style, had belonged to wealthy Batista-followers), we ran into Regis Debray, who had an Alfa (but without a driver) for his personal use, and Saverio Tutino. Tutino was an Italian journalist, and he had followed the Cuban Revolution for many years; he had just arrived from Chile. Tutino knew Padilla well; I told Padilla later that I was very much interested in hearing Tutino's impressions of Chile. Padilla said he would make arrangements with Tutino to bring him to the hotel to visit me.

During this time Padilla had had to move back into his apartment in El Vedado, on a street behind the enormous Hotel Habana Libre. Padilla's building, built in the thirties, was unbelievably dirty, dark, and shabby. The apartment he lived in with Belkis had three small rooms. One was entirely given over to discarded objects of all kinds—yellowing magazines, tattered books, broken chairs, torn posters. The second room had a round table that seated four people, a battered gas stove (whose malfunctions obliged the couple to waste long periods of time in lines at restaurants and coffee shops), and a dishwasher. The third room, which was very narrow, was both study and bedroom. The walls were lined with books and photographs, among which there was found, as in virtually every house I visited in Cuba, a photograph of Fidel Castro. One might criticize or make jokes in a whisper, believing oneself out of the range of the omnipresent microphones, but that photograph of Fidel in a place of honor was unfailing. It was like the chromolithographs of the Sacred Heart of Jesus in old homes in Chile, looking down upon the sinful inhabitants of the house with a mute reproachfulness that engraved itself upon one's very conscience.

In every corner of Padilla's house there were piles of papers, letters, manuscripts. As he sat in his apartment voluptuously savoring a cigar that I had brought him, twirling it in his fingers and moving it about between his lips as clouds of smoke billowed about us, and then rolling his eyes as he exclaimed, "*This* is civilization!" Padilla would jump up, dig furiously among the mountains of paper, and at last, with great exultation, unearth the very paper that he had wanted to quote in support of some affirmation (not necessarily political) he had just made—a letter from Yevtushenko, Hans Magnus Enzensberger, or some other writer who is now famous today. The last time I went to visit Padilla, a short while before I left Cuba, I saw that on the corner of the main avenue just a few yards from the Habana Libre, in a spot that one almost necessarily had to pass in order to reach Heberto's house, there were standing persons vaguely connected to the literary scene, persons familiar to me, and who followed me with their eyes.

Padilla announced that he and Saverio Tutino would come to my hotel to visit me on Friday night, March 19. That Friday I opened the door to my suite and there, alongside Tutino and Padilla, stood a young man who was a perfect stranger to me.

"You know him," Padilla said to me, however, and the young man, smiling, gave me his hand to shake.

Tutino described the opposing forces in Chile, he talked about what had happened in China when the country emerged from the Cultural Revolution, about the problem of socialist constitutionality in Cuba. Padilla would take every subject and perform grand intellectual elaborations upon it; his performance was virtually lyrical. "Brilliant!" Tutino would exclaim in Italianate delight, "Bravo!"; it was as though he were applauding the performance of an opera.

Suddenly I realized that the young man they had brought along (and who had so far not uttered a word) was José Norberto Fuentes, the young writer I had voted to award the Casa de las Américas prize to in 1968. I would have liked to talk to him, but we were all hanging on the political and historical speculations of Heberto, who seemed to be at his most inspired. As we sat at a table covered with bottles and cigar-ends, fanned by the warm breeze that heralded the tropical spring, Heberto would trot out Marx, Nietzsche, Hegel,

Rimbaud, and a host of English and Latin American poets to buttress his ambitious synthesis of the contemporary situation of Cuba, Chile, the entire world.

Suddenly the telephone rang. It was Belkis, and her voice was controlled but anxious.

"Is Heberto there?"

According to their arrangement, she was calling to make sure he was all right and to reassure him that his novel, which as I mentioned earlier he always guarded now, was safe. It might be maintained that the periodic telephone calls were a provocation, that the fact of carrying that manuscript around everywhere they went, never releasing their grip on it or letting it out of their sight, was a provocation, that in fact the very existence of that novel was a provocation. If one goes down that road far enough, it is easy to conclude that any literary creation is by its nature a provocation. In crises, the role of the writer and that of the *provocateur* (which is not so much a role as a calling, a destiny, a fate) can be confused. José Norberto Fuentes had, in perfect innocence, already experienced this phenomenon firsthand, when he published his book *Condenados de condado* ("Condemned of the County") and in exchange had been violently attacked by *Verde Olivo*, the army magazine. The attacks had meant for José Norberto the loss of his job, exclusion from the life of literature and culture in Cuba. Now, as he listened to our conversation and observed the scene in silence, he was no doubt drawing his own conclusions about this whole affair. He may have suspected that his trials, in spite of his most prudent reserve, had not yet ended, as was proven just a few weeks later. In my memory, the silence of José Norberto Fuentes that Friday night, March 19, 1971, was more eloquent than the words of Heberto Padilla, which shattered like the spray from the ocean that I saw, out of the corner of my eye, as it rose in feathery waves all along the Malecón and then dissolved in mist into the darkness of the Caribbean night.

Raúl Roa had told me that he was going to invite me to a going-away dinner at his house. In early January, during the Congress of the International Organization of Journalists, he had told me that he was going to invite me to meet a Mexican gentleman. Neither of these announcements had led to anything, probably because Roa had known for a long time that I was *persona non grata*. Meléndez, on the other hand, called me on the morning of Saturday, March 20, to invite me and my successor to lunch at one of the Protocol houses. He would be by to pick us up early, because there were things to talk about.

At last I saw with my own eyes one of those Protocol houses that I had heard so much about, and so often. The house lay in the shade of large leafy trees, surrounded by well-cared-for gardens, in the heart of the elegant neighborhood of Cubanacán. The bourgeois family of the Batista years had even left its furniture and its porcelain dinnerware with gold-leaf monograms. An impeccable waiter brought us daiquiris in Baccarat champagne glasses.

I imagined the reactions of certain Latin American political leaders (those of the least political "maturity") when they were lodged, as often occurred, in these surroundings. I realized that Fidel controlled great resources that might be put at the service of his guests. He no doubt used these resources well, and fitted them to the importance of his guests with consummate skill.

As we sat down to lunch Meléndez told me that Raúl Roa, "who really likes you, *chico*," had wanted to have a little going-away affair for me, but sent his regrets, as just now he was terribly overworked.

"I wanted to have this lunch, though, to say good-bye to you, Edwards," he went on, unsmilingly, "and also to talk to you about a serious problem." He wasted no time in getting to the point, either.

"I want to warn you about your secretary, Lupe. We have proof that she's working for the CIA. She worked for a Mexican diplomat who later turned out to have been a CIA agent in Havana. She worked *closely* with him. I just wanted to put you on your guard."

We had already been put on our guard with respect to Lupe, but in another sense. We had been told confidentially that she worked for Cuban State Security. Now that Meléndez was telling us with such conviction that she was an agent of the CIA, we had no choice but to fire her. Did this mean that Lupe had accomplished her mission? That it had been decided to remove her from the Chilean Embassy in order to prevent the operatives of State Security from being contaminated by our all-too-contagious strain of liberalism? Or was this yet another wrinkle in the web of intrigue, intended to keep us guessing? This is another of the countless mysteries of my mission in Cuba.

At the end of the luncheon, Meléndez gave us each a copy of the book published by the Cuban government on that spy scandal involving the Mexican Embassy that Meléndez had earlier referred to. He was eager for us to read it.

The book was a hymn to the efficiency of State Security. It showed that everything the Mexican diplomat had done, from the moment of his arrival in Havana, had been kept under surveillance and recorded by State Security. But the book, of course, served as warning as well as praise. The Chilean chargé d'affaires whose tongue had been too loose, who had been betrayed by subjectivism and bourgeois-intellectual class prejudices, realized too late that every word he had spoken had found its way, writ large, into the secret files of

State Security. This lesson might serve his successor, if not himself, since a word to the wise was rumored to be sufficient. If the successor wished to carry out his mission to everyone's satisfaction, he had no choice but to behave himself in private as well as in public. His very thoughts would be overheard by the omnipresent bugs of State Security, so he had best keep his thoughts stashed away somewhere as soundproof as possible from the very outset. If he did, he would leave Cuba with career intact, indeed improved, and with the praises of the Revolution. If not . . .

That singular farewell luncheon ended, then, with the presentation to us of the gift of History Exemplified. My successor, who looked at the world with eyes from which the scales had long since fallen, took note of the warning. I, for my part, realized that my own case was lost, since I had been held up to my successor as the example *not* to follow. That was the message given us by State Security when it solemnized our luncheon with the presentation of their little book. It demonstrated, too, that State Security knew how to keep up the forms, as befitted one of the few well-organized institutions on the Island—even, as ironists would have it, the *only* well-organized institution on the Island. Lupe, meanwhile, under a cloud of accusation (a cloud not destined to erase her enigmatic smile, however), vanished from the scene.

I arrived at the hotel around five o'clock that last Saturday afternoon I was to spend on the Island; I wanted to lie down for a while, but the telephone rang. The Chilean woman at whose home I had met Regis Debray was almost desperate to speak to me; she had already called several times. It seemed that the person I had seen the first night I was in Cuba, the person I had met, the important person, the most important person of all—Did I understand? Of course I understood!—wanted to meet me at her house. My compatriot had spoken to Debray of my interminable problems with finding a suitable house for the embassy—problems so absurd, if one considered the importance to Cuba of relations with Chile, that according to my Chilean friend it made one wonder sometimes if the CIA might not have a hand in them—and Debray had communicated this concern to the important person in question, who now wanted to talk the matter over with me.

"When?"

"Around seven."

"I'll be there a little before seven, then."

I arrived before the seven; the household, which included my friend, her daughter and son, both of university age, seemed deeply moved to have been selected for the visit, the announcement of which had been made indirectly and somewhat mysteriously by telephone calls from persons allegedly close to the Prime Minister. I had heard my friend say that Fidel was a friend of hers, but I had gotten the impression that it had been a long time since she had seen him; the friendship seemed to belong to a far-away time that the Revolution had now put behind it.

The daughter would go down to the corner every few minutes and come back to tell us that the corner had been "taken"—a jeep was parked down in the next block and the arrival of Número Uno, whose secret movements were betrayed by signs that any inhabitant of Havana could spot a mile away, must be imminent. The son was taking things more calmly, but he too had noted some signs in the neighborhood.

"There's no doubt in my mind," my Chilean friend said. "They called to be sure you were coming. I told them you were going to have some dinner with us, I told them you had been a friend for years and I didn't have anything special to fix for dinner. They said they would send dinner, then."

But the promised food did not come, and as the hours passed the whole affair began to be disconcerting.

Around midnight I went over to the house of some other Chilean friends that lived not far away; they had invited me over to say good-bye. I returned right away to my friend's apartment, but still nothing. At 2:00 A.M. I said I was going back to the hotel. My friend insisted that Fidel might arrive at any moment. I no longer thought so. In fact, it seemed more likely that on the eve of my departure State Security had seen to it that I was out of my suite so that they could search my rooms and read the letters that my friends were no doubt going to entrust to me. Any time a person left Havana to go abroad, his acquaintances loaded him down with letters. There was no more efficient way of breaking the postal blockade.

My successor, the consul, and the consul's wife had been invited to dinner at the home of a Cuban couple who had recently been doing everything they could to see to their needs. Perhaps too much. And I recalled one occasion when I wanted to leave a cocktail party only to find that Tomás, my driver, had disappeared. After half an hour of waiting, the correspondent for a Polish news agency had offered to give me a lift home. The consul and his wife, who were in a suite just opposite my own, had later told me that they had heard noises in my rooms. Since they didn't know I had gone out, they had given little thought to the incident.

Both on that occasion and now, as I arrived back in my rooms from my Chilean friend's apartment, I found nothing unusual. Nonetheless, the German who had been seeing to the provisioning of the *Esmeralda*, and whom Raúl

Castro had wanted nothing to do with since the man was a citizen of West Germany,[2] had said something to me on the second day of his stay at the Habana Riviera. "They've been through all my papers," Helmut told me; "They put everything back exactly where they found it, but I had sprinkled some special powder on the papers so that you could tell if they've been moved." The German had later told the consul that he knew something about bugging techniques. According to him, the silvering of the mirrors was a very modern sort of antenna, whose broad surface made it possible to pick up the slightest sounds that were made in the rooms. And the metal rings around the bases of some of the lamps were also microphones.

How did this Helmut fit in? Did he really know about these things, or did his information come from the 007 movies? In the last few days, the invisible presence of State Security had begun to take on mythic proportions. The large mirrors were the eyes of an ultramodern Polyphemus. They penetrated my dreams and my most intimate thoughts. The immobility of the lamps with their aluminum rings was disquieting. I would leave my room and come up against the impassive façade of the elevator operator, the smiling clerk at the front desk, the correct and friendly headwaiter in the dining room, who ushered me in through the people waiting their turns, seat me at one of the choice tables, make some small-talk about the menu or the weather or the news of Chile that was published that day in *Granma*. In my car there was Isidoro, my new driver. And to top it all off, someone had hinted to me that one of the people who frequented those get-togethers I attended with Pablo Armando, Pepe Rodríguez Feo, Heberto Padilla, and others, a certain person who passed himself off as a literary colleague and friend of ours, and who had somewhat obsequiously invited us to his house several times, would inevitably record the conversations that took place there.

I felt that my head was about to burst, that I would never find my way out of this labyrinth. The world outside the Island began to seem a fiction to me, unreal and unreachable. The hot season had come, and I couldn't get my breath. I would wake up at night in fear, bathed in sweat, my heart in my throat, and there were those blank mirrors, capturing the wan light of the moon, the reflection of the Caribbean, and my room.

During the time of my stay in Cuba, Capitán Duque Estrada, who had been named Director of the Americas Section of the Ministry of Foreign Relations,

---

[2] And Cuba only sustained relations with the German Democratic Republic, East Germany.

had been friendly and cooperative toward me, which was a tremendous difference from the slippery Meléndez. During the period when Meléndez was "unavailable," Duque tried to help me look for a residence for the Chilean ambassador.

Duque had come from managing a sugar plantation and processing plant. Someone told me he had fought with the guerrillas and had been a friend of Camilo Cienfuegos and Ché Guevara. He did not give the impression of having a political intelligence of any great scope. Once when I visited his office he talked to me about an article in *Punto Final*. The article had described the revolutionary energy inspired by the land takeovers in southern Chile. Even as Duque spoke, those takeovers were causing the Allende government terrible headaches. In spite of the fact that the Castro government had changed and was beginning to cement its alliance with the Soviet Union, *Punto Final*, whose links with Cuba and with Prensa Latina were no secret to anyone, continued to defend points of view openly contrary to those of the Chilean Communist party and almost identical to those of MIR. *Punto Final* had predicted Allende's "inevitable" electoral defeat and the victory of Alessandri. It had predicted that if Allende should by some miracle win, the forces of the bourgeoisie would never allow him to take power. After failing in both of its oracular pronouncements, it had set about chanting hymns of praise of the revolutionary actions of MIR to the indian campesinos of the south of the country. Some people said that the man backing *Punto Final* in Cuba was Comandante Manuel Piñeiro, Red Beard.

In spite of these differences of outlook between us, Duque struck me as a person of good intentions. Since he had formerly been "in sugar," as a capitalist might say, I asked him to take me to a sugar-processing plant. A few days before my departure, he called and offered to give me this tour on Sunday, the twenty-first, the day before I was to leave. He called three or four times to confirm our date, with an insistence that only later made sense to me. I told him I'd have to pack my bags and turn over all the affairs to the new minister-counsel, and asked him if we could be back by around three in the afternoon.

"Don't worry, Edwards! We'll be back in plenty of time."

On the telephone, as a prelude to our tour, he had stopped using the formal *Usted* with me and was now using the much more informal *tu*.

The night before, after the mysterious announcement of the visit from Fidel, I had been in my Chilean friend's house until two o'clock in the morning. Duque Estrada came by for me early, so I had no time to talk to my writer friends that had wanted to say good-bye. I hadn't seen Pablo Armando and Pepe Rodríguez Feo in days. I had last seen Padilla that Friday night two days ago when he came to my hotel with Saverio Tutino and José Norberto Fuentes. During the last week María Dolores, the Cuban ex-wife of Enrique Lihn, had been somewhat insistent in her attendance on me. In perfect candor, María Dolores said that Pilar and I, as diplomats, had given her social standing a little lift. I had also been visited often during these last few days by two young Chilean women, Lucía and Isabel. Isabel was the woman whose ex-husband wouldn't give permission to take their daughter to Chile. Lucía was studying at the university and lived in the student dormitories.

These two young women had reserved a table for us that last Saturday night at the Hotel Nacional, as a going-away gesture. I had looked forward to the dinner, but the wait for the elusive Prime Minister had forced me to stand them up. Of the writers, meanwhile, I had heard almost nothing, which was a little puzzling on the eve of my departure.

Duque was waiting for me at the door of the hotel in a Chevrolet Impala that was in perfect condition. There was a kid with him that he introduced as his driver, but instead of getting behind the wheel, the young man, looking only about half-awake, crawled into the back seat, and stayed in the back seat throughout our trip.

To judge by certain explanations he gave, Duque was going to take me to lunch at a sugar plantation and processing plant. I assumed, since I had to be back early, that the plantation would be near Havana. I had already visited the sugar plant called "Camilo Cienfuegos" and spoken for a long while with the workers there, who called up the ghost of the layoffs of the years before the Revolution. But Duque (along with an American engineer named Henderson who had remained in Cuba after the Revolution) had worked untiringly at solving the problems of mechanization, and I didn't want to miss the experience of visiting a sugar plantation in his company.

After more than an hour of driving, we stopped to look at a machine that cleaned the sugarcane and lifted it onto railcars, at a place that was called a collection center. The machine was quite interesting; it had been invented, Duque explained to me, by technicians of the Revolution—but this stop was fortuitous, since we had just happened to pass the machine by the side of the road. We speeded onward, then, until after some three and a half hours (and repeated questions from me about our destination) we came to the Zapata Swamp, not far from where the Bay of Pigs invasion had taken place. I realized suddenly that Duque was not taking me to any sugar processing plant, he was taking me to the beach at Huamá, which had been built up out of swampland by the Revolution. As a pre-departure trip, this was most interesting in all sorts of ways!

After mingling with groups of Soviet women and children (no doubt the family members of Soviet experts living in Cuba) we took a look at the famous crocodile hatcheries that Fidel Castro had ordered built, and then we boarded a

small ferry that took us over to the beach, which was a string of small islands
with wooden cabins for tourists, and which was separated from terra firma by a
wide lagoon. I kept insisting that I wanted to get back to Havana soon, but
Duque had been possessed by a sudden lassitude, a drowsy sluggishness that
was not only immovable in itself but impervious to any pushing from me.

"Naturally!" I thought to myself, "why should they be interested in showing
me any more of their problems with sugarcane?" Of course, I could not
imagine that they knew of my report on that year's harvest that I had sent to the
Chilean Ministry of Foreign Relations in January of that year. Now, with the
paranoia that I acquired, ironically, right there in Cuba, I would not be at all
surprised to find out that Duque had long since read a copy of that confidential
report that summarized the information I had gathered and my own opinions
on the 1971 harvest, the first harvest after the sensational failure of the ten-
million-ton harvest of 1970.

After lunch in the restaurant on the beach (which wouldn't have been worth
making a ten-minute trip for, let alone three and a half hours!), Duque led me
off to a cabin—*to rest!* I was not interested in a nap; what I wanted to do was
get back to Havana, but Duque, suddenly half-witted, only smiled. I finally
managed to get him out of the cabin and moving toward the central area of the
beach. Somebody said we might find a boat there. My optimism briefly
returned.

"Wouldn't you like a cup of coffee, a glass of orange juice?" Duque
inquired.

No! Heavens no! All I wanted to do was get back to Havana! What was I
doing in Huamá, when I hadn't packed my bags, hadn't turned things over to
my successor, hadn't said good-bye to my friends? But Duque drank a cup of
coffee, and then, taking a chair on the terrace and sprawling in the sun, began
to babble trivialities.

The promised boat turned up at last. It rode low in the water, and the hull
looked none too seaworthy, but it might get us across the lagoon to our car. We
boarded—Duque, his aide, somebody from the beach who ran the boat, and I.
The engine, after several tries, started. We traveled a few yards across the
lagoon and suddenly the engine's noise ceased; the boat drifted to a stop. The
man running the boat (which began taking on water) said the engine was shot.
We rowed back to the beach and got out. Duque, meanwhile, never lost his air
of slow and imperturbable laziness. The little ferry that had brought us across
originally was now fast approaching the dock on our side. I had already opted
for safety before speed—I had had the fleeting image of drowning in this
idiotic lagoon, and then of being devoured by crocodiles—but this means of
transportation seemingly provided both.

Suddenly, Duque recovered his energy. We traveled the hundred or so miles back to Havana with the Chevrolet floorboarded. Night began to fall, and the road, weaving along the coastline, was full of trucks. Duque overtook and passed them at a hundred miles an hour, never lifting his foot an inch off the accelerator. Not a word was spoken between us. If he had wanted to fake an accident, his life would have been in as much danger as mine. Yet we were surely in danger: He would pass the long trucks with a minimum of visibility, and there was the constant risk of meeting an oncoming vehicle.

Much later, when I had a complete picture of the events of that weekend, it occurred to me that his purpose (or the purpose that someone had charged him with) had been to subject me to severe nervous strain. Someone, in obedience to perfectly rational techniques and in pursuance of perfectly well-thought-out goals, was trying to wear me down, tire me, soften me before the decisive encounter came—and the encounter must have been foreseen long before that day. I knew nothing, could have known nothing, but my intuition told me to stay as calm as possible, and certainly to *appear* as calm as possible.

I looked out at the landscape of low rolling hills, palm groves, sugarcane fields, and blue sky turning violet, and I recalled the emotional words of Lezama Lima: "This is the most beautiful landscape on earth!" By thinking of such things, I managed to block out the senseless speed of the Chevrolet and to avoid showing nervousness or insisting on slowing down. I imagined myself in a horse-drawn carriage, half a century ago, riding through the farm described in Lezama's *Paradiso*.

I suppose Duque finally tired of showing off his prowess as a race-car driver. We stopped at a café packed with truck drivers; you could lay a coin on the counter and get a cup of coffee there, the way you could in any café in the world. I had the dizzying sensation for a second that all my observations as to the shortages in Cuba were false, the product of a stubbornly and perversely prejudiced mind.

We made the rest of the trip at a more normal speed, and we arrived in Havana sometime after eight. I said good-bye to Duque at the door of the Habana Riviera but his aide went with me to pick up the short-wave radio that Duque had lent me at the beginning of my stay in Havana. I glimpsed three friends sitting in the lobby waiting for me, looking extremely anxious, and as soon as they saw me they stood up, as though they were spring-loaded, and came toward me with discreet signs not to talk. I told them to come up to my suite. Duque's aide went up with me to pick up the radio.

The aide said good-bye very politely and left. I closed the door and went into my sitting room. My friends immediately began to make frantic signs to me, pointing to the invisible bugs, and handed me a piece of paper on which the following words were written: "Heberto and Belkis were arrested yester-day. We don't know the reasons behind it. Their apartment is under seal by the Ministry of the Interior."

We burned the piece of paper, flushed it down the toilet, and talked about the beauties of the beach at Huamá, the preparations for my trip. My friends were pale, and terribly upset.[3] There was a banging on the door and Pablo Armando burst in; he was shaking, and he looked a wreck. I had to talk to my successor for a few minutes, and also to the consul, who was readying a diplomatic pouch in that torrid office with no air conditioning or natural ventilation, where I had stewed in my own juices for three and a half months.

I went into my office to find that Y. had arrived. Y. was that young revolutionary who in a drunken stupor had wanted to accuse Cristián Huneeus and me of being potential agents (or agents by calling, to coin a phrase) of the CIA. Was he sorry for that? Had he come on some new State Security mission? Was he trying to get his place in government back, after his failure in a high-ranking position? He told me he needed to talk to me, and I, lacking any tangible proof against him, decided to continue to believe in his good faith.

My suite was now full of people, including two or three people who did not yet know about Padilla—among them, the Chilean writer and university professor Carlos Santander. Santander and I went out into the hall with Y.

I told Y. that I was very depressed about this spot Heberto was in; there was no doubt that his contact with me had hurt him, and I was in no position to help.

"Well," Y. said, "that's the way things go."

He asked me if I had noticed anything strange recently. Somebody in a room down the hall at that moment stuck their head out the door, so we stopped talking.

"I'm not sure," I said, when the head disappeared again. "I haven't noticed anything here in the hotel."

But I did tell him about that strange "appointment" of the day before, and the pointless trip that had consumed my entire Sunday.

"I imagine they didn't want you to know anything about Heberto's arrest." Y. shrugged his shoulders in a gesture of uncertainty. "The whole charade was probably staged so they would have plenty of time to search your rooms without worrying about your coming in unexpectedly."

---

[3] I later learned that one of them had called my wife Pilar in Santiago and talked to her about the good weather we were having and the occasional drizzle. It was a warning, and Pilar, who took it as one, didn't rest easy until she heard from me directly.

I remembered that the new chargé d'affaires and the consul and his wife had also gone out Saturday night; they had been the guests of a Cuban couple that had shown unctuous and somewhat suspicious attentiveness to the new Chilean diplomats. That is, the coast had been clear for several hours, during which it would have been quite easy to search the rooms of the entire Chilean Embassy offices and staff. The only person who remained behind was the baby sitter for the consul's children—the oldest was only two or three years old—but that detail might mean, almost surely meant, that she was a part of the system too.

We decided that my friends would all go to César López' house and wait for me there for our last good-byes. I would go as soon as I could get away, no matter how late that might be. While María Dolores and the two young Chilean women helped me pack my bags, the phone rang in room 1813, which was an unoccupied bedroom in my suite. It was Meléndez, who told me that the Minister of Foreign Relations urgently needed to talk to me, at eleven. Where would I be at that hour?

I told him I would be waiting for his call in my room or the consul's room. I said good-bye to the Chilean women and went down to the lobby for a few minutes. Like every Saturday and Sunday evening, the lobby was full of festive, milling people, who took over the space as though it had been some small-town square in the provinces. I went into the bar, and the France Presse correspondent, who had a girlfriend with him, asked whether it was true that Padilla had been arrested.

"I don't know," I told him.

"But you heard it, too?"

"Yes," I said.

"So I can report it," he said, "with the qualification that it hasn't yet been confirmed."

We had a drink together and I said good night. Then I went into the dining room to tell my colleagues from the embassy that I had been summoned by the Minister of Foreign Relations. We'd talk when I got back.

I went back up to room 1813, and a few minutes before eleven the phone rang. Meléndez said he was waiting for me downstairs.

We got into Meléndez' chocolate-colored Volkswagen, the same car that had taken me off to meet Fidel the night I arrived in Havana. My Alfa, driven by Isidoro, followed.

The Ministry of Foreign Relations was located in a building whose Greek columns and neoclassical sobriety made it resemble every millionaire's mansion in Latin America—and in fact it had once belonged to a sugar magnate. There were three or four lighted windows in the building that night, and two Alfa Romeos parked beside the entrance. In the shadows I made out the darker figures of several soldiers armed with machine guns.

My aide in the Protocol section, who had often attended me before, led me to the diplomats' reception room. After that piece of paper that had been handed me in my hotel room, I could well imagine the nature of this untimely summons. I was exhausted, and depressed, but during the three minutes' wait for the minister I managed to collect my energies and calm myself. The door opened and the aide showed me into the minister's office.

Standing in the middle of the room, dressed in olive-green fatigue uniforms and with pistols strapped to their waists, Fidel Castro and Raúl Roa were awaiting me.[4] Fidel gestured to a place on the couch and when I was seated took the chair to my left. Roa had always been cordial with me, and we had gotten on well, but now he was extremely tense and serious-looking. According to the notes I made three or four days later, I had entered the Ministry building at exactly 11:25 P.M. I will now try to reproduce that meeting, which though one or another detail may escape me is forever engraved on my memory.

"You recall our conversation that first night that you arrived," began the Prime Minister.

"Of course!" I replied.

"That night I took quite a liking to you. I enjoyed that conversation, and I was, as you will recall, quite courteous. But now I must tell you that we were mistaken about you. Because you have shown yourself to be a person hostile to the Cuban Revolution! And hostile to the Chilean Revolution as well! From the first day, you allowed yourself to be surrounded by counterrevolutionary elements, enemies of the Revolution, persons whose interest it was that you be given a negative view of the current Cuban situation, so that you might communicate those views to Chile. We learned all this immediately. As you will fully understand, it would have been stupid of us not to have kept you under a degree of surveillance. We have followed every detail of your meetings, your walks, your conversations—we have followed your every step. By

---

[4] In Geneva, Raúl Roa later told a mutual friend of ours, Vicente Girbau, a publisher and international diplomat from Spain, that he, Roa, had been wearing a dark blue suit and a tie. "Tell Edwards he made a mistake," he told Girbau. I don't know whether he was serious or joking, but I do know that my memory would have to be playing grave tricks on me if he was serious. Unless by calling attention to the one "false" detail Roa had wanted to confirm all the rest.

the time of the arrival of the *Esmeralda*, I was already quite well informed about you, and you will have noted that I made my displeasure with you evident when I shook your hand on the deck of the ship. Now, after the warmth I showed you on the day of your arrival, I did not want to let you leave without telling you how deeply displeased and disappointed we have been by your behavior here. We should, no doubt, have declared you *persona non grata*, but we didn't want to do that; it would have damaged our relations with Chile. But you should know that we have communicated our opinion of your mission here to Salvador Allende."

Fidel seemed to want to make his point about his irritation and end the conversation there. He supposed, I imagine, that the news that I had been reported to Salvador Allende would be a mortal blow to me, at least as far as my career was concerned, and that I would be dumbstruck by it. I think that mistaken belief stemmed in the final analysis from his ignorance of Chile and the Chilean way of life. In Chile one can survive even inside the administration in spite of the enmity of the head of state.[5]

I took advantage of the first pause that offered, and I said:

"Prime Minister, I don't think I have allowed myself to be surrounded by a group of counterrevolutionaries, as you call them. I am a writer first and a diplomat second, and I have socialized with the Cuban writers who are friends of mine, and who have been my friends since before my diplomatic posting here, from the time I first came to Cuba as a guest of the Casa de las Américas in January 1968—in some cases, since even before that. I am convinced that I have not met with any counterrevolutionary or enemy of the Revolution. It may be that these friends have critical views of the Revolution's present moment; but there is a very clear difference to me between an intellectual who criticizes a regime and a counterrevolutionary or an agent of the enemy."

Fidel was listening gravely. Suddenly, in fury, he interrupted me and began to openly attack. In spite of this, I insisted that he let me continue, and finally, led perhaps by curiosity to learn my version of things, he did.

"With regard to my alleged hostility to the Cuban Revolution," I went on, "I can tell you, Prime Minister, that the major difficulties I have experienced in my diplomatic career have been due precisely to my support for the Cuban Revolution. In 1965 and 1966, after relations were broken off, at a time when you were violently attacking the Frei government, I was the only South

---

[5] This sentence was written, according to the dates in my notebooks, in April 1972—a year and a half before the military coup d'état.

American diplomat in Paris[6] who maintained ties with the Cuban Embassy. The American invasion of the Dominican Republic occurred, and I signed the manifesto published by Cuban intellectuals. My signature appeared in *Le Monde,* and that, as you may imagine, did not sit very well with my boss, the ambassador from the Frei regime. During those years I accepted an invitation from the Casa de las Américas and I came to Cuba in early 1968 even though relations had been broken off between Chile and Cuba and even though I was a career diplomat for the government of Chile. It is true that Gabriel Valdés, who was at that time our minister of foreign relations, approved my trip, but that didn't keep the trip from causing no end of headaches for me at the time and later. My immediate superiors very much disapproved of my coming here, and I suffered a setback in my career because of it. And during all those years I was a contributor to the magazine *Casa de las Américas* and corresponded constantly with its editors. How can you say, given all this, that I have been hostile to the Cuban Revolution?"

I looked at Raúl Roa out of the corner of my eye; he was very serious, watching me, not saying a word. He had always been, as I say, very cordial to me; I felt, therefore, that this scene must be more unpleasant and perhaps more dangerous for him than for anyone else. I never learned, and probably never will learn, what thoughts, what reactions my words provoked in him. Fidel, on the other hand, was following me intently, and his expression hid nothing of what he was thinking and feeling.

"That said, Prime Minister," I continued, "I must explain to you what happens to a Chilean of good faith, a person who has never skimped on his friendship for the Cuban Revolution, who arrives in Cuba today as the representative of the Unidad Popular. A Chilean reads in the situation of Cuba today one of the possibilities of his own country's future. To speak with complete frankness, I think it is only natural that this Chilean not particularly enjoy contemplating that future as it may be seen in the situation of Cuba today. Nor would the people of Cuba have much enjoyed contemplating that future if they had been able to anticipate in 1959 what Cuba would be like in 1971—if, for example, twelve years of a revolution had passed in Ecuador or some other country in Latin America and the Cuban people had been able to look at it and find there the situation that I have found in Cuba today. Because I recall very vividly the predictions that were made in Cuba in 1966 and 1967 about the economy of Cuba in 1970. A huge economic boom was predicted, a boom that would banish forever the specter of foreign economic dependency. There was

---

[6] At the time I was first secretary of the Chilean Embassy.

to be a sensational increase in agricultural production, and it was promised that Cuba would export coffee, that no sugar harvest after 1970 would be less than ten million tons."

Fidel stood up in uncontrollable irritation.

"And you don't know the problems that Cuba has had to face! You don't realize that we have been subjected to a merciless blockade, that the most savage imperialist regime in history lies eighty miles off our coast! You seem not to want to recognize that the sole desire of Yankee imperialism is to destroy us, wipe us off the face of the earth, destroy the Cuban Revolution and all it stands for to the nations of the earth, and that this Yankee imperialist government is the richest and most powerful regime that has ever existed!"

"But I do recognize that," I said. "That is why I wouldn't want to see Chile go through the same experience."

"And do you think the Chilean experiment is going to be so easy?" Fidel broke in. "Do you think that the reactionary forces in Chile will fail to organize themselves, with the direct aid and support of the Yankee imperialists? Haven't you heard of the Djarkata Plan?[7] So far Allende has only conquered the government—which means he has only breached the first walls of power. When the inner bastion begins to give, the confrontation will be inevitable."

In other words, the Chilean Revolution was still to be won. The electoral process, our historical innovation, was but a prelude, an apparently favorable accident, although it could well turn out to be a two-edged sword. If Allende was not to bog down in the quicksand of constitutionality, his only alternative was to radicalize the process, take it to the point of rupture. It must be granted that when the MIR faction cooled before September 1970, Fidel allowed Allende to play his electoral trump, but this didn't mean that Chile had discovered the formula for a peaceful transition to socialism. Far from it. The Chilean situation had not led Fidel to revise his theories, as some people naively thought, but rather to refine them, and to confirm them by another route. I recalled that phrase from our first encounter: "If you Chileans need help, just ask for it. We may not be much good at producing, but we're great at fighting!"

Later, during his visit to Chile, it was at first believed that Fidel really had changed.

---

[7] Rumors of the existence of the so-called "Djarkata Plan" appeared often in the newspapers at this time. This was allegedly a plan by the CIA to organize right-wing death squads to kill Communists in Indonesia (and, by extension, any country) should there be a left-wing coup.

But all it took was the "empty pot" demonstration[8] (pots well salted with personal insults against Fidel from the right-wing press), and the Comandante, who theretofore had shown his most conciliatory face in all his public statements, became the Fidel of old. At the end of that day, the protest of the furious housewives, banging their pots and pans in the streets of Santiago, had turned into real street battles between the followers and the enemies of the government. He spent the night of the demonstration beside his machine gun, surrounded by his own armed guards, waiting with exasperated patience, in the internationalist spirit of Latin American revolution, for the Chilean government to ask him for help. But Allende kept his head, and the next morning Fidel discovered, to his rather noisily expressed surprise, that a regular-army general was in charge of the state of emergency. Chile was hopeless! In the National Stadium, while some members of his audience got up and left after the hours of Fidel's speechifying that they were wholly unused to, Fidel confessed that he was leaving Chile "even more radical" than he'd come, and "more of a revolutionary" than ever. He attempted to demonstrate this renewed revolutionary zeal later by inviting Miguel Henríquez, leader of the MIR party, to Cuba shortly afterward, and going to the airport personally to greet him.

Fidel, in sum, seemed, in spite of certain indications to the contrary, not to believe in the real possibility of success via the evolutionary, constitutional route that Chile had chosen. And the most serious thing about all this was, as one might see from Fidel's reaction to the "empty pot" episode, that Fidel's lack of confidence might create further problems for Chile. In a film of a conversation that Fidel had with Allende, one can see Castro acknowledge that his trip to Chile was a "voyage from one world to another." Yet there was little indication that he had reached all the possible conclusions from that observation. Of course such conclusions would have implied more modesty than Fidel could probably have mustered.

As a Chilean diplomat, and one accused of hostility toward the Cuban Revolution, I did not think it my place to enter into theoretical discussions regarding a country's choice of political strategy. Instead, I returned to the subject of my relationship with the dissident writers, since that was the most serious charge leveled against me during that singular conversation with the Cuban head of state at midnight on Sunday, March 21, 1971.

---

[8] During which a large number of middle- and upper-class Chileans, especially housewives, demonstrated against Castro and the Allende government by banging on empty pots, which symbolized the economic chaos of those years. These demonstrations became frequent in the last years of Allende and caused much concern among the Unidad Popular government.

"I refused to turn my back on my friends," I said. "I knew they were expressing opinions critical of the government, and that their relations with the government had become somewhat antagonistic, but they have been my colleagues and my friends for years. I have probably acted more like a writer than a diplomat. It is quite possible that after this experience, and this conversation, which I am certain I will always see as very important to me, I will leave the diplomatic service and devote myself to literature. I'd like nothing better. I recognize that I've been a bad diplomat in Cuba. But I have one excuse: The real relations between Chile and Cuba have been carried on in Santiago. My presence here has been only symbolic. I insist, furthermore, that my writer friends, however much they have criticized the current situation, are neither *gusanos* nor counterrevolutionaries. And I've met with writers of every stamp, you know, not just with the most critical ones."

"That much is true," Fidel interrupted. "We know that you have been in contact with writers on our side."

I had noted that in one way or another one would often be reminded of the efficiency of secret-police surveillance. The little book about the case of the Mexican diplomat, the TV program on the "CIA operative" Olive, the speech by the Dominican journalist in which he publicly confessed that he was a double agent, were all manifestations of that reminder. With this last statement, Fidel had not only demonstrated his personal knowledge of my "case" (for incredible as it might seem to a peaceful citizen of Chile, my stay in Havana had become a "case" within a socialist country), but also that the agents of State Security were very efficient at their jobs.

"But let's take the case of Heberto Padilla," I then said. "His criticism is always predicated on a standpoint within the Left. He once quoted Enrique Lihn to me, who said that when one leaves Cuba, the Revolution begins to grow larger and more imposing as one looks at it from a greater distance. Heberto talked to me about a period of volunteer labor he had done on a citrus farm, about a year ago. The leader of the project was, according to Heberto, the perfect example of the revolutionary. He wanted the best for his group, he wanted it to thrive and prosper and to live in the best possible material circumstances, and he had even designed the furniture in the project's living rooms and bedrooms. He made sure there was fresh orange juice every morning for breakfast. And at the same time he was a theorist, a great reader. Padilla cited that case in contrast to others who think that discomfort, carelessness of details, can be remedied with high-sounding phrases."

"Excellent!" said Fidel, for whom the mention of Heberto Padilla produced frank displeasure. "Excellent! But I feel I must tell you that Padilla is a liar.

And a turncoat! And, *and,"* said Fidel, raising his eyebrows and his index finger, and looking me straight in the eye, "he is *ambitious."*

He fell silent after this last phrase, as though giving me time to draw all the appropriate conclusions. It was true that Padilla was given to suggesting the existence of certain mysterious links between himself and secret higher powers. He had given me to understand on more than one occasion that he stayed afloat relatively successfully thanks to the power struggles between factions within the government. Whenever he made these suggestions, he would laugh uproariously and look very self-satisfied.

I always thought, and continue to think, that Heberto's ravings were no more than a game of vanity he played, mostly with himself. Fidel's last phrase, though, intrigued me. It confirmed, of course, that in early 1971 there actually was an underground factional power struggle going on. Had Heberto taken part in this struggle somehow? What fantastic version of things had been reported to Fidel? And how had my own actions, Heberto's contacts with me, been used?—for one had to wonder whether those contacts had intentionally, and with some mysterious plan, been made easier by that hidden hand which had sufficient power to assign people rooms in the Habana Riviera. The list of mysteries in this book, mysteries for which I can only give the most hypothetical sort of explanations, is already long. The fact is that I had learned no more than a few hours ago that Heberto had been arrested, and I was trying, out of conviction and out of simple friendship, but without much real hope, to help him.

"I insist on one thing, Prime Minister," I said. "I am convinced that Heberto Padilla is not an agent for anybody. He is a difficult man, I'll grant you—he is willful, and capricious, and he has a sharp critical bite. But he has never been anything but a man of the Left, and his criticism has come from the Left. And the relationship between the state and the writer has never been anything but troubled, anyway. It can't help but be. The *raison d'être* of the State and the *raison d'être* of poetry contradict one another. Plato said that one should listen to the beautiful words of poets, one should crown poets, anoint them, and then carry them outside the republic's walls the next day. He knew that if they stayed inside they'd cause nothing but trouble! But Plato intended his words ironically, too, since he was not only a philosopher but something of a poet as well. And socialism will just have to learn to live with its writers. That is important for the writers, but it is even more important for socialism."

"And you think that there are real poets in Cuba?" the prime minister asked.

He seemed to have serious doubts about that, but he did not consider himself the best person to decide the issue—not because he did not trust his own critical judgment (I suspect, on the contrary, that his was the only critical judgment he did trust) but because he didn't want to run the risk that an over-generalized and relatively negative pronouncement from him as to the quality of Cuban literature should later be quoted by me.

"We recognize that it has now become quite fashionable in Europe," he said, "among those that call themselves leftist intellectuals, to attack us. We don't care about that! Those attacks mean absolutely nothing to us! Until now we've had no time in Cuba, faced as we've been by the immense amount of revolutionary work to be done—and that needed our *immediate* attention—to worry about the problems of culture. Now we will begin to work at creating a popular culture, a culture for the people and by the people. The little group of bourgeois writers and artists that has been so active, or at least talked so much, up till now, without creating anything that's been of any real worth, will no longer have anything to do in Cuba. Look—every socialist country has come at some point in its development to the stage that we have come to now. The Soviet Union first and China not long ago, with the Cultural Revolution. There's no socialist country that hasn't passed through a stage like this, a stage in which the old bourgeois culture, which managed to hang on after the Revolution, is supplanted by the new culture of socialism. The transition is hard, but as I say, the bourgeois intellectuals are no longer of any interest to us. None! I'd a thousand times rather Allende had sent us a miner than a writer, I'll tell you."

Fidel would not expressly mention Stalin, but his suggestion was clear, perhaps in order to intimidate me, and through me my Cuban friends, and to warn us all that the cultural policy of the Revolution was entering its Stalinist phase. He knew what hackles this would raise in Europe, and among precisely those intellectuals who had previously supported Cuba enthusiastically, and he was declaring from the outset that criticism from that quarter, even an all-out attack, would not change his course one jot. He knew, too, that the criticism had already begun; at this point he opted to take the offensive and precipitate the rupture himself. The pretext, as always, was the need to lay the foundations for a proletarian culture. Why hadn't Allende sent him a miner? It occurred to me that a Chilean copper miner, some worker from the mines at Chuqui or El Teniente, would have been even more disillusioned than I at seeing the absenteeism, the volunteer work turned forced labor, the unpaid hours, the long, grave faces in the lines in Old Havana, the broken and potholed streets, the cracked and peeling walls, the broken windows. But I couldn't be insulting, even if Fidel was; I had to keep the discussion on another plane.

"It's true that there's a certain leftist fashion," I said, "but I, personally, have been pretty reluctant to follow political and literary fashions."

Fidel was disconcerted by the *sangfroid* of my replies, and the tone of the conversation, in spite of his aggressiveness, had begun to change. I took advantage of the moment to bring the talk around to more personal topics. I gave Fidel a history of my education, in order to try to make him understand that I had arrived by a process of natural, organic evolution at my left-wing stance, and that it was not some intellectual fad I had just recently taken up. My early and perhaps emotional rejection of my Jesuit education (the same education Fidel had received) had become more rational, more intellectual. Teenage reading had led me to refutations of those proofs of the existence of God that my professors of apologetics gave us, and from that to losing my religious faith was a short step.

"It's rare to lose one's faith through a purely logical process," Fidel interrupted.

"There was a rejection of Catholicism, at least as it was taught and practiced at the time, that was instinctive, of course, and not at all rational, but the arguments of modern philosophers gave the rejection a rational coherence. I think the strongest motivation after that was my support for Latin American nationalism. I performed my first political act when I joined a demonstration to protest the invasion of Guatemala in 1953 or 1954."

"You must have been pretty young!" Fidel said, his voice surprised and almost friendly.

I smiled.

"Later, as I said, I began, very, very enthusiastically, to follow the Cuban Revolution. After the Twentieth Communist Party Congress in the Soviet Union, when the Soviets were in the full swing of de-Stalinization, Cuba seemed to me to be setting an example for a different sort of socialism. That example thrilled a lot of us. It's true that the period that you are talking about now, the period that you now see as a necessary step in the evolution of the Cuban Revolution, has been taken in every socialist experiment. But that doesn't mean that it's inevitable, much less desirable. On the contrary. We must not abandon the quest for another kind of socialism. That, in fact, is the significance of the Chilean experiment. Marx tried to find a way to the integrated liberation of man, liberation at every level and in every aspect of life; no true socialist, no socialist of good faith, can give up on that ideal without falling into the blackest kind of pessimism. Remember that the entire intellectual thrust of Marxism is to dissolve the repressive apparatus of the state. One of its primary concerns was peace in Europe. Marx lived in an age of wars between nations, he was intimately familiar with the Prussian state, and he had come to the conclusion that the main causes of war were bourgeois states, with their repressive apparatuses that tended to lead them into conflict with each other, and their struggles for power, and their territorial expansionism. Marx conceived the dictatorship of the proletariat as an essentially temporary historical stage that would lead to that final stage when all traces of the bourgeoisie were destroyed or assimilated by the working class, when the state would be dissolved, and, in consequence, when there would be peace among the nations. The dictatorship of the proletariat would of necessity be much less repressive than the dictatorship of the bourgeoisie, which in Marx's time was totally inhuman, savage; it would be the dictatorship of the vast majority, come to replace the dictatorship of a tiny minority."

"As Marx conceived it," Fidel said, "socialism would triumph first in the most developed countries—Germany and England. Marx's socialism was conceived to be applied in the advanced industrial countries of his time. The factory workers would take over the reins of power and the control of the means of production. The historical experience of socialism, however, has been different. And that is why we face the problems that we do in applying socialism to the challenges of underdevelopment. Believe me, there are very serious problems, and you Chileans will be facing them very soon yourselves."

At this stage of our conversation, we had both stood and were pacing the office. The atmosphere had lightened considerably. I insisted that I had acted in good faith, with no ulterior motives or underhandedness—though I confessed that I had not always acted with the tact essential to any diplomat.

"Yes," Fidel said at one point, "I believe you. I wish we'd had this conversation before. I think it might have helped. But one is always so very busy. How can one find time? The problem is that I have already sent a message about you to Allende."

I said nothing. Fidel seemed to think that the news of his accusation would crush me. He looked at me out of the corner of his eye as he paced with long strides back and forth across the room. But what could Allende do to me? He could order me home to Chile, which would neither frighten nor displease me. He couldn't throw me out of the diplomatic service without the required administrative hearings and an order to that effect signed by the Comptroller-General. The subtleties of our bourgeois institutions! And if he did manage to have me expelled from the service, he could hardly keep me from breathing, living, writing, publishing whatever I felt like, at least at the current stage of our own Revolution—a stage which Fidel, without the slightest doubt and in fact precisely because of this "softness," scorned, and considered essentially fragile and temporary. When he realized that I was basically indifferent to his charges, Fidel reacted very naively—unless, of course, he astutely proposed to explore an area that had so far not been dealt with in our conversation.

"I see you don't care about Allende," he said. "But you do care about Neruda. I'll report you to Neruda!"

I smiled again. I refused to tell him that the Cubans had already denounced Neruda himself, and that they had spread the denunciation to the four corners of the globe, in a campaign they had never used even against their worst enemies. Fidel knew that perfectly well, and so he knew that the idea of "accusing me to Neruda" was pure bravado. During this part of our interview, as we paced in opposite directions—Fidel had the habit of walking while he talked, especially at crucial moments of the conversation, and so did I—back and forth across the office of the minister of foreign relations, who was observing us in absolute silence, something quite funny happened. Fidel was talking about Cuban agriculture, and he contended that back in the days of the Sierra Maestra he had been the only person to oppose an agricultural reform based on the mere subdivision of land, with the aid of a system of cooperatives. That, he said, would create a privileged, and profoundly conservative, class of campesinos.

"Yet I was in Princeton, Prime Minister," I put in, "studying international policy, when you went to the United States in early 1959, and I remember your speech to a group of students and professors there very well. You spoke there, in English, about an agrarian reform that would create new property owners, a step which you said showed how original and distinct the Cuban Revolution was in comparison with the Soviet Union. And you added that that new class of campesino property owners, as they emerged from the backwardness that had been their lot up to then, would create an excellent market for Cuban as well as for American industry."

Fidel stopped short and looked at me in amazement.

"It wasn't at Princeton," he said, looking at Raúl Roa. "It was at Yale or someplace. I don't remember too well anymore."

"I heard you speak at Princeton, Prime Minister," I insisted, imperturbably.

"It wasn't Yale?" Fidel asked Roa.

After a moment's silence, Roa, who spoke no other word the entire night, said: "It was Princeton."

Fidel then looked at me wide-eyed, in an expression approaching or pretending to approach childlike wonder, and went from the formal *Usted* to *tu.*

"And you were there!" he exclaimed.

At another point in the conversation I spoke to him about Chile's criticism of his government. I told him that on the Chilean Left, sharp criticism was the norm. It was precisely this habit of sharp criticism that had brought the Unidad Popular to power. Criticism of reactionary regimes had led to the electoral triumph of the Left. But this habit of criticism wouldn't just go away, just stop, from one moment to the next, I said, simply because a popular government was in power. Besides, Chilean experts who had worked in Cuba had taken away a very critical view of the Cuban situation.

"But they never aired those views outside!" Fidel exclaimed.

"Nor have I," I replied. "I never invited my writer friends to any of the official receptions I held, in spite of the fact that they were invited to other embassies. Our discussions were strictly private and personal. There is nothing more natural than that a diplomat who is at the same time a writer should get together with his literary brethren in the country he is posted to. That always happens. We writers, especially in Latin America, are almost a family, and people know each other across national borders. How was I supposed to avoid seeing these people in Cuba? Of course we talked, we talked a great deal, and we are by nature a sharp-tongued lot."

"Now I'm even beginning to think," Fidel said, turning to Roa, "that he's a pretty good diplomat!"

Fidel kept returning to the subject of writers, for whom he had what seemed to me a strange distaste.

"Why do you people have to keep appointing writers as diplomats?" he suddenly asked me.

I explained to him about the Chilean tradition of writer-diplomats and politicians: Vicente Pérez Rosales and Alberto Blest Gana.

"Pérez Rosales was active at every step of the building of the Republic," I said. "He was a journalist, a diplomat in Europe charged with handling German emigration, a colonizer of the south, a senator. At the end of his life he wrote his memoirs and produced the best book of his time, better than the work of professional literati. It's as though somebody had taken part in the Revolution and been minister, been put in charge of agriculture in the provinces, been taken into the diplomatic service, and then were to write a book based on his own experience."

"And the book turned out to be better than the writers'," crowed Fidel, who seemed taken with the idea.

"Yes," I said, "but Vicente Pérez Rosales had a real literary calling, frustrated in part by his life as a man of action, and he prepared himself for years for the task of writing."

"You have to send me that book," Fidel said. "Remember that you promised to do that."

I had in fact promised that. It was during the time of the *Esmeralda* visit, and Fidel had just given another demonstration of his prodigious memory.[9]

---

[9] Months later, in Paris, I was having lunch with Monsignor Zacchi, who was still papal nuncio in Havana at the time, and I gave him a copy of *Recuerdos del pasado* ("Memories of the Past") to take for me to the Prime Minister.

At another point in the conversation Fidel had asked me, almost sarcastically, if I thought *I* might someday write something worthwhile.

"I've never thought about the subject that way," I said. "I try to be true to my calling as a writer, and to write the best I can. I may never write a book of any real worth, as you put it, but results aren't everything. A writer writes out of certain personal obsessions. When those obsessions coincide with the great issues of a particular historical moment, the result may be a lasting work of art. The artist in that case becomes an interpreter of his or her time. The only thing I can assure you, for my own part, is that for good or ill I will keep writing."

The Prime Minister looked at me in surprise again, as though the imperturbable tone with which I answered him were utterly unheard of. He told me that when I wrote a book I considered worthwhile I should send it to him. He promised to read it![10] Later, confirming my impression as to his bewilderment throughout most of our conversation, he said, and these are his exact words: "Do you know what I've been most impressed by in this conversation?"

"What, Prime Minister?"

"Your calmness!"

I raised my eyes and looked straight into his eyes, but I did not say a word.

The last thing he said to me, with great seriousness, before shaking my hand warmly, was that he hoped we'd meet again someday. I understood by those words that he meant that he hoped that in spite of everything I would continue to count myself among the friends of the Revolution.

"I hope so too," I said.

Fidel walked me to the door and closed it slowly after me. The aide from Protocol was still outside in the large reception room waiting for me. I had gone into the minister's office at 11:25. It was now 2:45; the conversation had lasted three hours and twenty minutes.

On the sidewalk outside, near the armed guards, Meléndez was waiting.

---

[10] The book that followed this conversation was this book. I sent Castro a copy of the first edition, with a respectful dedication that mentioned his request. I sent it by way of a Cuban ambassador in Madrid. I learned later that Carlos Altamirano, the Chilean Socialist politician, had been in the Comandante's office at one point, talking about Chile and other subjects, and the two men's eyes had suddenly, and by pure coincidence, fallen on the book, which had little slips of paper marking some of the pages. "This kind of thing—naturally I don't read this," the Commander-in-Chief said, making a gesture as though to brush it away with his hand and moving quickly on to other subjects. "Naturally"! Other bits and pieces of gossip, however, have made me think that he had read it carefully and even vainly, as he seems to have been irritated by my description of the lined, tired face he showed during our first encounter. As some of my Spanish friends might say, "Read us? We're nobody!"

He'd no doubt assumed that I would emerge from the conversation within minutes of entering, shattered by the Comandante's attacks. I walked up to him calmly, inwardly savoring his perplexity, which he could not altogether mask.

"Well, Meléndez," I said, "Adios!"

Meléndez looked at me for an instant, his eyes troubled, and then looked quickly to one side. My attitude seemed to indicate that his accusations, his files, his tapes had not been fully successful in landing me among the "bad guys," in some lower circle of the Revolution's Inferno, and that recognition unnerved him. Something had happened in the world that his philosophy, like Hamlet's friend Horatio's, had not dreamt of.

"Adios, Edwards," he said, though his eyes were turned away. "Bon voyage!"

I briefed my successor and the consul on the conversation, for the proper functioning of the embassy in the future. My successor stared at me, wide-eyed and pale. I made no comments; they could draw their own conclusions. Fidel had revealed to me, in the course of the conversation, that they had "studied" my replacement and that in their view he was the person "least indicated" for the job who could have come, a person who by temperament and habits would not like Havana.

"He is an old-time diplomat," I had replied, "a man whose career means everything to him. He will try to act professionally. Consequently, he will work to make relations between Cuba and Chile the best that they can possibly be, since his professional success depends on just that."

"You're right," Fidel had finally said.

It was quite likely that my defense would help my colleague; but I said not a word about this part of the interview to him, so as not to make him more nervous than he already was.

There was a note for me on my bed. The young Chilean woman who couldn't take her daughter to Chile was asking for work at the embassy. She hadn't had the courage to ask for work before, but the job would be a lifesaver for her. I suddenly understood the anguish with which she had approached me recently. She, too, naively, had believed, as had many others, that I could help her. I called the hotel telephone operator to ask to be waked up at six, and I lay down to try to get a couple of hours' sleep. My bags were packed and sitting at the door. My ticket, my passport, and the keys were on the dresser. I looked out at the ocean, thinking I wouldn't be seeing that ocean again for a long, long time, perhaps a lifetime, and I closed my eyes and tried to sleep.

*   *   *

There was always a large crowd in the small passenger lounge at the airport: delegations just coming in or departing; men and women invited to Cuba from all parts of the world, sometimes emerging from the underground, or even a long prison term, to breathe the free air of the airport; foreign diplomats and international officials of all kinds. Some of the faces belonged to the airport itself: a Protocol officer who rushed with professional and imperturbable kindness to find me a seat on the plane; the representative from UNESCO, tanned and invariably smiling; a few muscular, short-haired men of indefinite occupation; a Western ambassador; a delegation from some institute of culture that was arriving from Chile and who greeted me with a hint of reticence, the unequivocal sign that the accusations that Fidel Castro had mentioned a few hours ago—during that interview that now, in the harsh light of the sun, in the midst of these familiar, or at least vaguely familiar, faces, seemed slightly unreal—had begun to produce its effect.

I pushed back the curtains in the lounge a bit to look out at the streets of Rancho Boyeros, perhaps for the last time, and I saw Meléndez and Duque Estrada jogging along together, as though they had forgotten something. The fact that they were together, and that they had not come up to say good-bye to me, gave me pause. On one occasion, Duque Estrada, who seemed to be willing to give me the facilities that the head of Protocol so evasively kept from me, had told the director of the Diplomatic Corps in Havana to explain to Meléndez the problems that I had encountered and looked for a permanent home for the embassy, all this because of a house we'd gone together to see. From that detail, I had gathered that Estrada preferred to avoid direct contact with Meléndez. Now, though, they were jogging lightly along together down the sunny sidewalk, and both of them had avoided sticking their heads into the lounge where there'd have had to say good-bye to the person who was still, at least officially, the chargé d'affaires of Chile.

The Yugoslav ambassador and the papal nuncio, Monsignor Zacchi, came up to shake hands and stay with me for a few moments while I waited for the plane. The namesake, or near-namesake, of Stendhal came over, too, M. Henry Bayle, the ambassador from France. The representative of the Kampuchean People's National United Front, who before being Prince Sihanouk's ambassador in exile had been an aging student of mathematics in Paris, came over and, as he always did, spoke insistently to me of the necessity of relations between the United Front and Chile. This was a declaration which, in spite of its brevity, had the virtue of giving M. Bayle, the Yugoslav ambassador, and Monsignor Zacchi an excuse to move away. Behind the Cambodian, waiting his turn to talk to me in the name of his ambassador, was a member of the embassy of the Democratic Republic of Vietnam.

They called my flight, and as I walked down the narrow corridor that led outside to the runway I said good-bye to one of those muscular, short-haired types that I had come to recognize on my continual trips to Rancho Boyeros (the places for entertainment best-known to a diplomat in any major city are the airports) and to the Protocol officer posted there, the man who had tried, perhaps presciently, to expel me from the VIP area on my first day in Havana. As I walked out onto the runway, staggering under the weight of my suitcases packed with books and bottles of rum, I thought that there was an amazing, and very revealing, symmetry between my arrival and my departure—both times I was loaded down with pointless bags and packages, and both times, by virtue of a tacit decision made in some mysterious and inaccessible realm of government, I was denied the official favors of Protocol. This time at least I was accompanied by the Chilean consul to Cuba.

"Good luck, wise-ass!" were the delicate last words, muffled by the roar of the engines as they began to turn, of my friend the consul. I learned that not long afterward the young Chilean ambassador from the MAPU Party, after a two-hour conversation with the first vice minister of the interior, Comandante Manuel Piñeiro, had said jokingly to the consul, "I hear the bourgeois wish each other good luck!"

"What?" the consul queried.

It seems the ambassador was alluding to those last little words of my friend the consul—they had been reported to the impressionable ambassador by the vice minister, who cited them as yet another example of our incorrigible subversiveness! But unless I was unwittingly wearing a bug in my tie-clasp, or the aircraft mechanics who were supposedly readying fire extinguishers in case the engines caught fire could read lips . . . of course it's likely that one of those short-haired breed had, without our realizing it, been nearby at the time, and that the vice minister had simply wanted to use that small detail to show the ambassador once again how extremely efficient the services of State Security were.

The seat reserved for me by the Protocol officer was about the middle of the plane, on the aisle, next to a very young, fat couple who examined me with barely concealed curiosity. The Iberia plane, a Boeing 707, rolled down the runway, leaving behind the buildings of Rancho Boyeros that I had come to know all too well in my three and a half months' residence in Cuba. My residence had lasted from December 7, 1970, to March 22, 1971, to be precise, and I will not deny, now, in fairness to the truth, and even though the confession may be used as a further argument against me, that at the moment of takeoff I was swept by a wonderful, unmistakable feeling of freedom. This feeling was, however, deceptive, the product of my recalcitrant, if not altogether incorrigible, naiveté—for the tentacular ramifications of my Cuban experience were to continue to pursue and entangle me.

This book ought by all rights to end here, with my departure as unremarked by Protocol as my arrival had been (though, of course, I now knew that the oversight was deliberate, whereas when I arrived I couldn't know that), and with the moment of the Iberia plane's takeoff from the soil of the "First Free Territory of the Americas" to the considerable relief, as I was to learn in the course of the flight, of many of its passengers. I must, however, like in all those nineteenth-century novels, add a summary of the events that followed, and of some which although I only learned about them later were linked to this story and now may help to fill it out.

When we were less than an hour from Madrid, the obese young couple sitting next to me, and who had almost literally never taken their eyes off me, spoke. They were leaving Cuba forever. From Madrid they were flying to the United States to join the rest of their family.

I was careful to say nothing. I was not in the sort of mood that would have been proper for talking to my seatmates, as I might have done on a flight from Chile to anywhere. But I did suddenly realize that Meléndez, as one last delicate gesture, had ordered his staff to put me in the part of the plane reserved for *gusanos*. My seat assignment, then, corresponded to a political judgment!

Padilla was right when he said that everything in a situation such as Cuba's was reduced sooner or later to politics. Everything—even the smallest joke, even what one did *not* say in given circumstances, even one's seat in tourist class on an airplane! I had left Cuba among those who Meléndez considered my peers.[11]

At Barajas Airport in Madrid, while I wandered around lost, trying to find the commuter flight for Barcelona, I was approached by a neat-looking gentleman of middle age who spoke with the eclectic accent of Latin Americans who have lived their lives in several different countries. This gentleman very courteously told me that he was with the Prensa Latina office in Madrid and

---

[11] I later discovered, furthermore, that Castroist sectarianism lumps all exiles into one indiscriminate mass, and then uniformly and stubbornly rejects that mass. In exile there is everything from Batista-era torturers to the writers, intellectuals, and professionals who represent the best that Cuba possessed, but they are all *gusanos*.

that he had instructions from Havana to interview me. I asked him to give me a moment to call Mario Vargas Llosa in Barcelona first, since when Mario passed through Cuba recently he had invited me to stay at his house. He answered the phone half asleep (it must have been close to two in the morning), and a little bewildered: He had completely forgotten that I had told him about a month ago in Havana that I would be coming to Barcelona today. When I hung up with Mario I invited the Prensa Latina correspondent to have a drink with me while I waited for my plane.

The reporter asked me trivial questions and wrote down my answers in a little notebook, as though this were the most natural interview in the world— and the most insignificant. I presumed that his questions were purely for police purposes, since I couldn't see what possible interest Prensa Latina could have, this late in the game, in interviewing me. Still, I was later told that the interview was published in Cuba, and that in it, as a "human-interest" detail, there appeared my telephone call and late-night flight to the house of Mario Vargas Llosa in Barcelona. In the subsequent attacks on intellectuals who protested Heberto's arrest, Mario became a sort of general scapegoat. Haydée Santamaría, who had given me a magnificent box of cigars on the eve of my departure, knowing, I presume, of my pernicious friends and my imprudent tongue, had sent Mario, on the other hand, a frenzied and overwrought letter in which she maintained that she had always wanted to stand beside Ché Guevara, firing off cannon-blasts against the enemy.

I boarded the little mail plane that made the 2:00 A.M. flight between Madrid and Barcelona. In the seats beside me there were two thin, pale young women in high black boots and long overcoats who seemed to me, at that moment, the most refined and decadent expression of the consumer society. There was also a man reading a newspaper. It suddenly occurred to me that he was a police agent, and he might in fact have been. Were there not plainclothes police officers in Francoist Spain? But the point is that such a suspicion would never have occurred to me before: In three and a half months I had discovered the seamy secret-police side of the world—I had discovered the existence of State Security! And in the tiny mail plane that bumped along the runway at Barajas Airport for what seemed forever before it took off for Barcelona, there very well might be a bomb planted by Meléndez' goons!

Two hours later, at 4:00 A.M., Mario, in his bathrobe, and with the patience of a saint, listened as the torrent of words rushed out of me, the story of my last weeks in Cuba. Mario followed me with his eyes as I paced the living room of his apartment like a caged lion—and then suddenly stopped, in alarm, and looked all about the room. "Are you sure there are no bugs in here?!" I exclaimed. Mario, who had not yet had the privilege of discovering the parallel

State Security universe, could only roar in laughter. It might be that I was the one whose mind had been twisted by experience, and his the mind in balance. But it is also possible that his was a state of pre-police innocence. I had tasted the fruit of the tree of knowledge; my experience had been the contemporary equivalent of the experience of original sin. When viewed from a great enough distance, one sees that all revolutions go through the same stage: After the spontaneous innocence of the first years, they take a bite of the forbidden fruit which the serpent of history puts before them . . . But I am talking allegory, and that goes to prove that the style of Heberto Padilla has taken over some corner of my mind. From the Heberto Padilla of earlier years to an act of public self-criticism. . . .

When I later read Padilla's letter of self-criticism and self-accusation, written just before he was released from prison, I thought I was imagining things. And I was not the only one who had that reaction. But the strange part of it, for me, was that I could still hear the echo of Padilla's laughter, his delighted invective aimed at the hidden microphones while the rest of us gestured at him to shut up. The letter provoked a wide spectrum of interpretations: torture, methods similar to those used in the Prague trials, a diabolic subtlety on Padilla's part, aimed at imitating the style of Stalinism and thereby at sending a coded message to his friends in the outside world. My own imagined scenario was that he had been ordered unexpectedly into a room, as I had been, except that Heberto would have been softened up first with a few days in solitary confinement (which they couldn't do to me for reasons of protocol), and that Fidel himself, who had just gone to the University to announce that he was taking personal charge of the matter, had turned to Heberto, suddenly revealing to the awestricken poet the side of him from which the entire fearsomeness of his imposing, thundering, and accusatory humanity could be seen, and had scolded Heberto, with maybe a couple of slaps for good measure, like some terrible *magister* of old. What more torture would be needed? Fidel would then have invited the poet, whose nerves must have been in a state all too easy to imagine, to discuss the possible letter of self-criticism with one or two chosen intellectuals tutored for the occasion by State Security. Then he would have left the poet alone, in a room more comfortable than his first isolation chamber, with paper and pen and perhaps, to aid inspiration, a discreet supply of tobacco.

Thus would have come to the poet his revelation, a revelation communicated to his colleagues in that memorable public session of the Writers' Union—a poem he said he had written as he sat before the window of the hermitlike cell in which he was being allowed what might be called his spiritual retreat, a poem to Spring, to blooming flowers and the song of a bird.

The transcription of the public session contains some pretty incoherent moments. The tongues of those who were called to the stage, tongues which had once been free enough in my rooms at the Habana Riviera, suddenly became twisted and thickened, perhaps in panic. This panic was probably unjustified, since poets tend to be scared by ghosts. The ghost might be called Stalin, but Cuba, in spite of the fevered imagination of its poets, lay in another clime, at a latitude and in circumstances very different from those of the Soviet Union in the thirties and forties. Although Cuba too had developed a tropical and somewhat half-hearted cult of personality . . . The proof of this difference was given by a young writer whose first manuscript had been discovered in 1968, in a six-foot-high by six-foot-wide stack of manuscripts, by the author of this chronicle, and who defended with luminous simplicity the cause of good faith and the power of literary creation. But the master of Padilla's public humiliation, José Antonio Portuondo, declared that the words of that young writer, José Norberto Fuentes, had been the only blot on those otherwise inspiring proceedings—a judgment which shows that in questions of style Portuondo suffers from a lamentable lack of taste.

Fidel had told me that our conversation on that last night had been useful, that he was sorry not to have had it before, but that he had already denounced me to President Allende. He meant by this, I presume, that nothing was to be done for it, that my fate was sealed. But aside from the indiscretion of entirely private remarks, I had committed no breach that could justify my being expelled from the diplomatic service by an administrative indictment. Nor could our intrepid Comptroller-General take into account the testimony of Cuban State Police officers who had kept me under surveillance and recorded my conversations, which had been initiated in many cases when their own volunteer or not-so-volunteer agents had done everything in their power to loosen my tongue. The maximum penalty allowed by our much-maligned "bourgeois constitution" was that I be summoned to Chile and put on the budget list of those paid in Chilean pesos, adding to that a universal ostracism by the unconditional followers of Fidel in Chile, who had already been given the name, though I did not yet know it, of the "Cuban lobby." This ostracism had, along with its various inconveniences, certain advantages: It would serve as a process of natural selection of my friends, since I have reached an age that demands that both unnecessary reading and unnecessary acquaintances be avoided; it would also give me more free time to write this book.

Meléndez' boss and friends spared no effort in sending me off to that new creative life-after-retirement. They sent to Chile a rich and varied repertoire of recordings, among which Padilla's speculations on power and the labyrinths of History, which usually elicited some approving remark from me, occupied a privileged position, especially whenever the intellectual level of the discussion fell to risqué examples of our personal and immediate knowledge. They also sent, by way of our young and inexpert MAPU-Castroite ambassador, a voluminous file that included even the smallest details of how I spent my free hours.

This attack served to reveal something not only to me but to Meléndez' group as well: My direct superior, the minister of foreign relations, would not so much as listen to secret-police accusations; he did not believe that the professional fate of a government official could be allowed to depend on the testimony of bugs hidden in private rooms. This was a sign, ominous to Meléndez and his followers, that the so-called "Chilean route" to socialism might be more than an empty phrase. The minister was subjected, as one might imagine, to all sorts of pressures, but he remained steadfast. Not to mention the fact that the leaders of the Chilean Communist Party knew from personal experience what it meant to be in disgrace and to be subjected to police surveillance in Cuba. But these are political elements of the situation, and this chronicle, even when some may misinterpret it, is a far remove from a political history.[12]

Apart from these elements I have mentioned, there was one further factor that might have had an influence in one way or another on my "case" and the way it was dealt with. The friends of Meléndez knew about it, but I did not: It was the experience of some Chilean experts who had worked in Cuba and who now were working, often in important positions, in Chile. These people's departure from Cuba had been more trying, more humiliating than my own, and that was a revelation to me.

The first case I learned about was that of X., a brilliant Chilean economist

---

[12] This paragraph of my notebooks had been taken out of the book, yet it seems to me important. This is not an essay on Cuba, but a literary text which falls into the genre of memoir and autobiography—*testimonio,* as the word has it in Latin America. It is much closer to the novel than anything else, even though nothing in it is invented (in the traditional meaning of the word "invent"). All it invents is the way of telling the experience. Thus, when Carlos Barral, its first publisher, asked me for a phrase by which to define the book, I told him, "A nonfiction political novel."

who in his younger days had been a militant member of the Communist Party. His enthusiasm for the Cuban Revolution led him to volunteer early on to help with the new regime's economic policy. After two or three years he realized that the general economic theory espoused in Cuba was mistaken: The system of purely moral incentives to production would lead to absenteeism and underproduction; the forecasts from the Cuban administrators were rosy, but lacked all realism; gigantic projects were begun, but they had no solid under-footing. Within a very few years, X. said, the sugar economy, and the Island's entire economy with it, would enter a period of severe crisis.

After long hesitation, X. decided to write a letter to Fidel, telling him of his belief that there had to be a change in direction, and that it was urgent that the change be undertaken immediately.

Two or three days after sending the letter, on an otherwise unremarkable afternoon, Fidel walked into X.'s office. "I received your letter. There are some interesting observations in it, but you're completely wrong. I'd like to take you out and show you some of the things the Revolution has accomplished."

Fidel took X. out for a drive in a jeep; they drove all around Havana. Fidel, as he was in the habit of doing with VIP visitors, showed X. his experiments with cattle hybridization and his artificial insemination laboratories; he had him taste the cheeses and savor the various milks that tasted of almonds or roses; they inspected some citrus groves, the construction site of the new Engineering School, etc. X. looked, but he spoke little. He was one of those reserved, taciturn Chileans; he was not one to be impressed by appearances, and in Chile he had been accustomed to exercise his critical faculties. X. returned to his office the next day and submerged himself in his work. The tour with Fidel had not changed his opinion about the Island's economy.

A year passed, and there was no sign of a change of economic direction. Over a period of time, X. had begun to get together every Saturday evening with another Chilean expert, Y., to drink beer and talk. At these Saturday night chats X. liked to put his tensions aside and drink until he was drunk. He talked about every subject imaginable with Y., with no restraints, in total confidence. Naturally the central and virtually obsessive pole around which all these conversations revolved was the current state of affairs in Cuba, "the little issue," as my literary friends put it. These Saturday nights, after countless bottles of beer (a commodity not yet rationed), the two economists and some Chilean friends would chew on the little issue almost *ad nauseam*.

One Saturday X. came in with the draft of a second letter to Fidel. It was a long, no-punches-pulled analysis of the state of the economy. X. insisted on the need to change the economic direction of the country, and it now seemed even more urgent to him to do so than it had a year ago.

Two or three days later, just as he had the first time, Fidel entered X.'s office. "You're a stubborn one, X.! You're pretty hardheaded!" Fidel then turned to the rest of the people in the office, who were enjoying Fidel's apparently joking exclamations: "Have you people ever seen anybody any more hardheaded in your lives? It's incredible!" Gales of laughter. "Well, all right," Fidel went on, with an air of resignation, and as though wanting to demonstrate his infinite patience and allow X. to try to convince him yet a second time, he invited X. once more into his jeep. Once again they toured the farms and ranches around Havana, giving even more time to the ride than they had previously.

That Saturday night, in the café where the group of Chilean friends met, Y. asked X.: "How was your tour with Fidel?"

"There's no convincing that mule!" X. exclaimed, drinking his beer with a gesture of bitterness.

Around this time there was to be a birthday celebration for one of the many Chilean professionals who were working for the revolution. The organizer of the party was a Cuban official whose relations with the Chilean community were very good, as he had spent some time in Chile. This official offered his house for the party. X., naturally, was among the first people on the list of guests.

During the course of the party, X. drank several glasses of rum, as he was in the habit of doing on Saturday night; tying one on on Saturday night was also a particularly Chilean custom, as the host had discovered during his stay in Chile and from his frequent contacts with Chileans in Cuba. The host had also observed that X. was a methodical, quiet man who worked twelve or more hours a day during the week, never touching a drop of alcohol, but who let his hair down on weekends, drank tremendous amounts of beer or rum, and talked a very great deal.

A while after midnight the host invited X. into the kitchen for a talk. He asked him, quite insistently, what his opinion was of several people in the government. The drinks had had their effect, and X.'s comments were biting. The Cuban friend, who listened in what seemed total agreement with X.'s remarks, took pains to keep X.'s glass filled. If the conversation lagged, he would throw X. another question, and X. answered them all.

Around noon on Sunday X. woke up with a headache and the confused recollection of what he had talked about the night before. Monday morning he was summoned to the Presidential Palace by President Dorticós. It was not the first time that Dorticós, as the person finally responsible for the Island's economy, had called X. in to talk about problems that the country might be facing.

The door to the president's office opened, and there was a group of people sitting around a large table. Dorticós was presiding. X. had been saved a seat at the opposite end of the table. Beside Dorticós was the host of Saturday night's party, the friend of the Chileans. Several of the Chilean experts were among the group around the table.

"I am going to read a letter," began Dorticós, "which compañero So-and-so (and here he named the Cuban "friend" of the Chilean experts) has written to compañero Prime Minister Fidel Castro."

The "friend" stated in his letter that he felt obliged to inform the Prime Minister, Comandante Fidel Castro, of the many counterrevolutionary ideas and opinions disrespectful to the leaders of the Revolution that X. had expressed in his presence. The letter did not fail to mention a pejorative phrase that X. had applied to Dorticós himself, and Dorticós read all this aloud, to the absolute silence of the listeners.

When he had finished reading the letter Dorticós employed that same subtle strategy of public denunciation that Padilla would also use on the stage of the Writers' Union after his twenty-eight days in purgatory in the State Security prison—he asked the Chileans present there to comment on the case. All, crushed and overwhelmed, contributed their grains of sand to the mounting accusation against X.

"Do you have anything to say?" Dorticós asked at last, when all the rest had finished.

X., with all the stubbornness of a modern martyr (even though one must admit that the torture was "only" psychological), gave a long speech in which he repeated and amplified on the views of the Cuban economy that he had expressed to Fidel Castro in his letter.

After that session in the office of the president of the republic, X. received his documents to return to Chile in twenty-four hours. His story has been known to very few. A direct witness of the events, after hearing some of the details of my diplomatic mission in Havana, told me not long ago about the case. I was told that in spite of X.'s initial defiant outburst of anger, the experience later had brought on a profound emotional crisis, which he still, after several years and in spite of being appointed to an important post in the new Unidad Popular administration, had not entirely gotten over.

Y., the Chilean expert who would get together with X. in a Havana café on Saturday nights, was the protagonist of a story perhaps less spectacular in its outcome, but no less dramatic and significant. Y. is also a quiet, simple man, of considerable professional stature. After finishing his coursework in economics at the University of Chile, his Communist militancy prevented him from finding a job in keeping with his qualifications. Just then—this was during the very early years of the Cuban Revolution—he met a young man who had come to Chile to recruit experts to work with the Island's economy, and Y. signed up at once. Although he still had not done his thesis, which he needed for graduation, he decided that he would take advantage of this opportunity to travel to Cuba and do a thesis on an original topic, for which he would have privileged access to information: the transformation of the Cuban socialist economy.

Y. worked quietly, for years, on his thesis. One of his few distractions were those Saturday-night talks with X. Throughout all this time he was gathering observations, data, information, but also critical observations, warning signs as to the need to follow a different path toward building the economy of an underdeveloped socialist country than the one Cuba was now following. The time came when he was to return to Chile for his degree. He requested a visa and he was granted it. He began to say his good-byes to his friends and to put his affairs in order for his return. Everything seemed to be going along perfectly normally.

On the eve of his departure, Y.'s wife went off in one direction to some ministry office for something or other that had to be done at the last minute, while Y. went off in another direction to get a paper signed. Their apartment was left in the care of a Cuban housekeeper who through the years had become almost a member of the family. But something very unusual had happened to the Cuban housekeeper that day: She had received a message that her son had to be taken to some ministry office, too, for some vague paperwork that needed doing. They had agreed that when Y. or his wife got back, the housekeeper would leave, but the message had scared the Cuban woman; it was as though she sensed that something serious was going on. Y. had had to calm her before he left on his errand.

Y. came back that afternoon and noticed that some wooden slats in a window were broken. Nervous about this, he opened the door and found that his apartment had been ransacked: there were lamps broken, books scattered on the floor, the furniture was all overturned. He discovered that a camera and a new portable radio had been stolen. Then suddenly he thought of the manuscript on the transformation of the economy in socialist Cuba, which he kept in a drawer in his desk. He ran to look, and saw that it too had disappeared.

In the neighborhood police station, after giving his report of what had happened, he was made to wait two or three hours in a windowless inside room. After a while the delay and indifference of the police, though it was masked by feigned concern, began to worry him. Suddenly, as we say in Chile, "the potato fell on his head." That is, the light dawned.

"Since we're not used to these police state tactics, it had never occurred to me that this was a political robbery. I went up to the police officer in charge and told him I was withdrawing my report. 'I'm very busy,' I told him, 'and besides, it's not that important.'

" 'What!' said the police officer. 'This is very serious! You are a foreign expert. We can't allow a foreign expert's house to be robbed like this. This is a matter of the greatest concern to us, and of the greatest seriousness!'

"I had to argue for a long time to convince him that I really wanted to withdraw my report. They wouldn't let me leave the police station. When I finally managed to leave, the only thing I cared about was getting on that plane and getting out of Cuba. I gave my thesis, which I had worked on for years, up for lost."

The leadership of the Revolution dismissed these cases out of hand: The victims (of both robbery and the system more generally) were social democrats, liberals, not real revolutionaries. Fidel summed up my own case to a leftist Chilean politician in one sentence: "He is a bourgeois intellectual." As a summary of the problem, it couldn't be simpler, and my politician compatriot seemed quite willing to leave it at that. "Bourgeois intellectual" was the label given those who dared to dissent, to think for themselves, whatever the thoughts might be. The others, the unconditionally committed, the good officials, received as reward the crown of revolutionary purity.[13]

The attitude shown by the Chilean ambassador, the first ambassador to assume that post after my stint as chargé d'affaires and my replacement, was not only comic but revealing as well. I have this story from a good source. After studying the sugar problem, I had reached the conclusion that it would be tough to reach a harvest of six million tons of sugarcane in 1971, when Fidel had set the goal of seven million tons and then, as the harvest started coming in, lowered his sights to six and a half. I reported my conclusions, through confidential channels, to the Chilean Ministry of Foreign Relations in early January 1971.

The ambassador read my report in Chile, before his arrival in Cuba to assume his post. He said that my reports were flawed, in fact invalidated by my prejudices against the Revolution. He went so far as to add, as in the accusations directed against himself by Padilla, that they were also the product of vanity and subjectivism. Even when he took over the mission in Cuba, when it was possible for him to verify my conclusions at first hand, he clung to the idea

---

[13] In October 1973, when I inserted the stories of X. and Y., which had been in the "Parisian Epilogue" of my Paris notebooks, it occurred to me that I didn't know what had happened to the two experts after the September coup d'etat. I later learned that one of them was sent to Dawson Island, a prison island off the coast of Chile, and the other went into exile.

that my reports were in error, and that the goals set by Fidel would be met.

When the results of the harvest were known, and they came in at a little under five million nine hundred thousand tons, the ambassador said the goal had not been reached because of sabotage. That is, I had foreseen in early January that there would be sabotage! As for the solid and simple reasons that I implied in my January report would be responsible for the low harvest (without insisting that these reasons were necessarily determining)—absenteeism, low yields, insufficient progress in mechanizing the harvest—the ambassador dismissed them out of hand. The bourgeois subjectivist, however, was me, and the dialectical materialist the ambassador! Such are the mental gymnastics that conformism engages in, whether it be on the Left or on the Right.

Meanwhile, I had gotten reports from Cuba. Someone, for example, had written me while Heberto Padilla was still in prison:

> Everybody's worried here: Everybody thinks repression is coming, and that this time it's going to be large-scale. I'm not so sure, because I've always said that nobody's really got the slightest interest in culture. I think he's been arrested as a warning, that's all.

In a later letter, that same person wrote the following:

> Well, the storm has passed. He has performed his act of self-criticism and he has been forgiven. The Revolution was very generous with him. What's bad is the repercussions from all this, the harm he's done many of his friends. I saw him before he left for Santa María for a week, and he looks fine. Belkis is fine, too—she acts like nothing's happened. Soon this whole disagreeable episode will be forgotten, because when all's said and done, literature is a pretty unimportant issue here.

Later, toward the end of 1971, the same faithful correspondent wrote, among other things:

> Everything's quiet here. Padilla is in pretty delicate shape with a bad kidney; he had to quit his job in Las Villas because the doctor ordered complete rest. Now a friend tells me he's in the hospital with it. I'm going to try to find out today how he is. His health is not good, since he's also got a nervous problem, and apparently they haven't been able to improve his health in that respect.
>
> Belkis is all right. She's on leave from UNEAC and is more or less dedicating herself to looking after Padilla. I'm now reading *The Great Terror*, by Robert Conquest, to diversify my reading habits—I think it was translated into French not long ago. It's in Penguin, and I recommend it. It's the most complete work on

that period in the USSR. Conquest is a novelist and distinguished English poet, too.

Well, that's all the news . . . Best regards from all your friends who love and miss you here . . .

A Cuban musician passed through Paris several months after I received these letters and told me that Padilla was fine, that he had a good job now in the Book Institute, that he took part in literary talks and whatnot and was very good-humored about his self-criticism, which he compared to some of the classical self-criticisms of the history of socialism. He said, for example, that his was better than Yevtuchenko's, but that he forgot one very interesting detail that Lukács included in his second one, and that in any case the best self-criticism of them all—Padilla recognized that he didn't manage to best it—was Eisenstein's, the great master of early Soviet film.

As one sees, there was some fear during the time of Padilla's imprisonment that large-scale repression was on the way. Fidel's unblinking prediction that I and my friends would suffer new and serious disillusionments with the Cuban Revolution made me fear the same thing, and especially since Fidel made it plain that our foreseeable reactions to the Revolution's promised new get-tough tactics left him totally unconcerned. Still, large-scale repression did not occur. My friend, in "diversifying his reading," was delving into Stalin's reign of terror, whose glacial, Asian proportions were profoundly alien to the way of life (so courteous, in spite of all) of the island long called the Pearl of the Caribbean. Padilla had emerged from the experience with his health somewhat affected, but his theatrical voice and his stentorian laughter once again resounded in the literary circles of Havana. That was not to say that the Revolution's errors no longer served as inexhaustible food for his wit. When all was said and done, the Revolution, as my friend said, had been quite generous with him.

The upshot was that nothing had happened—or, to use the words of my persevering correspondent (who, by the way, hasn't written me for over a year, no doubt from the simple effects of forgetfulness), "they all act like nothing has happened."

Paris, April, 1971
April 30, 1972
Santiago, Chile, January 1993

Epilogue[1]

When I reached Barcelona, I called Pablo Neruda. I wanted to stay a few days in Barcelona to rest, to "unwind," as the Americans say, from my Cuban experience, which had put my nerves to quite a test, but Neruda told me I was scheduled to accompany him when he went to present his credentials to President Pompidou the next day. I was obliged, then, three days after my departure from the airport at Rancho Boyeros, still vividly seeing my friends' exhausted faces in my memory, hearing the hoarse voice of Fidel Castro, reliving my discovery that Meléndez' staff had put me in the *gusano* section of the airplane, fearing the imaginary microphones in Mario Vargas Llosa's Barcelona living room, to enter once again into the ceremonies of diplomacy. I had not had time to breathe, and I was now to be plunged again into the eighteenth-century gilt, the grand mirrors, the white-painted paneling, the Gobelin tapestries of the Elysée Palace, where M. Pompidou would recall his past as a university professor as he welcomed the author of the *Canto General,* this Victor Hugo of the Spanish language come from a distant land of earthquakes, archipelagos, and volcanoes—a land whose politics, it now had to be admitted, was as extravagant as its geography, for it had raised a Marxist to power in free elections. *Hélas!*

---

[1] What follows is the text that I wrote in October 1973 in Barcelona and Calafell after learning of the events of that September in Chile; I was preparing my 1971 and 1972 notebooks for publication as a book. In the first editions of the book, I inserted the last pages of my notebooks into this epilogue, but now I prefer to restore all of it—the 1971 and 1972 notebooks, which constitute *Persona Non Grata per se,* and this separate "Parisian Epilogue," which was written when the original text was already in the hands of the publisher.

Dressed in the *de rigueur* suit of dark blue, Neruda spoke in his address of his brothers Louis Aragon and Paul Eluard, and he held aloft the letters which accredited him as ambassador extraordinary and plenipotentiary from that new Revolution in Latin America, a Revolution not lacking, in fact, in certain French ingredients, as could be seen by the respect for constitutional law which it had inherited in the last analysis from the French Revolution—though whose mixture of Liberalism and Marxism no doubt produced a slight twinge in the collective liver of M. Pompidou and the members of his government. Indeed, to the French palate the flavor of that mixture must have been *piquante,* and no doubt in certain circumstances might even turn explosive. All of us who were gathered there amid the Louis XV decor were aware of the danger for Franco-Chilean relations, but we all smiled, while our hosts exclaimed over the fact that President Allende had chosen a great representative of culture and letters to fill the post of ambassador to Paris.

In the Jardin d'Honneur the avalanche of journalists was of proportions never seen before at such ceremonies. The poet replied in his slow, almost ritual voice, and tried to make his way through the crowd without offending anyone. I, meanwhile, looked out over that garden in the heart of Paris, the mass of journalists, the discreet and obsequious smile of the Protocol officers who bowed as they showed the ambassador the way to his car, the red, black, and blue-uniformed Republican Guards whose unsheathed swords gleamed in the pale early-spring sun, and it seemed to me incredible that I had departed the Habana Riviera and its surroundings, which I had almost come to fear I would never leave again, incredible that I had left behind the contemplation of the waves that crashed and broke across the Malecón and whose salt spray gnawed at the unpainted, cracked and peeling faces of the buildings of the city.

At this time, in spite of the disease that was now beginning to undermine him, Neruda still maintained most of the euphoria of his best years. It is likely that as soon as we arrived at what Neruda called the "mausoleum" on the avenue de la Motte-Piquet (that is, the Chilean Embassy), we immediately took off our lugubrious dark suits and went out to celebrate his official investiture at Chez Allard, his favorite restaurant, with a *cassoulet Toulousain,* a hearty dish of beans with pork or duck that is the French equivalent (enriched with various sausages) of the Chilean *poroto granado.*

I told Pablo that once before in Paris, during the days of General de Gaulle, when I was second secretary of this same embassy, I had taken part in a similar ceremony. I had the memory of a tall old man whose facial muscles had been moving constantly while his gaze remained fixed, impassive, and immobile.

"It would be much better for our relations with France," I told him, "if de Gaulle were still here. I guarantee it!"

The French ambassador in Havana had told me once that General de Gaulle had given him strict orders to forge the best relations possible with Cuba, with no political coyness or demurrals of any kind. And the representatives from the Kampuchean United Front had told me that General de Gaulle had gone so far as to warn Sihanouk of a coup that the CIA was preparing to launch against him.

"Perhaps!" said Pablo. "It's very possible."

But Pablo was not much interested in speculations, especially when there was no possible practical way of testing the hypothesis.

As for my vicissitudes in Cuba, I had told Pablo my story the night before, in great detail, as soon as I arrived. My mind would not seem to let the subject go; I found that I couldn't concentrate on other matters, couldn't sleep; in the most confidential conversations with Pablo I kept returning to it, with new anecdotes, thoughts about it inspired by the most varied and apparently distant words.

"I feel like writing a book," I told him, "even if it's never published. Otherwise I'll never free myself of this obsession."

"Write it!" Pablo said. "Write it, and leave out nothing of what you've told me. And don't even think about publishing it! Someday you'll find you can publish it, and it will be an important book, a necessary testament."

I had brought with me from Lima, and had kept with me in Havana, on the large table in my room, the draft of a long novel that I had begun in Chile in 1969. Now I decided that the novel could wait.[2] The months in Cuba had plunged me into a severe crisis; I would not be able to resume the creative part of my writing if I didn't first get those experiences down on paper, and try in passing somehow to explain them all to myself.

So I bought an alarm clock, rented an apartment on the ninth floor of a building so that I could be far away from the noise of the street, bought a coffee pot and a coffee-grinder, and set to work. The alarm clock was set for six o'clock in the morning, and the coffee pot would be waiting in the kitchen, with the water measured out and the coffee, which I would have ground the night before, already in it, so that all I would have to do was turn on the gas. A half-hour later, braced by the liquid air of the early morning in the heights of Passy, with the Eiffel Tower before me, I would relive on paper the wild rides with Agustín or Tomás, the adventures of the Mysterious Visitor, the grandiloquent exclamations of Heberto Padilla, the beach at Santa María with its white sand, pine groves, and blue sea. Meanwhile, in real life, the representatives of

---

[2] This was the first draft of my novel *Los convidados de piedra* ("The Stone Guests").

the Unidad Popular would come by the embassy and I would detect in some of them a suspiciousness toward me which could only have its origins in Cuba. Pablo was worried, and I knew that he was defending me much more than he confessed. I later learned that during this time he had kept from me some pretty harsh internal attacks, so as not to increase my distress.[3] Abroad, meanwhile, the scandal brought on by the "Padilla affair" was at full zenith, though my name was never mentioned in connection with it at any time. There was only one American journalist who was visiting Cuba at this time who confusedly speculated, from conversations among the diplomatic corps, the role the Chilean representative had played in the "affair." Upon his return from Cuba he telephoned me from Washington; my replies, in the best diplomatic fashion, finished the job of disorienting him.

The pages of the book, handwritten each morning in a drawing-pad, with the solitary company of the fragrance of the coffee and the sight of the Eiffel Tower standing in the snow or rising through the pristine, transparent air, were the secret of my serenity, my equilibrium in the midst of the scandal and the internal accusations (which I had little suspicion of, I must admit, since they bounced off the solid shield of Neruda in Paris and also found in Chile no ready ear in Foreign Minister Clodomiro Almeyda) and the problems in the embassy that kept piling up.

I was an experienced diplomat, with a law degree from the University of Chile; I had some idea of business and international finance; and my parallel life as a writer and friend of Neruda made me the most appropriate person to assist him. Was there, in consequence, any real interest in pursuing these accusations? What sense did it make to create a problem in Pablo Neruda's embassy? Some people, in the upper echelons of government in Santiago, shook their heads: He screws up in Cuba and he's rewarded with a plush job in Paris! What had the world come to? Fidel, however, had made a remark to me during that conversation on the eve of my departure from Havana; it showed a curious sort of pragmatism. "It's possible," he said, "that the same factors that make you unsuitable for the job in Cuba will make you a good diplomat in Paris."

Someone once said that poets take refuge in the cracks that develop along

---

[3] What he had kept from me was a letter from Salvador Allende about me—against me, rather. "So as not to make you any more nervous than you were," he later explained. I also learned that Allende had drafted a cable ordering me out of the embassy; he left it on his night table and the next morning he tore it up. These were the consequences of the accusation that Fidel Castro told me about. The truth is that the matter went no further.

the fault-lines of the government. I had found my little niche in the dusty
embassy on the avenue de la Motte-Picquet, which was now spruced up with
posters touting agrarian reform and the nationalization of copper and with
weavings of burning yellow pecked by Chilean hens, bright greens and deep
blues cut by the boats of peanut-vendors. These weavings had been produced
by women plying their craft on Isla Negra, Neruda's *real* home, and he had
scattered them, in an act of artistic aggression, throughout the salons of the
Second Empire, among the frayed curtains. There was shock over these works
among the army colonels passing through, though generally they kept a
discreet silence. One had one's way of knowing, though, that they were
astonished that a person as renowned as the ambassador should have such
vulgar and infantile taste in wall-hangings. Why, the hens were bigger than the
people, and their eyes weren't even in the right place!

But the repercussions of the "Padilla affair," though not always visible, did
leave their mark on the cultural life of Chile and Latin America. Chile was
never to experience the artistic euphoria that Cuba had known since 1968.
Fidel had told Clodomiro Almeyda in Havana, half in jest and half seriously,
that "we went through that stage of writer/diplomats ourselves!" Fidel was
alluding to my particular problem, but he was generalizing, and he had
obliquely taken a shot at a sacred cow that he himself had little reverence for—
Pablo Neruda. In other words, experience had taught Cuba to distrust writers,
and even though it was hard to learn from other people's experience, Chile
ought to take a lesson. Fidel Castro was saying this to Clodomiro Almeyda,
one of the most independent politicians of the Unidad Popular. What would he
have said to his more docile Chilean supporters! After the "affair," a certain
passivity would reign in Chile, a relative indifference to questions of culture.

Some Chilean writers had been in Cuba before me, and had seen its true
situation at first hand. Now they shut themselves up in their university burrows
and kept their mouths closed. They were not, of course, the favorites of
Quimantú, the new state publishing house—"the publishing house of the
people of Chile," as the pontiffs of the enterprise proclaimed, or the first step
toward state censorship, as someone else, a writer from the East, once whispered in my ear with a grimace of disappointment.

Almost all intellectuals in Latin America gave fervent and hope-filled
support to the Allende government, but the Allende government paid them
very little attention. In Lima, for example, Mario Vargas Llosa was invited to a
cocktail party at the Chilean Embassy in honor of President Allende while the
president was making an official visit to Peru in 1971. An enthusiastic but ill-
informed Chilean official, seeing the novelist leave the party with the president
and his wife, had the unhappy idea of inviting Vargas Llosa to Chile. Mario

accepted, and everyone in the presidential party seemed delighted. But then later, the invitation was discreetly tabled. Mario had made a protest about the "Padilla affair" and had broken off his relations with the Casa de las Américas! As one can see, the mechanism for distancing one's natural friends, which had begun in Cuba years before with an official letter against Neruda, now surfaced again in Chile, where its effects were repeated. The disease took shape among us Chileans in a relatively benign way, but the dissociating and excluding virus now existed, and it wound up engendering the savage antibody that we knew later.

Every day dozens of letters arrived at the embassy with requests for interviews with the ambassador, or for autographs, books, biographical information, introductions to books of poetry, phrases for an album. His presence was requested for radio programs, art exhibits, afternoon teas, round tables to discuss the Third World, Quaker assemblies, wine festivals in Bourgogne, acts to honor Chile in provincial villages all over France.

"Why don't you go?" Pablo would say.

"You're the one they want to see and touch," I would reply. "If I go their faces will be a mile long."

Neruda's disease, in the meantime, was advancing, but its symptoms were vague, scattered, and left just enough room for uncertainty. The news from Chile allowed one to think that apart from the artificial agitation created by what were disparagingly called the "mummies," the fossilized politicians of the Right, things were really going pretty well. The increase in general consumption was bound to create shortages in some areas, but the factories were working, for the first time in Chile's history, at full capacity. The embassy received eyewitness reports from private industrialists who were happy, who confessed to be earning higher profits than ever before. Well then? Pablo reached the conclusion that one mustn't let oneself get depressed. A house in the country would cure all his ills. In Paris he was besieged, he was not allowed to sleep, the intrusions of boors and bores was getting totally out of control, and the fact of living and having offices in the same building, just when Chile had become the latest fad, made one little better than a slave to one's position.

The autumn was upon us, and newspapers had begun to talk about the next Nobel Prize. Neruda's name appeared, as it always did, on the short list. One afternoon I was in my office and I received a telephone call from Stockholm, from Sun Axelsson, a Swedish writer who was a friend of ours.

"I think Pablo will get it this time," she said. "I've learned that those enemies of his who always voted against him before are going to abstain this year."

I told Pablo about this conversation, and added: "I'm sure this time they're going to give it to you."

Since Pablo didn't believe it, or pretended not to, I offered a bet.

"I'd rather not bet you," he said. "You can't afford what the bet would cost you!"

Sun Axelsson had told me that the vote would come on Thursday, a week before the prize was announced, and that that same Thursday she had a dinner date with one of the members of the Swedish Academy. I called her house in Stockholm at midnight, figuring a Scandinavian dinner would be over by that hour. Sun came on the phone immediately and in her halting Spanish told me that Pablo had won, sure enough.

"How do you know?"

Her friend in the Academy, who was going to vote for Pablo, had arrived at dinner with a grin from ear to ear.

"Who won?" Sun had asked him.

"André Malraux," her friend had replied, and then, after a moment, in turn asked: "What books have you translated of André Malraux's?"

Sun Axelsson, one of the best-known Swedish translators of Neruda, had immediately answered: "The *Elementary Odes.*"

"Well, you should tell your publishers," her friend said with a smile, "that they should get André Malraux's *Elementary Odes* out into the bookstores right away."

I had been having dinner with Pablo in the embassy residence when I slipped out at midnight to phone Stockholm. Though I told him of this second conversation with Sun he still insisted on not putting any stock in the story. Nonetheless, the next day after lunch he invited me to go with him for a ride—to look for a country house.

He had pretty much given up the search and was quite dejected, when at last he was shown, in the western part of Normandy, just at the edge of the village of Condé-sur-Iton, a house that seemed built to order for him: it had a tile roof, a large living room with strong old exposed beams, windows that opened onto a lovely canal that ran so near the house it appeared almost to lap at the walls. Farther off, there was a lake and a woods from which the only sound to be heard was the cry of wild ducks. He named the house La Manquel, the Araucan word for "eagle," and there he wrote some of his last poems on autumn and on wood, two of the recurrent motifs of his poetry: autumn, the decline of life, and wood, in whose immutable, petrified substance the poet sought to escape the erosion of time.

Sometime afterward, Francisco Bulnes, who had a reputation for being one of the most cultured members of the right wing of the Chilean legislature, would accuse Neruda in the Senate of having bought a castle, while *La Prensa,* the Christian Democrat newspaper, reproduced a photograph of the manorial castle of Condé-sur-Iton, which had once belonged to the dukes of Rohan-Chabot. The Chilean right wing, which is far from living in huts, could not bear to see the great poet of the Spanish language, the winner of the Nobel Prize for Literature, possess a country home.

In the midst of this campaign over the "castle," Foreign Minister Almeyda passed through Paris. Neruda carefully engineered a practical joke for him. He persuaded the mayor of Condé-sur-Iton to open the great wrought-iron gates of the manorial park for us, one Sunday when Almeyda and I were invited to lunch at La Manquel. Pablo called me in Paris that morning and gave me very precise instructions: I was to arrive with the minister by the road past the cemetery, turn into the drive through the grounds, and take the road to the real castle.

It was a cold, gray morning, and there were patches of fog. I was driving the minister and his secretary. I turned in through the wrought-iron gates and took the drive through the enormous park. The tall spires of the towers and the parapets of the magnificent medieval castle rose up out of a green, grassy hillock, with a dense wood behind. The minister and his secretary looked out at this spectacle in silence, with a mixture of astonishment and incredulity. At the end of the fog-wet path, among the meadows, there was a great nineteenth-century pavilion.

"And this?" the secretary asked.

"This is the library," I replied straight-faced, and my passengers' silence spoke volumes.

But the path led us immediately out of the park, which Pablo always said was filled with the romantic and tragic atmosphere of Alain Fournier's *Le Grand Meaulnes.* Pablo was waiting for us beside the fireplace, in which a warming fire had been lighted, as delighted as any child with the joke he had played on the minister.

The evening before the Nobel Prize was to be announced, the newspapers said that Neruda's candidacy was assured. The day of the announcement I arrived at the embassy early and Manuel Cuevas, the septuagenarian door-man, rushed out breathlessly to meet me.

"There are fifty reporters in there waiting to see the ambassador!" he exclaimed.

There were journalists waiting in the cafés on the corner, in nearby streets. Manuel Cuevas, a doorman of the ancien régime, had taken the precaution of putting a double lock on the doors, but the intrepid reporters seemed ready to climb in through the windows, down through the skylights, along the rain-gutters . . .

"It would be absurd to make a statement before receiving official word," Pablo said. "What if they decided at the last minute to give the prize to somebody else?"

At eleven o'clock Manuel Cuevas reported, from his front-line post at the door, that he could not hold back the attacking hordes of journalists. We told him to open the salons: We would retreat to the residence on the second floor. Around noon, the first scouts from the reporters began to peek up the stairs; caution had been thrown to the winds, and they were moving. The French press were not the only ones there; there were German and Swedish television crews, Spanish and American correspondents. The fact that the near-certain Nobel Prize-winner was at the same time the Chilean ambassador to France, when a year had not yet passed of Allende's Unidad Popular regime in Chile, multiplied the interest the story held. When the telephone rang I answered it, and it was the announcer from a radio station in Buenos Aires who wanted a statement.

"The official notice has not yet come," I told him.

"That doesn't matter!" the announcer cried.

"Yes, but Señor Neruda cannot make any statement yet."

In that case, couldn't *I* make one? No, I couldn't either! For the same reason.

"But this call is costing a fortune!" the announcer said, losing his patience.

"I'm terribly sorry."

Then there was a not terribly polite word in reply, and the announcer from the banks of the Río de la Plata hung up.

Reporters from European television began to run cables, set up spotlights and all sorts of unwieldy equipment. Pablo, Matilde, and I decided to retreat to the last place left in the house: the bedroom. But how were we to hear the news of the prize from there? Matilde remembered that in one of the drawers of one of the desks there was a little transistor radio. It might even still be working. We turned on the radio and through the whoops and buzzes of static we heard a French voice announce that the 1971 Nobel Prize for Literature had just been awarded by the Swedish Academy to the Chilean poet Pablo Neruda. Matilde embraced him and said, "You can go out now, Pablito." The flashbulbs flashed and the TV cameras began to roll.

The France Presse correspondent in Havana queried the Cuban writers about Neruda's prize, and they said they would have to meet to discuss their opinion before they made it public. An official of France Presse in Paris sent our embassy the copy of the press release that was finally issued, with the following words handwritten on the bottom: "They had to find out what Writer Número Uno thought first . . ." Still, there were signs that Cuba in fact wanted to attempt a reconciliation with the Chilean poet/ambassador. Neruda told anybody who wanted to listen that he had nothing against the Cuban Revolution. Quite the contrary! His long poem *Canción de gesta* had been the first important poem in Spanish written in its defense. But he would not reconcile with the people that had signed the letter until they wrote a retractation and published it internationally.

At the same time (in a "simultaneity" that appeared anything but simple coincidence), the accusations against me had suddenly stopped. Some Chileans, with characteristic excess of zealousness, overran the embassy, thinking to find me missing; when, somewhat taken aback, they discovered that I was still there, head intact, they approached me with the sort of politeness that Pablo called "oleaginous." A reporter from Cuba assured me that the climate had improved greatly since I had left: There was more of everything, and one no longer found long lines at the cafés and restaurants. After the terrible crisis in the sugarcane harvest, the economy had begun to recover. The ominous black clouds of a large-scale repression had melted into the air. The country was working well, and the writers could cheer themselves in their useless talks, or sing hymns to spring.

After long decades of irreconcilable division, there were signs in France for the first time of a possibility of a *rapprochement* between the Communist and Socialist parties. The union of these two groups had worked in Chile without there coming to pass the widely predicted fate that the Socialists would be "devoured" by the Communist Party when the Communists came to power. It was the Socialists, in fact, that had won the most votes in the April 1971 municipal elections. For these reasons, as 1971 went on, interest in things Chilean on the part of the French political press increased dramatically. This, of course, had all sorts of repercussions in the embassy, which soon became one of the most watched and sought-after embassies in Paris, and therefore found itself besieged in countless ways by the most varied people and groups.

The leading figures of the French Left began to travel to Chile in order to study the Unidad Popular's accomplishments and problems on native ground. One of the first to go was Jacques Duclos, who was accompanied by other Communist leaders. I recall very well a remark he made to me on his return, at a cocktail party at one of the Eastern European embassies: "You people in Chile have to keep the middle class from becoming a political base for fascism.

That's why the relations with the Christian Democrats are one of the key issues for the Allende government."

François Mitterrand (leader of the Socialist Party though not to be elected President of France until 1981) also went to Chile in late 1971; with him went the Socialist mayor of Marseilles, Gaston Deferre, and a delegation from his party, which he had just joined in order to take over the post of first secretary. Neruda invited Mitterrand and his group to lunch at the embassy. There was talk on that occasion of the possibility of a union of the factions of the French Left. Pablo had pointed out to me many times that he detected in his comrades of the French Communist Party stubborn resistance to Mitterrand and the Socialists, in whom the Communists thought they saw unyielding anti-Communist sentiment. Overcoming all that mutual touchiness and guardedness would not appear an easy thing to do. At our lunch, Mitterrand broached the subject without hesitation. He said that the political picture in Chile, what Mitterrand in the current French political jargon called the "*éventail des partis politiques*," the "fan" or "spectrum" of parties, was extraordinarily like the political picture in France. Without overlooking the tremendous difference in the level of economic development, the political problems of the two Lefts were quite similar. So if the various groups on the Chilean Left had managed to unite and come to power through democratic elections, why couldn't the same thing be done in France? Mitterrand mentioned the reciprocal distrust and suspicion that one saw everywhere during those days, and said, smiling, "I am the only French Socialist who's never been anti-Communist." All the members of his group raised their heads from their plates in surprise, and some stammered protests.

Mitterrand was packing his bags when it was announced that Fidel Castro had just begun his official state visit to Chile, which has in the aftermath become famous for its length and for having culminated in the "empty pot" demonstration organized by the middle- and upper-class housewives of Santiago. In the avalanche of news and press releases about Fidel (which ranged from lyrical exultancy to savage denunciation), the presence of Mitterrand, Deferre, and their group passed largely unnoticed in Santiago. The French press, however, followed the Socialist group's brief visit with interest, and soon was calling François Mitterrand the "French Allende."

The unification of the French Left took place to the tune of explicit allusions to, and warm greetings from, Chile's Unidad Popular, and from that moment on, the politicians of the French government began wanting to examine our "case" in more detail. The first politician to go to Santiago was Edgar Faure, who upon his return went on a radio program and drew a very flattering picture of the Unidad Popular experiment. About a year and a half later, the news concerning our economic situation was not so optimistic. "Tell President Allende," Faure told me once when I went to see him in order to discuss our foreign debt, "that one must give the campesino a sense of the private ownership of the land. Socializing industry is easy, but in agriculture one must tread much more cautiously."

In mid-1972, one of General de Gaulle's former ministers, Alain Peyrefitte, went to Cuba and Chile on a parliamentary mission. He had to interrupt his visit to Chile after two days in order to return home to take charge of the center-right Gaullist party. At the Pudahuel airport in Chile, he gave a rather sly statement to the correspondent from France Presse: He stated that Fidel Castro had told him that Allende could not carry out his experiment unless he broke out of the too-tight bounds of bourgeois respect for constitutional processes. Fidel Castro's skepticism as to the possibility of a peaceful transition to socialism in Chile was well-known. It had been made more than clear in his speech at the National Stadium in Chile, after the "empty pot" demonstration, at the end of the longest visit made to the country by any foreign head of state. In that three-hour speech (so long that many of the bleachers were left scandalously empty), Fidel had said that he was leaving Chile more revolution-ary than ever, more "radical" than ever, since he had seen the face of fascism up close. Yet it was quite another thing to say those words to a representative of the bourgeoisie and the government of France.

The France Presse correspondent's cable dispatch to Paris was followed by a series of denials and clarifications: from Peyrefitte to the correspondent, and from Fidel Castro to Peyrefitte. Still, Peyrefitte came to the embassy to speak with Neruda, and during the conversation, at which I was present, he did not deny that Fidel Castro had made that statement, even when he accused the France Presse correspondent in Santiago of breach of trust, since the corre-spondent had not kept his word to let Peyrefitte see and approve the text of the article before it went to press.

There is no doubt that Peyrefitte's indiscretion was a perfectly deliberate internal policy move. The French public had to be made to think that socialism could be arrived at by repressive and violent measures, but not by the peaceful road followed by Allende in Chile and proposed now for France by Mitterrand and the Communists. The "establishment" could fairly easily tolerate social-ism in countries as far away and of such curious political habits as Cuba or China, but not in the sort of parliamentary democracy that had also become, within limits, the goal sought by the French Left.

During that conversation with Neruda, Alain Peyrefitte said several interest-ing things. He drew a general parallel between de Gaulle's attitude toward the former French colonies and that of the United States toward Latin America.

According to Peyrefitte's analysis, de Gaulle had been able to accept the independence and socialism of Algeria, and had even wound up, in spite of everything, imposing that same attitude on French capitalism. The United States, on the other hand, stubbornly refused to accept either the independence or the socialism of any Latin American country, as the cases of Cuba and Chile demonstrated.

Peyrefitte quoted de Gaulle's opinion of John F. Kennedy. Kennedy, according to de Gaulle, was a skillful young politician of great talent and good intentions, but he lacked the qualities of a true statesman. The statesman was a man who knew how to cut through Gordian knots. Kennedy had come up against the Gordian knot of the U.S. policy in Cuba, and he had not been able to cut through it, agreeing instead to the blockade and the Bay of Pigs invasion. He had come up against the Gordian knot of Vietnam, and once again had not been able to cut through it. And he had faced it again, without being able to find the solution, in the case of civil rights.

Peyrefitte posited a difference between the Chilean and the French situations which was quite to the taste of the politicians of the current government. We had already heard this difference defined, in very similar terms, by Edgar Faure. France, Peyrefitte said, enjoys the full use of its natural resources; its agrarian reform took place almost two hundred years ago; nor can it be shocked at a few nationalizations and state-run industries, since it had intimate knowledge of such things at the end of World War II. Chile, on the other hand, is just now going through its process of economic liberation. That is why the politics of the Left may be valid for Chile but unnecessary in France, where their implementation would inevitably bring about industrial paralysis.

Later, when the Pompidou government was about to confront a united Left in the legislative elections of 1973, Peyrefitte coined an evil little phrase, which merited the middling glory of the pages of *Paris Match*: "On vous promet le Pérou. Vous aurez le Chili!"—"They promise you Peru. But you'll get Chile!" In French slang, Peru was synonymous with gold, abundance. . . . Given the French system of a double round of elections, in which the slate of candidates is narrowed down in the first round, the election results in Chile would be able to serve as political propaganda in France for their second round, since our voting, on March 4, would coincide with the first round of elections in France.

The French establishment, however, made an error in its calculations, an error shared to some degree by the French (and even by the Chilean) Left. It was widely thought that economic problems were going to translate into a low voter turnout for the Unidad Popular. A huge publicity campaign was based on that prediction. Paris was filled with posters auguring that if the siren-songs of

Mitterrand and Marchais were followed, the same dark fate awaited the French as awaited the Chileans. Allende's electoral defeat, coming into a field already prepared with posters, newspaper articles, and radio and television polemics, was supposed to render the *coup de grace* to the French Communists. I protested this use of Chile's good name, and the Quai d'Orsay responded that such-and-such a poster, signed by a Gaullist shock-troop committee, or that such-and-such a TV program, were just accidents, that they in no way altered our excellent relations. But in the middle of a campaign growing more heated every moment, in which the government was for the first time facing a unified Left and in which the Chilean experiment had taken on considerable significance, the Quai d'Orsay could only offer polite words. One afternoon I ran into one of my contacts at the Quai in the street, and I soon realized that we were conversing under one of those unfortunate anti-Chile posters. My interlocutor cleared his throat, raised his eyebrows with an air of perplexity, shrugged his shoulders, straightened the collar of his impeccably-tailored overcoat, and continued on his way.

At midnight on March 4, 7:00 P.M. Chile time, French television, which still did not know the results of our elections, began to crow about Chile. At one o'clock in the morning, with the first results from Chile coming in and Allende showing strong, the French announcer, taken with a sudden case of amnesia, forgot about my country's existence. I myself had an appointment to be interviewed for television at the embassy at five o'clock on Monday afternoon. In spite of the fact that the French are famed for their punctuality, the television crew also forgot about their appointment and stood me up.

In Chile as well as in France, the result of the elections took virtually everyone by surprise. Some months later, a well-informed person told me that winning the elections had sealed Allende's fate. Allende was willing to try to find a compromise with the Christian Democrats, but the far left wing of the Unidad Popular, after the March election results, had refused to accept any deal. And the Right, their hopes for regaining power through the elections dashed, had decided to prepare a coup d'état.

The distinction that the French politicians in power made between a Third World country implementing a national economic liberation program and the problems of implementing socialism in an industrialized country seemed valid enough to me. One of the Unidad Popular's errors consisted of giving great publicity to their program of expropriation of private property, especially agricultural holdings—that is, the destruction of the economic power of the bourgeoisie—(or allowing that element to be given great publicity) instead of giving more emphasis to such foreign-affairs aspects of the program as national economic liberation, the struggle against foreign monopolies, and so on, so that a wider spectrum of social sectors might be brought into sympathy with the government. Fidel Castro pointed in that direction when he told me that night in the *Granma* offices that we ought to begin by nationalizing copper, "and doing it in such a way that every Chilean will be able to see his own personal interest involved in the issue, while leaving socialism for later."

I now think that while Fidel Castro was not mistaken in that point, what he was not so familiar with were the internal conditions under which a policy of that sort could be carried out in Chile. Fidel, who at the beginning of the revolution had invited to Cuba an indescribable group of center-right senators and congressmen (these were the Alessandri years), and had had countless clashes and misunderstandings with them, too easily discarded our parliamentary system. And yet it was true that the power of Parliament created problems for Allende. The one third of the Parliament who was Allende supporters could, with the presidential veto, effectively block the opposition's initiatives, but they were not strong enough to implement their own, positive, legislation, to give solidity and coherence to the government's program. Now, though, as he began his own term, Allende could count on the group led by Radomiro Tomic, the candidate of the Christian Democratic Party that had just been defeated in the presidential elections, and on the committed collaboration of some of the leaders of the Army, for help in putting his policies through, which included the nationalization of natural resources, state control of the banking industry, workers' active participation in industry, and the implementation of the existing agrarian reform law in its entirety, a reform that had been halted earlier by the Frei regime. The result would have been a Revolution similar to Peru's, more advanced, and with the participation of the whole gamut of popular-type parties in Chile.

But such a policy clashed with that of the extreme Left, which supported the formation of an armed popular power which would begin preparing for the "inevitable confrontation" and which urged direct and perhaps unconstitutional takeover of agricultural lands. Neither the Army nor the Christian Democrats could accept such a thing. Consequently, for Allende's strategy of cooperation with Tomic and the army to work, the extreme Left would have to be restrained and deprived of power. But the extreme Left couldn't be restrained because land expropriation had already found a ready ear in some members of Allende's Socialist Party, winning it over, and had begun to infect the Christian Leftist party and the MAPU, breakaway parties from the Christian Democrats.

For its part, by late 1970 Cuba had begun to move away from the theses of Ché Guevara, but the change had still not entirely taken effect, and could not be seen, for example, in Cuba's relations with Chile, whose peaceful experiment had been greeted with well-publicized skepticism. During his state visit, Fidel had presented President Allende and the MIR leaders with some symbolic machine guns, a gesture which revealed the premises on which his thought was based and which did not, of course, escape the attention of our military establishment. Upon his return to Havana, his first measure had been to invite Miguel Henríquez, the undisputed leader of the MIR party, to Cuba. That is, after seeing the Chilean experiment on its native grounds, Fidel had thrown his support to the extreme Left, whose policy was to all appearances completely incompatible with the government's major strategy.

That was the Gordian knot that Allende had to face. There was no doubt about it. The ultra-Left now reproaches Allende, not only in Chile but throughout the world, for not having better armed the people of the country, for not having consciously fostered and developed a parallel, popular power. The tragic outcome of the experiment appears to justify the reproach. But in spite of the apparently general opinion (expressed with all the tyrannical overtones of left-wing conformism), I believe that the correct line of reasoning is precisely the opposite. Any attempt at creating a people's army would have weakened the government's policy and condemned it to inconsistency. How was one to gain the Chilean Army's confidence and at the same time support a policy which when all was said and done sought the destruction of the Army as an institution? How was one to gain the confidence of an institution in which on principle one had no confidence? The Army was not fascist *a priori,* as many people today affirm. It had respected the results of the elections and allowed Allende to take power. The kidnapping of the commander-in-chief of the armed forces, General René Schneider, had been attempted precisely in order to push the army into fascism—but that was exactly the opposite result produced by Schneider's murder. Later, the conflict between those army leaders who favored the law and those who favored a coup had festered. But the policy of the ultra-Left, tolerated in spite of a few verbal attacks on the part of Allende, ended up leaving the generals favoring the constitutional system with nothing to answer the "hardliners."

The military junta talked insistently about the Cuban "intervention" in Chile. The Cuban presence, altogether too visible, was extremely ineffective for the purpose it was supposed to further. The action of the United States was just the reverse: invisible and incredibly effective. When the doors to the vaults of credit were closed, housewives were left without detergent, without cooking oil, without toothpaste; truckers were left without parts for their trucks; audiences were left without American Westerns; generals were left without tanks. Who would dare (or be mad enough) to think that the invisible hand of

Washington was behind the empty shelves, the stores without shirts or shoes? But it was, and the thumbs-down from the head of the American delegation to the Club of Paris was more imperative (and more dangerous to Chilean self-determination) than several divisions of Marines. Beside that power, the machine guns waved around by MIR only served to discredit the power of President Allende in the eyes of the army, whose loyal leaders found themselves growing more and more cornered every day.

The news from Chile, after a year and a half, began to be disturbing: Inflation was spiraling out of control; the problem of supplying the country with goods was no longer merely a story for the bourgeois press. But one of the most respected economists of the country contended in private that inflation would produce one important benefit: It would destroy the power of the bourgeoisie. When he heard this opinion, Pablo was indignant. "How stupid! Inflation will destroy us all!"

Pablo also received about this time a letter from a large landholder whose agricultural holdings had been expropriated. The letter troubled Neruda. He knew that this sort of agriculture was a modern kind of exploitation, that it rendered high yields, and that it was very different from our old feudal estates. But I could see that Pablo spoke to me about these misgivings with a certain reserve: He perhaps feared that my Cuban experience (or conflict, really), combined with my lack of party militancy of any kind, would make me lose a fair perspective on things.

At any rate, there was an anecdote about the Russian novelist Ilya Ehrenburg that Pablo liked to repeat. According to Ehrenburg, American propaganda was totally off the mark in its short-wave broadcasts to the Soviet people, talking about democratic freedoms and such poetic matters. "If they said that every peasant ought to have the right to own three cows, *then* we'd see the Soviets in trouble."

Back in 1966, the old days when I was secretary of the embassy in Paris, I had had lunch one day with Neruda and Ehrenburg at La Coupole, the meeting place for several generations of artists and intellectuals. I had asked Ehrenburg about the fate of the works of Isaac Babel, one of my favorite writers, who had died in a concentration camp during the first waves of repression under Stalin. Ehrenburg had replied quite straightforwardly that his posthumous "rehabilitation" had been only very partial; his stories had been published in an edition of ten thousand copies, and when that edition had sold out in twenty-four hours the authorities had used the excuse of a paper shortage in order not to reprint it. And one of his stories, "My First Pay," was still censored for "moral reasons."

In that story, the adolescent Babel visits a prostitute for the first time in his life, and in the heat of the conversation he tells the prostitute of his sad, impoverished, orphaned (and perfectly fictional) life. The prostitute, moved by this autobiography, not only does not charge the young man for her services, she gives him a coin: His first payment as a storyteller. Of course the Soviet bureaucracy had been totally insensitive to the tenderness of this story. What sort of lesson was this—a boy prostituting his talent even so far as tricking a prostitute—for the youth of the world's first socialist state?

In that semisolitary lunchtime corner of La Coupole, Ehrenburg, thin, graying, dressed in a tweed jacket as wrinkled as his face, considered the effect of this story on Pablo with an ironic smile on his face. Ehrenburg had ordered six oysters to begin. The waiter set before Pablo a plate of robust *boudins*, blood sausages very similar to those sold in the markets in southern Chile.

"*Pablo!*" Ehrenburg cried, adding with strong guttural Gallic *r*'s, "*Tu es un barbare!*"

"*Et toi!*" said Pablo, sinking his fork into the steaming sausage, unruffled save for a sardonic twinkle in his eye. "*Tu aimes la pourriture occidentale!*" — You go for Western moral decay!

Ehrenburg had gone to Chile to celebrate Pablo Neruda's fiftieth birthday, during the presidency of General Ibáñez, and the police had detained him at the airport, searched his luggage, and at last confiscated a couple of records of Russian folksongs, declaring to the press that they contained instructions from Russia for Pablo Neruda. "*Pablo!*" Ehrenburg would say each time the incident was brought up, "*ton pays n'est pas sérieux!*" ("Your country is not serious!") That was what they thought in Europe, too, when our military junta accused *Time, Newsweek,* Prime Minister Palme of Sweden, and Senator Edward Kennedy of being part of an "international Marxist conspiracy against Chile"!

When we received contradictory instructions at the embassy, or we were asked to book the hall at the Olympia for a singer arriving the next afternoon, or we discovered that someone had "revealed" to the press that Picasso was going to build a complete wing of a museum for his paintings and give it to Allende's Chile, or we had to shepherd around a delegation of seventeen congressmen of every party, along with their wives and daughters (the types to turn up their noses or sniff in displeasure when the embassy could not put at their disposal the embassy car that did not exist), or when a revolutionary was put out because Matilde didn't have time to accompany her on a shopping trip for perfume, or a reactionary protested because instead of being given the seat of honor at the right of the host (a seat which as chairman of some committee or other he had a right to) was put to the host's left, etc., upon all these varied and constantly recurring circumstances, Pablo would raise his finger, and in a voice of philosophic resignation say, *"Pablo! Ton pays n'est pas sérieux!"*

With regard to the Soviet Union, Pablo Neruda was convinced that it was capable of transforming itself. He described the country as a large elephant, slow to react but headed in the right direction. After the Nobel Prize there was talk of a trip to Moscow, and Neruda confessed to me that he would like to talk to the highest Soviet leaders about the plight of Solzhenitsyn and the dissident intellectuals. "Solzhenitsyn is touchy," he said, "and thin-skinned, a very difficult person. Still, all my friends agree that he is the great contemporary master of the Russian language. Why do we Western Communist writers always have to take the rap for the nonsense of the bureaucrats in the USSR? Why do we always have to have the Pasternaks, the Solzhenitsyns, so many others, thrown in our faces?"

Neruda had talked about the issue with his colleague the Soviet ambassador Abrassimov, whose reaction had been utterly disappointing. But just at that time the poet Andrei Voznesenski was passing through Paris, and Clodomiro Almeyda, the Chilean Minister of Foreign Relations and Socialist Party militant known for his relatively pro-China stance, had also arrived on some official trip. The lunch organized by Abrassimov gathered a somewhat heterogeneous leftist group: Neruda, Almeyda, Voznesenski, the Cuban ambassador Baudilio Castellanos. I recall Voznesenski as a man with short hair, dressed in a dark turtleneck and black leather jacket, looking like some young Moscow biker who'd just bought a new suit and found himself a little lost in the eighteenth-century *salon* which had once been the embassy of the Tsar of All the Russias. There was also a very stout, happy sort of woman, the daughter of some famous Soviet personage, whose name I did not catch.

Baudilio Castellanos, the Cuban ambassador, had been a member of the 26th of July Movement in Oriente Province in the days of the anti-Batista struggle. He had been ambassador to Paris since 1967. In his first years as ambassador he had been called on to implement a policy of openness toward the world of artists and intellectuals, and this policy had culminated in the transfer from Paris to Havana of the Salon de Mai in 1967 and the large delegation to the Cultural Congress in early 1968. He still had many friends in those circles, but the "Padilla affair" had also created conflicts and brought him enemies. A short while after my arrival in Paris, Castellanos had made a courtesy call on Neruda, returning Neruda's first protocol visit to him.

"Comrade ambassador," he had said to Neruda at one point, "what security measures have you considered taking in your embassy?"

"None!" replied Neruda in surprise. "I don't think that will be necessary."

Neruda, a skeptic in matters of security but a man with a clear sense of the political responsibility of high-ranking officials, had been irritated by that question. Afterward his opinion of Baudilio Castellanos improved greatly: "He is absolutely free of any contamination by literature," Neruda remarked to me, "and he's a better person for it." Literary backbiting and resentment had pursued Neruda ceaselessly, ever since his younger days when he won the poetry prize given by the Chilean Students Association for "La canción de la fiesta" ("The Song of the Fiesta"), and he considered mediocrity and envy deadly poisons. He had great insight into the disease of envy, and he held it at an irrevocable distance. At the same time, he actively cultivated solidarity with any writers who were free of the disease. He said that a true writer should never attack another. That was why he had never been able to forgive the attack by the Cuban writers, even when he knew that it had been set in motion by a small group of bureaucratic writers acting from motives of political opportunism.

The toasts with Russian vodka followed one after another at that luncheon in the Soviet Embassy in Paris, but suddenly a white-and-gold door opened and a noiseless official entered on tiptoe and said something in the ambassador's ear. Abrassimov, serious, excused himself to go and take a telephone call. When he returned to the dining room he said he had to leave for Moscow immediately: The Four Powers had just reached an agreement on Berlin, in preparation for which the ambassador had worked very hard, since he had been ambassador to East Germany before being posted to France, and he was being called to the Kremlin to take part in the signing.

Almeyda and I had a conversation after the luncheon in which he showed the worldly, somewhat acerbic sense of humor so typical of the old guard of Chilean politicians. He was perhaps the most sensible of Allende's ministers, and his role within the Unidad Popular tended to be the conciliator and peacemaker between factions, trying to forestall unnecessary disagreements. In foreign affairs he tried to maintain a clearly balanced program of national independence and nonalignment with the various power blocs. His handling of Chile's relations with Moscow were extremely realistic, and did not preclude cultivating a friendship with China. At the same time he was trying to avoid an embargo, working hard to develop economic and trade understandings with the countries of Western Europe, and especially with France, Spain, and Italy. In Latin America he had achieved privileged relations with Peru, Argentina, and Mexico. Later, when the time came, he would favor direct talks with the United States, but there he would find that the Nixon government used Chile's nonpayment of compensation to the copper companies as pretext pure and simple, a pretext that we had handed them on a silver (or copper) platter. Washington's real intention was to destroy the Allende experiment.

None of this prevented Almeyda, after the coup, from winding up on Dawson Island, a prison-island near the South Pole, where he was subjected to heaven only knows what humiliations and to material conditions that threatened his health and life. That is, he paid with his freedom for the attempt to carry out an independent international policy.

The military junta considered itself the continuation of the legacy of Diego Portales, an early-nineteenth-century founder of the republic. But Portales, the autocratic first prime minister of the nation, was a sworn enemy of the Monroe Doctrine, which attempted to sanctify the supremacy of the United States over the entire continent, and was the creative genius behind a system of civil power that freed Chile for a full century from the military *caudillismo* that in the aftermath of the continent's wars of independence swept all of Spanish America. A short while before the 1973 coup, the military establishment accused the Unidad Popular of falsifying the history of Chile in its textbooks. In part they were right: Quimantú, the state publishing concern created by the Allende government, was not at all exempt from sectarian pressures. When he heard about it, one of my Cuban friends had said to me in Havana that it was the beginning of censorship! But now the military would be obliged to do the same thing!

Pablo traveled to Moscow at the end of the year, but he was in no condition to talk to anyone. His disease had recurred, and he had to be hospitalized. Upon his return, however, it was clear he had recovered his good spirits. He brought fresh caviar and bear meat from Moscow with which to celebrate the New Year's at La Manquel. He informed me that his first great project would be a huge dinner, like in the old days at Isla Negra. But times had changed, and we soon realized that the guests would be invited not so freely as before, but rather out of a process of elimination: One person was struck from the list because he was a bore, another because he was too intellectual, another because he was too sad, another because he had a bad liver and couldn't drink. The daily obligation of meeting countless people had turned us misanthropic. Finally just six of us—the Colombian poet Camacho Ramírez and his wife, the Nerudas, and myself and my wife—found ourselves sitting at the big round table under the heavy beams of the ceiling at La Manquel, an enormous bowl of caviar in the center of it. The caviar was superb, and the bear meat had a forest taste that was strong and slightly bitter.

The only person who seemed ill at the party that night was Camacho

Ramírez, who had been turned by an attack of bronchitis into a gasping, coughing wreck. While his lungs labored, whistling alarmingly, he lay prostrate on a couch and looked out at our happy carryings-on with skeptical eyes. We drank, we put on costumes, we sang, we recited poems, and we danced until the wee hours of the morning.

That was the last moment of great happiness that I ever knew Pablo Neruda to have. During that time, in 1972, he would turn silent, reflective, pensive. He would often sit at the window in the embassy in the afternoon and take up the old ship's telescope he had bought at the Thieves Market and gaze up at the gold-leaf cupola of les Invalides. "At first I didn't like it," he would say, "but you know something? After looking at all its figures, its decorations, its gold leaf, its roundness, I've come to love it."

Sometimes there would rise to the surface a clue as to what he was meditating on. He contemplated the future with perfect lucidity, without the slightest pleasure. He saw that darkness described in the poem in *Residence on Earth*: "The heart entering a tunnel dark, dark . . ." He had told a close friend that his disease looked bad. Bad—I had learned that the doctors' diagnosis in Moscow had not been encouraging.

With regard to the Chilean situation, Pablo was also not overly optimistic. He thought that the opposition press, which was violently attacking the Allende regime, was a terrible enemy, while the leftist press, which was generally boring and predictable, did nothing to stop the right's overwhelming influence. The cure, of course, was not to be found in closing down the right-wing dailies, but in producing left-wing journalism of high quality. But who was to do that? How was it to be done? Pablo did not delude himself about a foreign attack, either: He believed that the pressure from the United States would be implacable, and that it would drag many Western European nations along with it, not excluding France.

During those days of early 1972 he got the first real sense that his worst fears might come true. Chile had had to suspend payments on its foreign debt in November 1971. The world price of copper had dropped through the floor. After the "ITT papers" had revealed that in October 1970 ITT had discussed creating economic chaos in Chile (with the aid of the CIA) for the purpose of toppling Allende, how was one not to suspect that the invisible hand of the large American copper companies, whose installations in Chile had been nationalized, was not behind the plummeting price of copper? It was calculated that every cent the price of copper fell on the world market represented in those days a loss to Chile of approximately $15 million per year. So if copper, which had been at more than eighty cents a pound in 1968 and 1969, sold in late 1971 and early 1972 for less than fifty cents, that meant a loss to Chile's budget of nearly $400 million a year! The cost of nationalization! And to make matters worse, the rise in consumption fostered by Allende's social policy meant that more food and raw materials for industry had to be imported. And Chile, whose total annual foreign-currency income was some $1 billion, was supposed to pay out $500 million a year to serve the crushing debt, amounting to more than $4 billion, that had been incurred by past administrations.

The group of Chile's Western creditors, elegantly called the Club of Paris, met during those first weeks of 1972 to consider our request to renegotiate the debt. Pablo Neruda, sick, suffering from the severe anemia that he now could not seem to overcome, presided over the Chilean delegation at the inaugural session. After the standard greetings, Mr. Hennessy, the chairman of the large American delegation, asked for the floor. This discreetly but elegantly dressed young man who spoke with the somewhat affected self-assurance of a graduate of Yale or Harvard contended that Chile did not recognize all its debts, since it showed not the slightest intention of paying compensation to the two major copper companies that had been nationalized: Kennecott and Anaconda.

Chile had recognized the principle of compensation, but it had made deductions for equipment that was in poor condition and for excess profits. In the cases of Anaconda and Kennecott, the deductions for those two items had surpassed the price of the nationalized installations. One example: Kennecott, through its subsidiary Braden, which was set up at the mine called El Teniente, had in the last few years shown a profit of 50 percent of the capital investment. In 1967, during the so-called "Chileanization" carried out by the Christian Democrats, the government of Chile had paid for 51 percent of the stock in El Teniente, an amount larger than the total value of the mine as carried on the company's books. Furthermore, it had assumed the company's debts, which were still being paid by the Allende administration. In spite of the 1967 Chileanization of the mine, in 1971, the year of total nationalization, its management and the control of the sale of copper were still in American hands.

It would take a long time to tell the story of Kennecott Copper in Chile. Spruille Braden, the son of the famous American secretary of state, had purchased the El Teniente mine in 1906 and had formed the Braden Copper Corporation, which was now a subsidiary of Kennecott. The mine was located in the lower mountains of the Andes, near the coast, on an enormous hacienda belonging to the Concha family. According to Araucan Indian tradition, fabulous riches were hidden in these mountains, but the owners of the hacienda used their land only for grazing their goats, so they had sold the mineral rights to Braden at a risible price, keeping the rich flatlands of Rancagua and Graneros, whose crops were managed in the early twentieth century as they had been for three hundred years.

Braden's purchase occurred at a time when the nation's economic development, a source of pride for Chile in the nineteenth century, had lost its steam. After President Balmaceda's defeat in the civil war of 1891, the country had entered a stage of absolute economic and cultural colonization, had been sold, as it were, for the Biblical mess of pottage. After setting up at El Teniente, Braden Copper paid not one cent of tax to the government of Chile until 1930, when the worldwide depression forced the Treasury to tax exports. In spite of this measure, one minister of the treasury, who was simultaneously a lawyer for Braden Copper and a leading politician in the old Liberal Party, confected a statute giving special treatment to all the nation's copper companies. After all, since they were foreign, they could hardly be expected to make the same sacrifices as the Chilean exporters.

In World War II, as Chile's way of contributing to the Allied cause, the nation agreed to a price on copper that was markedly lower than the international price. To compensate the American companies for their losses, Washington paid them a subsidy. Chile, on the other hand, the net loser in the operation, was supposed at the end of the war to buy goods and equipment from the United States at prices that had doubled.

A while after the Club of Paris meeting, Pablo Neruda was invited to New York by the PEN Club, a prestigious literary organization with headquarters in New York. There he was asked to give the inaugural speech for the meeting, and he spoke about the strange and sibylline atmosphere of that other Club which was deciding the fate of Chile. On the map Chile looks like an albatross in flight, noted Neruda, and the American delegate, with his after-dinner name, reminded him of Coleridge's ancient mariner, who kills an albatross and is condemned to wear it around his neck for the rest of his days. Neruda warned Mr. Hennessy in his speech that he ran the risk of wearing Chile around his neck for eternity.

At one of the Club of Paris sessions, Hennessy came up to me and said that Neruda's accusations seemed terribly unfair to him. "I have never intended to do Chile any harm. My wife, who is Paraguayan, is a great admirer of Sr. Neruda, and we have a collection of his works in our home." But the prediction has come true, and I believe that Mr. Hennessy, in spite of his good intentions, knows it. According to Coleridge, his only possibility of redemption will be through discovering love for all nature, for all things that live: At that moment, the leaden weight of the albatross will fall from his neck and sink into the sea.

The sessions of the Club of Paris ended with a cocktail party in the *salons* of

the French Minister of Finance. The Spaniards, the Italians, the Scandinavians, and at first the French helped us, and the champagne bubbles tended to
make us forget that the American position had not budged one inch. Pablo, the
poet, was perhaps more lucid than the diplomats and experts. "American
pressure will be unbearable," he said. "Don't fool yourself. Our theory of
excess profits, however much we like it, will never convince the Americans. It
is a theory which is repugnant to the capitalist system itself: Capitalism lives
on excess profits."

As 1972 went on, we found ourselves faced in France with another embodi-
ment of the United States' attack on Chile. French jurisprudence is perhaps the
most conservative in Europe with respect to the nationalization of industry.
The precedents set with the decolonization of Algeria naturally favored French
capitalism. Kennecott therefore went to the Cour de Grande Instance in Paris
and obtained an embargo on a shipment of El Teniente copper that was on its
way to Le Havre.

I recall the first public hearing at the Palais de Justice in Paris, in a room
located to one side of the great Salle de Pas Perdus. Neruda's disease continued
its irregular and surreptitious progress. That day he was not well, but he
wanted to attend the session and hear the arguments. Solidarity with Chile was
manifest all over Europe. The dockworkers of Le Havre and Amsterdam had
refused to unload the copper, and the ship had wandered for a week across the
northern seas, futilely pursued by the press. The measure obtained by Kennecott was one of subtle effectiveness: it did not affect the cargo *per se* but
rather its price, which the buyers were forbidden to pay us.

Pablo and I sat in the benches on the right side of the courtroom, behind our
lawyers. On the left side was the Kennecott lawyer, a tall, graying man with a
flushed face and thick glasses. He had taken advantage of the opportunity to
come to Paris from New York with two or three of his young children—round,
smiling kids as healthy-looking as could be; he was combining work with a
de luxe vacation at the Hotel Continental on the rue de Castiglione. One of the
finest jurists of Chile had come to Paris, too, expressly for this hearing, and he
was staying at a small hotel in the St-Germain-des-Prés. The yearly budget of
Kennecott Copper, the company fighting our expropriation measures, was
probably not a cent less than the entire national budget of Chile!

The Cour de Grande Instance, represented by its president and two assistant
judges, had no latitude for error: On the one side sat the powerful, octopus-like
Kennecott Copper Company and on the other the impoverished state of Chile,

whose economic problems in October 1972 began to reach and even surpass the point of crisis. The presence of the gravely ill ambassador, with his sallow face illuminated by the tall Renaissance windows of the room, was a profound and melancholy symbol. There were many journalists and lawyers in the room, as well, who had come in from the adjoining courtrooms to listen to the arguments.

Maître Cueff, the French lawyer for Chile, presented a long, solid argument, though there was a certain technical dryness about it. The government of Chile, as a sovereign power, had immunity from the jurisdiction of this court, and therefore could not capriciously be dragged into it. The nationalization of copper had followed all the procedures set forth in a constitutional reform approved unanimously by the Chilean Congress, including those votes from the extreme right wing. How could Kennecott claim as its property a mineral extracted more than a year after nationalization had taken place, and extracted from soil which, even before, in virtue of legal provisions that dated from more than a hundred years earlier, had been the property of the state, who had simply granted a concession to exploit it, and not the property of the private foreign or domestic mining companies themselves?

Kennecott's French representative, Maître Loirette, was a fit-looking young man who was a member of one of France's most prestigious law firms specializing in international trade. When it came his turn to speak, he stood, wrapped himself in his cape, looked majestically at the judges and the members of the audience, friendly or hostile as the case might be, and launched into an eloquent and fine-sounding speech; it was an exposition of the law which was truly mediocre, filled with quips and witticisms that the sunny children of the Kennecott lawyer enjoyed immensely, rubbing their hands together and giving each other looks of triumph, as though their favorite baseball team, at bat, were giving the other team a good rout. The lawyer said, and repeated *ad nauseam,* that Allende was a Marxist and that the nationalization of the copper industry in Chile had been a simple confiscation, a scandalous, semi-legalized, plunder. What else could be expected from such a regime, where an extreme left-wing Marxist held the reins of power? His counterpart had shown a report from the eminent Professor Batifol upon which was based the alleged immunity from jurisdiction that protected the government of Chile: Why had Professor Batifol not been asked to report on the legality of nationalization? And the Kennecott lawyer gazed around the courtroom with a look of cunning and contempt. Many of those present were aware of the very traditional ideas of Professor Batifol with respect to nationalization. After all, everyone knew what his opinion had been in the case of the Algerian nationalizations!

Pablo signaled to me that he was tired and was going to leave. He rose with difficulty and went to the door on tiptoe. I accompanied him across the solitary Salle de Pas Perdus. "Our lawyer's argument was good," he said. "The other one was just trying to scare the judges with all that stuff about Marxism." But Pablo was not carried away with optimism, either. "In Chile," he said, "somebody organizes a mass demonstration and everybody is happy, as though that could influence a French court." He believed that until we paid some sort of compensation the copper companies would never release their stranglehold on us. "Immunity from jurisdiction and all those other arguments don't convince the French. All they want to know is whether we've paid or not. As far as they're concerned, the whole issue comes down to that."

"Immunity from jurisdiction seems a very impressive obstacle," the president of the court told me a few days later, in a private audience to which he had summoned the lawyers and direct representatives of the two parties. Pablo Neruda had had to undergo an operation the previous day and had not been able to come. "When one examines the case more closely, however, it becomes a fragile obstacle. You understand that if I admitted the argument of immunity, that would mean that at a practical level the other party could not have been heard in any court, and that is repugnant to the judicial conscience.

"So then, if the question of immunity is removed, where are we? Chile has nationalized the copper industry and has recognized the principle of adequate compensation, but then has proceeded to deduct certain sums corresponding to excess profits and other items, to the extent that in the case before us the Kennecott Company and its subsidiary Braden will receive no payment whatsoever, since the amount of the deductions is greater than the amount of compensation. The burden of proof, then, lies with Chile, to demonstrate the factors which justify the deductions and above all to demonstrate the excess profits, the alleged amount of which is what determines that the company will not in practice receive any payment."

The judge's reasoning seemed impeccable, and he expounded it elegantly, looking at us directly, with a slight nervous smile, as though giving us to understand that he did not wish us any harm, and even that if we were sufficiently willing he could help us—but we had to be reasonable as well, "put yourselves in my position!", etc., and the thick glasses of the judge (a good Catholic, well-respected in his diocese, a scholar in matters of law) gleamed as though the friction between the two parties' positions gave off sparks. For ourselves, before all else it was imperative that the embargo be lifted. We could not go to court with a gun held to our head.

The Kennecott lawyer was at this meeting, too, of course, that graying, red-faced man who had brought his round-cheeked children to the hearing so they could see Maître Loirette make chopped meat out of those Communists from

Chile. Also in attendance was the president of the Braden Copper Corporation, a fat, almost swollen-looking man with the puffy face of the inveterate drinker. The president of Braden did not understand a word of French, and with visible nervousness he asked the help of one of his lawyers. Beside him, Maître Loirette, sitting with one leg crossed over the other, still maintained his aplomb, and cast sidelong looks at us. The president of the court had asked whether we were willing to submit to international arbitration and Loirette had sprung forward triumphantly (since he knew we would be obliged to refuse) to say that his client would be happy to do so, that that was precisely what they were seeking.

"We ask that the embargo be lifted, M. le President. Eighty percent of the foreign-currency income of Chile derives from copper. As Chile has suffered reverses in recent decades in its agricultural production, we need that currency for buying wheat, meat, milk. In other words, the embargo on the copper exports of Chile is a question of life or death. There is no proportion between the repercussions for Chile and the guarantees sought by the Kennecott Corporation. Chile is obliged to sell the largest part of its copper production in the Western market. If the embargo were first lifted and then Kennecott should at the end of an arbitration hearing receive a favorable decision from the court, Chile would have no difficulty paying compensation with the money earned from its exports. Therefore the embargo does not in any way improve the assurances that Kennecott may have in the case that the decision favor them. On the other hand, it threatens to ruin an entire country."

One saw that the argument had impressed the judge. When the argument had been translated into the ear of the fat man with the martini-drinker's face, he showed immediately that he had been hit. "Sixty percent of Chile's copper goes to socialist countries!" he cried, in obvious bad faith. But the representative from Codelco, our state copper corporation, had the figures at hand, and he showed up the fat man before the judge. The president of Braden squirmed in his seat and a slight shadow fell over the arrogant smile and bright glance of Maître Loirette.

Forced to decide between the interests of a large American corporation invoking the classical principles of international law in matters of nationalization (the same principles argued by the forces of French capitalism against Algeria), and the interests of a country as friendly to France as Chile was, all the president of the court wanted to do was find some formula that would let him pass the buck. His job was much more diplomacy than jurisprudence at that moment, and there was no doubt that the Quai d'Orsay had whispered a word or two in his ear. The judge could not simply discard the principle of indemnization for nationalized property, but he could also not be responsible for the strangulation of the Chilean economy, where the French were attempting to fill part of the vacuum left by the withdrawal of the Americans. The judge's eyeglasses gleamed as his eyes turned in anguish in on himself, in search of some impossible means of reconciliation. He spoke to me once more, to insist, almost implore, that we not utterly repudiate the idea of arbitration.

"We cannot accept arbitration between a private company and the government of Chile, which has made the sovereign decision to nationalize the copper industry."

In spite of all, the judge pleaded that we make an effort, a gesture of good will.

"We are opposed on principle to arbitration," I said, "but as a sign of good faith to you, I offer to consult my government."

The hearing ended on that note. The offer to consult my government gave the magistrate at least a momentary way out of his anguished impasse—an impasse which could imply some danger to ourselves, as well, of course.

We later learned that a certain officious person, one of those people who seem to feel a vocation for meddling in others' problems and who give a great show of humility but at bottom believe themselves to hold the universal panacea and so treat everyone else's solutions with contempt, had announced in Chile that in the private audience with the judge I had delivered up the national sovereignty of Chile on a platter. Indirectly and at a certain distance, the remark reflected the consequences of the Cuban accusation of me, which had enveloped me in a cloud of confused suspicion and, in that subtle way, made me vulnerable. Carried away by an odd mixture of ultra-Left zealousness and jingoism, this officious person, who had actually had some access to information, maintained that I had agreed to "talk" to the judge, without inflexibly standing upon the principle of immunity from jurisdiction.

The accusation, if truth be told, had no particular effect in any personal way, but during all this period the handling of any problem concerning the nationalization of industries in Chile was met with an over-technical, rigid adherence to the principle of immunity from jurisdiction, as though it were an infallible judicial shield. Before the next audience, Neruda, who had recovered somewhat, received a diplomatic note that he was ordered to deliver to the president of the court without any further comment. The note stated that Chile would not allow its sovereign acts of nationalization to be examined by foreign courts. The court must immediately recognize the principle of immunity from jurisdiction that protected the government of Chile, and dismiss the case.

"We will not allow our nationalization to be examined by foreign courts," Pablo remarked when he received the notes, "but in fact it is being examined, and copper is still embargoed. Selling copper throughout the world: That is the definition of the exercise of our national sovereignty!"

The order from Chile was clear and peremptory, and we had no choice but to obey it, even though our lawyer believed that delivering the note would not help our case with the judge in any way. Pablo presented Chile with the lawyer's objections and his own. The order, as we had foreseen, was repeated.

Pablo Neruda's illness exhausted him, but still he attended the second audience in the judge's chambers, and at the end of it he took the note out of his pocket and said: "M. le President, I have received instructions from my government to deliver this note to you, which summarizes the position of Chile with respect to this entire matter."

The magistrate read the note, furrowed his brow, and said: "Very well. I see that there is nothing further to discuss. I will inform the lawyers as to the date when this court's decision will be known."

During those days Pablo often said that the real Vietnam of the moment, a different, silent Vietnam, was Chile. It was there that the fate of socialism in one entire region of the world would be decided. And Pablo sometimes insinuated, even with all his confessed pro-Soviet sentiments, that the Soviet Union seemed not to be fully aware of what was at stake. They were spending in one month on the war in Vietnam what they were spending in one year in Chile. I would tell him that we didn't need tanks or anti-aircraft guns. We needed dollars, and wheat, and the Soviet Union had a terrible shortage of both. Pablo, at that, would fall silent, swallow, and contemplate, with implacable lucidity, the big, black clouds gathering on the horizon. In Chile the crippling truckers' strike went on; workers had taken over several factories; the country seemed paralyzed by divisions, and at the brink of ripping itself apart.

We were supposed to be preparing ourselves for the renegotiation of the debt, and there was not the slightest indication that Washington's position had improved. In the series of bilateral negotiations that had followed the first meeting of the Club of Paris, talks aimed at reaching agreement on payments for servicing the debt in 1972, the only creditor with whom we had reached no agreement whatsoever was our principal creditor, the holder of 50 percent of the debt, the United States. Of the members of the Club of Paris, only Spain, Italy, Holland, and the Scandinavian countries remained altogether favorable to Chile. In France, the establishment looked at the alliance of Socialists and Communists, by which the long political isolation of the Communists was ended and the Left was made a real political alternative, and it found that the Unidad Popular experiment might be more dangerous than it had thought. In Germany something had happened early on that had hurt us in their eyes. A liberal member of the German congress, related to families of German descent in the southern part of Chile, had invested large amounts of money not long ago in an hacienda in that region, and the hacienda had been expropriated in the Allende agrarian reform. The German congressman had become a dangerous enemy of the Chilean government at a time when the liberals' votes guaranteed the fragile majority of Chancellor Willy Brandt. A paint factory had also been taken over, and it was realized too late that it, too, belonged to German capitalists. In spite of everything, however, these problems with Germany were overcome, and toward the end of 1972, in one of its assemblies, the Social Democratic Party approved a resolution in support of the Chilean experiment.

Nevertheless, even with the inclusion of Germany, the group of creditors that showed unhedged good will toward Chile represented no more than 30 percent of the debt. And at the end of 1972, an objective, tangible problem presented itself, and it would not fail to be taken into account by all our Western creditors: runaway inflation, and the severe deterioration of our financial capabilities.

After stops in Mexico and the United Nations, from whose offices he had made a discreet but unsuccessful attempt to meet with President Nixon, President Allende had flown to Moscow in search of aid. The Soviets had granted him important credits for the purchase of equipment and a limited loan of free currency, though hardly enough to solve our problems.

Shortly afterward, perhaps as a way of balancing the president's visit to Moscow, the minister of foreign relations, Clodomiro Almeyda, had gone on an official visit to China. The Chinese government had also agreed to grant Chile a loan of currency. Besides the loan, which like the Soviets' would not solve many problems, the Chinese had given Minister Almeyda a piece of advice. Jou En-lai had told him that the Unidad Popular was going too fast; it was trying to do in two years what they, the Chinese, had done in ten. They knew Yankee imperialism, a paper tiger, but capable of giving a mortal blow with its claws! Jou counseled prudence.

United States Senate committee hearings in March 1973 gave a crude demonstration of the depth and danger of the anti-Chile sentiment in the United States. The multinationals, and especially ITT, whose gross income is larger than the entire Chilean budget, feared that the example of the Unidad Popular would extend throughout the continent, and they were ready to stake everything they had on destroying it. An eighteen-point plan proposed by ITT to the government in Washington in late 1971 stated: "Everything necessary should be done, quickly but effectively, so that Allende cannot remain for longer than the next six months, which will be crucial." The plan proposed that all loans to Chile, both from American and foreign banks, be suspended; that discontent be fostered within the Chilean armed forces; that obstacles be set in the way of Allende's diplomatic initiatives; that *El Mercurio,* a newspaper threatened with expropriation, be subsidized; and that "together with the CIA, ways of keeping up the pressure for six months be studied." The fate of this ITT plan is not known, but the very fact of its existence is revealing.

After those last months of 1971, the leaks of ITT documents stopped, and this may indicate that their strategy for dealing with the Chilean experiment had been refined and perfected. It seems anything but coincidental that the copper embargo had been secured by Kennecott precisely when the large transport strike in Chile began. It had probably been agreed to with other multinationals and included in a global action against Chile.

How would the multinationals be acting in concert with the CIA, their most loyal ally, in the decisive months of 1973? It is now known that the CIA, taking a new tack after the fifties and sixties, at this time was beginning to place its people inside the huge multinationals rather than in embassies. It is also known that in the case of Chile their actions were determined by one primary concern: Keep the intervention invisible.

In dealing too rigidly with the problem of compensations to nationalized companies at the beginning, the Unidad Popular had given the world an excellent pretext for the blockade. The idea of nationalization or expropriation without compensation is contrary to the most deep-seated mental habits and judicial principles of the capitalist world. The theory of excess profit, though ingenious and even to a point novel, did not convince those sectors of the Western world that needed to be won over.

In Paris we learned that Henry Kissinger had had a conversation with Orlando Letelier, at that time the Chilean ambassador in Washington, and had told him: "Pay a dollar, but pay something!" That dollar would, of course, from the moment we agreed to the principle of payment, become many dollars, but the point was that our theory of excess profit had hit a nerve in the body of capitalism. So long as we remained unbending, we would be given no quarter, and the possibility of our defending ourselves, given the problems in the agricultural sector and the acute crisis in the balance of payments, was virtually nil.

In order to free itself from the threat of imminent financial strangulation, the Allende government at last accepted the idea of paying some sort of compensation to the nationalized copper companies, but it was too late. The multinationals and the CIA had seen that their economic pressure was beginning to yield results. With the March elections, the worst crisis faced by the political system that had governed Chile for decades had begun. The democratic, peaceful experiment of the Unidad Popular, in spite of the last desperate efforts of some moderates, breathed its last.

But the climate of civil war had begun to be felt even as early as the second half of 1972. Cardinal Silva Henríquez passed through Paris during that time on a private visit, but he made it known that he wished to speak with Pablo Neruda. Pablo felt obliged to meet with the cardinal in his bedroom, from his sickbed.

"I'll tell you," Pablo afterward said, "there was even talk of the possibility that Allende would resign and new elections be called in order to avoid civil war. But I reminded the cardinal that should we come to such a pass, the first condition would be that Frei, who is the person most responsible for bringing on this crisis, should also refrain from being a candidate."

The decision of the Parisian Cour de Grande Instance was handed down just after Pablo and Matilde had returned to Chile. I called Pablo in Isla Negra to tell him of it. The court had rejected the argument of immunity from jurisdiction but at the same time it had lifted the embargo and named an expert to study all possible precedents, especially including those that might help to bring the two parties to an agreement. "I think that's excellent!" Pablo said, in a voice that somehow managed to be as strong as ever, even while the disease gave it a slight hesitancy. He had not been at all certain that the court would lift the embargo. It seemed, within its ambiguities and sticking points, the least bad decision possible. Pablo went on to tell me that Isla Negra was wonderful, that he never wanted to leave it again. He had recently written a French friend of his that he had wasted two years of his life as ambassador.

In the early days of 1973 I had a partial revelation of what was going on inside the Chilean Army. The upperclassmen of the War Academy, captains, colonels, and generals all, with the director of the academy at their head, came through Paris on their way home from an official visit to Moscow. As interim chargé d'affaires, I greeted them at the airport and invited the entire group to the embassy that evening for drinks.

After more than two weeks of seclusion in a Moscow military institute, the atmosphere of Paris and the flowing whisky quickly loosened their tongues. There was general fault-finding with the director, who was apparently known for his friendship with Allende. I was standing beside the wrought-iron balustrade of the embassy stairs when a little past midnight one of the officers came up to me and with no preamble whatever said: "I presume you're with us—you do belong to the resistance?"

"What resistance are you talking about?"

The officer, a bit perplexed, raised his eyebrows and walked away. The officers were talking about life in Moscow, the sadness of the city, the lack of places to go and enjoy oneself after nine o'clock at night, the infinite slowness of the restaurants.

"It may be all right for them," someone concluded, "but that system's no good for us."

During that period, when the Army still had a part in the government, the director described himself as one of the very few generals left who believed in constitutionality. He talked to his officers about being loyal to Allende, and said "politics ought to be left out of things" in Chile, that everyone ought to be working toward the "reconciliation of all Chileans." I noticed that the mere mention of Allende's name provoked a muted, sullen sort of exasperation in the officers.

A few weeks later it was my duty to receive in the embassy General Carlos Prats,[5] who was also on his way back home from Moscow. Under his bonhomie and his reserve, I thought I could detect deep concern. Prats believed that in preventing us from resupplying the army, the blockade on foreign credits created severe national security problems. In Moscow he had had a long conversation with Marshall Gretchko, the armed forces minister. Gretchko had asked Prats how we could allow strikes in an industry as vital to Chile as the copper industry. "Imagine!" Prats said to me, with a skeptical smile. Aided and abetted by the opposition with every means at its disposal, a large percentage of the laborers and office employees of El Teniente, the mine that had (coincidentally!) belonged to the Braden Copper Corporation, had been on strike for weeks, in an action that cost the Treasury millions of dollars. Gretchko had immediately offered Prats tanks, which could be paid for over a very long term.

"And what did you think of the Soviet tanks, general?" I asked him.

"They were good," Prats said.

"Well then?"

Prats did not speak. Then he made it very clear that if we purchased Soviet armor, which of course also implied technical assistance, experts, a more or

---

[5] The commander-in-chief of the armed forces after the murder of General Schneider.

less permanent relationship between the Chilean and Soviet armies, the tanks would never even make it to the shores of Chile.

Meanwhile, virtually all Western credit had been cut off. The latest report from the International Monetary Fund painted a dark picture of the Chilean economic situation. Skyrocketing inflation and the crisis of agricultural production were having disastrous effects on our balance of payments. Until Chile adopted drastic measures to rectify the situation, the Club of Paris would not begin to consider new credits.

We arrived at the latest meeting of the Club, during the second week of July 1973, ready to propose some of those measures. The system of agricultural compensations was going to be changed, by introducing bonuses that would encourage production. In other words, the repugnance for material stimuli to production—which had had its origin in the times of Ché Guevara in Cuba and which, in spite of the objections of some Chilean economists who had seen the Cuban experiment close up, had been adopted immediately in Chile—would be put aside, at least in the area of agrarian reform. Our deficit derived in part from the need to import foodstuffs, at an annual cost of more than $400 million.

We also informed the Club of our intention to establish trade incentives for nontraditional exports: shoes, fruit, textiles, etc. Up until then, import incentives had been in place, as a means of maintaining the level of consumption.

We announced some other measures, but we couldn't obtain any real concessions from the Club unless we drastically cut back on imports and put a brake on wage increases, which would have the practical effect of reducing consumption even further.

Our delegation emphatically rejected these demands, and the Club decided to adjourn, giving time for the measures aimed at rectifying the economic situation to be implemented and begin to work.

Today the extreme Left in Europe, in order to contend that the economic crisis had nothing whatever to do with the coup and that the coup, in consequence, was inevitable, maintains that in August 1973, the Chilean economy was on the road to recovery, that the credits from Western Europe were at last beginning to flow, that the government officials of Chile looked forward to the next meeting of the Club of Paris, set for October of that year, with great confidence.

What confidence? I ask myself. Without a decrease in consumer spending, on the one hand, and without the legal measures that would have entailed an accord with the Christian Democrats, there could be no "correction" that the Club would accept as sufficient. In 1972, pressure from smaller creditors had forced the United States to agree to a general accord in Paris, even though later, in bilateral conversations with Chile, the U.S. had not yielded an inch. In July 1973, however, the economic crisis in Chile allowed the United States to take the bull by the horns. Were creditors going to grant new credits to a country that showed not the slightest ability to pay—a country which in 1972 had offered to pay 30 percent of the service to its debt (an offer which it had kept) even though in mid-1973 it had come back to the same negotiating table, with practically the same negotiators, and with a straight face offered to pay 5 percent; a country with an inflation rate of 300 percent, and going even further out of control, since the Chilean citizen had to get rid of the *escudos* that were shrinking in his very hands as fast as he could; a country with a foreign-currency budget deficit whose amount it was better not even to ask about, as it might cause vertigo? Monsieur Nebot, the president of the Club of Paris, shook his bald head that reflected the fluorescent lights of the meeting room, gestured almost paternally, and told the Chilean delegation to be reasonable, because given the current conditions there was not the slightest foundation for agreement; he told us to come back for a talk, like good children, at the end of the European summer—October, say, since a date had to be set, and even though M. Nebot did not appear to believe that from July to October we could make any great progress in all this.

So I ask again: How could we have looked forward to such a meeting with confidence? Was the postponement not a U.S. stalling tactic, when time, in this quiet but terrible battle, worked to the advantage of the United States and against that of Chile? Mr. Hennessy had not been seen again at the meetings, but he had fired the first shot, and it was he who was going to have to carry the dead albatross around his neck.

After the meeting there was a reception for the participants in the Ministry of Finance offices next to the Louvre, with the shadow of the Arc du Carrousel crowned by Julius Caesar in his chariot in the background, and farther on, the Tuilleries in the shimmering haze of a late afternoon in July. As we chatted and sipped our champagne, I could feel the vise of foreign interests squeezing Chile. That adjournment of the Club, indefinite and without appeal, was one of the most sinister signs of it. So long as there was no decision from the Club, there would be no foreign credits, and so long as there were no foreign credits . . . The problem of supply was already grave, but what was going to happen when the economic crisis worsened and there were shortages even of the essentials—wheat and bread, milk, cotton, medicines? Could the government survive that? Allende was seeking a dialogue with the United States on foreign affairs and with the Christian Democratic party on domestic matters, but did the interests of those two parties embrace such a dialogue, now that they saw their adversary in such trouble? Julius Caesar and his motionless spirited steeds, profiled in shadow against a glowing sunset, gave mute answer to my questioning.

The representative to the Club of Paris from the International Monetary Fund, a French friend of ours, and given to black humor, came up to us and said: "You Chileans have still not broken the record for inflation. The absolute record is held by Indonesia, with 10,000 percent . . ."

"Yes," I said, "And you know what happened in Indonesia."

Our French friend raised his eyebrows and looked away, as though the reminder of the bloodshed sickened him. Not long before there had been a coup attempt in Santiago led by the tank regiment of one Colonel Souper. General Prats had easily put it down, but what had happened immediately afterward was much more serious. Most of the regiments throughout the country also showed signs of revolt, and there were demands for Souper's release from custody. Before flying to Paris some of the members of our delegation had had to sleep away from home; that kept all the major government officials of Chile from being easily arrested during the nightly curfew imposed after Souper's coup attempt.

After the Club of Paris cocktail party, and almost by way of consolation, our French friend from the International Monetary Fund invited the Chilean delegation to dinner at La Méditerrannée, a restaurant with wonderful seafood on the place de l'Odéon. He took us after dinner to a party at the studio of a sculptor on a little street near the boulevard de Montparnasse. There was a long narrow garden with plants along the walls. It was a warm night, the eve of Bastille Day, and there was an animated gathering of pale women with long legs and naked backs, middle-aged men with full heads of graying hair, all dressed in the most heterogeneous mixture of costumes and colors, and all talking and drinking gaily. One went down three or four steps to reach the dark studio, where there was a drawing table covered with bottles and dirty glasses full of wet cigarette butts floating in the dregs of wine, and where several couples were dancing acrobatically to the sound of two very powerful speakers.

"And you!" an Argentine painter I had not seen for a long while asked me, "what's up with you?"

"I've just come from a meeting with Chile's creditors," I told him.

"¡Mi madre!" the Argentine exclaimed, shaking his hand in that Latin American way that means you've just touched something hot.

Later in our conversation he told me that President Cámpora's resignation in Argentina, which had just been announced, was a strike from the Right engineered by the Peronists.

"And I was just getting ready to go back to Argentina," the painter said. "Imagine! This has blown my plans all to hell!"

Meanwhile, I had requested a two-year leave without pay from the Foreign Ministry. As I had told Fidel in our conversation the night of March 21, 1971, I wanted to step back a little from government and take up my pen again, full time. It had been Cuba, in fact, with Allende in power in Chile, that had brought me, in the most irrefutable way, to my conviction that diplomacy and literary creation were, at least for me, incompatible. I had told Fidel this, and Fidel had asked the following question: "And do you think that you can write something worthwhile?" I didn't know, of course—one never knows beforehand—but my decision to take the plunge was final.

The Foreign Ministry gave me the leave, after I explained the reasons for my request to my friend Orlando Letelier (then foreign minister, later imprisoned by the military junta on Dawson Island, and finally murdered in the streets of Washington, D.C., on September 21, 1976, by an agent of Pinochet's secret police). My successor, who left a similar post in London, was to arrive in Paris on August 1. At 8:30 A.M. on July 14, Bastille Day, after the adjournment of the Club the day before and the party at the sculptor's studio, I was dressed in morning coat and tails and on my way to the reviewing stands on the Champs Elysée to attend the military parade and bid my adieux to diplomacy, perhaps forever.

Afterward, I attended the traditional reception in the gardens of the Elysée Palace. It was a splendid sunny morning.

Those diplomatic receptions seemed designed to give one the sense that nothing has changed, nothing happened, that time has stood still and that we live in the best of all possible worlds: the same *hors d'oeuvres* on white tablecloths, the heavy silver candlesticks, the tables along each side of the lawn; the same ambassadorial faces; the same gold braid on the military men; the same waiters dressed in black. The representatives of Yugoslavia, Rumania, and Algeria talked among themselves in one tight little group. The Chinese delegate, recently arrived, and in his predictable blue, advanced toward me with a smile, followed by his faithful interpreter. The military attachés from Brazil and Ecuador were talking and laughing with the military attaché from Chile. Prime Minister Messmer, a white-haired gentleman standing straight and motionless in the middle of the lawn, was speaking with unquenchable optimism about some matter of internal policy. The ambassador from the Philippines showed off his excellent Spanish to the ambassador from Panama. In all the world, it seemed, there was nothing but ambassadors, peaceful military men making small talk, white-haired ministers, obsequious waiters, tables freighted with gastronomic abundance. Suddenly the thought came to me that I had been dreaming when I considered leaving these circles, and especially doing so in order to follow a vocation that was a sort of mental illness, a shameful vice contracted in some now-distant adolescence. Outside these circles lay only desert! Outer darkness! And the expressions of the curious, who watched me advance through the double file of Republican Guards, depart the palace pale, pensive, dressed in strict gray and black, and slip into the official dusk of the waiting car, made me suspect that the universe, once one had left the periphery of those receptions, was formless and unknown.

In the embassy, the members of the Chilean delegation to the Club of Paris had taken over the meeting rooms and the dining room, poring over figures and exchanging remarks about the meeting of the Club. Everyone seemed aware that the situation was desperate, but no one wanted to acknowledge the fact aloud. I had only known this group of officials from the Unidad Popular in their roles in the renegotiation of the debt. They were all well trained as economists, and they were tireless, selfless workers, every one. One had become the true hero of the renegotiations, traveling around the world, his portfolio under his arm, analyzing columns of figures day and night, weekdays and holidays, trying indefatigably to find the solution to a problem no less difficult than the squaring of the circle.

They were, moreover, a group that was hardly political in any narrow sense at all; they were pragmatists, but given the circumstances, their pragmatism naturally became tinged with irony. Some of them, in the first few months of the Allende administration, had told Allende that the first economic measures adopted would lead to uncontrollable inflation. Someone who had attended that meeting had taken the floor to answer in the following way: "Are we here to govern a capitalist economy well or to forge socialism?" As one very powerful and influential group within the Unidad Popular insisted, Chile had to "advance without retreating."[6] Events would show that those who were going to

---

[6] "*Avanzar sin transar*": literally, "go forward without compromising." The rhyme in Spanish makes this a slogan, not a policy, and fossilizes the message irremediably. The

advance without retreating, running over and crushing everything that got in their way, were the other side.[7]

I turned over the office with the feeling that I was freeing myself of the weight of tons of dusty paper, and I headed off for the beach at Calafell, south of Barcelona. I had first come to that beach years ago, in a time that now seemed infinitely far away. In Calafell I worked every morning beside the changing, azure waters of the Mediterranean, as an occasional boat sailed by and the clouds in the distance piled up into thunderheads thousands of feet high.

At noon I would walk into the village to buy the newspapers and read the news of the strike that was wearing away my country. The strike had been joined now by wider and wider circles of professionals, and it was marked by that anonymous, diffuse terrorism in whose stubbornness and skill one could hardly help but see the shadowy foreign hand at work. Western credits were cut off, and since transportation was also paralyzed very soon there would be no wheat, and the supply of bread would simply run out. President Allende had had no choice but to announce this to his people.

In spite of everything, there still operated in me that mentality of the average Chilean who had lived in the days before September 11, 1973, the mentality that "nothing ever happens in Chile." Every morning I would sit beside the immutable sea at Calafell and work on the final revision of this book, and I would often sit there until four or five in the afternoon. On one of those afternoons my daughter came running in, her eyes like saucers, and gasped that somebody had just called from Barcelona, that there was a revolution in Chile and the air force was bombing the presidential palace.

The entire world knows the rest, except perhaps about the stupor, the disorientation, the strange befuddlement a citizen feels when he discovers he belongs to a country that he no longer recognizes.

At first I believed the story about Salvador Allende's suicide. I have traced through some of the pages of this book the parallel between the Allende period and that of José Manuel Balmaceda, the nineteenth-century president of Chile who committed suicide when he was defeated by the alliance of the oligarchy, with its stranglehold on parliament, and the navy and the machinery of English imperialism. The similarity between 1890, when the civil war of 1891 (a war

---

phrase "advance without retreating" tries to capture that catchiness-become-inarguable-dogma.

[7] One leader who did not join in the general euphoria, and found himself therefore shunted a bit to the side, said later that that phrase *"avanzar sin transar"* had become in practice *"avanzar sin pensar"* —not "advance without retreating" but "advance without reflecting."

perhaps bloodier even than the war between Peru and Bolivia) was being hatched and there was no turning back, and the last year and a half of the Allende administration was clear. On many occasions Allende had shown that he himself saw the similarity, with all that it held of premonition and dread. That—an overly geometric conception of history—is why I thought that it might be true that Allende had shut himself up in the presidential office and pulled the trigger.

During the last two years it had been the Right whose interests were best served by showing the parallel was a false one. The Right had maintained that Balmaceda had never dreamed of nationalizing the nitrate industry, in spite of the legend propagated by some Marxist historians. As usual, the Right was spreading half-truths. Balmaceda, who knew that the available Chilean capital at the time would be insufficient to exploit the nitrate deposits, had been careful to nationalize the nitrate railroads, not the deposits themselves. Their control of the transport of nitrate to the ports was what had allowed the English to drive off all competition, foreign or domestic. At the same time, Balmaceda had wanted to attract French, German, and even (an innovation at the time) United States capital. That had been his way, the methods of his time, to combat the British monopoly on nitrate.

Defeated in late August 1891, Balmaceda sought asylum in the Argentine legation and committed suicide on September 19, the day his term as president officially ended, as the national celebrations were being held that day. It was his way of saying that he embodied the legitimacy destroyed by its adversaries. Those adversaries understood the message immediately, as one can see in an odd document that I read years ago in Paris in the archives of the Quai d'Orsay. In a report to his government, the French ambassador to Chile, in Santiago, stated that he had gone to an official dinner on September 20 and was seated next to the new administration's minister of the interior, Isidoro Errázuriz. Every few minutes a curtain behind the minister would open, a man would enter, and the minister would be given a little piece of paper. Errázuriz explained to the French ambassador that when the rumor of Balmaceda's suicide began to spread a crowd had gathered in front of the Argentine legation. It was then that, following the instructions that Errázuriz whispered in the ear of the man who kept popping out from behind the curtain, the cadaver was taken out a rear door of the legation into an alleyway behind and hauled off in a police wagon, as fast as the wagon would go, to the cemetery.

The French ambassador learned later, and so informed his government, that the *carabineros* had been about to throw Balmaceda's body into a common grave, but the Uruguayan ambassador, one Sr. Arrieta, who was married to a

Chilean woman, had managed to rescue the body of his old friend the president, who had begged this favor of him, and put it to rest in his wife's family's tomb. The French ambassador added a macabre detail to his report: Balmaceda was very tall, and his height had prevented the body from fitting in the first coffin Arrieta tried.

I now think of the quick burial of Allende's body, in the presence only of his wife and a handful of soldiers, in the cemetery in Valparaíso.

The shadow of José Manuel Balmaceda hung over all of modern Chilean politics: over the movement of 1920, over the Popular Front, and later over the Unidad Popular. In 1969, a short while before leaving Chile, I visited his tomb and I discovered that it was covered with inscriptions, prayers, and *mandas,* the sort of vows people in Chile make to saints. The Chilean people had transformed Balmaceda into one of their few sacred, sacralized heroes.

It now seems more likely to me that Allende had defended his legitimacy with machine gun in hand, dying by his assailants' bullets in that fight. The proofs of his suicide offered by the junta are extremely fragile. He has thus joined the pantheon of our tragic heroes, along with my own forefather José Miguel Carrera, an anarchist *caudillo* in the wars of independence who was shot to death in Mendoza, Argentina, as he was trying to cross into Chile, and with José Manuel Balmaceda. All three have been criticized in Chile's recent and more distant past for their lack of political realism. And yet beyond the myths of history, all three have left irreversible achievements: Carrera, the country's first printing press, the Instituto Nacional, and the freeing of the children of the slaves; Balmaceda, an impressive list of public works and schools, not to mention the very modern idea of putting controls on foreign capital; Allende, the nationalization of copper, before which Chile, in spite of its ostensible independence, had 70 percent of its export industry in the hands of private American companies.

A good part of the European press let itself be swept away by the hysteria, and one had to take its reports with a grain of salt; some accounts from the inside, however, were fated by their simple and terrible veracity to burn themselves into one's memory with letters of fire. One of these was published by the Barcelona newspaper *Tele/Express* on October 19, 1973, and was the news of the death of Joan Alsina, a priest who had been born in Gerona, Catalonia, and which was reported by some other Gerundians who had managed to get out of Chile:

The nights of September 10 and 11 Alsina spent in the National Health Service Hospital in Santiago, where he was chief of personnel. From the twelfth on, he began sleeping again in his room in the rectory of the church of San Bernardo, where he remained all day September 18, the Chilean national holiday. On the morning of the nineteenth, much against the advice of some of his friends, he returned to his job at the hospital where he met with Msgr. Pablo Laurin, episcopal vicar of the southern region of Santiago, who in giving the homily at the funeral services recalled the conversation the two men had had during that last encounter. "I have nothing to fear," Alsina had told Msgr. Laurin, "because I have nothing to reproach myself for in my work. I am going to my brothers, because I know that there are many who will suffer and I want to show that I am with them. Pray for me, Pablo."

He knew when he said those words that three people from his own office had been arrested, and there were indications that the noose was tightening around him.

Throughout the morning of September 19, Joan Alsina worked in his office; he ate there at the hospital with two young men who were witnesses to his arrest. This occurred at three o'clock that afternoon, and was carried out by an Army captain and two soldiers.

At eight o'clock that night, an anonymous telephone call to the church of San Bernardo reported that Fr. Alsina was being held at the Barros Arana lyceum [high school]. Beginning on September 20 numerous attempts were made to locate him, but in spite of the kindness and diligence of the first secretary of the Spanish consulate in Santiago these attempts were fruitless. Finally, on September 27, a second telephone call asked that one of Alsina's co-workers go to the Forensic Institute in order to identify the body of Fr. Alsina, which had been taken there at 10 o'clock on the morning of the twentieth, along with other bodies found in the Mapocho River near the Bulnes Bridge. The coroner certified that the fingerprints of the body matched those of Fr. Joan Alsina on file in the Identification Archives. The body had ten bullet wounds in the back.

In his room in the rectory at San Bernardo some lines written by Alsina were found: "If the grain does not die, it will never yield fruit. A scorched mountain is terrible. But one must hope that from the wet ashes, black and sticky, new life will spring."

In mid-October, thanks to letters sent to me or other Chileans (and often arriving mysteriously), I began to receive more direct news of home: A well-known professional, a Communist, had died in a hospital after several days spent in the National Stadium; another had been left in the stadium for twenty-four hours naked, in order to humiliate him; the friend of a friend, accused of belonging to the MIR (which he did not actually belong to), had been surprised eating lunch at his mother-in-law's house, taken away, and his body found the next morning three blocks away; Victor Jara, the singer, had been murdered; a woman had visited the morgue in search of her electrician's son and had found one hundred seventy fresh cadavers piled on top of one another in a small room; a doctor had been beaten by the police; there had been no word from Angel Parra; Enrique Bello, the art critic and most peaceable of men, a champion of the struggle against socialist realism during the days of Stalin, had been arrested.

A group of representatives of the Socialist International, members of the English Labor Party and the Swedish and German Social Democratic Parties, reported that they had been held at gunpoint at the tomb of President Allende when they were about to lay a wreath on the tomb, and that for several hours they believed their lives to be in danger. That item reminded me of the tomb of Balmaceda!

Thus it was that "normalization," a return to "constitutional order," came to Chile. It came with the approval of the powers that be, the guilds and unions, the housewives of the upper class, those women that had once been called the country's living strength.

Newspapers reported one day on an operation carried out in a central area of the city where my own house, my own library was located: Great bonfires were kindled with unclean books. The generals announced that they were going to rid the country of foreign ideas, and as the land of the Araucans has never been noted for engendering new doctrines, the task of purification promised to be long and vast. Weeks later I learned that my books, in boxes in a cellar, had been saved by a hair; twice the soldiers had gone down into a neighbor's cellar and found nothing. None of the books in my library would easily have avoided being branded subversive, from Plato, Fernando de Rojas, and Cervantes to Baudelaire, André Breton, and Pablo Neruda. All were fated, from their conception, to be fodder for inquisitions, whether those of earlier times or our own modern ones.

An acquaintance of mine, who in his youth had voted for Allende, was on the point of denouncing the leftists in his neighborhood. The filmmaker Patricio Guzmán had wound up in the stadium from some report a neighbor had made on him. One person who loved to read, and who in his younger days had shown some inclination toward a literary life, went out into his back yard and burned all his books of suspicious political coloring. Better to keep the plague from spreading than to cure it! But an old great-aunt of mine, more sensible than many other people, wrote me from her European refuge that she "thought a great deal about us and our dear unfortunate and mistreated Chile, plunged into this shocking tragedy." She wanted a return not to constitutional order but to the order of families: She wanted none of her relatives, friends,

and acquaintances to have to suffer these "painful circumstances." She had
emotions which the new upper classes of Santiago had lost, as was so sadly
shown by their abject celebration in the midst of gunfire, beside the river on
which every night, among the dead rats and garbage, cadavers floated down-
stream.

And then a Chilean friend showed me a letter sent her by someone who
attended Pablo Neruda's funeral:

> A few days earlier they had searched all of Neruda's houses, and I don't know
> whether they turned a pack of fanatical vandals loose in them or not, but Neruda's
> house was completely destroyed: windows broken, lamps smashed, chairs en-
> tirely destroyed, paintings and prints destroyed too, some of them with awls
> punched through them. Plus—I imagine intentionally—the stream of the canal
> that ran by the house was turned so that all the rooms in the lower story were
> flooded. One room was burned, and all that was left were the remains of the
> columns and pieces of unrecognizable objects. They had scattered glass and
> pieces of pottery everywhere—ceramics, pitchers, Pomaire and Quinchamalí
> pottery. They laid out Neruda in the room where there was the least broken glass
> and pottery, and to get there you had to walk through glass shards that crackled
> under foot.
>
> Today was the funeral, which was very moving. There were not many people,
> given the circumstances. Most of the people that should have been there have
> been arrested and sent off to various islands or the National Stadium. Inside the
> cemetery, in the procession toward the mausoleum he was put in temporarily
> (because he had asked to be buried on Isla Negra, but it took too long to make
> arrangements), there was a silent anger, and a sense of combativeness, which
> suddenly became embodied in shouts like "Comrade Pablo Neruda—present!",
> "*Compañero* Salvador Allende—present!", and there were shouts for Victor Jara
> as well, who had died in the National Stadium. The widow was in the procession.
> I had never experienced such a powerful moment in the arena of politics, or one
> so moving.

I now recall my encounter with Neruda after Allende's victory, in one wing
of that same house on San Cristóbal Peak. Neruda was surrounded, as in all his
houses, with objects that he loved: pieces of wood, pieces of colored glass,
primitive paintings, ships in bottles, pottery, little brass hands pointing toward
some secret place, or pasteboard eyes with huge eyelashes, filled with wonder,
and hanging from a beam, swaying in the light breeze.

After spending almost all of 1970 in Peru, I had come home to a Chile
deeply shaken by Allende's victory. I had had lunch one day at the victorious
candidate's house on Calle Guardia Vieja (the Old Guard, indeed!), and while
we were alone in the little study with its portraits of Fidel Castro, Ché Guevara,

and Nicolás Guillén, conversing after lunch, he told me he had information that an attempt was going to be made to assassinate him. "The prudent thing would be not to show myself, but a candidate who's won the elections can't go into hiding. The very idea! Day after tomorrow I have a rally in the Plaza Victoria in Valparaíso, and I've already told them I would attend."

In spite of the revolutionary impatience (or petulance) showed by the ultra-Left, one had to see that such measures as the nationalization of copper, the state control of the banking industry, the full-scale implementation of the agrarian reform were going to shake the country to its foundations, and release all the good and evil genies pent up under the surface. Violence, a specter virtually unheard-of for the last twenty or twenty-five years, was now stirring, breathing new air.

Later, when Neruda was up to his ears in the political battle in his various roles as ambassador, poet, and militant, he would recover his optimism. The return to Isla Negra from Paris, especially, would give him one last injection of vitality. Looked at from the point of view of Paris, the difficulties of the Chilean situation appeared more alarming. In a letter of November 1972, written just a few days after his arrival, he wrote me:

> Dear Georgius, the matter stands as follows:
> Buttery cheese with olives.
> Sea urchin, brimming plate, huge fresh sea crab.
> Fried eel or paella with eel and shrimp, or a filet with peppers, onions, tomatoes, and green peppers.
> Very happy *chirimoyas.*
> Las Encinas white 1969, Concha y Toro Reserve red 1954, from the cavernous wine cellar of don Jaime.
> These and other things are what four of us had for dinner at the Santa Elena Inn. *Grande cuisine!*
> Apart from that, everything is roses, including the sea. The sky totally blue, except at sunset, when it is dyed a thousand colors.

One month later, in a letter written at the end of December, the optimism of the first moment of his arrival had given way to concern over the frontal attack by the political Right:

> The country is no more definable than ever. The mummies have achieved a level of insolence verging on the criminal. All you hear is right-wing radio stations breathing fire, insulting the government and demanding freedom of expression. All the government's legal actions in the courts against these acts of contempt wind up in the garbage can.

As for supplies, what I told you in my last letter still stands, though a bit improved. Everybody manages for victuals, while the mummies hoard huge quantities of goods. The CIA flooded the country with dollars in order to support the Owners and Employers Strike, and the dollar dropped on the black market.

And that's all for now from your Esso Reporter.

The Esso Reporter was one of the best known news programs on Chilean radio. In April 1973, Pablo Neruda wrote again. The success of the March elections had given him renewed confidence:

The mummies are as touchy as horses in the circus frightened by the tiger of the people. Still, there's "raised consciousness," and constant ground being gained.

I'm writing well, and a lot. This prescription works wonders on this marvelous coast. The country is tonic, nervous, stimulating like none other. Living anywhere else seems parasitic after this. How foolish to stay away so long! While it is true that there is much to remedy, such good things happen before your eyes, in the midst of a battle that is basically calm.

But even in the time before all these battles, when I visited him at his house on the peak of San Cristóbal that mid-October of 1970, Pablo Neruda seemed to sense with every pore and antenna of his body that destructive wave that was gaining strength far out at sea. He could sense, feel, the breath of inert matter, the soft curve of the clayey soil, the veins in the wood, the dark life of the plants motionless in the garden, their large leaves trembling, erect, and wet, and the idea of a mysterious, Vandal-like force that would descend upon the country from outside and disrupt the balance of things and nature brought him intense, if silent, agony. "It all looks black," he said at one point. Some months later, talking with Fidel Castro about the Revolution's problems on the eve of my departure from Havana, I told him what Neruda had said, and Fidel immediately replied: "Neruda saw clearly."

But presentiment, divination, was one thing, and brute, implacable events another. Events now forced us to rethink everything. I still believe, however, that black and white is not the only way, that the world is not solely divided, as Robespierre thought, into the good and the bad citizens. I believe that in the analysis of recent history we should resist the temptation offered us by Manicheanism. The first, easy reaction leads one to think that the Allende experiment was impossible from the beginning, that the idea of a peaceful, democratic transition to socialism was pure dream, or self-delusion. For my own part, I continue to be convinced that if the rules of law had been played out, without double-dealing and, of course, without useless provocations of one's opponents, and if the economy had been managed intelligently, without allowing the spirit of destructiveness to prevail as it so often did over the spirit of constructiveness and creation (which in no way excludes audacity, risk-taking, at the right time), then the experiment might have been pulled off.

"Then it wouldn't have been a *revolutionary* experiment at all!" cry the indefatigable theorists of revolution from their trenches in the Western press, or in the universities, or on Mont-St-Genovieve or on the Left Bank of the Seine. But Theory, which is of course an indispensable ingredient, should only be poured into the Revolution in moderate amounts, or the recipe turns sour, even poisonous. Revolution corresponds to the instinct of life, yet revolution-ary romanticism, so dear to the inhabitants of Mont-St-Genovieve, of the Latin Quarter in Paris, is often accompanied by suicidal tendencies, as though it were rather a reflection of the instinct of death.

Meanwhile, between the newly invested chargé d'affaires who almost three years ago had flown first class on Canadian Pacific Airways from Santiago, Chile, to Cuba by way of Mexico, bidden good-bye at the Pudahuel Airport by a gentleman of the banking and horse-racing industries, full of genuflexions and condescending smiles, happy to be near someone who had to a degree been anointed with power, even if that power were not necessarily altogether to the liking of that horse-racing gentleman—between that fledgling and the person now writing this Epilogue, there have intervened very, very profound changes. Experience, exhilarating and hard, can hold some useful lessons. The Manicheanism that still today dominates the Left would demand that the transcription of that experience onto paper should be kept under strict lock and key, so as "not to give arguments to the enemy." Everything connected with socialism should be rose-colored, and everything connected with capitalism, blackest black. And yet events show that the enemy, when it comes to that, does not take time out for debate, while the Left does have an urgent need for reflection and maturation.

I think about Cuba now and I tell myself that in spite of everything, in spite even of appearances, I hold no grudge. Perhaps I hold no grudge precisely because I transferred that hard experience, with its many uncertainties and moments of wavering, to the pages of a book. I think I even share some of the nostalgia of those former European diplomats in Cuba who would go to a cocktail party in Paris and invariably wind up together off in a corner some-where reminiscing, talking, making jokes about that one eternal subject. I can still see the waves breaking over the Malecón during that desolate winter, and still hear the warm voice of the hotel operator on the phone, still see the smile of Tomás, my driver, moving in some slow internal rhythm toward the Alfa, commenting between his teeth on something I said just before he screeched off along the seawall—and who, just before he was brusquely replaced (perhaps because he no longer gave assurance of absolute independence from me), had phoned me one afternoon to ask how my health was and whether there had been any news from my wife since her return to Chile, "news from Pilar," as he said. "She must be happy to be with her kids again." I understand the terrible dilemmas of the Revolution better now, in spite of the many things that I would still like to change about it (and although neither the one side's excesses nor the other's justify anything), than on that day I first set foot on the runway at Rancho Boyeros as chargé d'affaires and discovered, at first with relief, but immediately afterward with disappointment, that out there on that runway, in that blazing tropical sun, no one was waiting for me.

Barcelona-Calafell, October 1973
Santiago, Chile, January 1993

Index of Names